God's Wounds

Hermeneutic of the Christian Symbol of Divine Suffering

VOLUME I

DIVINE VULNERABILITY AND CREATION

Princeton Theological Monograph Series

K. C. Hanson, Charles M. Collier, and
D. Christopher Spinks, Series Editors

Recent volumes in the series

Kevin Twain Lowery
Salvaging Wesley's Agenda: A New Paradigm for Wesleyan Virtue Ethics

Michael S. Hogue
*The Tangled Bank: Toward an Ecotheolgical Ethics
of Responsible Participation*

Charles K. Bellinger
The Trinitarian Self: The Key to the Puzzle of Violence

David C. Mahan
*An Unexpected Light: Theology and Witness in the Poetry and Thought
of Charles Williams, Micheal O'Siadhail, and Geoffrey Hill*

Jeanne M. Hoeft
*Agency, Culture, and Human Personhood: Pastoral Thelogy
and Intimate Partner Violence*

Christian T. Collins Winn
*"Jesus Is Victor!": The Significance of the Blumhardts
for the Theology of Karl Barth*

Paul S. Chung
Martin Luther and Buddhism: Aesthetics of Suffering, Second Edition

Steven B. Sherman
*Revitalizing Theological Epistemology: Holistic Evangelical
Approaches to the Knowledge of God*

Mary Clark Moschella
*Living Devotions: Reflections on Immigration, Identity,
and Religious Imagination*

God's Wounds

Hermeneutic of the Christian Symbol of Divine Suffering

Volume I

Divine Vulnerability and Creation

Jeff B. Pool

PICKWICK *Publications* · Eugene, Oregon

GOD'S WOUNDS: HERMENEUTIC OF THE CHRISTIAN SYMBOL
OF DIVINE SUFFEREING
Volume 1: Divine Vulnerability and Creation

Princeton Theological Monograph Series 100

Pickwick Publications
An imprint of Wipf and Stock
199 W. 8th Ave., Suite 3,
Eugene, OR 97401.

www.wipfandstock.com

ISBN 13: 978-1-55635-464-9

Cataloging-in-Publication data:

Pool, Jeff B., 1951—
    God's wounds : hermeneutic of the christian symbol of divine suffering, vol. 1,
    divine vulnerability and creation / Jeff B. Pool.

    xviii + 360 p. ; 23 cm. — Princeton Theological Monograph Series 100
    Includes bibliographic references and indices.

    ISBN 13: 978-1-55635-464-9

    1. God as creator. 2. Human nature—Religious aspects—Christianity.
3. Love—Religious aspects—Christianity. 4. Divine passibility. I. Title. II. Series.

BT83.78.P66 2009

Manufactured in the U.S.A.

Dedicated to

MY FORMER GRADUATE STUDENTS
IN THEOLOGICAL STUDIES

With whom I examined most of the practical and
theoretical problems and concepts that the following
studies explore in various ways.
My conversations with them,
individually and during many classes,
deeply enriched my thought and conclusions
about the Christian testimonies to God's wounds
from which I have reconstructed the rationality
of the Christian symbol of divine suffering
that this work elucidates.

Contents

Preface

EXPERIENCES OF SIN, SINFUL SOCIAL FATEDNESS OR EVIL, AND TRAGIC
reality often disintegrate human lives, leaving some of them, at best,
apathetic in the face of the tremendous burdens that they must bear.
Other people respond to similar experiences quite differently. Within
the latter category, however, many persons, including both Christians
and persons from other religious communities, have responded to their
negative experiences, to their experiences of affliction, evil, and sin, with
testimonies to a God who suffers with them, for them, and because of
them.

In three volumes, I have focused my attention upon the Christian
symbol of divine suffering through an examination of Christian attestations or testimonies to the suffering God, under the following over-
arching title for this work: *God's Wounds: Hermeneutic of the Christian
Symbol of Divine Suffering.* The present book constitutes the first volume
of these studies: *Divine Vulnerability and Creation.* The two volumes of
studies that will follow also occur under the general title, but carry parallel titles for the individual volumes: *Evil and Divine Suffering* (volume
two); and *Divine Suffering and Tragic Reality* (volume three).

For the main title of these three volumes, I have employed a metaphor, "God's Wounds," an archaic English oath often uttered in surprise
or even in anger.[1] As I have studied the Christian symbol of divine suffering, this symbol has often delighted and surprised me, eliciting from
me responses with the *heuristic sense of that oath.* On numerous other

---

1. William Shakespeare, for example, used variations of this oath as well as related
oaths throughout his works. His characters, Iago, Hotspur, and Poins, occasionally use
"zounds" (*Othello, the Moor of Venice* 1.1; *King Henry IV: First Part* 1.3; 2.4). Hamlet
uses one variation of this oath, "Swounds" (*Hamlet, Prince of Denmark* 2.2), while
Gremio uses another variation, "gogs wouns" (*The Taming of the Shrew* 3.2). Related
oaths also refer to God's blood and God's body: Iago, Hamlet, and Falstaff use the term,
"'sblood" (*Othello, the Moor of Venice* 1.1; *Hamlet, Prince of Denmark* 2.2; *King Henry
IV: First Part* 2.4); another character uses "'Odsbody" (*King Henry IV: First Part* 2.1).

occasions, however, as I have struggled to understand this symbol, when some aspect of this symbol kept eluding me, and especially during moments when this symbol felt much more like a burden than a gift, this symbol also has sometimes distressed and bewildered me, evoking from me responses with the *imprecatory sense of that oath*. Nonetheless, this work required from me both the delight and the distress, both the surprise and the bewilderment, for its completion. For both experiences through these studies, I remain grateful.

Walter Benjamin describes the storyteller as "the [person] who could let the wick of his [or her] life be consumed completely by the gentle flame of his [or her] story."[2] With abandon, I some time ago gave myself to the study of the story held within the Christian symbol of divine suffering. I have listened to this story hundreds, perhaps thousands, of times by storytellers who knew and told various versions. So often have I forgotten myself in hearing these attestations to God's suffering, that, before I realized it, this symbol's flames had already engulfed me. More than once since my realization of being gently ablaze with my studies of this symbol, I have suspected that its story would slowly yet completely consume the wick of my life; and, in spite of my best efforts and the efforts of many others to extinguish that quiet conflagration, the fire continued to burn.

While I began my studies of this symbol by following Horace's counsel, carefully choosing a subject that appeared equal to my strengths, I soon discovered that this story weighed far more than my shoulders alone could bear.[3] Nonetheless, the burden of this story that I cannot bear alone has permitted me to discover even more about this story's mystery, to experience more deeply this symbol's sublimity. Now, precisely because this story has both overwhelmed me with its weight and consumed me in its flames, I can re-tell it to others. I hope that my narration of the story in this symbol adequately re-presents the traditions that I have discovered and interpreted, regardless of and perhaps through the re-shaping that they have received from my perspective.

My efforts at a comprehensive interpretation of this symbol, however, most certainly leave areas unexplored; variations on the three main forms of divine suffering, for example, require additional

2. Benjamin, *Illuminations*, 108–9.

3. "Sumite materiam vestris, qui scribitis, aequam viribus, et versate diu, quid ferre recusent, quid valeant umeri" (Horace, *Ars poetica*, 38–40).

clarification and fuller elaboration. Furthermore, despite my best efforts to hear all testimonies to the suffering of God, I know that numerous voices remain in a variety of cultural, religious, social, moral, political, philosophical, and theological contexts about which I have not yet even heard, much less have I carefully studied. I can only apologize for these and other rather serious weaknesses, weaknesses to which I need not alert even the average reader, and weaknesses over which I have little control simply because some of them result from the conditions and limitations of finitude itself.

I have endeavored to write also on the basis of another guideline from Horace, to proceed in these studies without defying Minerva.[4] Sometimes, however, as characteristic for humans in our sinful, ambiguous, and strenuous (even if also astonishing, joyful, and beautiful) creation, I have studied this symbol *invita Minerva*, without inspiration. Hence, in spite of the many persons who have tried to help me think carefully, coherently, clearly, and responsibly about this amazing Christian symbol, I assume full responsibility for the final results, either satisfying or disturbing, that this work contains. Although I have also listened to Horace's caution, and know that, once I have published this work, I cannot erase these studies, I venture them as topics for public discussion.[5]

I have labored on these studies *in medias res*, in the midst of things, truly, *in transitu*, in a journey of many years, through a series of social, political, religious, and academic contexts. The original form of this project arose as the dissertation for my Ph.D. degree at the University of Chicago, which I began writing during the year that I spent as a Junior Fellow in the Institute for the Advanced Study of Religion (now the Martin Marty Center) of the University of Chicago Divinity School.[6] Even my doctoral dissertation, however, had emerged from my initial interest in this topic as an undergraduate student, when I first encountered the concept of the suffering God in Dietrich Bonhoeffer's letters from prison. Although I have published other books both before and since I completed my dissertation, my long-standing fascination with

4. "Tu nihil invita dices faciesve Minerva: id tibi iudicium est, ea mens" (Horace, *Ars poetica*, 385–86).

5. "Delere licebit quod non edideris; nescit vox missa reverti" (Horace, *Ars poetica*, 389–90).

6. Pool, "God's Wounds."

this subject has continued to nourish my hope to publish a more comprehensive study of the Christian symbol of divine suffering, the hope
that this three-volume work now realizes.

No sooner had I begun writing my doctoral dissertation, however, than I also accepted my first full-time academic position, teaching
theology and ethics at Phillips Theological Seminary, a traditionally-
liberal Protestant seminary of The Christian Church/Disciples of Christ.
I completed the final portions of my dissertation, however, as Assistant
Professor of Systematic Theology in my second full-time academic post,
Southwestern Baptist Theological Seminary, a formerly conservative,
but now fully and militantly fundamentalist, seminary of the Southern
Baptist Convention. I mention this second academic context precisely
because the seminary's administrative reaction against and opposition
to the content and conclusions of my dissertation (which I also had explored during classes with my students there), especially as contained in
my interpretation of the role of divine suffering in the traditional teaching about the meaning of the crucifixion of Jesus (found in volume two
of this work), elicited a refusal from the Dean of the School of Theology
at that time to recommend me for tenure in the mid-to-late 1990s. This
reaction to the rationality of the Christian symbol of divine suffering
also occurred, of course, during the final stages in the fundamentalist
conquest of the Southern Baptist Convention.[7] While I will not develop
here an exposition of the relationship between this challenging symbol
and the re-emergence of fundamentalist/dogmatic cultural, religious,
moral, social, and political realities, this incident illustrated poignantly
many of my conclusions about the rejection of the Christian symbol of
divine suffering by the dominant classical Christian theistic traditions,
about the radically-different concepts of power at the basis of Christian
testimonies to divine suffering, on the one hand, and classical Christian
theistic testimonies to divine activity, on the other hand, at which I had
arrived in my doctoral research on this symbol. The studies of these
volumes will clarify this illustration for the reader.

7. I have published studies of the confessional traditions of the Southern Baptist
Convention, in which I have analyzed the complex (and often camouflaged) relationships between the political and the theological factors that formed the ecclesiastical
context for my vocational mission at the time and the situation for me that resulted
from my commitment to the calling of that moment (see Pool, *Against Returning to
Egypt*; idem, "Conscience and Interpreting Baptist Tradition," 1–36).

I have initiated this large project for publication in my present academic and pastoral context at Berea College, where I currently serve as Associate Professor of Religion, Director of the Campus Christian Center, and College Chaplain. In this academic institution, I have experienced for the first time a community in which its radical historic mission and vision, its institutional structures for governance and academic life, and its real practices remain relatively consistent with one another and genuinely support and promote complete academic freedom and social justice, not only in the larger world but also within the College itself. For these reasons, the institutional mission, vision, governance-structures, and practices of my present academic and pastoral context, more than any of the institutions in which I previously have served and taught, remain genuinely compatible, if not always fully consistent in finite reality and also among fallen humans, with the vision of a community shaped by the vision of the suffering God, as reflected in the rationality and logic that I have discerned and tried to elucidate through my interpretation of the Christian symbol of divine suffering.

As with all such works, various persons from these many different contexts, as the networks of interdependence that nourish, shape, challenge, and inspire me, deserve my thanks for their contributions to and support during my journey toward the publication of this project. I begin by expressing special gratitude to several people who helped to shape both my approach to and my thought about this symbol. In this respect, I first remember with genuine affection and the most profound gratitude the late Professor Langdon Gilkey, my advisor during the entire course of my doctoral studies and the co-advisor of my dissertation. I also thank Professor David Tracy, who served as the other co-advisor of my dissertation, as well as Professors James M. Gustafson and Anne Carr who also served on my dissertation committee: *Salus ubi multi consiliarii*—where there are many advisers there is safety. In this connection, I especially thank Professor Gustafson for his careful reading of the initial overview of my interpretation of divine suffering, which I presented to him as a lengthy research paper for his year-long seminar in theological ethics in 1983–84 on the theme of love in the Christian Tradition. Professor Gustafson deserves my special thanks for so profoundly shaping the methodological direction of my dissertation by his comments on that initial research, but especially for his close and critical reading of that paper of slightly more than 170 pages. Each of these advisors, however, patiently helped me to bear the burden of my passion for the Christian symbol of divine suffering.

I also thank the University of Chicago Divinity School for my appointment as a Junior Fellow in its Institute for the Advanced Study of Religion or the Martin Marty Center (1987–1988), now a full two decades ago. I thank the other Fellows of the Institute during that academic year for their discussion and criticism of this work's earliest drafts. I especially thank the Director of the Institute at that time and also one of my dearest graduate teachers, Professor Bernard McGinn, for his encouragement, counsel, and kindness to me during that year and in subsequent years.

Since my days as a doctoral student, many other people have contributed to my work on the Christian symbol of divine suffering. I especially thank my traveling companions in El Salvador and Nicaragua during the summer of 1991 as well as my *compañeras* and *compañeros* in the barrios, base communities, farming cooperatives, and resettlement communities in those still struggling and troubled lands. My experience with them significantly enriched my interpretation of this Christian symbol. I also thank my friend and former colleague, Dr. Robert Bernard, for his expert help with Latin. Additionally, I convey my gratitude, permanent affection, and sincere respect to my graduate students in theology and ministry, those with whom I have explored most of this work's central concepts during courses, social occasions, and office hours. Other friends have contributed to my work in a variety of ways too numerous to catalogue here. With gratitude, I mention two of these friends, whose friendships with me have persisted since our days together in undergraduate courses in philosophy and theology, because of their gifts of time, conversation, confidence, and even material resources at various points during our journeys together: Rev. Ron Kafer and Professor Doyle Walls.

In addition, I offer gratitude to the two institutions that have supported my publication of this project in various ways. I especially thank Berea College and Dean Stephanie Browner for the supportive academic context in which to complete the writing of this work, as well as for both resources and an environment of academic freedom to bring this project to publication. I also thank Charlie Collier, Acquisitions Editor of Wipf & Stock Publishers, for both his confidence in the value of this large project and his efforts to bring this project into reality as three published volumes of studies.

My family has provided for me the greatest material support as well as the immeasurable resources of confidence and love that have sustained and nurtured me during the years that I have labored on this project. I owe every member of my family debts that I can never fully repay. I thank each one of them for their patience with me in my struggles with this work on the symbol of divine suffering. I suspect that my suffering over this work has caused them more suffering than they would have experienced, if I had chosen another profession. With the deepest love, I thank my parents, Billie Faye Hughes Pool and Roger Lee Pool, always ready with whatever resources that I have needed and that they possessed to share, their confidence never wavering in such a different, perplexing, and often difficult son. With a love proven by the trials, suffering, joys, and accomplishments of life together, I also thank Laurinda Lynn Littlejohn Pool, my spouse, for her tenderness and enormous sacrifices for me throughout my involvement with this project, especially when the conclusions of this work seriously affected the course of my academic career and the quality of our shared life. With affection that has emerged from entire lifetimes with one another, I remain grateful for the ever-encouraging support and the many conversations with my sister, Karen Diane Pool Dansby, and my brother, David Bryan Pool. With similar affection and deep appreciation, I also thank my brother-in-law, Dick Dansby, and my sister-in-law, Glenna Pool, for their humor, generosity of spirit, patience, and confidence.

With all my love, finally, I especially thank my children, Kristen Michelle Pool Lew and Jonathan Gabriel Pool, who have lived with my work on this project since their childhoods. During my work on this project, in its initial form as a dissertation, they patiently endured my research and writing; as children, they listened to me read aloud far more of this work than children should have to hear. Their affection in those years often soothed my fiery struggles. They trusted me as their father, in my obsession, even when they did not always understand the obsession itself. As young adults and now the dearest of my friends, they have listened to me continue my thoughts about this subject and have made their own contributions to my thoughts in many conversations. Their confidence in and love for me, but especially their own creativity and accomplishments, have genuinely inspired me to bring this work into publication. They have truly suffered with me as I have suffered God's wounds, the Christian symbol of divine suffering.

Finally, I mention those to whom I have dedicated this volume of studies. While the book as a whole carries a dedication, both part one and part two also carry dedications.

I have dedicated this entire first volume of studies to my former graduate students, those who enrolled in and completed the courses that I offered in theology at several educational institutions: Phillips Theological Seminary in Tulsa, Oklahoma; Southwestern Baptist Theological Seminary in Fort Worth, Texas; International Baptist Theological Seminary in Prague, The Czech Republic; and Brite Divinity School, also in Fort Worth, Texas. These former students, a number of whom now have completed doctoral degrees of their own in social ethics, philosophy, theology, psychiatry, counseling, and music, who also teach at various colleges, universities, and seminaries, and many of whom serve congregations as pastors or in other contexts of ministry, contributed significantly to my work on and thought about the large cluster of problems, questions, and theoretical and practical issues that accompany the Christian symbol of divine suffering. Their contributions through discussions during classes or in my offices genuinely helped to advance my thinking about this symbol: we learned much together, even when we disagreed about specific questions, issues, doctrines, religious practices, or ecclesiastical politics.

I have dedicated part one of this book, which addresses various important methodological issues and concerns, to my four major teachers during my doctoral studies at the University of Chicago: Langdon Brown Gilkey (1919–2004); Paul Ricoeur (1913–2005); David Tracy (1939–); James M. Gustafson (1925–). Their influence on my approach to theological, philosophical, and moral questions profoundly helped to shape the method by which I studied and interpreted the Christian symbol of divine suffering, especially as the chapters of part one demonstrate.

I have dedicated part two of this book to my parents. I dedicate this portion of the book to the memory of my father, Wilson Corley Mauldin, for the ways in which his own curiosity about the world positively elicited from me a corresponding desire to explore and to value other cultures and people that differed from me, as well as for the biological contribution that he made to my own life. I remain grateful for my re-discoveries of my father: for the grace and healing that we both experienced in the mid-1970s from my efforts to re-connect with him after more than a decade of his absence; and for the bittersweet surprise that I experienced in 1998, when I learned of his burial in a cemetery very near my home, after another twenty years had lapsed since our last contact with one another. Most especially, though, I dedicate part two of this book to my mother, Billie Faye Hughes Pool, and my step-father, Roger Lee Pool. My step-father, Roger, has served as a model of exploring practical ways of solving real problems, demonstrating to me from my youth the meaningfulness of work, quality of endeavor, and persistence, encouraging me in various ways to discover my own way through difficulties and questions and to realize my own creative potential. Finally, I dedicate this portion of the book to my mother, Billie Faye Hughes Pool, who, more than anyone, represents the most profound continuity across the course of my entire life: conceiving and giving birth to me, guiding me into adulthood, and always remaining ready with spiritual, emotional, and material support for me, and later for my own children and her grandchildren, when we have experienced severe challenges, pain, or suffering of our own—an inestimable, invaluable, influence on my life for creativity, goodness, truth, and beauty—and an utterly irreplaceable gift of God to our world, but most specially to me.

Prologue:
Terrible Sublimity of the Christian Symbol of Divine Suffering

THE ULTIMATE GLOOM, VULGARITY, GRIM SEVERITY, HORROR, EVEN apparent conceptual paradoxes, in Christian testimonies to divine suffering repel many people in their initial encounters with various forms of this Christian symbol.[1] Such revulsion for language that attributes

1. One mid-nineteenth-century (classical-theistic) response to Edward Beecher's theology of divine suffering (Beecher, *Concord of Ages*) illustrates this theological revulsion for the idea that God suffers. "Some of the language which Dr. B. uses on this subject is terrible. There is nothing scarcely which he hesitates to apply to him. 'In spirit,' he says, 'God is humble, benevolent, and self-sacrificing.' His manner of handling this subject, the character of God, is positively repulsive. . . . He carries his anthropomorphism to extreme lengths. He has not the slightest regard for the feelings of others in these matters, but seems to glory in trampling upon them" (Vermilye, "Suffering of God," 25, 26). As H. Maurice Relton said in his essay entitled "Patripassianism," first published in 1917 and later included as a chapter in one of his books, "this picture of a suffering God may at first sight revolt us" (Relton, *Studies in Christian Doctrine*, 82). Hastings Rashdall also acknowledged this point: "the medieval language about God's blood and God's wounds has already become distasteful to modern Christians" (Rashdall, *Idea of Atonement in Christian Theology*, 451).

I employ the term "symbol" with a meaning that resembles a long history of usage among some continental European philosophers and American revisionist theologians: as examples, Paul Ricoeur, Paul Tillich, Langdon Gilkey, Edward Farley, David Tracy, Sallie McFague, among many others. I have used the term "symbol" in place of terms like "doctrine" or "dogma" on the basis of the following rationale. Precisely because the earliest ecclesiastical conciliar decisions designated the notion of divine passibility (in the cross or otherwise) as heretical/unorthodox in various ways, the churches never had an official teaching, doctrine, or dogma about God or divine reality as passible in any real sense. For that reason, although I could have used the term "doctrine" instead of the term "symbol," the notion or concept of God's suffering has never appeared as official Christian doctrine or dogma. Therefore, I have avoided the term "doctrine" to refer to the concept of divine passibility. Chapter 1 contains a section in which I clarify my use of the term "symbol" with respect to the concept of divine suffering. In my usage of the term, though, I merely apply the language of divine suffering to a concept long in use by theologians like Tillich, Tracy, and Gilkey. Gilkey, for example, refers

suffering to God, however, may surprise contemporary Christians who easily attribute all sorts of emotions and experiences to God and may lead such Christians to criticize classical Christian theism itself, when they discover how the vast majority of official teachings and dogmas of orthodox Christianity (Eastern Orthodoxy, Roman Catholicism, and many of the major Protestant denominations that emerged from the reformations of the sixteenth century) have defined the Christian concept of God in opposition to the notion that God or the divine nature (even in Christ) suffers. The responsibility for eliciting reactions against the Christian symbol of divine suffering, nevertheless, does not reside only with those Christians who have accepted and developed the conceptual strengths and resources of classical theism.[2]

---

to "theological symbols" such as "creation, providence, incarnation" or "God" (Gilkey, *Through the Tempest*, 58–59, 69, etc.).

2. Classical *Christian* theism belongs to the larger family of classical theism. Various understandings of classical theism, however, abound. Some identify this designation with the convictions of piety, without showing how the beliefs of that piety became intertwined with various categories and concepts from Hellenistic philosophy. Hence, for those who espouse this first and rather indiscriminate way of understanding, classical theism describes God with some or all of the following central characteristics or attributes: omnipotence, omniscience, omnipresence, eternity, omni-benevolence, aseity, perfection, and so on (e.g., Barnhart, *Religion and the Challenge of Philosophy*, 61). Of course, the scriptures of many religious traditions, including those that originated from Christian piety and reflection, characterize God with most or all of those attributes. Nevertheless, such descriptions do not adequately represent the entire conceptual network of classical theism. Other central and even more definitive features of classical theism include technical concepts that early Christian theologians inherited primarily from Hellenistic philosophies: impassibility, immutability, simplicity, incorporeality, incomprehensibility, indivisibility, and so forth. These latter characteristics or attributes, plus those mentioned previously, more fully reflect the essential characteristics of the classical-theistic concept of God. Other characteristics become necessary to qualify a system of beliefs as any particular variety of classical theism: such as classical *Christian* theism. More careful analysts of classical theism perceive, in the history of various religious traditions, phenomena in which the symbols and images of religious piety combine with more refined philosophical concepts. In this respect, see the excellent collection of examples from Jewish, Christian, and Islamic theologies (Philo, Maimonides; Augustine, Anselm, Aquinas, Descartes, Leibniz, Kant, Channing, von Hügel; Al-Ghazzali), and their philosophical precursors (Plato, Aristotle), with which Charles Hartshorne and William L. Reese illustrate various religious traditions in the family of classical theism (Hartshorne and Reese, eds., *Philosophers Speak of God*, 38–164). Numerous careful analyses of classical Christian theism address these issues: Grant, *Gods and the One God*, 75–83; Prestige, *God in Patristic Thought*, 1–24; Kelly, *Early Christian Doctrines*, 14–28, 83–87. More recently, other scholars have studied the relationship of classical Christian theism to the modern and contemporary worlds

According to Christian scriptures, Peter, the disciple of Jesus so prominent in the eyes of later Christian communities, rebuked Jesus when Jesus predicted his own death by religious persecution.[3] Furthermore, testimony from one of Jesus' earliest disciples memorializes the cowardly responses to Jesus' suffering from all of the disciples, including his closest friends, Peter, John, and James: ". . . they all left him and fled."[4] While both religious and political authorities interrogated, isolated, scourged, beat, humiliated, and then crucified Jesus, his friends and disciples hid or sought anonymity. Even Peter denied his friendship with Jesus while, in the midst of a group of people, Peter warmed himself beside a fire.[5] According to Christian testimonies, only after Jesus' resurrection from the dead did his disciples begin to regard their crucified friend and teacher as something other than a shattered messianic hope. Only then did even the apostle Paul describe the crucified Christ as God's wisdom and power.[6]

That Jesus' closest disciples abandoned him, fleeing both from his embrace of his own crucifixion and from its meaning for the God whom Jesus had disclosed to them, also typifies the primary and characteristic response of most subsequent Christian thought to Jesus' crucifixion. Ironically, the story of this symbol's rejection by Christians begins in narratives among the texts that constitute the founding Christian attestations to the suffering God. Still, orthodox Christian communities dogmatically described Jesus as both divine and human.[7] With respect to all dimensions in the Christian symbol of divine suffering, histories of Christian thought largely narrate the story of how "they all left him and fled," indeed, how the majority of Christian theologians actually have sought to discredit various concepts of the suffering God, judging

---

(Gilkey, "God," 88–113; also, idem, "The Christian Understanding of God," 69–88). Also see G. A. Cole's careful though brief description of classical theism (Cole, "Towards a New Metaphysic of the Exodus," 75–76).

3. Matt 16:21–23; Mark 8:31–33; cf. Luke 9:22–27.

4. Mark 14:50 NAS (New American Standard).

5. Mark 14:66–72; John 18:12–40.

6. 1 Cor 1:18–24.

7. More than a century ago, Edward Beecher drew this analogy between the refusal of suffering to Jesus by his disciples and the refusal of suffering to God: "as the Jews had idealized their Messiah as coming to triumph by resistless force, without humiliation or suffering, so the pride of Gentile Christians has idealized God" (E. Beecher, *Concord of Ages*, 23).

those concepts as heretical or heterodox. Post-biblical Christian thinkers and writers of Late Antiquity, in their efforts to conceptualize and
safeguard the Christian God's perfection in light of the crucified Christ,
contributed central concepts that they had principally inherited from
Hellenistic philosophies (such as immutability and impassibility), but
also images of divine transcendence that had originated from the Hebrew
scriptures and Jewish piety, toward developing the classical-*Christian*-
theistic concept of God. Such intellectual and religious contributions
led to concepts of deity that emerged as completely incompatible with
suffering of any kind. Thus, very early in the development of Christian
orthodoxy, although Christian theologians and ecclesiastical councils
acknowledged and insisted upon Christ's suffering in his human nature,
the church officially and emphatically rejected and condemned the claim
that Christ's divine nature suffered at all.[8] For centuries, this tendency
repeatedly reinforced itself through ecclesiastical dogmas, creeds, confessions, and their theological interpretations in the various Christian
communities.[9] Consequently, and despite the wonderful conceptual

---

8. As a Protestant example, see a classic statement of the *communicatio idiomatum*
in the "Solid Declaration" of the Lutheran "Formula of Concord" (1577): "on account of
this personal union, without which such a true communion of the natures is unthink-
able and impossible, it is not only the bare human nature (whose property it is to suffer
and to die) that has suffered for the sin of the world, but the Son of God himself has
truly suffered (although according to the assumed human nature) and, in the words
of our plain Christian Creed, has truly died, although the divine nature can neither
suffer nor die" ("Formula of Concord," "Part II: Solid Declaration," 595). Earlier, Martin
Luther, with a slightly different emphasis, had accepted this classical Christian theistic
doctrine as well (Luther, "On the Councils and the Church, 1539," 103). Although both
Luther and the "Formula of Concord" distinguished between a "real exchange" and a
"verbal exchange" of attributes, while accepting only the former, their distinction between Christ's two natures (in their opposition to Monophysite tendencies to blend the
two natures into one) activates an inertia that seems to pull them back to the traditional
theism that Luther's staurocentric theology so radically though implicitly opposed in
many ways.

9. Catholic conciliar decrees consistently define divine immutability and impassibility (in regard to every member of the divine Trinity) as ecclesiastical dogmas, anath-
ematizing those who deny them. A Latin anathema, upon those who describe Christ's
deity as changeable (*convertibilem*) or mutable (*demutabilem*), accompanies the creed
formulated by the Council of Nicea (325 CE) (Denzinger and Schönmetzer, eds.,
Enchiridion Symbolorum, 126 [53]; hereafter cited as *DS*). "The Creed of Epiphanius"
(fourth century CE) declares both that the divine nature of the Logos did not alter or
change during the incarnation and, further, that nothing altered the Holy Spirit (*DS*, 44,
45 [31–32]). One Council of Toledo (400 CE) produced a creed in which this council

riches and linguistic precision that Christian theologians had received from Hellenistic culture, Christians who attest to a suffering God usually assume a deeply critical posture toward the Hellenistic heritage of Christian thought. The critical reception of that Hellenistic heritage, at least by theologians of divine suffering, resembles the Trojan response to the Greek gift of the large wooden horse: *"quidquid id est, timeo Danaos et dona ferentis."*[10] Although official ecclesiastical and theologi-

---

anathematized those who believe that Christ's divine nature suffered. A later Council of Toledo (447 CE) slightly emended this creed with an anathema upon those who believe in the mutability or passibility of Christ's divine nature (*DS*, 196.6; 197.7 [76]). One Lateran Council (649 CE) condemned those who do not confess the Trinity's immutability (*DS*, 501, canon 1 [171]). The Roman Council (860, 863 CE) professed that, during the crucifixion, Christ suffered only in his human flesh and remained impassible in his deity: "passionem crucis tantummodo secundum carnem sustinuit, deitate autem impassibilis mansit" (*DS*, 501, 635). Leo IX (1049–54 CE) declared, in his "Professio fidei," about the Christ: "impassibilem et immortalem divinitate, sed in humanitate pro nobis et pro nostra salute passum vera carnis passione et sepultum" (*DS*, 681 [225]). The Fourth Lateran Council (1215 CE) reiterated faith in an unchangeable (*"incommutabilis"*) Trinity (*DS*, 800 [259]). The Second Council of Lyons (1274 CE), in its "Professio fidei Michaelis Palaeologi imperatoris," with slight alterations, reaffirmed Leo IX's christological formulation: "impassibilem et immortalem divinitate, sed in humanitate pro nobis et salute nostra passum vera carnis passione, mortuum et sepultum" (*DS*, 852 [276]). The Council of Florence (1438–45 CE), in its "Decretum pro Iacobitis," both reaffirmed an unchangeable (*incommutabilem*) Trinity and similarly formulated its faith in Christ: "immortalis et aeternus ex natura divinitatis, passibilis et temporalis ex condicione assumptae humanitatis" (*DS*, 1330, 1337 [337, 339]). Even in the First Vatican Council (1869–70 CE), the Roman Catholic Church reiterated its faith in an unchangeable (*incommutabilis*) divine creator (*DS*, 3001 [587]). In the twentieth century, several Christian communities authorized doctrinal commissions to study contemporary interests in, testimonies to, and discussions of divine passibility and impassibility: *Doctrine in the Church of England*, 55–56; Commissio Theologica Internationalis, "Theologia-Christologia-Anthropologia: Quaestiones Selectae," 20–24; and *We Believe in God: A Report by the Doctrine Commission of the General Synod of the Church of England* (1987), viii–ix, 157–60. Although the earlier Anglican doctrinal commission briefly noted the Christian theological rationale for divine suffering, and affirmed this doctrine's value, the latter Anglican doctrinal commission attended much more carefully to the broad range of issues that accompany this doctrine. The latter doctrinal commission, as a consequence, formulated a much more sophisticated attestation to divine suffering.

10. One may translate this phrase as follows: "Be it what it may, I fear the Greeks [Danai] even when they offer gifts" (Virgil, *Aeneid*, 2.49). In the legend of the fall of Troy, the seer Laocoön, like Cassandra, detected the carefully-crafted Hellenic equine deception, but could not convince the Trojans of the danger. Adolf von Harnack's influential work develops this mythical caution into critical analyses of both the essence of Christianity and its Hellenistic elements (see Harnack, *What is Christianity*, especially

cal flights from the Christian symbol of divine suffering have attempted hermeneutically to neutralize this symbol's theological and ontological potency, in the religious life of numerous Christian communities, through liturgy, sermons, hymns, devotional literature, prayers, art, and so forth, vital testimony to God's suffering persists.[11]

Nevertheless, forces within modernity launched deliberate and sustained critical attacks against all concepts of deity, both the dominant deity of classical Christian theism and those lesser concepts of deity that even the dominant Christian tradition had subjugated to itself.[12]

---

the second part, "The Gospel in History," or lectures 9–16). My comments, however, require at least a double qualification. By no means, on the one hand, do I intend with these comments to idealize the Christian scriptures, by construing them as free from Hellenistic conceptual influence and, therefore, as purely Hebraic in thought-form—as if only such cultural purity might guarantee the authenticity, adequacy, and authority of the symbols and concepts within those writings. As Frederick Grant noted some time ago, "the beginning of this Hellenization of the gospel can be traced in the New Testament" (Grant, *Roman Hellenism and the New Testament*, 162). On the other hand, neither do I intend to demean the genuine and manifold positive contributions of ancient Greek thought to Christian theology. Nonetheless, much Hellenistic conceptual inheritance and influence had a negative impact upon Christian thought, as Frederick Grant also perceived: "as a consequence of this Hellenistic-Roman influence, much of the vast potency of the gospel became neutralized, insulated, and has never been set free to this day" (Grant, *Roman Hellenism and the New Testament*, 164). Grant continued by stating that this Hellenistic influence channeled the Christian community's interests and energies into "fruitless controversy and sectarianism," a situation that Grant described as "the tragedy, over which God himself must weep" (Grant, *Roman Hellenism and the New Testament*, 164, 171). Theologians of divine suffering almost unanimously share and consistently articulate these suspicions of Christianity's Hellenistic conceptual inheritance. For instance, ". . . Christian theology as a whole, and the doctrine of God in particular, have suffered because of the lack of caution which theologians in every age have shown in their too ready acceptance of the gifts which the Greeks have brought" (Pollard, "Impassibility of God," 353; also see, Scheffczyk, "Die Frage nach der Hellenizierung des Christentums unter modernem Problemaspekt," 195–205; idem, *Tendenzen und Brennpunkte der neueren Problematik um die Hellenisierung des Christentums*).

11. Even images of the divine "father's" suffering begin to appear frequently in Medieval art (Boespflug, "Compassion of God the Father in Western Art," 491–93). Also see Henri J. M. Nouwen's interpretation of Rembrandt's painting, "The Return of the Prodigal Son" (Nouwen, "Vulnerable God," 28–35).

12. "Whatever is God to a man, that is his heart and soul; and conversely, God is the manifested inward nature, the expressed self of a man,—religion the solemn unveiling of a man's hidden treasures, the revelation of his intimate thoughts, the open confession of his love-secrets" (Feuerbach, *Essence of Christianity*, 12–13). "A people that still believes in itself retains its own god. In him it reveres the conditions which let

More recently, philosophers and theologians have challenged even the meaningfulness of religious language.[13] In short, even Western culture has abandoned the dominant classical-Christian-theistic notion of deity that Western culture itself had produced. Of course, the classical-Christian-theistic concept of deity did not suffer alone from this cultural rejection. No concept of deity or ultimate reality has remained immune to the forces that threatened classical theism. Thus, the concept of the impassible, unaffected deity has suffered as much loss of credibility, at least in Western culture, as the symbol of the suffering God had suffered under the dominance of classical Christian theism. As a result, within the contexts of modernity and then post-modernity, the notion of God's death has acquired new meaning. For the modern world, this phrase signified the death of an unnecessary explanatory factor or influence in a material universe, a universe predisposed to empirical or scientific investigation, a universe quite adequately and thoroughly understandable from that perspective.

Perhaps, then, this cultural rejection of classical Christian theism's deity represents a sort of contemporary cultural analogy to the severe reprimand that Jesus issued to Peter for his refusal of Jesus' intention to suffer and die as the Messiah. Several recent and contemporary Christian theologians argue that the advent of modern and contemporary atheism, the death of God in Western culture, has resulted from the incompatibility of this inherited concept of impassible deity with reality as experienced by humans in modern and postmodern worlds. Some theologians, like Eberhard Jüngel, have taken this one step farther,

---

it prevail, its virtues: it projects, its pleasure in itself, its feeling of power, into a being to whom one may offer thanks. . . . The Christian conception of God . . . is one of the most corrupt conceptions of the divine ever attained on earth. It may even represent the low-water mark in the descending development of divine types. God degenerated into the *contradiction* of life, instead of being its transfiguration and eternal Yes! . . . God—the deification of nothingness, the will to nothingness pronounced holy!" (Nietzsche, "The Antichrist," in *The Portable Nietzsche*, 582, 585–86). "The psychoanalysis of individual human beings, however, teaches us with quite special insistence that the god of each of them is formed in the likeness of his father, that his personal relation to God depends on his relation to his father in the flesh and oscillates and changes along with that relation, and that at bottom God is nothing other than an exalted father" (Freud, *Totem and Taboo*, 147).

13. See, e. g., Ayer, *Language, Truth and Logic*. See the even more recent literature on deconstructive philosophy and theology (e.g., Caputo, *Radical Hermeneutics*; M. C. Taylor, *Erring: A Postmodern A/theology*).

claiming that the classical Christian notion of God paved the way for its own demise by holding within itself the seeds of atheism.[14]

Edward Beecher, a North American Christian theologian from the mid-nineteenth century, regarded the impassible deity of classical Christian theism as a false view or a misconception of God's character. Beecher described this misconception as "an obscuration or an eclipse of the glory of God" and of the true conception of God, as well as "a cloud between God and the mind" and "an interception of [God's] legitimate influences on the soul."[15] Beecher advocated replacing that misconception with a more biblical view of God, the concept of a God who suffers.

Dietrich Bonhoeffer, one of the twentieth century's most provocative, if not enigmatic, European witnesses to divine suffering, also regarded the classical-Christian-theistic concept of deity, a concept that he characterized as *deus ex machina* or "God as a working hypothesis," to be "a false conception of God."[16] Bonhoeffer, unlike Jüngel, did not directly try to show how this "false conception of God" subverted itself in modern culture. He indicated, however, that his understanding of "the development towards the world's coming of age" did away with the concept of God as the *deus ex machina*.[17] The "development toward the world's coming of age" involved, according to Bonhoeffer, the realization of human autonomy in politics, ethics, science, and so on, and, therefore, the rejection of "God as a working hypothesis," the divine explanatory factor. With his concept of the "world's coming of age," Bonhoeffer described the human exercise of freedom and responsibility in all areas of life, the awareness "that we have to live in the world

14. "It is precisely the absolutist monarchical understanding of God which has given rise to atheism as a righteous revolt" (Berdyaev, *Slavery and Freedom*, 85). Similar discussions appear in a variety of works by other theologians of divine suffering: e.g., Williams, "Deity, Monarchy, and Metaphysics," 51–70; and Jüngel, *God as the Mystery of the World*, 43–152.

15. Beecher, *Concord of Ages*, iv, v, 1, 55, 58. J. R. Lucas holds a similar view: "Once we cease imputing to the suffering God of the Christian religion the supposed perfections of the God of the philosophers, we can see how it is that God can be God without thereby depriving us of freedom and responsibility" (Lucas, "Foreknowledge and the Vulnerability of God," 128).

16. Bonhoeffer, *Letters and Papers from Prison*, 360, 361.

17. Ibid., 359–61.

etsi deus non daretur," " 'even if there were no God.'"[18] Furthermore, and perhaps most importantly, Bonhoeffer claimed that God desires the human awareness and exercise of this freedom and responsibility. "God would have us know that we must live as [humans] who manage our lives without him. The God who is with us is the God who forsakes us (Mark 15:34). The God who lets us live in the world without the working hypothesis of God is the God before whom we stand continually. Before God and with God we live without God." Hence, for Bonhoeffer, the true God desires "the development toward the world's coming of age," even seeks to motivate the growing acknowledgment of human and worldly autonomy. This development, this awareness, eliminates from the world a dominating though false conception of deity. For Bonhoeffer, the elimination of false concepts of deity establishes the possibility to discover the biblical God, "the suffering God."[19] Consequently, whatever the source for the demise of the concept of God in classical Christian theism, Bonhoeffer's most creative insight remains: *the death of deity (including classical theism) in Western culture provides the first condition of possibility for encounter with the concept of God to which the Christian symbol of divine suffering attests.*

Whatever the accuracy or inaccuracy in Bonhoeffer's theological assessment of the suffering God's relation to modern Western culture, classical Christian theism's crisis in Western culture—the so-called "Death of God"—has helped to clear the space for alternative Christian symbols of the divine to appear and to speak. Hence, I return to the Christian symbol of divine suffering, because it appears to hold significant resources, paradoxical as this thought may seem, as a figure of hope in post-modern and post-Christian worlds. My perception, however, only faintly echos Heinrich Heine's more eloquently articulated sentiments. "Eternal praise is due to the symbol of that suffering God, the Saviour with the crown of thorns, the crucified Christ, whose blood was as a healing balm that flowed into the wounds of humanity. The poet especially must acknowledge with reverence the terrible sublimity of this symbol."[20] Beecher, earlier in the nineteenth century, had

18. Ibid., 359, 360.

19. Ibid., 360, 361. Cf. Krötke, "Teilnehmen am Leiden Gottes: Zu Dietrich Bonhoeffers Verständnis eines 'religionslosen Christentums,'" 439–57.

20. Heine, *Religion and Philosophy in Germany*, 26. Such attestations to divine suffering and the sentiments about them, of course, obviously contradict classical theories

similarly announced that ". . . the most sublime, glorious, and powerful development of the character of God is found in the fact that he can and does suffer in consequence of the sins of his creatures."[21] Some theologians significantly stress this symbol's terrible sublimity on a revised Anselmian basis: the God who surrenders in love, suffering in response to creatures, is the God "than whose power of love nothing greater can be conceived"; or the suffering God is "'that than which a greater cannot be thought'; it is the unsurpassable self-definition of God" or also is "the greatest that the mind of man can conceive."[22]

Heine's rhetoric, of course, refers to Jesus' crucifixion, which he understood as the symbol of divine suffering. In light of the great variety in Christian attestations to divine suffering, however, testimony to the crucifixion of Jesus constitutes only one facet, albeit the central one for Christian experience and reflection, of Christian attestations to

---

of the sublime. For example, about Homer's description of the battle among the gods in *The Iliad*, Longinus says the following. "But although these things are awe-inspiring, yet from another point of view, if they be not taken allegorically, they are altogether impious, and violate our sense of what is fitting. Homer seems to me, in his legends of *wounds suffered by the gods* [italics mine], and of their feuds, reprisals, tears, bonds, and all their manifold passions, to have made, as far as lay within his power, gods of the men concerned in the Siege of Troy, and men of the gods. . . . he portrays the gods as immortal not only in nature but also in misfortune" (Longinus "On the Sublime," 9.7, in *Critical Theory since Plato*, 81–82).

21. E. Beecher, *Concord of Ages*, 87.

22. E. Johnson, *She Who Is*, 268; Kasper, *God of Jesus Christ*, 194; E. Beecher, *Concord of Ages*, 87. Also, in 1938, the doctrinal commission of the Anglican Church published the following statement. "It is also true that the revelation in Christ discloses God as taking on Himself in the Person of His Son the suffering involved in the Incarnation. We recognize that this carries with it a loftier conception of the Divine Majesty than that which would deny that suffering can enter at all into the experience of God" (*Doctrine in the Church of England*, 56). Also, see the similar position advanced by Jüngel. "The death of Jesus Christ, which forced a differentiation between God and God, has been properly understood only when one experiences, on the basis of the resurrection of Jesus Christ, that the divine[s] [sic] modes of being, Father and Son, which in this death separated into such a great differentiation than which nothing greater can be imagined, now so differentiated relate to each other anew *in the Holy Spirit*. Next to the Father and the Son, the Holy Spirit is a third divine relationship, namely, the relationship between the relationships of the Father and the Son, that is, the relationship of the relationships and thus an eternally new relationship of God to God. This eternally new relationship of God to God is called, christologically, resurrection from the dead, and is ontologically the being of love itself. Only in the *unity* of the giving Father and the given Son is God the *event* of giving up which *is* love itself in the relation of lover and beloved" (Jüngel, *God as the Mystery of the World*, 374).

the suffering God. With two comments, however, I qualify my anticipation about the unused resources of this symbol within contemporary contexts, although even this qualified anticipation motivates my studies of this symbol.

First, I acknowledge indebtedness in my own interpretation of this Christian symbol to human communities that both *have* thought and *continue to* think about this symbol. While I hope that a renewed interpretation of this symbol will yield new aspects of its structure or meaning, I refuse to claim, by focusing upon this symbol as an object of interpretation, either that I have discovered a new object of study or that the results of my work upon this symbol reflect complete originality of perspective. In this respect, Augustine's wise and prayerful caution guides my studies: "for whosoever claims to himself as his own that which Thou (God) appointed to all to enjoy, and desires that to be his own which belongs to all, is forced away from what is common to all to that which is his own—that is from truth to falsehood." Second, in my re-interpretation of this symbol, I have tried to avoid simple endorsements of popular contemporary ideas. La Rochefoucauld reminds readers that "most things are praised or decried because it is fashionable to praise or decry them."[23] Obviously, many more theologians in the nineteenth, twentieth, and twenty-first centuries have accepted this Christian symbol's validity, meaning, and theological appropriateness than did theologians in the preceding, combined eighteen centuries. In previous centuries, however, several factors prevented this symbol's theological acceptance and development that more recent years have produced. Platonic, Neoplatonic, and Aristotelian ontologies inhibited the discovery of ontologies that could adequately account for the dynamism in ultimate reality that Christian attestations to divine suffering have announced and implied. Furthermore, the elevation of those Hellenistic ontologies, in their patristic and medieval theological forms, to the status of ecclesiastical dogmas prohibited the development of ontologies on a theological level that would permit positive assessments of attestations to divine suffering. Modernity, however, challenged in many ways both that ecclesiastical authority over the dissemination of ideas and those dominant ontologies that precluded positive assessments of testimonies to divine suffering. Hence, voices that Christian

23. Augustine, "Confessions," in *A Select Library of the Nicene and Post-Nicene Fathers of the Christian Church*, 12.25.34; La Rochefoucauld, *Maxims*, 108, maxim 533.

cultures had spiritually, politically, and intellectually silenced or marginalized in former centuries have more recently found and taken their
opportunities to speak. I add only a small voice to the ever-widening
discussion among those who have chosen and continue to choose positively to re-evaluate the Christian symbol of divine suffering. Thus, I
join the community of those who question the wisdom and authority
that have empowered efforts either to silence or to discredit attestations
to a suffering God. Especially since the nineteenth century, Christian
theologians in large numbers (at least as compared to previous centuries) clearly have begun to think seriously about the symbol of divine
suffering.[24] That this shift became possible may have resulted, in part,
from the severe criticisms that religion and religious language have suffered in modern, post-modern, and post-Christian cultures, especially
insofar as that critical scrutiny has focused upon classical Christian theism as one of its principal objects of analysis.

I join the community of those who seriously and expectantly
encounter the Christian symbol of divine suffering. Interpretations of
this symbol, however, can assume a multitude of forms, may move in a
number of directions, and may entertain a vast variety of issues. Where
an interpreter begins and with which issues or problems the interpreter
begins, when studying the Christian symbol of divine suffering, both
depend quite significantly upon factors within the contemporary context and may deeply affect that context as well. Many problems and areas of inquiry arise in connection with the Christian symbol of divine
suffering. What status does such language about God possess? What
ontological implications does such a symbol entail? What treatment has
this symbol received in the history of debates between its theological
defenders and the conservators of the classical Christian concept of divine impassibility? If God suffers, how can such a God help humans who
also suffer with their own needs? Asking and answering any one of the
previous questions about this symbol supplies any study of this symbol
with a specific object and, therefore, with particular shape and direction. Obviously, the previous questions touch only a few of the many
issues that thinking about this religious symbol involves. Additionally,
one series of studies cannot possibly address adequately every one of

24. Daniel Day Williams regarded this revolutionary change as a "structural shift in
the Christian mind" (Williams, *What Present Day Theologians Are Thinking*, 172).

even the few questions that I raised previously. In my studies of this symbol, therefore, I do not pretend to answer all of those questions.

I propose a task for my studies of this symbol both more modest and more ambitious. All of the previous questions presuppose Christian attestations to divine suffering. Due to the more modest impetus for my studies, then, I ask only one question: *What is the Christian symbol of divine suffering?* I propose, therefore, only to answer this question by describing this symbol and clarifying the contours of its structure and dynamics. Arising from the more ambitious impulse for these studies, however, I propose a radical re-interpretation of this entire symbol, not just one or two of its central features.

Due to this ambitious impulse, I have developed a phenomenological hermeneutic of the Christian symbol of divine suffering under the following general title: *God's Wounds: Hermeneutic of the Christian Symbol of Divine Suffering.* I have organized my study of this symbol into three separate volumes: Volume 1, *Divine Vulnerability and Creation*; Volume 2, *Evil and Divine Suffering*; and Volume 3, *Divine Suffering and Tragic Reality.*

The present work constitutes Volume 1, *Divine Vulnerability and Creation*, which consists of two major parts. In "Part One: Orientations for Encounter with the Christian Symbol of Divine Suffering," I delimit the questions through which I have chosen to encounter or address this symbol (chapter 1), outline the method with which I have embarked on this particular path of inquiry (chapter 2), and hypothetically though briefly sketch the broad contours of this symbol's structure (chapter 3). Although these first three chapters address specific methodological and epistemological issues, they arise from the nature of the object of study itself. In that light, because the Christian symbol of divine suffering emerges from the larger root-metaphor of God as love, this metaphorical core figures prominently throughout the entire symbolic network and, therefore, supplies the guiding metaphor for my phenomenological hermeneutic of this symbol. In "Part Two: Presuppositions of the Christian Symbol of Divine Suffering," through two major divisions, I excavate and reconstruct the two major symbolic presuppositions of the Christian symbol of divine suffering. These two presuppositions represent the essential, yet often only implicit, conditions of possibility for the various aspects of divine suffering to which numerous expressions of the Christian symbol of divine suffering attest. Division One,

"Divine Lover: Self-Limiting Divine Creator," develops an exposition of the divine creator as the self-limiting God of love, first uncovering the characteristics of the divine life itself (chapter 4), then describing the features of the divine life actualizing itself as love in creation (chapter 5). In Division Two, "Beloved Human: *Imago Dei* and *Imitatio Dei* as Love," the present work develops an exposition of the beloved human whom God has created as *imago Dei*, with the being or life of love (chapter 6), the beloved human actualizing the *imago Dei* as love in terms of *imitatio Dei* or imitation of God (chapter 7), followed by an exposition of the human as part of the cosmos or world itself, rather than the world as only the context and resource for the human's life as *imago Dei* (chapter 8).

Volume Two of this project, *Evil and Divine Suffering*, will include two major parts that examine this symbol's construal of the first two divine wounds, the divine experience of and response to human sin and its consequences: "God's First Wound: Divine Grief" (Part One); and "God's Second Wound: Divine Self-Sacrifice" (Part Two). The third volume of this work, *Divine Suffering and Tragic Reality*, will constitute a study of the third moment or dimension of divine suffering: God's third wound, divine affliction. With that final set of studies, I will complete this particular approach to interpreting the Christian symbol of divine suffering. The final volume of studies examines the divine relationship to and experience of the tragic region of reality and experience (as distinct from the realities and experiences of evil): creaturely affliction by the created features of finitude itself, as distinct from evil, or the region of tragic reality and experience and the twofold afflicted divine response of divine distress and divine compassion.

The studies of these three volumes, then, supply central arguments in support of my claim to develop a relatively-more-adequate interpretation of the structure and dynamism in this religious symbol than most interpreters have developed in previous and alternative expositions. Hence, I endeavor to liberate something more of the complexity and profundity, that which Heine described as "the terrible sublimity," that people may experience through encounter with the Christian symbol of divine suffering. Most assuredly, whatever sublimity emerges through this study, it will challenge the usual notions of human experience of the sublime. For this reason, these studies constitute a serious responsibility with respect to both the larger history of the Christian traditions and contemporary Christian communities. In this task, I take seriously the seemingly unhesitating enthusiasm in Martin Luther's discerning judgment: the person ". . . who contemplates God's sufferings for a day, an hour, yes, only a quarter of an hour, does better than to fast a whole year, pray a psalm daily, yes, better than to hear a hundred masses."[25]

I note, however, that, while Luther often wrote about divine suffering, and even said that "God died for us" or that ". . . Christ, the true paschal lamb [I Cor 5:7], is an eternal divine Person, who dies to ratify the new testament," nevertheless, his doctrine of God remains within the classical theistic paradigm, especially insofar as he continued to utilize the classical-Christian-theistic concept of *communicatio idiomatum* with which to construe the place of Christ's sufferings in the two-natures christology of classical theism: "for God in his own nature cannot die; but now that God and man are united in one person, it is *called* [italics mine] God's death when the man dies who is one substance or one person with God."[26] The rhetorical power of Luther's language about divine suffering, however, has inspired many contemporary theologians in attempts to retrieve Luther's theology of divine suffering from his adherence to classical theism in other key respects. Jürgen Moltmann made such an attempt, by emphasizing Luther's modifications of the *communicatio idiomatum*. Ted Peters also similarly interpreted Luther's theology of the cross: "for Luther the divine nature was present throughout the earthly life of Jesus, suffering the slings and arrows of human fortune."[27] Nonetheless, while Luther's theological struggles with the cross indicate his ambiguous relation to the traditions of classical Christian theism, I do not perceive a significant advance in his use of this concept beyond even Tertullian's nascent use of the notion of *communicatio idiomatum*; and Tertullian never surrendered the classical-theistic paradigm, despite his criticism of philosophy.[28]

25. Luther, "Meditation on Christ's Passion, 1519," 11.

26. Luther, "On the Councils and the Church," 103, 104; idem, "A Treatise on the New Testament, that is, the Holy Mass, 1520," 85.

27. Moltmann, *Crucified God*, 231–35; Peters, *God—the World's Future*, 198.

28. For example, see Tertullian, *Adversus Marcionem*, 2.16; idem, *De Carne Christi*, 5. Luther's comments on Yahweh's grief, as written in Gen 6:6, also clearly indicate Luther's reluctance to attribute any sort of suffering to God. "One should not imagine that God has a heart or that He can grieve. But when the spirit of Noah, of Lamech, and of Methuselah is grieved, God Himself *is said* [italics mine] to be grieved. Thus we should understand this grief to refer to its effect, not to the divine essence. When, by

Isaak August Dorner insightfully perceived that, although the sixteenth-century Protestant reformers developed soteriologies that implicitly or latently contained "a better, yes, the true concept of God," those soteriologies (including Luther's) and those of their dogmatic heirs ". . . left standing a doctrine of God which, built up from other principles, was taken over traditionally from the pre-Reformation church and remained essentially consonant with the Roman doctrine, as if the purification from non-Christian conceptions did not have to extend also to this doctrine, whereas in fact the medieval doctrine of God in large part and clearly goes back to non-Christian sources."[29]

In these studies, then, I attempt to take Luther's assessment at least as seriously, and, I will venture, perhaps more seriously than Luther himself. More than likely, however, even if I should succeed in surpassing Luther in this matter, I probably have not yet taken the Christian symbol of divine suffering seriously enough. Nonetheless, I hope that the following studies will release afresh this symbol's terrible sublimity, something of that which has not yet fully disclosed itself within Christian theology.

---

revelation of the Holy Spirit, Noah and his father and grandfather perceived in their hearts that God hated the world because of its sins and intended to destroy it, they were grieved by its impenitence. . . . The inexpressible groanings of these outstanding men *are assigned to* [italics mine] God Himself because they proceed from His Spirit" (Luther, *Luther's Works*, vol. 2, *Lectures on Genesis: Chapters 6–14*, 49, 50). Luther similarly commented on Isa 63:10 (Luther, *Luther's Works*, vol. 17, *Lectures on Isaiah: Chapters 40–66*, 358). William L. Jaggar, discerning the aporia in Luther's understanding of the relation between God in eternity and God incarnate, argued similarly (Jaggar, "Passibility of God as Atonement Motif in the Theology of Martin Luther"). Also, see Dennis Ngien's study of Luther's theology of the cross, in which he argued that Luther claimed an ontological status for divine suffering, despite key texts in Luther's work in which Luther flatly denied that the divine nature suffers in any sense: Ngien, *Suffering of God According to Martin Luther's Theologia Crucis.*

29. Dorner, "Dogmatic Discussion of the Doctrine of the Immutability of God," 116.

Orientations *for* Encounter *with the* Christian Symbol *of* Divine Suffering

*I dedicate part one, with enduring gratitude and affection,
to my major teachers during my doctoral studies
at the University of Chicago:*

Langdon Brown Gilkey
(1919–2004)

Paul Ricoeur
(1913–2005)

David Tracy
(1939–)

James M. Gustafson
(1925–)

Introduction to Part One:
Approaching the Symbol

IN AN ENCOUNTER WITH THE CHRISTIAN SYMBOL OF DIVINE SUFFERING, a maze of problems opens before the inquirer, beckoning, with promises of both disclosure and transformation, the seeker to enter into its mysteries. The interpreter of this symbol must enter its maze carefully, always keenly aware of every clue, in order wisely to discern the next most favorable move to make through the ever more complex difficulties in an encounter with this religious symbol.

I intend carefully to follow this caution in my own journey through this maze of problems. To fulfill this aim, I have assigned two tasks to Part One of this book: (1) display the broad range of concerns and difficulties that any encounter with the Christian symbol of divine suffering entails; and (2) develop a relatively-more-adequate approach by which to engage this religious symbol. Part One accomplishes this dual task through a threefold orientation.

In order to provide the proper conditions for an intelligible and a fruitful encounter with the Christian symbol of divine suffering, Part One orients these studies in three chapters. Chapter 1 delimits the problem that constitutes the object of my studies. Chapter 2 describes the method by which I have engaged the problem. Chapter 3 identifies and develops the hypothetical threefold structure of this Christian symbol.

In my studies of the Christian symbol of divine suffering, this first part contains a series of orientations to my entire study of this symbol, while Part Two contains interpretations of the symbol's two principal presuppositions. The preliminary character of the studies in this book, therefore, requires a brief explanation of their relationship to one another. I have written Part One of this book only to prepare for a study of the Christian symbol of divine suffering, with a disciplined line of questioning and delimitations. Nonetheless, various portions from the chapters of Part One, but especially chapters 2 and 3, begin actively to engage in the study of this symbol despite the methodological constraints upon those chapters. I have developed the five chapters of Part Two as studies to commence my explorations into the Christian symbol of divine suffering. Again, nonetheless, the chapters of Part Two also display a peculiar quality in that respect: they do not actually begin to examine this symbol's theology of suffering. As the implicit structural components in the Christian symbol of divine suffering, however, I have derived the analyses and conclusions in chapters 4–8 from Christian attestations to divine suffering. Hence, I allow the concrete aspects of this symbol into the interpretations of Part Two, as well as into specific portions of Part One, but principally for epistemological reasons.

In the two major parts of this book, then, a process comes into view that also characterizes the movement between the three volumes of my larger work: the movement from the more abstract to the more concrete. Any *successful* phenomenological hermeneutic of the structure and dynamism in the Christian symbol of divine suffering will depend to a great degree upon the ability with which I have consistently maintained as well as rhythmically both released and restored a complex series of brackets around this symbol's various components and features. The first two parts of this larger study, which constitute this first volume, display the most abstract features of this symbol, as its eight chapters first orient an approach to this symbol, while taking clues from the symbol itself, that most adequately allow this symbol to exhibit its distinctive features. The five chapters in Part Two of this volume, then, initiate explicit studies into this symbol with an elaboration of its implicit fundamental presuppositions, presuppositions that the symbol construes as the conditions of possibility for divine suffering—divine vulnerability.

My studies in the two parts of this first volume, then, disclose *essential* structures and dynamics in the Christian symbol of divine suffering, elements that Edward Farley has described as "perduring features that constitute the being of something in its region or situation," ". . . not a static or timeless essence in contrast to process or change but its characteristic powers or ways of existing in the typical and extended situation of that thing."[1] In the second volume of studies, then, I will

---

1. E. Farley, *Good and Evil*, xix.

release one set of brackets, in order to study this symbol's construal of evil and the effect of evil upon the various essential structures and dynamics of this symbol. With Volume Three of the larger work, I will reintroduce the previous set of brackets, thereby withholding from consideration this symbol's attestation to the reality of evil in these essential structures (as in the studies of Volume Two); yet, at the same time, I will remove a second pair of brackets to allow the perduring characteristics of the tragic region of reality and experience to appear within the essential dimensions of the symbol that Part Two of this first volume will disclose.

Thus, the first two parts that constitute this first volume of the larger work contain the most abstract studies in this project. Because of this feature in the two parts of this first volume of studies, their analyses differ from the series of studies that will follow in volumes Two and Three. In my expositions of this symbol's two major presuppositions, I have described their essential features as *dimensions*, material and formal. Whereas, in the latter two volumes of this study, although I also will follow the pattern of examining both formal and material features of those moments in this symbol, I have described those features as *characteristics*. I distinguish dimensions from characteristics to emphasize the highly abstract quality of the studies that appear in the second part of this first volume of studies.

Although the orientations and interpretations in the two major parts of this book remain more abstract than the studies that will follow in the remaining two volumes of studies, even the studies of this first volume display both the practical and the emancipatory cognitive interests within the Christian symbol of divine suffering.[2] The methodological abstractions operate to allow the full disclosure of this symbol; the operations of these abstractions, however, also liberate this symbol from a history of its theological, philosophical, and even socio-political

---

2. I borrow these distinctions between practical cognitive and emancipatory cognitive interests from Jürgen Habermas (Habermas, *Knowledge and Human Interests*, 301–17). Most pointedly, Habermas supplies a fifth thesis on knowledge and human interests: ". . . the unity of knowledge and interest proves itself in a dialectic that takes the historical traces of suppressed dialogue and reconstructs what has been suppressed" (Habermas, *Knowledge and Human Interests*, 315; cf. Campbell, "Critical Theory and Liberation Theology"). Farley locates his own anthropological studies on the map of Habermas, but only in terms of practical cognitive interests (E. Farley, *Good and Evil*, xix–xx).

suppression. Just as importantly, though, through the rhythm of the application, removal, and restoration of these abstractions, these studies also disclose *both* the symbol's critique of its own suppression *and* the symbol's self-critical capacity or tendency. This disclosive process begins with these first sorties into the Christian symbol of divine suffering.

1

Delimitation of the Problem

Introduction

BY DELIMITING THE PROBLEM FOR INVESTIGATION, THIS CHAPTER PRO-
vides the first orientation that an encounter with the Christian symbol
of divine suffering requires. I will delimit the problem for inquiry in a
series of steps. (1) In the first step, I will circumscribe *the question* with
which to approach this symbol. (2) Second, I will specify the meaning
of this symbol as a *Christian* symbol. (3) My third step will describe
the *concept of symbol* that I have employed to formulate the problem
that this larger study addresses. (4) In a fourth step, I will clarify the
nature and extent of this problem's *theocentric posture*. (5) The fifth
step will display the symbol's *various structural levels*, and their inter-
relationships, as examined through these studies. (6) Sixth, I will *contextualize this particular interaction with the symbol*, as conceived in the
particular problem that this larger study investigates. (7) Finally, my last
delimitation will formulate *the aim* for this particular encounter with
the Christian symbol of divine suffering.

Circumscription of Inquiry

In order to initiate delimitation of the problem for consideration, I
must answer a first question. With what sort of inquiry does one begin
through which to commence an encounter with the Christian symbol
of divine suffering, in order to understand this symbol most completely
on its own terms and with respect to the questions that it attempts to answer? One might assume that the first and most fundamental question
to articulate, by which to circumscribe this problem, logically should

take the following form: Can God suffer?[1] Following an affirmative answer to that first question, one might need to ask another series of questions prior to considering actual characteristics of divine suffering, such as the following questions. *Does* God suffer, if God *can* suffer? If God can suffer, does God have a choice of whether or not to suffer? An inquirer might extend this line of questioning almost indefinitely, thus postponing the even more pressing discussion about the characteristics of this symbol. Only after securing affirmative answers to the previous questions, at least according to that particular line of thought, can the inquirer begin to describe the characteristics of that divine suffering. Unfortunately, however, beginning with the question of divine suffering's possibility often elicits a negative and dogmatic answer, thereby at least inhibiting, if not entirely preventing, any thought about characteristics of divine suffering: in other words, one may already have identified such a concept as an impossibility.

More importantly, however, the previous questions fail to reach the foundation of this problem. Those questions already imply a presupposition of their very inquiries—the attestation of piety itself: "God suffers!" This attestation elicits the previous questions, rather than following them as an affirmative conclusion to the question that initiated the previous series of inquiries. Attestations to God's suffering certainly remain confessional, devotional, even liturgical, religious language of a first order. Precisely for that reason, however, language that testifies to divine suffering precedes all reflection or speculation about whether or not God can or does actually suffer.[2]

---

1. Many Christian theologians frequently approach the problem from this perspective, often answering the question from opposite perspectives on the spectrum: see Attfield, "Can God be Crucified." 47–57; Galot, *Dieu souffre-t-il*; Harrison, "Can the Divine Nature Suffer," 119–21; Kobusch, "Kann Gott Leiden," 328–33; Küng, *Incarnation of God*, 518–25; Owen, "Does God Suffer," 176–84; Stockdale, "Does God Suffer," 87–92; Torrance, "Does God Suffer? Incarnation and Impassibility," 345–68; Weinandy, *Does God Suffer*; idem, "Does God Suffer," 35–41.

2. Other scholars, such as Francis Fiorenza, perceive the only adequate approach to "the possibility of a theology of the pain of God" to be through the transcendental consideration of "the problem of the possibility of language about God and the meaning of such language," an approach which means "that we are first of all dealing not with God directly but with a question of our language about God" (Fiorenza, "Joy and Pain as Paradigmatic for Language about God," 75). Abraham H. Khan engages similarly with the question of the possibility for a theology of divine suffering, as a linguistic and epistemological problem, though from a Wittgensteinian and Kierkegaardian

Notwithstanding any validity in the previous claim, in a very important historical respect, such a claim requires qualification. In the intellectual world that received Christian communities at their births, an entire universe of philosophical reflection upon the nature of God had flourished for centuries, philosophical efforts that argued for *stasis* in the divine being: for example, that nothing external to God can change (divine immutability) or affect (divine impassibility) the ultimate reality. For example, one finds this line of thought in the biblical interpretation of the Jewish philosopher, Philo of Alexandria. This world of thought had developed from philosophical attempts by Greek thinkers to interpret the myths of Greek religion in such a way as to dispense with the cruder aspects of their anthropomorphic language about the gods. Christian thinkers quite readily, though also somewhat uncritically, adopted this approach to interpreting their own God-language, so that even they began to describe God as immutable and impassible.[3]

---

perspective (e.g., Khan, "God Suffers: Sense or Nonsense," 91–99). While the concerns that these approaches express remain very important for theologies of divine suffering, they remain equally important for all theologies. Most, perhaps all, theologians of divine suffering would not deny the importance of such approaches to this problem. Nonetheless, should theology remain preoccupied to such an extent with *talk about talking about God* that theology finally fails to talk about *God*? In these studies, for a variety of reasons, I have not approached the Christian symbol of divine suffering in a way that resembles Fiorenza's line of treatment. Thus, these studies do not focus upon Fiorenza's concern: the question about the possibility, meaning, or even viability of applying the language of suffering to God.

3. See the following works, as an introduction into the complexities and history of this rich tradition of discussion and debate: Abramowski, "Die Schrift Gregors des Lehrers 'Ad Theopompum' und Philoxenus von Mabbug," 273–90; Brasnett, *Suffering of the Impassible God*; Brown, "Schelling and Dorner on Divine Immutability," 237–49; Burnley, "Impassibility of God," 90–91; Creel, *Divine Impassibility*; Crouzel, "La Passion de l'impassible," 269–79; D'Arcy, "Immutability of God," 19–26; Dodds, *Unchanging God of Love*; idem, "Thomas Aquinas, Human Suffering, and the Unchanging God of Love," 330–44; Dorner, "Dogmatic Discussion of the Doctrine of the Immutability of God," 115–80; idem, *Divine Immutability*; Edwards, "Pagan Dogma of the Absolute Unchangeableness of God," 305–13; Grant, *Early Christian Doctrine of God*, 14–33, 111–14; idem, *Gods and the One God*; House, "Barrier of Impassibility," 409–15; Jones, "Immutability of God Considered with Reference to Prayer," 565–70; Kondoleon, "Immutability of God: Some Recent Challenges," 293–315; Maas, *Unveränderlichkeit Gottes*; Meesen, *Unveränderlichkeit und Menschwerdung Gottes*; Mozley, *Impassibility of God*; Mühlen, *Die Veränderlichkeit Gottes als Horizont einer zukünftigen Christologie*; Muller, "Incarnation, Immutability, and the Case for Classical Theism," 22–40; Norris, *God and World in Early Christian Theology*; O'Hanlon, *Immutability of God in the Theology of Hans Urs von Balthasar*; Pohlenz, *Vom Zorne Gottes*, 66–105;

Nevertheless, the previous claim remains valid. Even the language about the passions of the Greek gods certainly preceded the hermeneutical qualifications of that language by the early Greek and later Hellenistic philosophers. Although Christian communities originated within the Hellenistic world, even the Christian and Jewish language that attested to divine suffering definitely preceded the hermeneutical qualifications of that language by early Jewish and Christian theologians and philosophers.

In spite of the previous historical comments, however, I do not propose with these studies either to search for the origins or to trace the development of the Christian symbol of divine suffering. Naturally, much of that history will appear throughout these studies in notes and references. Nonetheless, I do not propose explicitly in this project to inquire into the origin of this symbol or idea, although that inquiry remains essential even if often implicit for the results of my studies.[4]

Pollard, "Impassibility of God," 353–64; Prestige, *God in Patristic Thought*; Prichard, "Immutability of God," 338–44; Randles, *Blessed God: Impassibility*; Robertson, "Does God Change," 61–64; Ryssel, *Gregorius Thaumaturgus: Sein Leben und Seine Schriften*, 71–158; Schoonenberg, "Chalcedon and Divine Immutability," 103–7; Slusser, "Scope of Patripassionism," 169–75; Taliaferro, "Passibility of God," 217–24; Thaumaturgus, *Ad Theopompum: De Passibili et Impassibili in Deo*, 363–76; Trethowan, "A Changing God," 247–61; Watson, "Problem of the Unchanging in Greek Philosophy," 57–69; Weinandy, *Does God Change*; Woodbridge, "God Without Passions," 42–61; Zoffoli, *"Mistero della sofferenza di Dio"? Il pensiero di S. Tommaso*

4. Thorough and accurate historical studies about this Christian symbol's origin and development remain lacking in both histories of Christian thought and systematic Christian theological efforts. Such studies would need to identify and assess numerous appearances and versions of this symbol in its vastly different geographical, cultural, social, political, and intellectual contexts: such as East Asia, Southeast Asia, Scandinavia, Western and Central Europe, Great Britain, Africa, the Americas, and so forth. One contemporary theologian of divine suffering suggests that this symbol originated in the Israelite exodus from Egypt (Exod 2:23–25; 3:7-8); nonetheless, he proposes neither to prove or defend this thesis nor to attempt such a comprehensive historical study (Frey, "Holocaust and the Suffering of God," 613). Other theologians claim, somewhat inaccurately, both (1) that the doubts about the doctrine of impassibility "have their earliest roots in British theology, where we can trace the passibilist tendency back to the last ten years of the nineteenth century" (Sarot, "Patripassianism, Theopaschitism and the Suffering of God," 363; idem, "Het lijden van God," 35; Sarot finds support for this conclusion in van Egmond, *De lijdende God in de Britse Theologie van de negentiende Eeuw*, 23–25), and (2) that English theology has "pioneered" the development of theologies of divine suffering "from about 1890 onwards" (Bauckham, "'Only the Suffering God Can Help,'" 6; cf. Schoonenberg, "De lijdende God in de Britse Theologie," 154–70). Even Moltmann makes a similar oversight, when he makes the following claim. "In

Two convictions support the rationale for the necessity of this study, therefore, both of which historical research validates. First, before the symbol of divine suffering could develop fully enough to stand on equal terms before and debate with the historically-dominant Christian ontologies, epistemologies, and axiologies, the intellectually-dominant representatives of the Hellenistic world had both asked and then answered negatively the question (and its related questions) as to whether or not God can suffer. This effectively (both intellectually and finally politically) stifled any fully adequate and convincing expressions of this symbol. An interested person needs only to survey the history of Christian thought on divine impassibility and immutability to perceive the extent of this situation. Second, although since the nineteenth century many theologians (and not only Christian theologians) have accepted, contemplated, and studied the Christian symbol of divine suffering, most of these religious and theological efforts remain sketchy or incomplete. Most of the earlier receptions and retrievals of this symbol have usually held positions in larger projects with broader theological agendas. Few of these theological studies have closely examined the fuller structure in the Christian symbol of divine suffering in any clearly systematic way. Thus, these facts, *both* the intellectual refusal and silencing of the symbol as a credible proposal prior to its adequate de-

---

the nineteenth and twentieth centuries it was English theology which carried on the theological discussion about God's passibility. Continental theology passed it by unheedingly" (Moltmann, *Trinity and the Kingdom*, 30). Not only does Moltmann fail to identify and acknowledge the historical North-American emphasis upon this theological theme, but he fails to perceive even its broader presence in European thought as well. As examples in European thought, see the works of Schoeberlein, Troeltsch (*Christian Faith*, 174–94), Erling Eidem (*Den Lidande Guden*; *Suffering God*), or even the philosopher, Hermann Lotze, who influenced the personalist tradition in the United States through Borden Parker Bowne. Admittedly, Bauckham does credit the North-American theologian, Horace Bushnell (ca. 1866), with "a good deal of influence on the English tradition" (Bauckham, "'Only the Suffering God Can Help,'" 6 n.2). Nonetheless, the North-American shift in the direction of divine passibility was much broader than even Bushnell's influence indicates. See, as examples from the early through the later 1800s in the United States, the works of Edward Beecher, Charles Beecher, Henry Ward Beecher, Harriet Beecher Stowe (Caskey, *Chariot of Fire*), and George Griffin (*Sufferings of Christ*), all of whom developed concepts of divine suffering. As other scholars study this symbol in other historical and geographical contexts as well, discoveries of such omissions will increase.

velopment *and* the less than fully adequate recent acceptance and study of this symbol, invite the present study.[5]

Given the historical factors that have contributed to the need for this study, and given the secondary character of the questions about the possibility of divine suffering, I orient this present encounter with the Christian symbol of divine suffering through the following question: *What is the structure, and what are the structural dynamics, of the Christian symbol of divine suffering?* By construing this question in another way, I amplify my intent: *What are the various modes of divine suffering, and how are they both distinct from, and related to, one another within the broader Christian symbol of divine suffering?*

With this line of questioning, I aim to provide the conditions for a more complete elucidation of this symbol's characteristics. I intend to initiate an encounter with this symbol that permits the symbol's full development, prior to any extended conversations or debates about this symbol with the classical Christian theistic tradition. Here, as Walter Bauer suggested for the historian, I attempt to comply with the following principle: "*audiatur et altera pars* (let the other side also be heard)."[6] Thus, I have bracketed the question about the possibility of divine suffering, a question usually addressed to traditions that already affirm divine suffering, as a topic for later conversation with classical Christian theism. Certainly, this question and the network of questions that relate to it remain important areas of inquiry. Nevertheless, the conversations (and finally arguments) in which those questions play significant roles do not determine the focus in my studies of this symbol. That conversation becomes equitably possible only following the completion of two tasks: (1) a more complete elucidation of this Christian symbol; and

---

5. See some of the more systematic interpretations of this Christian symbol: E. Beecher, *Concord of Ages*; Brasnett, *Suffering of the Impassible God*; Eidem, *Suffering God*; idem, *Den Lidande Guden*; Fiddes, *Creative Suffering of God*; Fretheim, *Suffering of God*; Galot, *Dieu souffre-t-il*; Griffin, *Sufferings of Christ*; Kitamori, *Theology of the Pain of God*; Krause, *Leiden Gottes-Leiden des Menschen: Eine Untersuchung zur kirchlichen Dogmatik Karl Barths*; Kuhn, *Gottes Trauer und Klage in der rabbinischen Uberlieferung (Talmud und Midrash)*; J. Lee, *God Suffers For Us*; Moltmann, *Crucified God*; idem, *Trinity and the Kingdom*; Ohlrich, *Suffering God*; Robinson, *Suffering, Human and Divine*; Thaumaturgus, *Passibili et Impassibili in Deo*; Scharbert, *Der Schmerz im Alten Testament*, 216–25; Varillon, *Humility and Suffering of God*; idem, *La souffrance de Dieu*; White, *Forgiveness and Suffering*.

6. Bauer, *Orthodoxy and Heresy in Earliest Christianity*, xxi.

(2) an elaboration of the contemporary *significance* of this symbol at several levels (ontological, epistemological, axiological, and praxiological). In this book, I take the first step in an elucidation of this Christian symbol (which I will complete in the next two volumes of this larger study) but do not attempt to fulfill the latter task. Nevertheless, only on those two bases, minimally, can one expect an intelligible and a genuine dialogue between the alternative Christian traditions of divine suffering and those of classical Christian theism. Hence, I have placed brackets around the conversation with classical Christian theism, thereby separating it from my present studies of this Christian symbol, at least as I herein conceive that encounter.

In these studies, then, I hope adequately to identify and elucidate the fundamental character of the structure and dynamism within the Christian symbol of divine suffering. Such labors necessarily precede inquiries into the validity, truth, value, or correspondence of that symbol to any and all levels of reality. One must listen carefully to the complete statement of one's partner in conversation before one can respond both fairly and intelligibly to the other perspective.

Christian Symbol

The question by which I have defined my approach to the problem of divine suffering more specifically delimits the problem by inquiring only about the *Christian* symbol of divine suffering. Such a qualification at least implies attestations, or the possibility of attestations, to some form or forms of divine suffering in other religious traditions.[7] I will inves-

---

7. One may find examples in both contemporary and ancient religious texts. In more recent decades, the teachings of the Unification Church supply one example. While possessing many of the marks of traditional Christian communities, the teachings of this community deviate radically from traditional Christian thought, most specifically at the key point, christology. Still, this community espouses a strong concept of divine suffering (Moon, *Divine Principle*, 10; Y. Kim, *Unification Theology and Christian Thought*, 36–40; Sonneborn, "God, Suffering and Hope: A Unification View," 163–239). Another contemporary version of divine suffering appears in the teachings of The Children of God (now known as the Family of Love or the Family) (e.g., as analyzed in, Richardson and Davis, "Experiential Fundamentalism: Revisions of Orthodoxy in the Jesus Movement," 397–425). Some Hindu thought about the issue of divine passibility resembles many classical Christian theistic defenses of divine impassibility except under certain conditions (Bhattacharyya, "Does God Suffer," 34–47). Also see a North-American Christian example: England, "Weeping God of Mormonism." 63–80. As examples from ancient religious traditions, consider the suffering deities in the *Enuma*

tigate, however, only that symbol of divine suffering that its witnesses represent as a *Christian* symbol: by virtue of their confession of Jesus as Christ, their participation in the broader Christian communities, their adherence to one or another of the very similar canonical scriptures of these Christian communities, and their explicitly-stated relationships with the God to whom all of these witnesses attest.

By contrast, at this point, many persons might reasonably object that orthodox Christian teaching has never supported any claim that anything external to God in any sense affects God or causes the divine nature to suffer.[8] Furthermore, the doctrine of divine impassibility (as

---

Elish, the Akkadian epic of creation (Enuma Elish, "The Creation Epic," 60–72). There, the gods, formed within Tiamat and Apsu (the two primal gods), by all of their activity disturbed and troubled their begetters (Tablet I, lines 22–23), so that Apsu decided to destroy those whom he had begotten (I.35–40). This plot grieved Tiamat, filled her with woe, so that she desired to deal kindly with her children (I.41–47). Apsu proceeded with his plan, but word of it reached the intended divine victims, who wept from fear and sorrow, whereupon Ea developed a counter-plot and killed Apsu (I.60–70). Other gods then persuaded Tiamat to avenge Apsu, since they themselves grieved over his murder (I.109–23). Tiamat agreed to their call for vengeance and elevated Kingu into the position of her consort and leader of the gods (I.147–54). When the usurper Ea learned of this, he became troubled and sought aid from his forefather Anshar; Anshar, having heard the gloomy report, became troubled (II.49–51). Finally, when the remaining gods heard of Tiamat's vengeance, they all sorrowed and extended their divine power and authority to Marduk, son of Ea and Damkina, to battle against Tiamat (III.125–28). Thus, Marduk and Tiamat battled, whereupon Marduk killed Tiamat (IV.98–106). The gods who had supported Tiamat wailed in fear (IV.113). Marduk created the world from the carcass of Tiamat (IV.128–40). Marduk then killed Kingu who was accused of contriving the rebellion of the gods: from Kingu's blood, Marduk created humanity (IV.23–33). Later, the praise of Marduk's heroics attributed great sympathy to Marduk (VII.155).

8. Bertrand de Margerie, in response to an official, and a somewhat sympathetic, Roman Catholic reassessment of Christian attestations to divine suffering (Commissio Theologica Internationalis, "Theologia-Christologia-Anthropologia: Quaestiones Selectae. Altera Series [Sessio Plenaria 1981, relatio conclusiva]," 20–24), argues that such attestations contradict revelation, Catholic tradition, and human reason (De Margerie, "De la Souffrance de Dieu," 110–12). De Margerie cites evidence from those sources to support his argument in that order. Nonetheless, although he begins with scripture, insofar as his ontological assumptions (e.g., ultimate reality's impassibility and immutability; and determined far more by tradition than by reason) require a particular hermeneutical approach to scripture, he finds in the scriptures only that which he already presupposes. On the one hand, he cites in this essay only one biblical text (Jas 1:17), although he might easily have cited more, to support his argument. On the other hand, he completely ignores those biblical texts that explicitly attest to various forms of divine suffering: such as Gen 6:5–6; Isa 63:9–11; and Eph 4:30. Nonetheless, given

well as its attendant doctrine, divine immutability) received dogmatic status in the earliest stages of the development of Christian thought,[9] has been consistently propagated and defended by all of the major Christian confessional traditions, and still marshals strong defenders of its claim to truth. As far as this objection goes, according to its understanding of that which constitutes *Christian* doctrine and dogma, it remains correct.

Nevertheless, although the Christian doctrine of divine impassibility has possessed, and still possesses, dogmatic status in many of the major Christian confessions, one may properly describe testimony to divine suffering in Christian thought as a *Christian* teaching. Certainly, Christian ecclesiastical authorities have officially judged Christian testimonies to divine suffering as heretical or heterodox. One inescapable reality, however, has always challenged such judgments: the presence in a variety of Christian canonical scriptures of testimonies to various forms of divine suffering. Ecclesiastical judgments, to which I have previously referred, upon the idea of divine suffering have relied upon hermeneutical methods by which interpreters have realigned such scriptural affirmations with the philosophical presuppositions that justified the condemnation of this idea or symbol in the first place.

Not only can one discover testimonies to divine suffering within the scriptural traditions that arose from the Jewish and early Christian communities. Throughout Christian history, piety has articulated such testimonies in a variety of ways, through hymns, liturgies, confessions, sermons, and theologies.[10] Since the early years of the nineteenth cen-

---

the theo-logic of de Margerie's symbolic framework, attestations to divine suffering do contradict revelation, Catholic tradition, and reason.

9. See examples from this history in the notes to the Prologue of this book. Studies of the definitions, creeds, confessions, and anathemas that appear in the earliest conciliar decisions of the Christian communities clarify this: see Mozley, *Impassibility of God*; Kelly, *Early Christian Creeds*; Leith, ed., *Creeds of the Churches*; Schaff and Wace, eds., *Seven Ecumenical Councils*; Denzinger and Schönmetzer, eds., *Enchiridion Symbolorum*.

10. Besides Christian ecclesiastical doctrinal studies that various Christian communities have commissioned to study this symbol (as I noted in the Prologue), Christians have explicitly organized entire consultations and conferences around this theme: see Cameron, ed., *Power and Weakness of God: Impassibility and Orthodoxy*; Smith, ed., "Seoul Theological Consultation 1979: Reporting the Event," 3–4. Furthermore, these consultations have occurred in Asia as well as in Europe. In Korea, the Seoul Theological Consultation adopted a theme with the following title: "The Hope: God's Suffering in

tury, this tendency has increased significantly. Presently, both theological and philosophical support for the idea of divine suffering has grown so strong that one writer has described the increase in this notion's popularity as "the rise of a new orthodoxy."[11] Hence, whether or not, and to what extent if so, one agrees with such an assessment, and while one may not speak (from an official ecclesiastical standpoint) about the idea of divine suffering as an *orthodox* teaching of all or most Christian communities, one yet truly can and should describe this teaching as a *Christian* teaching. Furthermore, this teaching continues to acquire, not only a religious and devotional following, but also a stronger theological and philosophical reception among Christian scholars.

Therefore, in this book, I will examine the symbol of divine suffering as attested by numerous voices within various Christian communities. Even on the basis of such a delimitation, however, numerous Christian interpretations of divine suffering demand attention, many of them claiming to be the most adequate understandings of the phenomenon to which they attest. Neither do all of these different Christian testimonies to divine suffering agree with one another nor can an interpreter harmonize all of them. All Christian witnesses to divine suffering, nevertheless, primarily ground their testimonies, as a rule, in the Christian scriptures.

Another facet of the problem attends this situation, a facet that further complicates any examination of this religious symbol: *Even the Christian scriptures contain competing traditions.* Referring to Christian scriptures, James Barr states this much more forcefully: "The Bible is more like a battlefield, in which different traditions strive against one another."[12] Thus, not only do Christian testimonies to divine suffering compete with one another, testimonies that principally originate from

---

Man's Struggle." The consultation in Korea also indicates the global proportions of this concept among Christians: case studies from Latin America, North America, Eastern Europe, the Middle East, Africa, and Asia followed its theological presentations.

11. Goetz, "Suffering God," 385–89. This claim, however, really expresses nothing more than that which perceptive theologians have expected for at least the last one hundred years. For example, in his essay entitled "Patripassianism," first published in 1917 and later included as a chapter in his book, H. Maurice Relton anticipated something similar to Goetz's claim: "There are many indications that the doctrine of the Suffering God is going to play a very prominent part in the theology of the age in which we live" (Relton, *Studies in Christian Doctrine*, 79).

12. Barr, *Scope and Authority of the Bible*, 115.

the Christian scriptures. One may also discover that even the Christian scriptures themselves contain testimonies to divine suffering which, at best, do not harmonize or, at worst, even conflict with one another.

Nonetheless, both the variety of testimonies to divine suffering in the Christian traditions and the sometimes-conflicting viewpoints within this variety contribute to the richness of the Christian symbol of divine suffering. To express any experience of the divine (especially experiences of the suffering God) requires repeatedly-renewed thought-experiments. As William James expressed this point, "without too much you cannot have enough of anything." At the basis of this insight, rests the practical conviction that "precious specimens" of thought only appear scattered throughout and lodged within mountains of sometimes partial, inadequate, inferior, misguided, or even banal alternatives and experiments. More positively, this means that, with James, I acknowledge the benefits of multiple thought-experiments about God, in this case about the suffering God of Christian piety. Multiple Christian viewpoints yield a many-faceted portrait of the God who suffers.[13]

In spite of the complexities involved when examining the different kinds of Christian testimonies to divine suffering, I here rely upon a wide variety of texts from the history of the Christian traditions. These texts, as Christian texts, comprise the primary source-material for my analyses of this symbol. These selected texts include texts from the two canons of Christian scriptures,[14] works by classical and contemporary Christian thinkers, and Christian liturgical, confessional, and credal writings. In addition, at certain points, I will examine texts from Jewish (and other) traditions for amplification of, or comparisons to, particular elements of this symbol's rationality. All of the post-biblical materials or sources for my interpretation of this symbol, therefore, principally interpret and re-interpret the primary testimonies to divine suffering that one may find in the Christian scriptures. I will examine these sources in order to contribute either to elaboration and development of this inter-

13. James, *Essays in Radical Empiricism and a Pluralistic Universe*, 316; E. Beecher, *Concord of Ages*, 40.

14. As examples, see Gen 6:6; Isa 63:9; Eph 4:30. One may refer to these two testaments as "the one" and "the other" testaments (following Beauchamp, *L'Un et l'Autre Testament*), as the first and second canons, or as the older and newer Christian canons or scriptures. I will sometimes use each of these categories as well as occasionally the more familiar distinction between "old" and "new," even though problems appear in connection with the usages of any of these distinctions.

pretation of the structure and dynamism of this symbol, to clarification of the methodological principles that I have used to study this symbol, or to both of these ends.

By further delimiting the problem for this work, as well as through a discussion of the procedural principles or method in chapter 2, I will clarify the procedure that I have used both to adjudicate between competing testimonies and to establish the core Christian symbol of divine suffering. The following chapter on method will also clarify more about the sources to which I have turned for these studies.

Operative Concept of Religious Symbol

I have cited enough evidence already by which to support my claim that various Christian witnesses attest in one way or another to divine suffering. If Christian testimonies to the suffering of God, however, compete with one another for the position as the most adequate witness to that phenomenon, and if most of the major Christian communities have consistently identified such testimonies as unorthodox (erecting in their places, instead, the ecclesiastical dogma of divine impassibility), then in two senses a question about the existence of an actual Christian understanding of divine suffering arises. (1) First, since official Christian ecclesiastical authorities have labeled Christian testimonies to divine suffering as heretical, are those testimonies not then, by definition, non-Christian? (2) Second, even should Christian ecclesiastical authorities award some kind of *Christian* status to testimonies to divine suffering, then, due to the often great differences between these various testimonies to divine suffering, may one convincingly designate one single construal of divine suffering as its definitive Christian expression? I have tried to open a way beyond the dilemma that this dual perplexity poses with two initiatives: first, by developing a distinction between symbol and doctrine, by which I limit this study to the notion of religious symbol; and, second, by elaborating this particular concept of religious symbol.

Religious Symbols and Religious Doctrines

Admittedly, to distinguish between religious symbols and religious doctrines artificially separates very similar phenomena from one another.[15] In one sense, at least, this *falsely* distinguishes very similar phenomena from one another. With religious doctrines, religious communities symbolize the realities to which those doctrines point and in which the symbols participate. This remains true even when religious doctrines become dogmas, when official ecclesiastical authorities of any religious community sanction them or prescribe adherence to them. In the dogmatic construal of doctrines, then, one will discover very little Christian doctrine that attests to divine suffering.[16]

In a second sense, however, while one may describe all religious doctrines as religious symbols, one cannot accurately describe all religious symbols as religious doctrines—at least not in terms of teachings that ecclesiastical authorities of religious communities officially sanction. In this sense, then, the distinction between religious symbols and doctrines helps rather than hinders. Many religious symbols challenge orthodox doctrines. While the heterodox status of some religious symbols often does not allow them to hold officially-sanctioned locations and functions within religious communities, nevertheless, many of these symbols retain central components of orthodox religious symbol-systems, components that permit, however marginally, these heterodox symbols to be defined in terms of the religious communities both to which those symbol-systems disclose ultimate reality and from which those symbol-systems have arisen. Hence, one can refer to the Christian symbol of divine suffering as a Christian *symbol*, without construing it as an officially-sanctioned Christian *doctrine*. Many Christian scriptures, hymns, poems, theological writings, other literary genres, as well as other human productions and experiences, testify that the Christian

15. David Tracy rightly warns against the too facile opposition of these genres (Tracy, *Analogical Imagination*, 293–94 n. 57).

16. Inasmuch as Christian confessions or creeds function as official doctrines within various Christian communities, occasionally, though very sporadically throughout Christian history, some of these confessions attest to divine suffering. For example, note the following early Anabaptist testimony to divine suffering. "Images and pictures are of no value. Therefore you should trust no longer in wood and stone, but in the living and suffering God" (Hübmaier, "Eighteen Dissertations Concerning the Entire Christian Life and of What it Consists," 20). Here, as also in most patristic writings, however, this phrase refers principally if not exclusively to the suffering Christ.

God suffers. Furthermore, often, leaders of religious communities communicate official religious doctrines almost exclusively to intellect and conscience, thereby obscuring the depth and breadth of their symbolic contact with the fuller range of human experience as a whole.[17]

For the previous reasons, I describe the object of my studies as the Christian *symbol* rather than the Christian *doctrine* of divine suffering. Still, the problem of competing testimonies to divine suffering persists. How can one speak of *the* Christian symbol of divine suffering? Finding an answer to this question first requires a description of the concept of religious symbol that I have employed in this larger study.

Describing the Concept of Religious Symbol

I begin by noting the complexity that any description of the concept of religious symbol involves. I specifically focus only upon the religious symbol, not upon either the nature of symbols in general or political, social, economic, and racial symbols. Nevertheless, because a religious symbol constitutes a type of symbol, several general characteristics of symbols require description as well. My focus, however, remains upon the fundamental features that characterize symbols as *religious*. In addition, although a symbol may be a religious symbol, a religious symbol may and usually does also possess political, social, economic, or even racial features. These other symbolic features may become objects of consideration when examining a religious symbol, but only insofar as their relations to the religious heart of the symbol may be traced to them and through them. Although not the point of this study, as I will show through the following inquiry into the nature of religious symbols, with careful scrutiny one may discern the religious dimension of all symbols—including political, social, economic, and racial symbols.

With the following description, I sketch the theory of symbol on the basis of which I have studied the Christian symbol of divine suffering. This description, then, elucidates a criteriology of *religious* symbols, by which one may identify and distinguish them from other symbols, identify their referential meaning, describe the strata of significance that reside in religious symbols, and observe the functions of these peculiar symbols.

17. Gilkey, "Symbols, Meaning, and the Divine Presence," 264; also in idem, *Through the Tempest*, 49–65.

CRITERIOLOGY OF RELIGIOUS SYMBOL

Any effort to describe a concept of religious symbol requires a set of criteria by which both to circumscribe the space of symbols from the space of all other signs and to discriminate further between religious symbols and all other symbols. With the following criteria, I sculpt a rough, but operational, theory of religious symbols.

First Criterion

Any element, aspect, or dimension of finite reality or ordinary experience may serve as a religious symbol, that in, to, and through which the Sacred, ultimate reality, or God communicates, discloses, or manifests itself, on the one hand, and, in so doing, transforms the finite, as the finite reveals through its own being the creative presence of the Sacred, on the other hand.[18] This criterion entails at least the two following corollaries.

1. If sacred or ultimate reality discloses itself through finite media, then humans always experience God indirectly. Ultimate reality always mediates itself and, therefore, hides or cloaks the divine presence in finite reality, even as it discloses itself in and through that medium.

2. If any aspect of finite reality may function as a symbol of the Sacred or God, and potentially at least every element of ordinary reality and experience may transmit disclosures of the transformative power of the divine presence, then (also because the Sacred or God grounds the being of every aspect of finite reality) each creature or each aspect of finite reality most authentically actualizes itself and fulfills itself as it symbolizes ultimate reality. As Langdon Gilkey has carefully stated, "each creature in its essential or natural being, as *itself*, is a 'symbol' of the presence of the holy, and it becomes its authentic self when the pattern of its life in faith inwardly and outwardly in action reflects that creaturely status and role as an image of God."[19]

---

18. Gilkey, "Symbols, Meaning, and the Divine Presence," 256. Paul Tillich stated this similarly: Tillich, *Systematic Theology*, 1:240.

19. Gilkey, "Symbols, Meaning, and the Divine Presence," 256. Paul Tillich summarizes this criterion most succinctly, perhaps, in his well-known formulation. A religious symbol "participates in the reality of that for which it stands" or "participates in the reality which is symbolized" (Tillich, *Systematic Theology*, 1:239; idem, *Systematic Theology*, 2:9).

Second Criterion

Even though all of finite reality may participate in the symbolization of the Sacred or ultimate reality, because of the human's universal alienation from its ultimate ground, from itself, and from other creatures, the Sacred discloses itself in particular forms—special and unique finite media—to specific historical communities, in order to re-awaken those communities to their own status as symbols.[20] This criterion entails at least the three following corollaries.

1. Although God or ultimate reality grounds human life, both as personal and as communal or social, sin obscures and distorts the Sacred or divine reality, the authentic self, the authentic other, and authentic relationships among all of these. Thus, human sin entangles the divine presence in a *double concealment*: the Sacred first conceals itself as it seeks to disclose itself through finite media; second, however, finite media obscure and distort the divine presence within and through themselves insofar as those creatures refuse their own authentic actualizations.

2. Specific historically-determined religious symbols *re-awaken*, through their disclosive power, the status of both individuals and communities as symbols of the Sacred. In so doing, a particular finite medium embodies the essential nature of the self, the other, and God, a disclosure through which the Sacred offers transformation as a possibility.

3. As a symbol of ultimate reality that embodies the essential nature of being human both personally and socially, a religious symbol *challenges* the sinful distortion of human selves and communities. Hence, religious symbols criticize and refine the social, political, economic, and even racial symbols that reflect and promote the various characteristics of human alienation.

Third Criterion

God or ultimate reality, disclosed in and through particular finite media or special events and persons, founds a community and transmits itself to that community; that community also transmits the sacred presence through its own communication about the Sacred. Religious symbols, then, communicate meaning to a specific community. Members of the

20. Gilkey, "Symbols, Meaning, and the Divine Presence," 258–59.

community communicate to the community about the founding symbol of divine presence, through communal acts or elements as well as with language.[21] Religious symbols, then, contain both linguistic and non-linguistic dimensions. In the latter dimension, the presence of the Sacred re-communicates itself to the community and re-awakens the community, only through finite media like the community itself: for example, as in Christian worship through the eucharistic bread and wine. Nevertheless, language announces the divine presence even within that non-linguistic dimension of the religious symbol. This criterion entails at least the five following important corollaries as well.

1. All symbols are signs. Every symbol, whether or not that symbol takes the form of some material object (such as a tree, a serpent, or an owl), communicates symbolically by coming to language, by expressing a linguistic moment—either in the spoken discourse of the worshipping community in which the symbol participates or in that community's written thoughts. According to Paul Ricoeur, symbols ". . . are expressions that communicate a meaning; this meaning is declared in an intention of signifying which has speech as its vehicle."[22]

2. Although all religious symbols finally communicate their meaning alongside and through language, and because religious symbols bind themselves to finite elements of the universe, language never fully succeeds in bringing to language that which seeks expression in language—the presence of the Sacred in which the symbol participates: "language only captures the foam on the surface of life."[23]

3. While all symbols signify something else, all signs do not operate symbolically. Only those signs symbolize, insofar as they conceal within themselves a double intentionality. First, the symbolic sign possesses a literal intentionality that depends upon a conventional sign—literal or ordinary descriptive discourse. Tied to this literal intentionality, however, a second intentionality points beyond the symbol to something that resembles (is *like*) the conventional sign, but is not that sign. The symbol supplies this second or figurative sense, however, only through

---

21. Ibid., 259–62.

22. Ricoeur, *Symbolism of Evil*, 14. See also, idem, *Interpretation Theory*, 54–57.

23. Ricoeur, *Interpretation Theory*, 63; cf., Geertz, *Interpretation of Cultures*, 91.

the sign's literal sense, thus implying the inseparability of the symbol's figurative sense from its literal sense.[24]

4. The phrase, "metaphoric process," identifies the linguistic strategy that produces the analogical bond between the literal and figurative senses of a symbol and communicates the meaning of this symbolization.[25] In the metaphorical process, a literal "is" that predicates an object of a subject implies both an "is not" and an "is like." Thus, a metaphor suspends ordinary or descriptive referentiality in favor of a secondary or figurative referentiality. Metaphor, then, promotes a split-reference and, in so doing, unleashes new meaning beyond the literal sense of the metaphorical statement.[26] Thanks to the metaphorical process at the heart of symbolization, ". . . the symbol is the movement of the primary meaning which makes us participate in the latent meaning and thus assimilates us to that which is symbolized without our being able to master the similitude intellectually."[27] One cannot separate the literal sense from the figurative sense of a metaphorical statement without the loss of symbolic meaning.

5. Before rejoining these brief comments upon the linguistic dimensions of religious symbols to my previous discussions, I need to distinguish other forms of language from symbols in general. First, the category of symbols does not include allegories; rather, allegorization represents a method for interpreting myths, not an analogical creation of meaning via the metaphorical process. Once an interpreter has employed an allegory to translate or interpret the meaning of a myth, the interpreter can discard the allegory. Second, the category of symbols, as developed previously, does not refer to the symbols of symbolic logic. Symbols of the latter type signify univocal meanings with mathematical characters, in order to dispel ambiguity and multiple interpretations. A symbol, with its central metaphorical process, by contrast, carries a surplus of meaning and, therefore, a creative ambiguity. Third, the concept of symbol that I have employed in my study of the Christian symbol of divine suffering, however, does include myths. Communities produce

---

24. Ricoeur, *Symbolism of Evil*, 17; cf. Tillich, *Systematic Theology*, 1:239–40; 2:9.

25. Ricoeur, "Biblical Hermeneutics," 75–106.

26. Ibid. Also, see Ricoeur, *Rule of Metaphor*, 216–313.

27. Ricoeur, *Symbolism of Evil*, 16. Compare this to the statement by Karl Jaspers: "in the cipher script, *the symbol is inseparable from that which it symbolizes*" (Jaspers, *Philosophy*, 3:124).

myths when they develop symbols as narrations and contextualize them within ". . . a time and space that cannot be co-ordinated with the time and space of history and geography according to the critical method."[28]

The previous criteria make possible the identification of religious symbols and their differentiation from other symbols. Through that criteriology, two features of transcendence have appeared that indicate the core of religious symbolism. First, a symbol transcends its literal sense through a figurative sense—the removal of either one of which from the other evaporates the symbolic meaning. Second, symbolic religious language expresses a relation in which an element of the universe, a finite aspect of reality, points beyond or transcends itself toward the Sacred or ultimate reality in which the symbol participates. These features indicate the dialogical relationships that operate among the divine presence, the human, and the world even in the symbolization of that relationship.[29] Not only, then, does the divine presence seek to share itself, to re-disclose itself to humans by choosing finite media for that purpose, but also humans choose finite media and language with which to open themselves to the divine reality that seeks disclosure. Hence, one need not choose between a Feuerbachian approach (that understands all language about God as a projection of human qualities) and a Barthian approach (that emphatically rejects *analogia entis* as natural theology) to religious language. The process of symbolization requires both divine and human creativity.

REFERENTIALITY OF RELIGIOUS SYMBOLS

Throughout the preceding criteriology for religious symbols, I repeatedly announced, either implicitly or explicitly, the fundamental referents of religious symbols. This stage in my description of religious symbols, then, sustains and develops from the preceding discussion this interest in the referentiality of religious symbols.

The question about the referentiality of religious symbols arises from larger questions that concern the meaning of religious symbols,

28. Ricoeur, *Symbolism of Evil*, 16–18; cf., Eliade, *Myth and Reality*, 18–19.

29. Tillich identified this when he noted the following about religious symbols. "They are directed toward the infinite which they symbolize *and* toward the finite through which they symbolize it. They force the infinite down to finitude and the finite up to infinity. They open the divine for the human and the human for the divine" (Tillich, *Systematic Theology*, 1:240).

more generally the meaning of religious discourse, and still more generally the meaning of all discourse. Briefly considering the meaning-theory of discourse will permit me to clarify my use of the term "referentiality."[30]

Leaving aside here the significant differences between written and spoken discourse,[31] one may discern the kinds of meaning in discourse through a simple, though profound, description of the discursive situation: *someone says something about something to someone*. An author or speaker expresses in language something about his or her experience of reality in an address to someone else. Thus, discourse possesses an event-character, often described as a speech-act. The meaning that discourse holds, then, contains subjective, objective, and inter-subjective poles. One can conceive the subjective and objective poles of meaning as the meaning-of-the-discourse-in-itself, while acknowledging the inter-subjective pole of meaning as the meaning-for-the-hearer-or-reader (the audience or partner in conversation).

Some linguistic philosophers describe the subjective pole of meaning as the "utterer's meaning." Discourse contains elements that direct the reader or hearer to the one who has uttered or written the discourse: for example, the self-reference found in the sentence, the illocutionary dimension of the speech-act, and the intention for recognition by the hearer or reader.[32] Both the speaker's or author's "particular vision" of reality and the speaker or author remain extra-linguistic referents, referents that appear through the discourse as the discourse's "self-referent" or "subject-referent."[33]

The objective pole of meaning, the "utterance meaning," contains two basic dimensions. The first dimension of objective meaning in discourse, the *sense* of discourse, concerns the "what" of the discourse itself, the relations between the signs, the grammar, and the sentences of the discourse itself. Discourse means something linguistically. The second dimension of the object-meaning of discourse, the objective

30. I follow Paul Ricoeur's theory of meaning in language: see Ricoeur, *Interpretation Theory*, 19–23; idem, "Naming God," 217; cf., Tracy, *Blessed Rage for Order*, 75–78.

31. See Ricoeur's important distinction between speaking and writing: e.g., Ricoeur, "Hermeneutical Function of Distanciation," 129–41; idem, *Interpretation Theory*, 25–44.

32. Ricoeur, *Interpretation Theory*, 19.

33. See Tracy, *Blessed Rage for Order*, 77–78.

reference, the object-referent of discourse, concerns the "about what" of discourse. In this second dimension, discourse means as it refers to something outside itself, to an extra-linguistic reality. The term "reference" designates the way, therefore, in which language transcends itself, relates itself to a world, and claims to be true. Written discourse *refers to* "the thing or the issue of the text," "the world of the text."[34] For discourse in general, then, reference designates the thing, the issue, or the world that discourse projects.

I describe the inter-subjective pole in the meaning of discourse, in parallel fashion, as "the meaning for the one to whom the speaker utters discourse," the meaning for the audience, reader, or hearer. This designates neither the sense nor the reference of discourse. Rather, as inter-subjective meaning, discourse communicates *significance* to the one with whom the speaker or writer communicates. The object-referent (the thing, the issue, or the world) of discourse incites the significance of discourse. This indicates a movement from discourse (whether written or spoken) into lived existence, that which Ricoeur has described as "the transfer from texts to life," "self-understanding in the face of the text," "the *application*, which will be as much political praxis as the labor of thought and language."[35]

Upon the basis of the preceding distinctions, several related perspectives contribute to a theory of meaning in discourse. Discourse communicates both linguistic and extra-linguistic meanings. The linguistic meaning of discourse designates the *sense* of discourse that remains immanent to discourse itself. The extra-linguistic meaning of discourse includes both the *reference* (both the object-referent, the world, the thing, or the issue of discourse and the subject-referent, the self-reference, the implied author, of discourse) and the *significance* of discourse for the one to whom the speaker communicates with discourse. Thus, the event-character of discourse promotes three kinds of meaning: (1) meaning as the sense of discourse; (2) meaning as the reference of discourse; and (3) meaning as the significance of discourse. The distinction between the latter two kinds of meaning in discourse enables me to distinguish between the referentiality and the significance of religious symbols.

---

34. Ricoeur, *Interpretation Theory*, 89–95.
35. Ricoeur, "Naming God," 226, 227.

The previous sketch of a linguistic meaning-theory, then, enables an identification and a description of the referentiality in religious symbols. To the extent that religious symbols communicate their meanings through language, the phrase, "referentiality of religious symbols," designates neither the subject-referent of those symbols (through which, the text directs the person in the presence of the symbols to an implied author) nor the first dimension of the objective pole of discursive meaning (the sense of a religious symbol's linguistic aspects in which the person before the symbol understands the symbol in itself). Rather, the phrase, "referentiality of religious symbols," describes the second dimension of the objective pole of meaning; it indicates that to which religious symbols point, that about which they speak, that extra-linguistic reality in which they participate, the object-referent.

Thus, a question arises: In which extra-linguistic reality do religious symbols participate? To which realities do religious symbols refer? I have already identified an aspect of that referentiality as the Sacred, the divine presence, the ultimate reality that or who transcends the finite. Before this question relaxes itself with the reception of such a basic and simple answer, however, I will press the question further by examining two somewhat different answers.

On one side, in some of his earlier work on religious language, Paul Ricoeur answered as follows. For him, the presence of a God-qualifier in poetic discourse characterizes that discourse as religious discourse.[36] For Ricoeur, however, the God-qualifier does not represent the ultimate referent of religious discourse. With the God-qualifier or the limit-referent, religious discourse redescribes the ultimate referent. Ricoeur describes that ultimate referent as "human experience centered around the *limit-experiences* of man," or "human reality in its wholeness."[37] Thus, Ricoeur understands human experience, as re-described by religious symbols and discourse, as the ultimate referent of religious symbols, not the Sacred to which the God-qualifiers in religious discourse attest. Such qualifiers only specify a certain variety of poetic language: *religious* language.

36. Ricoeur, "Biblical Hermeneutics," 33; idem, "Philosophy and Religious Language," 80, 82–83.

37. Ricoeur, "Biblical Hermeneutics," 33, 34, 108, 122, 127, 128. Ricoeur later modified this stance (e.g., Ricoeur, "Naming God," 217). Also, see the very similar position of David Tracy (e.g., Tracy, *Blessed Rage for Order*, 51–52, 77–78, 124, 134–36).

On the other side, in some of his earliest work, Karl Barth answered the previous question differently. Barth perceived the ultimate
referent of the Christian scriptures (or, in Ricoeur's terminology, "the
world of the text") as a "strange new world," "the world of God."[38] Barth,
like Ricoeur, acknowledged that religious language functions to present new possibilities for human and worldly life. Barth understood the
new world, however, as one that gathered around the God to whom
the scriptures refer. Barth emphasized that divine center when he wrote
about the referentiality of biblical language.

The two types of approaches to the primary referentiality of religious symbols, as roughly characterized, compete with one another for
the principal position in discussions about the linguistic dimensions
of religious symbols. The two approaches, however, both identify fundamental objects to which religious symbols refer: humanity and the
sacred or divine presence. Both of these objects, as well as a third, the
world (in both its socio-historical and natural or cosmic dimensions),
which contextualizes the interactions between humans and God, exhibit themselves as referents of religious symbols.[39] The question remains,
nonetheless: which aspect of this threefold referentiality of religious
symbols assumes the primary, ultimate, or fundamental position? The
primary referent of religious symbols remains the referent that qualifies
a symbol, and its linguistic expressions, as *religious*: for a religious symbol, the Sacred, ultimate reality, or the divine presence constitutes that
primary referent. As Langdon Gilkey perceived, "self-understanding
("the Christian mode of being in the world") is the *subsidiary*—though
very important—'referent' of the biblical symbols; the primary referent

---

38. Barth, *Word of God and the Word of Man*, 33, 37, 40, 45. I take these references
from his essay entitled "The Strange New World Within the Bible," which constitutes
the second chapter of his book. He originally delivered this chapter as an address in the
church at Lentwil in 1916.

39. Wolfhart Pannenberg argues similarly, when he observes that ". . . in the history
of religion every understanding of God corresponds to a particular understanding of
the world. It is impossible to associate any understanding of the world we like to choose
with an equally random idea of God. For it is one function of the idea of God to determine the understanding of the world in its own light. Thus the biblical idea of God as
the almighty Father also corresponds to a particular understanding of the world. This
is certainly variable in detail, but it is fixed in its basic character by the biblical idea of
God" (Pannenberg, *Apostles' Creed in the Light of Today's Questions*, 36–37).

is God, [God's] activity and so [God's] relation to possible modes of being in the world."[40]

Hence, religious symbols refer to a threefold extra-linguistic reality: human experience, the world, and the Sacred or God. Nonetheless, the first two referents of a religious symbol revolve around that third and primary extra-linguistic referent. An adequate understanding of the referentiality of religious symbols, however, will not designate one or the other of these three referents as the only referent. To abstract one of these referents from the other two referents threatens to distort the meaning of a religious symbol. Each of the referents that structure the referentiality of religious symbols remains woven into the fabric of the other two. Already within religious symbols, a correlative structure appears. The referentiality of religious symbols, then, describes the relational network that the referents of the Sacred (divine or ultimate reality), human reality, and the world (in both its socio-historical and natural dimensions) constitute. Consequently, religious symbols point to theological, cosmological, and anthropological referents.

STRATA OF SIGNIFICANCE IN RELIGIOUS SYMBOLS

Previously, I considered the theory of meaning in language, in order to clarify referential meaning or that to which religious symbols refer, their referents. My previous discussion of meaning-theory implies as well that religious symbols communicate something to someone. Religious symbols, therefore, also communicate meaning as *significance*. Those to whom religious symbols communicate experience four strata of significance in the communicative event.[41] Four strata of significance within religious symbols reflect the principal dimensions of self-understanding

---

40. Gilkey, *Reaping the Whirlwind*, 377 n. 23. See Gilkey's earlier discussion of this point (e.g., Gilkey, *Naming the Whirlwind*, 293–95). In later work, both Ricoeur and Barth slightly modified their positions. "God, who is named by the texts held open by my desire to listen, is, in a way still to be spoken of, the ultimate referent of these texts. God is in some manner implied by the 'issue' of these texts, by the world—the biblical world!—that these texts unfold" (Ricoeur, "Naming God," 217). Also, see similar developments in Barth's understanding (e.g., Barth, *Humanity of God*, 37–65). Mark Wallace develops an interesting comparison of Barth and Ricoeur on this and related points (Wallace, "World of the Text," 1–15).

41. I rely upon Langdon Gilkey's analysis of a symbol's meaning as significance: see Gilkey, *Naming the Whirlwind*, 247–304, 415–70; idem, *Catholicism Confronts Modernity*, Chapters 2–4; idem, *Reaping the Whirlwind*, 134–55; also see, Gilkey, "Roles of the 'Descriptive' or 'Historical' and of the 'Normative' in Our Work," 10–17.

that a religious symbol elicits from and within the one who encounters the religious symbol.

Eidetic Stratum

The word "eidetic" means the essential idea of something, its basic structure. The eidetic stratum of significance in a religious symbol refers to the meaning of that symbol within previous historical contexts: the past meaning of that symbol, both in its original scriptural forms and in the history of its interpretations and re-interpretations by its religious community. This historical significance differs from its experienced meaning in contemporary contexts, its present significance. Furthermore, the eidetic stratum of significance represents the past picture of the interrelationships of the threefold referentiality of a religious symbol, how previous communities formerly understood the Sacred, the human, and the world. Nevertheless, as *significance*, this eidetic or historical stratum represents the picture of the past meaning to the present as well. After an interpreter has observed and described the plurality of the various past understandings of a religious symbol, the interpreter identifies and renders the common features among them into a single picture, one fundamental symbolic structure, one that displays the essential *eidos* of a religious symbol. This rendering, by the contemporary interpreter, of the various interpretations of a religious symbol into one single structure yields a historical significance. This single structure, however, can differ in numerous respects from the entire variety of historical interpretations of the symbol, principally because the contemporary interpreter risks a historical reconstruction from his or her own perspective. This results in a historical significance for the contemporary interpreter, a reconstruction that begins to mediate this symbol to the present in such a way that the symbol offers its historical meaning as *contemporary* significance.

Epistemological-Experiential Stratum

A second stratum of significance arises from the aspects of actual contemporary human experience that a religious symbol both thematizes or discloses and shapes or directs. One can discern such significance in a religious symbol only insofar as the interpreter has successfully elucidated the religious dimension in actual contemporary experience, in the forms of the most important questions that constitute the depths of that experience. In that way, then, the religious symbol yields contemporary significance, for it supplies an answer to experiential questions of ultimate importance.

Ontological Stratum

In one conception of the discipline, ontology appropriates contemporary experience through its attempts to answer questions about the structure of finitude and reality as a whole, in categories that express present understanding. Although religious symbols themselves do not systematically articulate ontologies, they rely upon ontologies that the symbols themselves imply and that the linguistic dimension of religious symbols often disclose.[42] The ontologies that religious symbols presuppose remain part of the eidetic significance of those symbols. This third stratum of a religious symbol's significance, however, concerns how the symbol relates to the structures of finite reality and reality in its entirety as understood within contemporary contexts. The interpreter translates a religious symbol's ontology into concepts that relate both to that which contemporary contexts hold as true and to contemporary renderings of reality's contours.

Axiological-Praxiological Stratum

The word "praxis" designates the significance of a religious symbol in terms of its use as well as in terms of its projected activity, forms of actualizing existence, or potential modes of being in the world. That description implies values as the basis for a symbol's use, an axiology. Once again, even though religious symbols once had uses and values in the history of the religious communities for which they held significance, and even though those symbols projected new possible modes of being for that past world, those praxiological and axiological significances abide as part of the eidetic significance of religious symbols. In this fourth stratum, a religious symbol principally holds significance for contemporary praxis. Religious symbols exhibit a praxiological significance, in one sense, as their religious communities use them in wor-

42. See Tillich's discussions about the relationships between religious symbols and ontology: e.g., Tillich, *Systematic Theology*, 1:21; 2:12; idem, *Biblical Religion and the Search For Ultimate Reality*.

ship, morality, social and political relations, and in thought about the praxiological elements of human experience: thus, these symbols have an ordinary usage. In a second sense, religious symbols elicit praxiological and axiological significances both as they critically evaluate present forms of individual and communal or social life and as they creatively submit alternative proposals for human praxis. Such significance transfers to contemporary life, once again, only through the translation of the eidetic-praxiological significances of religious symbols into contemporary conceptions of the axiological and praxiological realities of creaturely experience.

Functions of Religious Symbols

The functions of religious symbols, like their strata of significances, do not confine themselves only to the hearers or audiences, the times, the places, or the situations, of their origins. Religious symbols, if they signify and therefore maintain themselves as symbols at all, function in contemporary experience as well. Broadly construed, religious symbols function in two ways.

1. First, religious symbols point beyond the finite referents with which they signify to the sacred or divine reality therein disclosed, through the specificity of the double intentionality in their linguistic dimension, in order to disclose the divine presence within all of ordinary (or secular) existence or in which all finite reality already participates. Religious symbols, then, function both to penetrate the sin-effected distortions of all finite reality, the distortions that obscure the Sacred's presence in ordinary existence, and to illumine the Sacred within the opacity of all finite reality. Religious symbols operate to dissolve the double obfuscation of the divine presence: the opacity of essential finitude and the distortions of faulted finitude. Thus, in religious symbols, the Sacred refuses to blast into human experience like something thrown from somewhere else into that experience; religious symbols *both* deliver or make explicit that prior presence in which all of finite reality already participates *and* give to that presence a specific religious form or name.[43]

---

43. Cf. Gilkey, *Naming the Whirlwind*, 464; idem, "Symbols, Meaning, and the Divine Presence," 261.

2. Second, religious symbols both critically challenge existing patterns of ordinary human life and offer creative proposals with which to displace the distortions that appear in both personal and social expressions of that experience. As critical challenges, religious symbols (also themselves already subject to the critical procedures of modernity) unveil the distortions and ideologies that the existing symbolic resources of contemporary culture both hide and protect. As new or at least different paradigms (models, norms, possible modes of being in the world), religious symbols promise to transform social and personal human life cognitively, emotionally, and volitionally, thereby providing resources with which human life can guide itself in these fundamental respects.[44]

Theocentric Posture

With another delimitation, I continue to narrow the focus of my study of this religious symbol. In the following elaboration of my continuing circumscription of the problem, my previous description of the operating concept of religious symbol in these studies provides the first ground for this delimitation.

In these studies, I deliberately adopt a theocentric posture. I have focused this interpretation of the Christian symbol of divine suffering upon God. I refuse to eliminate God from symbolic resources, for the purpose of denying the objective referent (God), through a philosophical proclamation that the Christian symbol of divine suffering really attests with a louder voice than usual only to human suffering. I refuse Feuerbach's reductive inversion of subject and predicate in the attestation "God Suffers." Unlike Feuerbach, here I listen attentively to the objective claims of this attestation: the Christian claim that God or the Sacred itself suffers.[45] On the basis of the insight that through religious symbols both the divine presence discloses itself and the human creatively opens itself to the invitation to that disclosure, here I listen to and observe the Christian symbol of divine suffering as that medium

44. Ibid.; cf. Geertz, *Interpretation of Cultures*, 87–125.

45. For Feuerbach, that attestation means that "to suffer for others is divine," that "feeling is absolute, divine in its nature," that "God is for man the commonplace book where he registers his highest feelings and thoughts, the genealogical tree on which are entered the names that are dearest and most sacred to him" (Feuerbach, *Essence of Christianity*, 60, 62, 63–64).

through which the Sacred discloses essential aspects of itself and of reality as a whole.

Still, both the character and extent of my theocentric posture within these studies require clarification. To construe these analyses as properly theocentric, therefore, requires me to define the term "theocentric." In order to approach a definition of this term and, thereby, to describe the theocentric posture of these studies, I first offer a typology of theocentric postures with regard to the referentiality of religious symbols.

Types of Theocentric Postures

In their interpretations of Christian symbols, scholars assume a variety of theocentric postures. In the discussion that follows, I have isolated and examined three major types of theocentric postures.

SOTERIOLOGICAL THEOCENTRICITY

In a first theocentric interpretation of Christian symbols, many theologians attempt to revitalize soteriology. Theologians who operate from this posture criticize those forms of soteriology that result in christocentric interpretations. According to this first theocentric approach, if God works to conquer the sin that concerns God in redemption, then one should acknowledge Christ's work as only "part of the whole work of God." This approach conceives salvation more consistently on a trinitarian basis.[46] Such a theocentric posture results from a suspicion of theological categories that have prevented the attribution of suffering, or of change that is essential to the emotional quality of life, to the divine nature of the God who became a human creature.

---

46. F. Robinson, *Redemption and Revelation in the Actuality of History*, 272–73. Robinson partially relies upon the work of Erich Schaeder (Schaeder, *Theozentrische Theologie: Eine Untersuchung zur dogmatischen Prinzipienlehre, Erster, geschichtlicher Teil*; idem, *Theozentrische Theologie: Eine Untersuchung zur dogmatischen Prinzipienlehre, Zweiter, systematischer Teil*). One can detect a related theocentric trajectory in Ricoeur's emphasis upon the christological dialectic between the celebration of total power in the first Christian canon and the confession of total weakness in the second Christian canon: "but the Cross does not allow itself to be spoken of or understood as the relinquishment of God except in relation to all the signs of God's weakness that belong to the whole naming of God" (Ricoeur, "Naming God," 224).

Cosmological Theocentricity

A second type of theocentric approach understands Christian theology as theocentric, only as long as this discipline focuses deliberately and critically upon the "all-pervasive reality" or the "strict universality" of the divine presence. This variety of theocentric thought impels theology to become public and informs "any theological analysis of the public character of theology." This approach derives the public character of theology from the universal participation of all reality, including all publics, in the divine presence that grounds all reality.[47] Because the divine presence pervades all reality without exception, the theologian must speak responsibly about God to the publics that are grounded in that divine reality and may do so with confidence because of her or his confidence in the all-pervasiveness of that divine ground.

Theological Theocentricity

Some theologians oppose a third type of theocentric thought to their assessments about the dominant form of piety and theological thinking in Western culture. This third type of theocentric posture understands that dominant form of piety and theology as human self-preoccupation, as anthropocentric piety and theology. The anthropological preoccupation of Western religious thought has focused upon human reality both as the measure of all things and as the central aim of the beneficent purposes of God for human life—human salvation and preservation.[48] This third theocentric posture proposes a shift of focus, in which "the proper orientation is not primarily toward self but toward God—to the honoring of God, and to the ordering of life in relation to what can be discerned of the divine ordering." Thus, this approach develops the following moral imperative: "we are to conduct life so as to relate to all things in a manner appropriate to their relations to God."[49]

47. Tracy, *Analogical Imagination*, 51, 52. One can also locate Tillich's thought within this type of theocentricity: for example, "God is not God without universal participation" (Tillich, *Systematic Theology*, 1:245).

48. "It is man's preoccupation with humanity and its spiritual civilisation or culture. It is the religious egoism of Humanity, i.e. man's absorption with himself, instead of with God, His purpose, His service, and His glory. . . . Everything has come to turn on man's welfare instead of God's worship, on man with God to help him and not on God with man to wait upon Him" (Forsyth, *Justification of God*, 18).

49. Gustafson, *Ethics From a Theocentric Perspective*, 1:110, 113. Gustafson's concept of God does exhibit some weaknesses, especially as related to the notion of divine suf-

Consequently, this approach significantly alters thinking about God *from* an almost exclusive concern with human salvation and well-being, as the principal divine purposes, *toward* attention to divine purposes for all of reality, in which human salvation and well-being may hold only minor roles in the divine aim, if any at all.

Theologians understand a theological approach as theocentric in a variety of ways, then, ways sometimes construed in opposition to one another. Theologians who espouse the three previous approaches to interpreting and using Christian symbols construe their own postures as theocentric. Each of these theocentric postures conceptualizes theocentricity in light of non-theocentric postures: (1) if one construes human salvation exclusively as *Christ's* work and Christ's experience of human history, while God observes from a distance the spectacle during which Christ appeases the divine wrath against sin, then one has developed a non-theocentric soteriology; (2) if one describes God as limited to shattering human history with one special event or several special events, and not as a universal presence in which all reality already participates, a presence that concrete religious symbols bring to awareness, then one has thought non-theocentrically about God; or (3) if one's talk about God focuses principally or only upon divine efforts to save and to preserve human life—and if one understands God to be orienting the entire cosmos around the human, to be dominated by

---

fering. One sympathetic critic of Gustafson's work attempts to modify Gustafson's concept of God, however, in light of Abraham Heschel's understanding of divine pathos. "There is no notion in Gustafson that what goes on in the world affects God; only that God is acting upon the world. What I want to reaffirm is that God's concern motivates God's activity. To put this in Gustafson's terms, God's rule or ordering activity, the norm, flows from God's concern for creation, the motive. To say that God is 'motivated' to act on behalf of creation is no more anthropomorphic than to say that God 'intends' the well-being of creation." This critic recalls that Heschel characterizes divine pathos as "absolute selflessness" (e.g., Heschel, *Prophets*, 2:5–6). "Pathos has a transitive not a reflexive character" (Glennon, "Divine Pathos and Human Sympathy," 246). The absence of a reflexive divine pathos, however, involves a suffering God precisely in that which Gustafson abhors—an almost exclusive soteriological (transitive) concern for the human. Heschel's theology of divine suffering weakens at this very point. Furthermore, even the Jewish scriptures indicate that God desires to maintain the divine being and glory. The prophet Ezekiel, for example, reminds the exiles in Babylon that Yahweh delivered them from Egypt, and would presently deliver them from Babylon, if only for the sake of the holy divine name (Ezek 20:9, 14, 22; 36:21–22). I find it difficult to regard this exclusively as a transitive divine concern, when it clearly reflects something of a reflexive divine pathos!

human life, to serve the good of human life—then one has not thought theocentrically.

Hence, if any single one of these viewpoints becomes the criterion by which to address the extent of the theocentricity in the other two approaches, then, depending upon the criteriological perspective from which one begins, one can construe all three approaches as deficient. In any case, all three viewpoints identify important elements for a theocentric posture. In the discussion that follows, I will note the contributions from each of these three approaches to a more comprehensive theocentric posture, the posture that I assume in the study of this Christian symbol.

An Alternative Theocentric Posture

Religious symbols refer to a threefold extra-linguistic reality: (1) the Sacred or God; (2) the world (in both its social or historical and natural dimensions) as the condition for and context of interaction between the divine presence and humanity; and (3) the human self and community. My previous discussions identify the Sacred as the focal point in this threefold referentiality. Here, then, I also re-emphasize the theocentric referentiality of Christian symbols.

For a variety of reasons, however, either the cosmological or the anthropological referents of a Christian symbol can become the central objects of a theological analysis. Nevertheless, such an analysis divests itself of theological content, if it fails to examine the special and determinate relations of either the human or the world to a Christian symbol's central referent—the Sacred or God.

As the previous theocentric postures make clear, even language about God might fail to qualify as theocentric depending upon how one discusses God or locates God in the discussion. For instance, on the one hand, some theologians may identify an approach as anthropocentric, either by virtue of its anthropomorphic or anthropopathic language about the divine presence, or by virtue of its fanatically-soteriological concerns with human life—even though that approach might claim that God carries the full responsibility for human salvation and preservation. On the other hand, some scholars may describe an approach as cosmocentric, either by virtue of its talk about God in terms that express natural growth and development, or by virtue of its understanding of

God as the structure of reality. Hence, although the desire for theocentric thought appears to be instinctive for theologians, theologians must carefully define their understandings and uses of the word "theocentric," for theocentricity in Christian thought exhibits several dimensions. I have attempted to distill from the Christian symbol of divine suffering three principal dimensions of theocentricity: theocentric internal relations of the divine presence; theocentric relations between God and the world (both historical and natural); and theocentric relations between the divine presence and the human.

First, the Christian symbol of divine suffering, with God as its central referent, refers to the ends, goals, or purposes of God. Admittedly, God's suffering correlates to situations in and circumstances of the creation. Nonetheless, through this symbol, one should not mistakenly construe God as oriented toward and for the human alone or even principally or preferentially in any sense. This dimension of theocentricity inquires as follows: What significance does the Christian symbol of divine suffering possess for the purposes, glory, and respect of God's own self? This question requires a theocentric posture from the beginning in these analyses of the Christian symbol of divine suffering.

Second, the Christian symbol of divine suffering refers to the cosmos as the context of and condition for, as well as a factor in, interactions between God and human reality. Although the cosmos provides—in its derivation from God—the condition of possibility for encounter between God and the human, the divine reality initiates a relation to the cosmos in itself (in which human life plays only a minor role). God orients this relation, however, toward fulfillment of God's purposes and ends. Inasmuch as the human originates within that context, the human depends upon the cosmos, in spite of the extent to which human freedom to master its context develops. Thus, as my study progresses, I endeavor to stabilize its theocentric character through a second question: What resources does the Christian symbol of divine suffering offer for indicating the place of the cosmos in the divine purposes? This dimension of theocentric thought acknowledges the Sacred's universal presence, in both non-human and human aspects of reality, in the cosmos as a whole. This theocentric dimension depends upon the first dimension in a theocentric approach to the Christian symbol of divine suffering.

Third, the Christian symbol of divine suffering, with its third referent (the human) focused upon God through its cosmological ground and context, dramatizes a fundamental quality of the divine purposes, through the characteristics in its representation of the relations and interactions between God and the human. Even though the cosmos contextualizes relationships between God and humanity, the cosmos also represents an end in itself within the larger divine aim, and in which the human's role becomes only one ingredient—perhaps an even smaller one than humans prefer to imagine. Hence, to some extent, one improperly describes the cosmos as the *context* for interactions between God and human life. Such a manner of speaking seems to define the cosmos as the expendable context in, through, and with which humans may fulfill their own superior purposes in God's scheme.

In the Christian symbol of divine suffering, however, if an emphasis upon human salvation appears, this neither necessarily implies a denial of a cosmological soteriology nor does it imply a declaration of the supreme importance of anthropological soteriology. God did not create the cosmos simply for the human's sake, but rather both for God's sake and for the world's own sake, just as God also created the human for the human's own sake. Nevertheless, any symbolic focus upon anthropological soteriology may suggest even more far-reaching divine purposes. God's salvation or healing of the human species may represent only one step toward the greater fulfillment of the cosmos itself; given the human propensity to actualize the *imago Dei* negatively, perhaps God can realize the greater divine purposes only through a divine healing of the human tendency to dominate, to distort, and to destroy the cosmos.[50] Hence, in order to prevent overlooking such insights into the divine purposes and ordering of relationships in the Christian symbol of divine suffering, I will avoid an exclusive focus upon the christological dimensions of divine suffering, by surveying the entire range of attestations to divine suffering as well as this symbol's symbolic presuppositions. With this in mind, I will maintain this interpretation's theocentric posture through a third question: What significance does the Christian symbol of divine suffering have for understanding both the place of the christological focus in the greater soteriological efforts of the whole divine life and the place of human salvation within the greater purposes of God for the cosmos as a whole, as well as for Godself?

50. The Yahwist imbeds this insight in the narrative of Yahweh's judgment of the earth through the flood and the following covenant with Noah (Gen 6:1—9:17): this text also contains a Yahwistic attestation to divine grief over human sin (Gen 6:6).

Structural Levels in the Symbol

I have delimited the focus of my studies in a fifth way. Both the threefold object-referent of religious symbols and that referentiality's theocentric character supply fundamental structural elements, elements that exhibit various structural levels and dynamics within the Christian symbol of divine suffering.

I do not elaborate here the specificities of the structure and dynamism in the Christian symbol of divine suffering. Rather, in this section, I briefly outline the general structural levels and relationships that I will analyze later. Only in chapter 3 does the particular content of these structural levels begin to assume a hypothetical shape.

The three object-referents of the Christian symbol of divine suffering (*theos, anthropos,* and *cosmos*) comprise the three principal elements, as abstracted from their relationships to one another, that generate the structure and dynamism in the Christian symbol of divine suffering. For the religious symbol that my study examines, the Christian attestation that "God suffers" summarizes the relationships between the symbol's three object-referents.

In the three volumes of this larger study, I seek to discover the major moments or modalities of divine suffering in that attestation. In addition, the dynamism that generates each of those major modalities invites elaboration. Finally, the dynamics that constitute the rich relational network among each of the modalities of divine suffering solicit interpretation as well. Thus, three structural levels require examination: (1) the basic modalities or forms of divine suffering; (2) the correlative structure between God and the creature in each of these principal modalities, the structure generated as each moment of divine suffering finds its occasion in the creature; and (3) the supportive principles or structures, the symbolic system that the attestation to divine suffering presupposes, that supply the conditions of possibility for the attestation that "God is love."

The previous structural levels indicate the central concerns in this large study. My focus intentionally precludes other structural dimensions, which might require other types of investigative procedures that derive from a variety of disciplines. Thus, I delimit this study by restricting it to the three structural levels that I have previously identified.

Contextualizing Interaction with the Symbol

I now return in this delimiting task to the very strange situation that I described in the prologue. Posing the following question initiates that return. Into what context does my attention to the problem of these studies, as heretofore delimited, insert itself? In what sort of situation does my present interaction with the Christian symbol of divine suffering occur? Here, then, I seek to delimit the context for my interpretation of this particular Christian symbol.

I take a preliminary step toward addressing this concern with a dual acknowledgment: (1) Christian attestations to divine suffering constitute a *Christian message*; and (2) this message ultimately addresses itself to *contemporary cultural situations and global concerns*. This dual acknowledgment supplies systematic Christian thought with its two major sources. The task of systematic or constructive theology, therefore, requires a mutually-critical correlation of these two sources to one another, in order to render or to transfer the symbol's meaning into significance for contemporary human life.[51]

---

51. The following works either develop or utilize correlative theological methods: Gilkey, *Message and Existence*; idem, *Reaping the Whirlwind*; Tracy, *Blessed Rage For Order*; Tillich, *Systematic Theology*, 3 vols.; also, cf. Farley, *Ecclesial Reflection*. Peter Hodgson's understanding of constructive theology even more closely approximates my own approach to the correlational task: "Theology, as a practice of the Christian community, is a constructive activity that requires critical interpretations and practical appropriations of faith's language about God in the context of contemporary cultural challenges and their theological implications" (Hodgson, *Winds of the Spirit*, 10). Most especially, my work has much in common, in terms of both method and content, with Edward Vacek's theology of love. Unfortunately, his work on love, very similar to my own work on divine suffering with its underlying theology of love, appeared the same year that I completed my dissertation. Thus, I did not have the benefit of reading his splendid work on Christian love before I completed my original thinking about this symbol. As I have had opportunity in this expanded study of the Christian symbol of divine suffering, I have shown where our two parallel studies have arrived at very similar conclusions. See his claim to develop a correlational theology of love: Vacek, *Love, Human and Divine*, viii n. 18. I have engaged this study of the Christian symbol of divine suffering with one version of a hermeneutical phenomenology and, in doing so, have developed in this three-volume work only an exposition of one pole in the correlative constructive theological task. My move to follow Tracy, with his emphasis on the theological method as "mutually-critical correlation" of the two major sources of theology, rather than Tillich (for example), indicates that I perceive significant theoretical and practical weaknesses in the method of correlation. In this study, although I have invoked a version of this method, I note (and readers will perceive this as well) the dissolution that this method experiences even from the beginning, as the following

Such a critical correlation relies upon the resources in interpretations of both the Christian message and contemporary experience, but remains wary of distortions that may lurk in both of them. In this sense, then, just as *the situation* receives judgment in the presence of the *Christian message* (as well as receiving possibilities of new modes or forms of existence in the world), so too ". . . the regeneration of freedom is inseparable from the movement by which the figures of hope are liberated from the idols of the marketplace."[52] Even interpretations of the Christian message require liberation from various distortions.

The Christian message stands between "the Christian fact, the revelation of God on which Christian faith is founded, and our present understanding of experience as a whole."[53] A mutually-critical correlation of the Christian message (here, the attestation to divine suffering) to the present cultural situation entails the following stages.

First, the Christian message requires an eidetic analysis. Such an analysis, in a *first stage*, abstracts the views of this present cultural situation from the prior understandings of God, the human, the world, and their relationships to one another that Christian symbols express.[54] An eidetic analysis operates on the basis of biblical and historical theologies. Such an analysis identifies and describes the experiential questions, the implied ontological structures of reality, and the social, moral, and political possibilities of that historical message. This operation, however, serves only to discover the questions and answers of that message for its own epoch or epochs, not the questions and answers of our contemporary world's understanding of experience as a whole. As a *second stage*,

---

chapter will demonstrate to an extent. As a result, my awareness of the weaknesses in correlative methodology closely resembles the perspective of William Schweiker. According to Schweiker, correlational approaches "must assume that somehow a text 'expresses' a meaning in symbolic form that can be correlated to common human existential experiences open to non-symbolic analysis. It is not at all clear that there are such experiences, especially in the time of many worlds, or that any human experience is unchanged by its expression through symbolic and linguistic forms" (Schweiker, *Theological Ethics and Global Dynamics*, xx). In this work, however, I will not address these methodological problems at length, but will retain correlative methodology, at least in part, for the duration of this study.

52. Ricoeur, *Conflict of Interpretations*, 424.

53. Gilkey, *Reaping the Whirlwind*, 143.

54. Ibid., 143. This resembles Tracy's "Historical and Hermeneutical Investigation of Classic Christian Texts" (Tracy, *Blessed Rage for Order*, 49–52, 120–45). In chapter 2, I attend more thoroughly to this stage.

then, an eidetic analysis reduces the plurality of historical viewpoints on any given topic or doctrine to one common symbolic structure. This symbolic structure, pointing to God's reality and activity, begins to mediate the Christian fact to contemporary understandings of reality.

Second, a contemporary understanding of experience as a whole requires numerous related analyses. The *initial stage* of this multiple analysis exercises a phenomenology of concrete or ordinary experience, through which to unveil those dimensions of experience that the Christian message thematizes, the religious dimensions present in ordinary experience in which dwell the most important questions and answers of human life.[55] A *secondary stage* in this analysis of contemporary experience involves an ontological analysis of the categories and structures of finitude in terms of contemporary understandings of reality, not in terms of the ontology implied or presupposed in the symbol itself (such an analysis would remain eidetic).[56] A *tertiary stage* entails a praxiological analysis of the contemporary situation, an analysis that examines the ways in which humans both positively and negatively actualize their freedom in morality, ethics, community, social science, politics, political science, and so forth. Thus, in the face of both stated and actualized human values, the Christian message appears as the possibility of both a critical challenge to and a creative transformation of actual contemporary life.[57]

Finally, interpretations of the two sources require mutually-critical correlations to one another. Such correlations require criteria for the evaluation of claims made both about the Christian message and about the contemporary situation.[58] In this larger project, however, I do not attempt such a critical correlation.

55. Gilkey, *Reaping the Whirlwind*, 144; cf. Tracy, *Blessed Rage for Order*, 47–48, 91–118.

56. Gilkey, *Reaping the Whirlwind*, 144–46; cf. Tracy, *Blessed Rage for Order*, 52–56, 146–71.

57. Gilkey, *Reaping the Whirlwind*, 138–39, 146; cf., Tracy, *Blessed Rage for Order*, 237–58.

58. For discussion of the issues that developing such criteria involves, see the following studies: Tracy, *Blessed Rage for Order*, 64–87; Gilkey, *Reaping the Whirlwind*, 146–48; cf. Ricoeur, "Hermeneutics of Testimony," 435–61; Nabert, *Désir de Dieu*, 265. I discuss criteria with which to evaluate claims about the symbolic structure of Christian attestations to divine suffering in chapter 2. "Such is the circle: hermeneutics proceeds from a prior understanding of the very thing that it tries to understand by interpreting

I have restricted my task to an eidetic analysis of the Christian attestation that "God suffers," in an attempt to discover this symbol's structure. That symbolic structure begins to mediate the revelation of God as sufferer, the originative Christian fact of divine suffering, to the contemporary situation. Although I have delimited this project to an analysis of the first source of Christian theology, I acknowledge the necessity of the many contextual analyses in order properly to construct a systematic theology. Nevertheless, even though I refrain from a formal interpretation of the contemporary situation here, I do offer a brief description of the contemporary situation that faces the Christian symbol of divine suffering.

The trajectory of flight from the crucified God in post-biblical Christian thought resembles the trajectory of flight away from God altogether (especially the dominant *Deus ex machina*—the impassible, immutable, and deterministic God) by modern Western culture: the former with its denial of divine passibility in any sense; the latter with its affirmation of God's death in every sense. The projectiles in these two trajectories, though strikingly similar, launch from opposite regions of experience. Yet, as the paths of these trajectories cross, the projectiles in these two flights collide with one another in a contemporary situation that massive forms of radical suffering for humans, other creatures, and the global environment have terribly disfigured.[59]

In this situation of massive suffering, then, the Christian symbol of divine suffering appears and speaks. On the one side, in an analysis of the contemporary situation, one should consider the following question: Has the situation produced, and if so to what extent, attestations to a suffering God, the message that God suffers? On the other side, one

it. But thanks to that circle in hermeneutics, I can still today communicate with the sacred by making explicit the prior understanding that gives life to the interpretation. Thus hermeneutics, an acquisition of 'modernity,' is one of the modes by which that 'modernity' transcends itself, insofar as it [modernity] is forgetfulness of the sacred" (Ricoeur, *Symbolism of Evil*, 352). "Still, if theology is the interpretation of experience through traditional symbols, it must include hermeneutics in this sense, for the places those symbols are to be found are texts or their equivalents, and thus they, and the texts that bear them, must be interpreted and their relation to ourselves discovered and established" (Gilkey, *Reaping the Whirlwind*, 134–35).

59. Many Christians have chosen the Christian symbol of divine suffering (in a variety of interpretations) as the way by which "to speak about God in the midst of suffering." Gustavo Gutiérrez discerns the task of formulating God-language in the midst of suffering as the theme of the Book of Job (Gutiérrez, *On Job*, 13).

should entertain another question: Has proclamation of God's death in Western culture originated from, and if so to what extent, Christian attestations to divine suffering? I have delimited my study to an interpretation of the Christian symbol of divine suffering, thereby, leaving an analysis of the contemporary situation to which that symbol responds (and from which, perhaps, it also originates) as a task for future additional studies. Since I have subjected the symbol of divine suffering to this analysis, however, the second question becomes an essential task for my analyses. Therefore, without pursuing this insight any further in this study, I discern already within the structure of the symbol itself a thematization of the contemporary situation's self-understanding.

Thus, I have identified the context for my interaction with the Christian symbol of divine suffering. For the purposes of my study, however, I have temporarily isolated my analysis of this symbol from a correlative analysis of the situation that both contextualizes it and will finally extrapolate significance for itself from the symbol.

Aim of Study

As indicated through my previous delimitations, an elucidation of the structure and dynamism in the Christian symbol of divine suffering constitutes the principal goal for this study. In this elucidation, I labor to bring into view the major structural features of this religious symbol as well as their corresponding relationships with one another.

Analogically, in one sense, my effort resembles an archaeological excavation. In such an enterprise, sometimes features or artifacts remain visible on, available on, or protruding through, the surface of a site. Whatever these features or artifacts may be, these signs lead an archaeologist to formulate specific hypotheses about the nature of a site. Then, the archaeologist begins to excavate. During excavation, the archaeologist studies various portions of the site, unearthing various cross-sections in the site. Through digging the trenches by which to unearth cross-sections of the site, on some sites, the archaeologist discovers the ruins of cities that humans had once constructed upon the ruins of other cities. When an archaeological team has completed enough excavation, archaeologists reconstruct the site's history—mapping its contours, its major structures, the relationships between the various structural levels, and so forth.

Similarly, in my studies of this symbol, I examine the features and artifacts that attest to divine suffering and that protrude through the soil of the dominant Christian traditions above and covering them. By performing theological excavations, I cut cross-sections through the site, whereby this symbol's major features and structures begin to appear. As on archaeological sites, certain connections between structures appear vague; some structural features may no longer be available or identifiable, as in some archaeological excavations where various circumstances or influences have damaged or destroyed structures.

Consequently, as in an archaeological reconstruction of a site's history, I venture informed inferences and judgments about the symbol's structural features and their inter-relationships. Nevertheless, due to the quantity and diversity of Christian traditions that attest to divine suffering, and because every approach toward interpreting the Christian message remains perspectival, therefore making retrieval of the tradition necessarily selective, my analysis and reconstruction of the structure and dynamism in the Christian symbol of divine suffering admittedly becomes a risk.[60] As a ventured depiction of this symbol, it remains incomplete, tentative, and vulnerable. As a consequence, I have applied a principle of inconclusiveness to my interpretation. As subject to such a principle, my interpretation invites criticism and reconstruction. Nonetheless, I aim to provide as complete and definitive an interpretation as possible of the structure and dynamism in the Christian symbol of divine suffering. Chapter 2 describes the method by which I will develop that interpretation.

---

60. For helpful discussions about the limitations of theological thinking, see the following: Gustafson, *Ethics from a Theocentric Perspective*, 1:141; Gilkey, *Message and Existence*, 18; idem, *Reaping the Whirlwind*, 143.

2

Procedural Principles

Introduction

I INITIATED THE ORIENTATION OF THIS STUDY BY CLARIFYING ITS OBject through a series of steps to delimit the problem. Building upon that first orientation, this present chapter more fully orients my work by outlining the major principles on the basis of which I have interpreted the Christian symbol of divine suffering.

The procedural principles that roughly define my method in this work constitute the outline of a strategy for a *Chaoskampf*, a struggle for the discovery of a pattern within the competing and often conflicting varieties of Christian attestations to the suffering God.[1] I have not formulated this strategy on principles that remain wholly external, however, to the religious symbol that constitutes the object of my analysis. Quite the contrary, I have largely adapted the strategy for interaction with the Christian symbol of divine suffering from both explicit and

---

1. This adjudication between various Christian testimonies to divine suffering initiates only the first stage of a larger *Chaoskampf*. A second stage would require an engagement with testimonies to God's suffering in other religious and philosophical traditions. A third stage would produce a more intense interaction still—from dialogue to debate with Christian and other religious traditions of divine impassibility. Such latter stages in the larger *Chaoskampf*, however, address concerns in mutually-critical correlations between analyses of the Christian message and the contemporary situation, both of which define the two principal sources of constructive theology proper. From more explicit and deliberate studies and interpretations of the second source, and thus from the mutually-critical correlations of the two sources, I have delimited my present task. With caution, I also remember the warning of Nietzsche. "He who fights with monsters should be careful lest he thereby become a monster. And if thou gaze long into an abyss, the abyss will also gaze into thee" (Nietzsche, *Beyond Good and Evil*, 97 [146]).

implicit tendencies that operate both in the broader Christian traditions and within the more narrow variety of Christian testimonies to divine suffering.[2] I will substantiate this claim both as I describe the method and then apply the method to this particular symbol.

Just as I have derived the method, in certain respects, from the object upon which it focuses, so too each of the procedural principles have inherited dimensions of abstraction in relation to one another. In order for these procedural principles to remain distinct from their object of analysis, as well as distinct from one another, they require each of these dimensions of abstraction. Thus, each procedural principle operates with the confidence of the ancient Scholastic axiom: "*abstrahentium non est mendacium*," or "abstracting is not a lie!" To isolate certain features in an object of study from their organic relationships to the remaining features of that object, for the sake of a more careful examination of those isolated features, does not misrepresent the character of the object that one analyzes, provided at least that this abstraction both identifies itself as such and finally reintegrates the various features. The following discussions of three procedural principles specify these moments of abstraction: eidetic, criteriological, and anthropological principles.

Eidetic Principle

With the eidetic principle, I examine the eidetic stratum of significance in the Christian symbol of divine suffering.[3] As I indicated in chapter 1, the historical stratum of significance in a religious symbol requires an analysis peculiar to itself. The eidetic or historical stratum of significance denotes that which religious symbols ". . . have meant, in all the ways that are relevant, in their original form in the biblical witness, and as they have been interpreted and re-interpreted in the life of the

2. "A method is not an 'indifferent net' in which reality is caught, but the method is an element of the reality itself. In at least one respect, the description of the method is a description of a decisive aspect of the object to which it is applied. The cognitive relation itself, quite apart from any special act of cognition, reveals something about the object, as well as about the subject, in the relation" (Tillich, *Systematic Theology*, 1:59–60).

3. I previously discussed the meaning of the term "eidetic" in chapter 1, as the first stratum of significance in religious symbols and as the object of analysis in the first pole of a correlational or constructive theology. I rely here upon Langdon Gilkey's concept of eidetic analysis, a concept that resembles Edward Farley's notion of "Theological Portraiture" (see E. Farley, *Ecclesial Reflection*, 183–216).

Christian community."[4] Eidetic analysis includes both objective and subjective dimensions. These two dimensions divide the analysis into two stages. Eidetic *abstraction* designates the first and more objective stage in the analysis, while eidetic *reduction* designates the second and more subjective stage in the analysis.

Objective Stage: Eidetic Abstraction

The first stage of eidetic analysis constitutes the objective side or dimension in the analysis. The objectivity in this stage consists in abstracting or separating the meaning of a religious symbol for other historical periods from its meaning for the contemporary situation (the experiential, ontological, and praxiological significances for contemporary human life). With an eidetic or historical analysis, one attempts to view religious symbols ". . . in their own terms, as they appeared to another time, as they *meant* to that time, unrelated to all else we know, value and hope to be true."[5] A symbol yields historical meaning both as reference and as significance. Hence, the first stage of an eidetic analysis supplies a twofold objectivity.

Meaning as Reference

First, an eidetic analysis discerns the religious symbol's *meaning-as-reference* in the past understandings of a religious community. Eidetic analysis inquires in the following way: What were the concepts, notions, or images of God, the human self, and the world to which those symbols referred in the past of a religious community? In this sense, eidetic abstraction endeavors, through a focus upon the symbol, to discover the extra-linguistic reality or realities to which the religious community formerly understood the religious symbol to refer.

Meaning as Significance

Second, eidetic abstraction examines the religious symbol's *meaning-as-significance* in the past experience of a religious community. This aspect of objectivity in eidetic abstraction inquires as follows: What was the subjective or existential and social significance (affectively, cognitively,

4. Gilkey, *Reaping the Whirlwind*, 140.
5. Ibid.

and volitionally) of this particular religious symbol for the people who lived in the past of this religious community? This question refuses to procure the significance of this symbol for *contemporary* human life, except insofar as an eidetic or historical re-construction possesses significance as knowledge for the contemporary inquirer. That quest for the *contemporary* significance from the results of an eidetic analysis concerns a later stage of the correlative theological task, a stage from which I have previously delimited this study.

Although eidetic abstraction claims to re-present the objective meaning of religious symbols, it somewhat cautiously engages that task. Biblical and historical theologies primarily explicate the eidetic meanings of religious symbols. A religious symbol that endures the passage of time, nevertheless, changes and develops as its religious community interprets and re-interprets it. One discovers, through the first stage of an eidetic analysis, numerous versions of any single symbol, from a wide range of historical periods and cultures. Thus, the persistence or endurance of a religious symbol requires from eidetic abstraction a continual assessment of new interpretations or re-interpretations of the symbol.[6] Nevertheless, such eidetic assessments yield a plurality or variety of understandings of any given religious symbol. Discerning the symbolic structure of a religious symbol requires, then, a second stage in an eidetic analysis, a stage in which the task shifts to a quest for a common pattern or structure within the many versions of a religious symbol.

Subjective Stage: Eidetic Reduction

The second stage of eidetic analysis remains historical, even though it entails a creative or constructive task as well. This constructive task authorizes a description of this second stage as the subjective dimension of eidetic analysis. In this stage, the task of eidetic analysis diverges from the task explicitly assigned to biblical and historical theologies. No longer does the systematic or constructive theologian remain content with the multiplicity found among the numerous versions of a religious

6. I concur with Edward Farley's perspective. "What is portrayed is something historical and therefore in process. Thus the portraiture is itself a constantly changing enterprise. It resembles an artist constantly redoing a portrait and even offering new portraits of a child who is growing up" (E. Farley, *Ecclesial Reflection*, 204).

symbol that the theologian discovers among the various historical attestations.

The subjective aspect of eidetic analysis, however, by no means refers to the quest for the contemporary significance of a religious symbol. To the contrary, such a move would be premature, as noted in chapter 1. The move to that second major stage of a correlative systematic or constructive theology, though, remains impossible without this second stage of eidetic analysis. As Langdon Gilkey has noted, ". . . before any Christian symbols can function creatively in contemporary theology, they must be 'reduced' from the plurality of their historical variations to some unity and coherence of form—to some unified meaning that represents *one* perspective of God, human existence, the world and the divine activity therein, not a multitude of divergent perspectives on each of those subjects."[7]

Such a reduction of the various viewpoints on a single religious symbol may violate the sensibilities of the historian who assesses the specificities of each unique viewpoint. Reduction in this sense, nonetheless, does not wholly forfeit its historical character. As reduction, though, eidetic analysis does search for a pattern, a common structure, by which to unify or condense the numerous understandings of the symbol's meaning.

Even the reductive stage of eidetic analysis, however, requires a basis upon which to operate. In order to reduce a plurality of viewpoints, the interpreter must supply the criterion or criteria for judgments about whether or not, and if so to what extent, a unified meaning conforms to the religious tradition from which the interpreter has abstracted it. At this point, the spiraling relationship between subject-matter and method appears with full force.[8] Still, the theologian discovers the necessity for a criterion, one required by the reductive stage in eidetic analysis itself.

The symbolic structure that the theologian discovers through this reductive stage, then, attests to past human experience and under-

7. Gilkey, *Reaping the Whirlwind*, 143.

8. Because traditions possess different kinds of status (such as, "a bearer of the content of theology," "a criterion," or "a field of evidence"), the relation between an object of study and the method that one abstracts from that object for its study produces a spiraling relationship rather than an impasse of circularity (cf., E. Farley, *Ecclesial Reflection*, 195).

standing of the relationships among God, the world, and human life. A Christian symbol's structure "mediates between the Christian fact, the revelation of God on which Christian faith is founded, and our present understanding of experience as a whole." In this sense, then, the symbolic structure receives the status, ". . . if not that of a norm, at least that of an indispensable source" for the remaining stages of a correlative systematic or constructive theology.[9]

Criteriological Principle

Tasks Antecedent and Subsequent to Eidetic Analysis

Initiating eidetic reduction, however, requires an antecedent task, whereas completing the reductive stage requires a subsequent task. The first task submits the various testimonies to the following question: Do these attestations to God's suffering possess a *Christian* quality, character, or nature? Expressed another way, by what measure or on what sort of basis can one understand these attestations as *Christian*? The second task adjudicates between the various *Christian* testimonies to divine suffering with the following inquiry: Do these many Christian attestations to divine suffering adequately and consistently exhibit the fundamental structure in the Christian symbol of divine suffering and, if so, which attestations do so and why, and, if not, which testimonies do not do so and why not? The following question construes the intent of this second inquiry in another way: Which Christian attestations to divine suffering are, or are not, internally inconsistent or illogical in terms of this particular religious symbol's rationality?

These two tasks, when fulfilled, bond tightly to the task of eidetic reduction. The first task necessarily precedes eidetic reduction, providing both stages of the first procedural principle with their raw materials, so to speak, a plurality of diverse *Christian* attestations to divine suffering. Thus, the commencement of eidetic reduction awaits fulfillment of the first task. The second task, which follows eidetic reduction, corresponds to the moment in which eidetic reduction judges whether or not a particular Christian testimony to divine suffering conforms to the common pattern that the theologian has already discovered among

9. Gilkey, *Reaping the Whirlwind*, 143; Farley, *Ecclesial Reflection*, 216.

the previously-submitted and various testimonies or expressions of this religious symbol.

Positioning the Principle

Accomplishment of the first task depends upon the presence of a criterion by which an interpreter can decide whether or not any given religious testimonies to divine suffering represent *Christian* attestations or testimonies.[10] In this sense, then, the criteriological principle constitutes an essential component in eidetic reduction, although an interpreter must derive the criterion that defines the formal content of the criteriological principle from the broader Christian tradition, prior to any examination of testimonies to divine suffering.[11] As a result, to examine in isolation the criteriological principle, as distinct though not separate from the eidetic principle, abstracts an essential component from the presuppositions of eidetic analysis. Eidetic reduction, the more *subjective* (creative and risk-oriented) stage of eidetic analysis, operates *without undisciplined subjectivism* only through its criteriological principle.

The criteriological principle, by which my studies of this symbol proceed, follows. *An interpreter may evaluate attestations to divine suffering as appropriate or inappropriate attestations to the Christian traditions, on the basis of their conformity or non-conformity to the following criterion: God most fully discloses the divine self as love in Jesus as the Christ.*

---

10. To discern, from among religious attestations to God, as to whether or not they qualify as appropriate to any particular religious tradition (e.g., Islamic, Jewish, Hindu, Buddhist, etc.) requires a similar criterion or similar criteria.

11. In my approach to developing this criteriological principle (as well as the other two principles of my method), I rely significantly on Ernst Troeltsch's concept of *Glaubenslehre*. Perhaps I have greater concern to demonstrate both why and how I have arrived at my particular understanding of the criteriological principle. Nevertheless, Troeltsch's thought influences my method significantly. I refer here, only as an example, to Troeltsch's "concept of the Christian principle." "'Principle' is simply a summary term for the many diverse religious and ethical ideas and powers of Christianity, signifying a highly diverse and yet individual formation that retains the capacity for continued historical development. This concept of the Christian principle replaces the old concept of biblical authority, while retaining the unity of the spiritual-religious life power that the biblical records express" (Troeltsch, *Christian Faith*, 10).

I propose a point of departure that resembles David Tracy's point of departure. "For myself, the major Christian metaphor 'God is Love' focussed on what love-in-suffering means in Jesus Christ would call forth in a full systematic theology: (1) first, a process understanding of the internal relatedness of God and world and an understanding of the 'suffering' of God focussed on the ministry, cross and resurrection of Jesus Christ; (2) an interpretation of the traditional Christian understanding of God's trinitarian nature by means of that focus on suffering love."[12] Despite the strength of Johannine testimonies, this criterion also draws from other important, perhaps even central, Jewish and Christian traditions that precede its Johannine base. First, the Hebrew scriptures of the older Christian canon supply this criterion with resources.[13] This

12. Tracy, *Analogical Imagination*, 443. Robert Grant claims that Jesus understood "the God who had revealed himself to Moses and the prophets" as characterized by "all-inclusive love." According to Grant, "the theme of love—he who does not love does not know God, for God is love' (1 John 4:8)—is one which philosophical theologians were going to treat only with difficulty, as we shall see. From the writings of early Christians after New Testament times we can discover relatively few references to God's love, though a few writers provide exceptions" (R. Grant, *Early Christian Doctrine of God*, 3, 4–5). To the contrary, Arthur McGiffert observes the following about Jesus and his teaching. "That he makes no specific reference to God's love in the Synoptic Gospels may therefore be a mere accident. At the same time it serves to remind us that the burden of his preaching was righteousness and judgment, a preaching entirely consonant with his own sternness and severity toward the self-righteous, the proud, the hypocritical, . . . and other sinners." Instead, McGiffert (I think wrongly) attributes this difference between the Christian and the Jewish concepts of God, the Christian emphasis upon God's love, to the teaching of the apostle Paul and the Christians who followed (McGiffert, *God of the Early Christians*, 13, 21, 24).

13. For example, S. D. Goitein, a Semitic and Arabic scholar, attempted to demonstrate, on the basis of extensive philological comparisons of Hebrew texts with Arabic literature, that the verbal root of the name "Yahweh" denotes both "strong feelings and passion" and "complete devotion either to one's own aims or to another person." He argued that the divine name "Yahweh" (e.g., Exod 3:14; 33:19; 34:6–7) derives from the root "*hwy*," which "expresses strong feelings and passion, mixed with the idea of personal ambition and arbitrariness." Hence, according to Goitein's theory, Yahweh's words from the burning bush to Moses (Exod 3:14) express the following meaning: "I shall passionately love whom I love." Nonetheless, the name "Yahweh" means far more than passionate love: "it conveys also the notion of exclusiveness and jealousy, in other words the emotional aspects of monotheism." As the imperfect form of the word "*hwy*," the name "Yahweh" means "the One who loves passionately and helps those that worship Him, while, at the same time, demanding exclusive devotion to Himself." Furthermore, Goitein also demonstrated how this perception of Yahweh requires love to characterize Israel's worship of Yahweh. "If God's own name means passionate love, it is natural that His worship should consist above all in love: 'You shall love YHWH,

criterion, of course, certainly rests upon a solid Johannine foundation (e.g., John 1:18; John 14:9; 1 John 4:8–9, 16b). With this principle, then, the interpreter guides eidetic reduction.

Source of Criterion in the Christian Fact

I have abstracted and condensed the formal content of the criteriological principle, the criterion, from the material content of the principle that richly underlies the criterion, like soil in which a tree roots itself. I have broadly construed the material content of the criteriological prin-

---

your God, with all your heart and all your soul and all your might' (Deut vi 5). As is well known, the command to love God occurs in Deuteronomy no less than ten times and already in Deborah's Song the worshippers of YHWH are simply called His lovers, Judg v 31" (Goitein, "YHWH the Passionate," 1–9; also see, Perry, "Jahweh, the God of Love: A Study in Old Testament Theology"). Few biblical scholars, however, readily accept this interpretation of the name "Yahweh." Theologians still mostly tend to argue that the divine name originates from some form of the Hebrew verb "to be" (e.g., Mettinger, *In Search of God*, 30–36). To what extent does the ancient Hellenization of the Mediterranean world continue to guide Christian scholars in this interpretive direction, since that Hellenization most certainly influenced such patristic and medieval interpretations of the divine name? Additionally, especially on the basis of the previous resources from the first Christian canon, texts from the second collection of Christian scriptures support this criterion as well. Perhaps the previous light, then, illumines Jesus' unspoken rationale for summarizing the entire divine revelation as complete love for God, neighbor, and self (e.g., Matt 19:16–22; 22:34–40; Mark 12:28–34; Luke 10:25–37; cf. John 13:34–35; 14:15–24; 15:8–17). The beloved human fulfills the entire revelation of God (Matt 7:12; 22:40; Mark 12:28, 33; Luke 10:25, 26, 28; cf. Rom 13:10; Gal 5:14), through authentic love for God, neighbor (cf. Rom 13:8–10; Gal 5:14), and self (see also, Deut 6:5; Lev 19:18, 34), both in terms of the mutuality that the Golden Rule (Matt 7:12; Luke 6:31) elicits and even in terms of a sacrificial love toward the neighbor as enemy (Matt 5:43–44; Luke 6:27). According to Jesus, this latter form of neighbor-love establishes a criteriology for perfect human love; in loving the enemy, the human loves perfectly or completely in the way that God loves (Matt 5:38–48; Luke 6:27–36). On the one hand, then, Jesus also interpreted God's holiness (Lev 11:44–45; 19:2) as love, a love expressed most powerfully as divine love for the enemy, the unfaithful though beloved human; on the other hand, Jesus interpreted the corresponding holiness (Lev 11:44–45; 19:2; cf. 1 Pet 1:16) of the beloved human's *imitatio Dei* also as love even for the enemy. From the perspective of Jesus, such love envisions or produces no limits to its forgiveness of victimization by the neighbor (Matt 18:21–35; cf. Luke 17:3–4). According to the Lucan evangelist, as Jesus died on the cross, he even forgave his own crucifiers (Luke 23:34), thus actualizing in his death that which he had taught during his life. Hence, at least in this light, McGiffert's dichotomy between Jewish and Christian concepts of God collapses.

ciple as "the Christian fact."[14] The Christian fact, however, refers to a dual phenomenon.

1. As the primary phenomenon of the Christian fact, the *originative Christian fact*, God discloses the divine self in Jesus as the Christ. More generally, this notion designates the event (broadly construed) of divine self-disclosure through the relationship between God and the people of Israel, as the context later for the life of Jesus as the Christ.[15]

14. I adopt this description from Langdon Gilkey and David Tracy (Gilkey, *Reaping the Whirlwind*, 143; Tracy, *Blessed Rage for Order*, 15, 60, 72, 250). I have partially modified this concept, however, more along the lines of clarification than of disagreement.

15. I repeatedly utilize this criterion, based as it is in the event of and testimony to Jesus as the Christ, as my study's epistemological window into the Christian symbol of divine suffering. The results of this usage, as displayed in every chapter of this work, exhibit a variety of my operative commitments to this criterion. Two highly significant concerns, however, surface about both the criterion and the twofold Christian fact from which I have derived it. First, a more general epistemological concern or question emerges: Is it possible, and to what extent if so, to extrapolate a symbolic system from any given religious symbol (specifically from the symbol of the Christ, Jesus of Nazareth, the one said most decisively to reveal God as love)? Moreover, what kind of validity do such extrapolations possess? Bernard E. Meland sharply stressed this concern. Although he conceded that the truth which religious symbols (as responses to an objective reality) grasped could yield to "logical elaboration or to scientific analysis," Meland insisted that such elaboration and analysis must express the insight of that truth "in the terms of logic and of science." To elaborate or, as I have expressed it, to extrapolate religious symbols "in terms that claim the character of logical deduction or of scientific observation" produces confused conclusions. "For it is not in the symbol, but in the experience of responsiveness, that the empirical qualities must be discerned." I do not attempt, however, to extrapolate conclusions about divine reality in contemporary experience from this christologically-focused criterion. With this criterion, I intend only to extrapolate the structure of the Christian symbol of divine suffering and the symbol-system in and with which it operates. One must take other steps along a correlative theological path, before one could make the moves that correspond to Meland's concern; I have briefly outlined these steps in chapter 1. Second, a more particular ontological concern emerges: In light of my use of a criterion that derives from the Christian fact, does, and if so in what ways and to what extent, such an analysis allow an extrapolation of resources from this symbol that either avoids the charge of anthropocentricity or at least illuminates the range of the symbol's resources that may extend beyond merely anthropological concerns? Meland asks both theological and philosophical versions of this question. As a theological question, he asks, "can the character of God be ascertained merely by learning the character of Jesus?" In that question's philosophical form, he asks, "can the character of cosmic reality be deciphered in terms of personality?" (Meland, "Toward a Valid View of God," 197, 198, 199). While my use of a christological criterion situates me to some extent in the category of *christocentric* theologians (e.g., see Bonhoeffer, "Concerning the Christian Idea of God," 181) in relation to whom Meland framed his question, nevertheless, I thoroughly share

2. The secondary phenomenon of the Christian fact, the *derivative Christian fact*, results from, and refers to, the primary reality or the event-character of the Christian fact. The derivative Christian fact includes the total witness to the event of God's disclosure in Jesus Christ, as this disclosure contextualized itself within the history of God's entire relationship to Israel. Christians construe this witness as the Christian tradition.

The whole derivative Christian fact, however, revolves around the apostolic witness: namely, the newer Christian scriptures or the second Christian canon. The derivative Christian fact, however, remains much larger than this, its pivot.

a. On one side of the pivot, the newer Christian canon interpretively attests to the event of Jesus as the Christ in light of the Jewish scriptures, which formed the larger textual context (as the principal witness to the event of God's relation to Israel) for the newer Christian canon and which Christian communities eventually re-named the "Old Testament." For the earliest apostolic attestations to Jesus as the Christ, Jewish scriptures constituted the founding textual witnesses to Jesus as the Christ.

b. On the other side of the pivot, Christian communities immediately interpreted and continually have reinterpreted the event of Jesus as the Christ through the newer or second Christian canon that witnessed to that event, thus, greatly multiplying the derivative Christian fact. Broadly construed, then, the derivative Christian fact—the Christian traditions—constitutes the principal mediating reality of the event of Jesus as the Christ to human comprehension in and of the contemporary situation.[16]

The pivot of the derivative Christian fact—the newer Christian canon—remains, then, the *norma normans non normata*, as the original authoritative collection of witnesses to the event of God's revelation in Jesus as the Christ. The newer or second Christian canon norms,

---

Meland's concern for a non-anthropocentric concept of God, a concept with a capacity to include all forms of life and created reality. Hence, although the criterion that I have chosen promotes an understanding of God with the qualities of personality, the analyses that follow disclose symbolic resources with which to address those broader concerns about God's relation to and purposes for the entire cosmos, as well as for the human portion of that cosmos.

16. See Tracy, *Analogical Imagination*, 237; Gilkey, *Reaping the Whirlwind*, 143.

but is not normed by, later or earlier witnesses to the event of Jesus as the Christ: (1) Christians hold accountable the witnesses to Jesus Christ in all later Christian communities, where *they* hold *themselves* accountable, to the witness of the newer Christian canon; (2) the earliest Christian communities—as represented by their testimonies in the newer or second Christian canon—held the earlier scriptural attestations (the Jewish scriptures) to God's self-disclosure in Israel's history accountable to the history of Jesus as the Christ, by understanding that series of events between God and Israel, and its derivative scriptural witness (the Hebrew bible and Septuagint), as the originating covenant and the Old Testament respectively. Thus, the core of the criterion's material content remains the Christian scriptures, which include both the newer or second and older or first Christian canons, with the centerpoint focused upon the newer Christian canon—the authoritative pivot of the derivative Christian fact. I understand this accountability to the authoritative pivot of the derivative Christian fact, however, in the sense of David Tracy's notion of "appropriateness" to the Christian tradition: ". . . all later theologies in *Christian* theology are obliged to show why they are not in radical disharmony with the central Christian witness expressed in the scriptures"; but appropriateness suggests neither that ". . . a later Christian witness must be found in identical form in the scriptures," nor that ". . . there can be no criticism of scriptural expressions in light of later developments."[17] Shortly, I will discuss more about appropriateness to the Christian tradition.

Twofold Character of the Criterion

The criterion within the criteriological principle expresses a twofold character in its interactions with attestations to the Sacred or God. As a critical tool, the criterion distinguishes and evaluates that which appears before it. Not only does this criterion indicate the reasons that attestations to God *are not* in radical disharmony with the pivot of the derivative Christian fact, but this criterion also indicates why certain attestations to God *are* in radical disharmony with that central Christian witness. The criterion places attestations within a continuum that moves from total non-conformity to complete identity. In this sense, then, the

---

17. R. Grant and Tracy, *Short History of the Interpretation of the Bible*, 176. See also, Tracy, *Blessed Rage for Order*, 73.

criterion both affirms and negates, both supports and corrects. The criterion identifies a witness's (including the newer Christian canon's witness) de-formation of the event to which it refers. Also, then, the criterion identifies a witness's con-formation to that event to which it attests. Thus, the criterion exercises the re-forming tendency that exists within the derivative Christian fact (a self-reforming tendency there), a tendency that it inherits from the event of God in Jesus as the Christ.

The event of Jesus as the Christ occurred in the midst of the wider processes and dynamics of God's relationship and interaction with Israel. Although faithful to the tradition that gave to him his identity, Jesus accused his own tradition of its de-formation of the events in God's relation to the people of Israel, while still affirming the tradition in the areas of its con-formation to those formative events. In this way, the event of Jesus Christ re-formed and, therefore, trans-formed the possibilities for all future witnesses to the event of God in Jesus Christ. Hugh Ross Mackintosh stated this similarly: "It is not the case that belief in Divine love has given credibility to the story of Jesus; it is the other way about."[18] This tendency toward self-reformation, the event of God in Jesus Christ transferred, delegated, and entrusted to the witnesses, to the derivative Christian fact. One can already perceive the presence of this tendency, for example, in the apostle Paul's use of the proclamation

18. Mackintosh, *Christian Experience of Forgiveness*, 220. Elsewhere, Mackintosh says the following: "There is no need to say that every true idea about God must be derivable from Christ; everything essential is secured if we say that no idea can be admitted which is out of harmony with Him" (Mackintosh, *Some Aspects of Christian Belief*, 38). This criterion, thus, finally supplies a basis for the development of a Christian systematic or constructive theology of love. Paul Ricoeur argues that a theology of love lacks power both "to integrate justice conceptually" and, more problematically, "to account for the position of evil in the world." In particular, with respect to the latter weakness, Ricoeur identifies "the concept of 'permission' (God "permits" evil, but does not "create" it)" as "the witness to this failure" (Ricoeur, *Symbolism of Evil*, 326). On the contrary, I hope to illuminate through these studies the symbolic and conceptual resources to develop a Christian systematic or constructive theology of love, resources that do possess the strength both to integrate justice conceptually and to provide a relatively more adequate account of evil's reality and place in the world. See especially the work of Edward Vacek, whose theology of love certainly shows how love integrates justice in terms of *philia*, rather than love and justice standing in contrast to one another (Vacek, *Love, Human and Divine*, 280–318). In this project, I also attempt to identify and to elaborate within the Christian symbol of divine suffering one of the conditions for "a kerygmatic reinterpretation of evil," as Ricoeur describes it: ". . . that the symbolic figure of God should preserve from the theology of anger only what can be assumed into the theology of love" (Ricoeur, *Conflict of Interpretations*, 351).

about Jesus' crucifixion, by which the apostle evaluated the piety and morality of the Christian communities to, with, and among whom he ministered.[19]

As a trust to be invested, handed down by the event of Jesus as the Christ to the witnesses of that event, the tendency toward self-reformation augments its portfolio of investment possibilities through its adoption and adaptation of public and sharable methods of explanation. Even though I do not describe and examine such methods in these studies, I characterize them, following David Tracy, as three broad methods: historical-critical, literary-critical, and social-scientific. These explanatory procedures serve as "major correctives of the constituting, mediating tradition."[20] Nevertheless, whereas these procedures operate as correctives of the tradition, the interpreter must employ them critically; the distortions within critical thought and procedures or methods also require identification, criticism, and correction, operations already present and active (as I have noted previously) within the criterion of the derivative Christian fact itself. Thus, the interpreter, even though acknowledging the tendency toward self-reform in the criterion's material content (through the interpreter's augmentation of that tendency with contemporary critical methods), must critically evaluate these critical explanatory procedures in light of the criterion itself, in order to use such critical procedures fairly and effectively upon the derivative Christian fact in all of its forms.

Risk in Identifying the Criterion

Thus, the criteriological principle, the principle within and presupposed by eidetic analysis, assigns the diverse Christian testimonies about divine suffering to their proper places within the continuum that ranges from mere total identity with the pivot of the derivative Christian fact to sheer non-identity with that pivot. I qualify this adjudicative operation, however, as somewhat risk-oriented. For, although I have abstracted the criterion's formal content from the various specificities of the criterion's material content (the pivot of the derivative Christian fact: the newer Christian canon's witness to Jesus as the Christ), my choice of that formal content—however justified by that material content's

19. 1 Cor 1:18–31.
20. Tracy, *Analogical Imagination*, 237.

attestations—remains a *choice* of one candidate among many. I utilize specific Johannine texts, within the pivot of the Christian fact, as the focal point in my choice of formal content for the criterion of the criteriological principle (that God discloses the divine self as love most fully in Jesus of Nazareth as the Christ). I do not necessarily assume, however, that Pauline, Petrine, Marcan, or Lucan theologies only contradict or subvert the Johannine testimony by their own testimonies. They often support rather than contradict. Instead, in this work, my search for a formal criterion *begins* from the Johannine confessional emphasis upon God as love, rather than from, for example, the Pauline emphasis upon justification by faith. I primarily derive the criterion of the criteriological principle, therefore, from powerful Johannine testimonies.

The event of Jesus as the Christ, then, refers to the entire event and history, including the teachings, actions, and destiny, of the person called Jesus of Nazareth. Through the character, actions, teachings, and person of Jesus, the principal character and qualities of God as love disclose themselves to the world. Through the event of Jesus as the Christ, God again presented the divine self in, to, and through the creation, the most decisive disclosure of the divine self as love in, to, and through finite realities. The derivative Christian fact mediates this reality to the world. Therefore, with this criterion, I attempt to hold attestations to divine suffering accountable to a basic *Christian* criterion, so that, by proceeding in this way, certain parameters appear by which to measure the appropriateness of attestations about divine suffering to the derivative Christian fact.

Anthropological Principle

Even after an application of the criteriological principle to the variety of religious attestations to suffering gods and goddesses, eidetic reduction still confronts a wide variety of *Christian* testimonies to divine suffering. Before eidetic analysis can begin to identify the common patterns and to reduce them to a unified symbolic structure, however, one further problem emerges—a problem that requires the development of a third methodological principle to address it.

I have formulated the problem in the following way. In an examination of Christian testimonies to God's suffering, the various *kinds*, *modes*, or *types* of divine suffering seem, at times, indistinguishable from one another. Probing the heart of this problem requires an answer to a first, very simple, question: What obscures the distinctions between the various *modes* of divine suffering in these Christian testimonies? The answer to that question resides in the *occasions* of divine suffering, as identified by the attestations to divine suffering themselves. Clearly, most Christian attestations to the suffering of God identify some aspect of human or creaturely reality and experience as the occasioning source for God's suffering. These attestations, however, seldom distinguish those occasions from one another. Thus, a second question indicates the heart of this problem: How can one distinguish the various modes or types of divine suffering from one another, in the face of their obscuration by the indistinct occasions for those modes of divine suffering? An answer to the second inquiry, then, requires distinctions between the *occasions* for divine suffering, occasions to which the *modes* of divine suffering correlate themselves as responses, in Christian attestations to the suffering of God.

　This leads, however, to another problem. How does one distinguish between these various *occasions* of divine suffering? The answer to this question releases the inquiry, to some extent, from its perplexity about how to approach the ambiguity in Christian attestations to divine suffering. This inquiry, nonetheless, requires a principle by which to distinguish the occasions for divine suffering from one another. Reflections both upon the human experience of the interwoven realities of evil and suffering and upon attestations to that experience in the Christian scriptures disclose a tendency that enables the development of an anthropological principle. On the basis of this double reflection, I will develop an anthropological principle (by which to distinguish between the principal occasions for the primary modes of divine suffering in Christian attestations to those phenomena), a principle rooted both in contemporary experience and in the material content in the criterion of the criteriological principle. Thus, within the eidetic principle, working alongside and through the criteriological principle, prior to the stage of eidetic reduction, resides the anthropological principle. This principle prevents the ambiguous character of Christian attestations to divine suffering from continuing to cloak the distinct moments of divine suffering in the symbol's structure. This principle, thus, enables an envisioning of that structure by disclosing the principal occasions for the various modes of divine suffering. In that which follows, then, two stages of reflection divulge resources with which to formulate an anthropological principle.

Practical and Epistemological Aporias in Human Experiences of Evil and Suffering

I initiate this first meditation upon human experiences of evil and suffering by considering the most innocuous realities of suffering—at least those realities that, at first, appear to be the most innocuous. These initial experiences of human suffering include the problems and results of such experiences as aging, deterioration of health, susceptibility to disease, accidents and injuries caused by human ignorance or inability, diminishment or loss of the senses, disability of all kinds, and so forth. I refrain in this initial meditation, however, from listing and discussing the specificities of the almost infinite permutations of suffering that one might observe in this sphere.[21] These forms of suffering, nevertheless, confront humans at every turn in their experience.

Max Scheler attempted to describe all forms of pain and suffering as subjective human experiences that reflected, and thereby correlated with, objective events of sacrifice, or ". . . effective tendencies, in which a good of a lower order is surrendered for a good of a higher order (the ontology of suffering)."[22] Although Scheler's contention, that all suffering contains a sacrificial character—whatever the response of the sufferer to the suffering, accurately describes one facet of suffering, analyzing the character of sacrifice requires more care. Scheler's understanding of sacrifice remains somewhat inadequate. Humans relinquish many things in order to accomplish certain goals or to attain specific goods. Sometimes, humans surrender things of a higher order for those of a lower order, thus disqualifying such acts as sacrifices, at least in the sense with which Scheler defined the concept of sacrifice. Nonetheless, such forms of relinquishment still may entail suffering. The reality of suffering abides—even when it does not conform to Scheler's conceptions of either suffering or sacrifice.

---

21. The Christian symbol of divine suffering also attests to this aspect of the human condition. In volume three of this work, *Divine Suffering and Tragic Reality*, I will analyze this occasion for divine suffering, which I construe there as *the tragic region* in creaturely experience.

22. Scheler, "Meaning of Suffering," 128.

As another example by which to unmask the deficiency in Scheler's notion of suffering as sacrifice, and his notion of sacrifice as the surrender of lower-order goods for higher-order goods, one might consider the process of aging. In that experience, a person's health deteriorates, bodily and mental functions diminish and often disappear, and so on. Can one properly designate that kind of suffering as sacrifice in the sense with which Scheler has endowed the notion? Toward which goods of a higher order does the surrender of such lower-order goods (such as, good health, mobility, or even sanity) aim? Furthermore, in these examples of suffering, does the human even participate voluntarily? Here, it seems, no greater end appears as the result of such suffering. Hence, whatever apologetic value disappears, the notion of sacrifice, in the sense with which Scheler has invested it at least, fails as the most adequate designation of suffering's essence. While suffering may entail sacrifices of some things in order to attain other things, one might more accurately refer to costs and gains in suffering.

Even if one could accurately describe suffering in all its forms as sacrificial in Scheler's sense of the term, the reality of human suffering remains even more ambiguous and problematic due to its ever-present companion, evil. At least since the work of Friedrich Schleiermacher, theologians have commonly distinguished between two types of evil: natural evil and moral evil.[23] *Natural evil* refers to the suffering and destruction that the elements and forces of the natural world (such as, tornadoes, hurricanes, floods, volcanos, earthquakes, droughts, blizzards, famines, diseases, deformities, accidents) represent and/or cause. *Moral evil* refers to the bad, wrong, or illicit actions, deeds, thoughts, or projects that persons conceive and enact: individually, socially or communally, and institutionally. If I momentarily stabilize this traditional distinction between the two types of evil, perhaps I can begin to clarify partially the complexity in the human experience of evil and suffering.

Many writers, and perhaps most people, commonly both describe all suffering as evil and identify all suffering as the result of either natural

---

23. Schleiermacher designated these two types of evil as "*natürliches Übel*" and "*geselliges Übel*." He refused, of course, to use the word "moral" to describe the second type of evil, preferring instead to use the word "social" ("*geselliges*"), by which refusal he aimed to prevent the subsumption of "the bad also as such" ("*das Böse*") under the concept of evil (Schleiermacher, *Christian Faith*, 184–89, 315–20 [§§ 48, 75, 76]).

or moral evils.[24] Such responses to the experience of suffering, however, invite inquiry at two critical junctures.

First, can one legitimately construe all suffering as evil? Certainly, one may accurately describe some suffering as evil, insofar as moral agents often intentionally inflict some forms of suffering. Such suffering, though evil, might produce good results, either for the agent that inflicts it or even for the victim of suffering. Thus, in one sense, one can experience, perceive, or understand even suffering that evil causes as good. On the other side, can one properly describe the suffering that results from good intentions as evil? Again, to answer this question properly, one should view such a situation relationally. For the victim, such suffering might produce either good or bad effects. For the one who inflicts such suffering, the resultant suffering could represent an evil precisely because the one who has inflicted the suffering did not intend to do so. Hence, even this simple sort of inquiry cautions against superficially describing all suffering as evil.

Furthermore, much suffering does result from moral evil. Certain actions and forms of irresponsible behavior by individuals and communities produce great suffering: as examples, the results of prostitution, murder, war, greed. Nevertheless, many people consider the suffering that individuals or societies experience, especially the suffering that results from their own evil intentions and actions, as deserved and, thereby, justified. Hence, many persons construe suffering as punishment—and not necessarily as evil. Others consider much suffering that arises from similar kinds of examples as unjustifiable—even though explainable—since it falls upon innocent victims or persons who have not caused their own suffering by such examples of evil.

Second, therefore, in light of the previous aporias in human experiences of suffering and evil, is the distinction between natural evil and moral evil a sound distinction? It appears that, inasmuch as evil remains a *moral* category, or a category that depends on the reality of freedom and responsibility in personal and communal agency, evil cannot become a *natural* category. For, if evil is natural, in the sense that it constitutes an essential dimension of finite reality, then one can-

24. For example, see the position of Baron Friedrich von Hügel, one of the most influential and often-quoted opponents of the idea of divine suffering. He understood suffering as intrinsically evil and, therefore, God as incapable of its experience (von Hügel, "Suffering and God," 199).

not genuinely hold persons or communities responsible for it. In the traditional perspective, then, evil constitutes something that happens, something merely instinctual, not something voluntary.

On the one hand, one could attribute to the natural world a will that resembles the human will with the possibilities of good and evil within it, thereby construing the natural world in personal categories. Moreover, advocating the concept of *natural* evil may imply that, from a theistic perspective, God is either not omnibenevolent or not omnipotent, since God created a natural order that either opposes God somewhat successfully or resembles its evil creator.

On the other hand, in order to understand evil exclusively as a moral or agential category, one must construe the natural world as impersonal, non-moral, or non-agential. Such a construal, then, identifies human reality as the source of evil. Thus, one may consistently construe evil in terms of either moral (agential, personal) or natural (cosmic, non-personal, instinctive, non-agential) categories, but not in terms of both categories. To describe evil as both moral and natural involves an interpreter, therefore, in a serious category-mistake.

If one perceives evil as a natural phenomenon, a phenomenon that people can observe in the processes of nature rather than as an aberration of nature, then the notion of moral evil makes no sense. Insofar as humans participate in the natural world, from such a perspective, human reality is naturally evil: an actual evil will appears from birth in every human being as something inevitable and inescapable. To elaborate this perspective further, however, contradicts human experience, experience that also includes good intentions, actions, and projects. Thus, one must qualify any concept that describes humans as fully determined to do evil. How can one understand the complex relationships between evil and suffering, however, if one reduces evil to the moral, religious, personal, or agential category? Although moral evil does not *effect* all suffering, the character and extent of moral evil does *affect* all suffering. Likewise, suffering does *effect* some evil, but also *affects* some, if not all, evil.[25]

---

25. Sylvester Paul Schilling also discerned problems in equating evil with suffering. "Thus evil and suffering are not interchangeable; yet in our total experience they overlap and interpenetrate, and probably most frequently they coincide" (Schilling, *God and Human Anguish*, 10–11). Numerous theologians of divine suffering express similar awareness of this distinction (see Hughes, *Christian Idea of God*, 215; D. White, *Forgiveness and Suffering*, 54).

Paul Ricoeur's thought assists in moving through some of the practical and epistemological aporias in human experiences of evil and suffering. Ricoeur began his phenomenological analyses of the human will, or the problem of human freedom, with an analysis of the structures of human willing; therein, he analyzed the human will's capabilities and limitations. In his analysis, however, Ricoeur bracketed the actual experiences of evil, that which he called the "fault." Thus, he identified both voluntary and involuntary dimensions in decision, motion, and consent: "the common keyboard serving both innocence and fault." Ricoeur regarded the fault or evil as an alien presence in a philosophical anthropology. The fault or evil is accidental, not an aspect in the will's essential structure, rather, only one direction in which the will exercises itself. In the second stage of his philosophical anthropology, then, Ricoeur partially removed the brackets, in order to examine "the constitutional weakness which makes evil possible." He described this constitutional weakness as "fallibility." At this second stage, Ricoeur had not yet begun to analyze the evil human will. He sought, instead, to disclose the condition of possibility for the appearance of evil. Fallibility meant, for Ricoeur, "that the *possibility* of moral evil is inherent in man's constitution," inherent because of the disproportion in human being between the infinite affirmation of and the existential negation of human freedom (the limitations of finitude), a negation that must mediate the infinite affirmation of human freedom in order for the human to actualize itself concretely. Finally, in a third stage, Ricoeur studied human attestations to the experience of fault with a phenomenological hermeneutic of the symbolism of evil.[26]

26. Ricoeur, *Freedom and Nature*, 21; idem, *Fallible Man*, xix, 203, 209; idem, *Symbolism of Evil*.

Tendencies within Christian Scriptures toward a Distinction between Faulted and Essential Finitude

A meditation upon the way by which to develop the abstraction of faulted from unfaulted or essential finitude into an anthropological principle also invites a brief inquiry into a similar tendency within the Christian scriptures. This tendency appears in both canons of the Christian scriptures. Both libraries of literature, however, house several interpretations of the relationships between evil and suffering. In the brief discussion that follows, by no means do I treat exhaustively the rich variety of biblical perspectives on the relationships between suffering and evil. Rather, I examine several of the main strands in those perspectives, through which a number of testimonies express the tendency toward a distinction, like that between faulted finitude and essential or authentic finitude, in the Christian scriptures.

In both canons of Christian scriptures, the principal responses to the presence of suffering most often identify the origin of suffering in human sin. Sin, as understood in the Christian scriptures, refers to two principal realities: *primarily*, disobedience of, turning from, rebellion against, or betrayal of God the creator and covenant-maker; *secondarily*, disruption of proper relationships among creatures themselves. Inasmuch as God the creator ordered those relationships, however, the secondary reality of sin becomes the historical way in which humans actualize the primary reality of sin.[27] Insofar as certain communities of faith regarded all forms of suffering as evil, thus anomalous to creation's goodness, these communities principally construed suffering as the result of sin—a religious and moral category.[28] For the most part,

---

27. See, as examples, Deut 30:15–18 (as a statement of the primary reality of sin) and Amos 5:12 (as a statement of the secondary reality of sin). One can find a similar relationship in the newer or second Christian canon. In Rom 1:18–32, the apostle Paul, however, construed the secondary reality of sin as God's judgment upon the sinner, a judgment that results from the primary reality of sin. God, as a result of human betrayal of God, surrenders humans (as judgment) to the secondary reality of sin as a disruption among the proper relationships within the created order. Thus, God judges sin (the first reality) by sin (the second reality). I will treat these themes more fully in the second volume of this study, *Evil and Divine Suffering*.

28. Various Christian scriptures interpret suffering in several ways: as expiation for sin, as God's discipline by which educationally to strengthen and enhance human life, as attacks from agents other than God or the human—hostile personal powers (spirits, Satan), as part of hidden and inexplicable divine purposes, or even as testing of

then, Christian scriptures describe suffering and its descendant, death, as punishment by God for sin.

This influential biblical understanding of sin's relation to suffering appears repeatedly throughout the various genres of both Christian canons of scripture. As examples, according to the Hebrew scriptures, the first Christian canon of authoritative texts, increased pain in childbirth, male domination of the female, and hardship in the toils for a livelihood originated from the sin of the first humans. The Yahwist narrates the story of a great flood that God sent to destroy the entire world, a world that had turned from God's purposes for it. King Solomon's prayer during the temple-dedication acknowledged the negative experiences and suffering that had resulted from the sin of the people. When Israel experienced Josianic reform, the Deuteronomist enumerated a series of curses (promises of specific experiences of human suffering) that God would invoke upon the people of the covenant, if this people violated the terms of its covenant with God. Both canons of scriptures contain additional and numerous examples.[29]

Some biblical interpretations of the relationship between sin and suffering also construe present suffering as resulting from the sins of previous generations: as punishment from God across generational lines, causing future generations to suffer for the guilt of that which they did not do.[30] Whereas such perspectives contain important aspects of truth with respect to the historical fatedness that sin produces, those perspectives largely depend upon notions of corporate personality in ancient Israel. Nevertheless, even in literature from the first Christian canon, challenges to those perspectives appear: "in those days they will not say again, 'the fathers have eaten sour grapes, and the children's teeth are set on edge.' But everyone will die for his own iniquity; each man who eats sour grapes, his teeth will be set on edge."[31] According to this

---

commitments to God's service (Gerstenberger and Schrage, *Suffering*, 103–16, 205–42; also see, Scharbert, *Der Schmerz im Alten Testament*).

29. Gen 3:16–19; 6:6–13; 1 Kgs 8:31–36, 46–50; Deut 28:15–68. As a prime example, the reality of death results directly from sin (Rom 5:12–21). See the following studies: Gilkey, "Christian Understanding of Suffering," 57; idem, "Meditation on Death and Its Relation to Life," 20; both studies republished in Gilkey, *Through the Tempest*, chapters 14 and 15 respectively.

30. See, as examples, Exod 20:5; Lev 26:39; Num 14:33; Job 21:19.

31. Jer 31:29–30 NAS. Also see the forceful development of this conviction and insight in Ezek 18:1–32. The challenge that the story of Job represents seems to contain this shift as well (e.g., Job 21:19).

later perspective, sin still results in suffering, but that suffering falls only upon the guilty party, not necessarily upon the sinner's descendants and not upon those who remain innocent of such transgressions.

These biblical perspectives attempt to trace direct causal relationships from present suffering to some prior sin or sins. Even a short survey of these perspectives, however, discloses an important tendency that fully blossoms in the literature of the second Christian canon.

The book of Genesis, for example, does not begin with the punishment that God inflicted upon the first humans for their sin. Rather, these narratives initially portray for the reader a good creation, one not yet affected by evil. Only then does the book narrate the process by which unfaulted finitude becomes faulted. In a mythical way, Genesis constructs and issues a distinction between essential and faulted finitude.[32] Despite the identification by other traditions within the book of a direct causal relationship between sin and suffering (as punishment for sin), other traditions within this book perceive some kind of distinction between essential structures of finite reality and the accidental actualities of sinful finitude or the intruder that ruptures essential reality.

The book of Job also challenges the religious axiom that understands all suffering as the result of sin. The epic's narrator immediately declares that Job ". . . was blameless, upright, fearing God, and turning away from evil."[33] Job's friends, when they finally speak, quickly repeat the ancient axiom of suffering, interpreting Job's suffering as discipline or punishment for sin. The narrator, nonetheless, has already informed the reader of the emptiness in such an assessment of Job's experience. Thus, the book of Job radically challenges all human confidence in its own ability to identify a necessary causal link between sin and suffering. Whether or not the concluding chapters of this epic offer a more adequate rationale for the suffering of the innocent, however, does not primarily concern me at this stage. More importantly for my purposes

---

32. Gilkey perceived the symbolization of this distinction in the myth of the human race's fall into sin (Gilkey, *Maker of Heaven and Earth*, 184, 186–87). Some theologians during the nineteenth century had already perceived this distinction—as in the following statement, for example: "Why is suffering a universal possibility? Does some one say because of sin? We doubt it. It was sorrow, and not pain, that came as a result of the fall. Pain and death were before sin. The very soil of the garden was a result of death in vegetation" (Stockdale, "Does God Suffer," 88).

33. Job 1:1 NAS.

here, the Joban epic insightfully declares that suffering does not always result from sin or as a punishment from God for sin.[34]

Attestations in the second Christian canon to the life and death of Jesus, which disclose God as love, also exhibit this critical tendency in interpreting relationships between sin and suffering. This tendency appears, on one level, in the *teaching* of Jesus. For example, when Jesus encountered the congenitally-blind man, the disciples confronted Jesus with a theoretical dilemma (a variation on the ancient religious axiom that suffering results from sin): whether this person's congenital blindness resulted from his own or his parents' sin. Both horns of this dilemma presupposed that suffering results from sin. Jesus refused both answers, because Jesus did not accept their common presupposition. Rather, Jesus responded, "It was neither that this man sinned, nor his parents; but it was in order that the works of God might be displayed in him."[35] Although this Johannine testimony indicates, as its central message, that God discloses the divine presence through the miracle by which a blind man gains his sight, implicit to the activity of Jesus remains his own conviction that all suffering does not result from sin. Finite reality entails its own risks quite independently from the well-known bad risks of sin.

To advance most deeply into the mystery, the *person* of Jesus as the Christ requires examination. Later apostolic meditation on Jesus' role led Christian communities to this conviction: "For we do not have a high priest who cannot sympathize with our weaknesses, but one who

34. Job's "soliloquy of curse and death" (Job 3) challenges the mythic order, as represented by the religious axiom (that sin always results in suffering as punishment for sin) that Eliphaz, Bildad, and Zophar repeatedly articulate and echo (cf., Perdue, "Job's Assault on Creation," 295–315).

35. John 9:1–3 NAS. Christian theologians of divine suffering often cite this text in order to refute the claim that human suffering results as divine punishment for human sin (e.g., Weatherhead, *Why Do Men Suffer*, 116–17). Another logion of Jesus similarly challenges the direct correlation between sin and suffering as the punishment for sin. "Now on the same occasion there were some present who reported to Him about the Galileans, whose blood Pilate had mingled with their sacrifices. And He answered and said to them, 'Do you suppose that these Galileans were *greater* sinners than all *other* Galileans, because they suffered this *fate*? I tell you, no, but, unless you repent, you will all likewise perish. Or do you suppose that those eighteen on whom the tower in Siloam fell and killed them, were *worse* culprits than all the men who live in Jerusalem? I tell you, no, but, unless you repent, you will all likewise perish'" (Luke 13:1–5 NAS). J. A. McGuckin acknowledges this point in his treatment of Jesus' understanding of sacrifice (McGuckin, "Sacrifice and Atonement," 650).

has been tempted in all things as we are, yet without sin."[36] Thus, according to the witness, God inflicted neither suffering nor death upon Jesus because of sins that he had committed against God. Some of his sufferings, most especially his death on the cross of course, did result from sin, but only from the sin of his adversaries. The tendency to distinguish between the suffering of essential finitude and the suffering of faulted finitude, then, appears most completely in the person of Jesus, who, according to Christian testimony, actualized human life most authentically because he did not sin, though he did suffer and die unjustly.

The scripture's tendency to affirm a distinction between essential and faulted finitude also displays an application of the material criterion's self-reforming character. Within the Christian scriptures, this distinction subverts the simplistic construal of direct causal relationships between sin and suffering, a simplistic construal already so forcefully present in the scriptures. This subversion, then, begins to clarify the complexities of the relationships between evil and suffering.[37]

36. Heb 4:15 NAS. Also see, Heb 7:26–28 and 2 Cor 8:8.

37. Recent and contemporary theologians of divine suffering also rely heavily upon the distinction between faulted finitude and unfaulted finitude in their efforts to circumscribe the relationships between evil and suffering. Whether or not such modern and contemporary efforts take as their point of departure the tendency toward that distinction in the Christian scriptures remains unclear (as examples, see Brasnett, *Suffering of the Impassible God*, 122–23, 160; Hughes, *What Is the Atonement*, 73–78). One can certainly observe the distinction, however, in the work of well-known theologians as well. The negative features of the created world, including destruction, sickness, and especially death, only constitute elements of the darker side of the created order, "the negative aspect of existence" (Barth, *Church Dogmatics*, 3.1: 372–76). "Light exists as well as shadow; there is a positive as well as a negative aspect of creation and creaturely occurrence." "It is true that in creation there is not only a Yes but also a No; not only a height but also an abyss; not only a clarity but also obscurity; not only progress and continuation but also impediment and limitation; not only growth but also decay; not only opulence but also indigence; not only beauty but also ashes; not only beginning but also end; not only value but also worthlessness. . . . Yet, it is irrefutable that creation and creature are good even in the fact that all that is exists in this contrast and antithesis. In all this, far from being null, it praises its Creator and Lord even on its shadowy side, even in the negative aspect in which it is so near to nothingness" (Barth, *Church Dogmatics*, 3.3: 295, 296–97). "But 'good' or 'evil' only mean that which furthers or destroys life where it is combined with the idea of responsibility. Evil (*das Böse*) is different from misfortune (*Übel*); evil is the destructive action of a responsible being. Thus evil is the negative aspect of responsibility" (Brunner, *Man in Revolt*, 115). Langdon Gilkey also makes this point (Gilkey, "Christian Understanding of Suffering," 58; idem, "Meditation on Death," 20–21). In volume three of this study, *Divine Suffering and Tragic Reality*, I will interpret this tragic region of creation, Barth's "negative aspect of existence" and Brunner's "misfortune," as the occasion for the third divine wound.

Yield of the Principle

The preceding double meditation has indicated the necessity of a distinction between essential and faulted finitude. Without such a distinction,
reflection on human experiences of evil and suffering cannot proceed
fruitfully beyond a variety of practical and epistemological aporias.
Furthermore, tendencies toward such a distinction expose themselves
alongside the counter-claims of direct causal relationships between sin
and suffering even within the Christian scriptures. Thus, the following
formulation of the anthropological principle receives its impetus, not
only from a meditation upon contemporary human experience, but
also from the tendency that the material content in the criterion of the
criteriological principle has suggested and disclosed.

I have formulated the anthropological principle, by which my study
of this Christian symbol continues, in the following way. *One can distinguish the occasions for the various modes of divine suffering, as found
within Christian attestations to God's suffering, from one another as one
views those attestations through the prism of the following distinction:
unfaulted finitude, the essential realities and structures of the finite world
as unaffected by the evil will, refuses an unqualified equation with faulted
finitude, the finite world as affected by the evil will.* With this distinction,
of course, this principle abstracts faulted finite reality from unfaulted
finite reality. In actual human experience, however, one cannot observe
finite reality as distinct from its faultedness. This abstraction unveils
essential characteristics of finite reality, as a result, aspects that remain
un-distorted in their essence. The structural characteristics and qualities
of unfaulted or essential finitude, therefore, are necessary to finitude,
while faultedness—introduced by the evil will—remains accidental, not
essentially (even though historically) necessary to finitude.

Although Scheler's understanding of suffering as sacrifice remains
inadequate, his analysis of the transcendental constitution of suffering
engrafts a helpful feature onto the distinction that I have utilized in
the anthropological principle. Finite reality in its essential structures includes the condition of possibility for suffering, that which Max Scheler
described as ". . . the conflict of autonomous and independent parts with
their functional position in a whole, the whole in which they are found
in solidarity and which is in solidarity with the parts, such a conflict
is always the most general *ontological basis for the (ideal) possibility* of

suffering and pain *in a world*."[38] Thus, even prior to any thought about the problem of faultedness in finite reality, the possibilities, as well as the actualities, of suffering already appear.

Equipped with this anthropological principle, then, one may interpret testimonies to divine suffering with an aim toward discovering, through this prism, distinctions between the occasions for divine suffering to which those testimonies also attest. Using this prism yields three main, though very general, *occasions* for the suffering of God. First, faulted human finitude, human sin or evil, appears as the most immediate occasion for divine suffering in attestations to that phenomenon. Second, a type of suffering that faulted human finitude experiences appears distinctly as an occasion that results from the first occasion, the misery of human sin. Third, still distinct from the first two occasions and resulting from neither of them, the suffering of essential human finitude exhibits itself as the least accessible and most problematic of the three occasions, and that mainly due to the mixed and unabstracted character of all human suffering in actual human experience as well as in testimonies to divine suffering: the affliction of authentic human life through the essential or created features of tragic reality and experience.

Chapter 3, which follows, will make evident the implications of my anthropological principle for the entire structure of the Christian symbol of divine suffering. Therein, I examine the entire range of Christian testimonies to divine suffering through these three principal *occasions* for divine suffering. To move into that discussion here, however, would violate the limits of this portion of my study.

As I have shown in reference to each of the three procedural principles, in certain respects, I have abstracted each of these principles from the Christian symbol of divine suffering upon which this method focuses and guides my attention. Furthermore, each of those procedural principles contain within themselves moments of abstraction that remain peculiar to each principle. The eidetic principle abstracts the meaning of the symbol for past historical periods from its significance for contemporary experience. Eidetic reduction, through its establishment of a unified picture, abstracts a common structure from the numerous Christian testimonies to divine suffering. The crite-

---

38. Scheler, "Meaning of Suffering," 129.

riological principle abstracts the formal criterion from the pivot of the
material criterion. I have abstracted even the pivot (the newer or second
Christian canon) of the derivative Christian fact from the many streams
of Christian traditions. The anthropological principle, then, abstracts
the structures and characteristics of essential finitude from the reality
of faulted finitude, as that which is accidental to reality and not essential
or necessary to it. In turn, the abstraction of faulted from unfaulted finitude allows the abstraction of the occasions for divine suffering from
one another, when one reviews attestations to God's suffering through
the anthropological principle.

More importantly, however, not only do the three procedural principles contain independent and isolated aspects of abstraction within
themselves, and not only are they (as methodological) abstracted from
the object upon which they focus their analyses. I have abstracted these
three principles from one another, in an effort organically and thereby
properly to understand each one of them. Each principle performs a
function, without which none of the principles can properly function.
They operate almost simultaneously in mutual inter-dependence upon
one another.

In a sense, all of the principles reside within the eidetic principle
as I have applied it to the Christian symbol of divine suffering. Eidetic
analysis cannot reduce the multiple viewpoints to one unified pattern
without both the criteriological principle to provide the framework
with which to exhibit that pattern and the anthropological principle to
initiate the illumination of the common pattern within the Christian
attestations to God's suffering. The criteriological principle cannot provide that framework for those historical attestations, without the refusal
of eidetic analysis to consider (or, at least, its determination to bracket
temporarily) the significance of the symbol for contemporary experience. Neither can the criteriological principle sharpen the picture of
the symbol's structure without the aid of the anthropological principle
that permits occasions for divine suffering to appear distinctly from
one another within those Christian testimonies that the criteriological
principle identifies. Finally, the anthropological principle cannot elicit
solid support in its contention for the necessity of a distinction between
faulted and unfaulted finitude, as applicable to Christian attestations to
divine suffering, without the reliance of the anthropological principle

on its discovery of this tendency within the material criterion of the criteriological principle.

Thus, the method of my study remains one piece with three necessary dimensions. Through this method, Christian attestations to God's suffering disclose a specific symbolic structure, one with its own form of rationality, but one not unconnected to contemporary experiences and understandings of reality. In the chapter that follows, I will briefly display the hypothetical structure in the Christian symbol of divine suffering on the basis of the method that I have developed in the present chapter.

3

Hypothetical Structure of the Christian Symbol of Divine Suffering

Introduction

ON THE BASIS OF MY PREVIOUS PREPARATORY STEPS, THIS CHAPTER supplies a third, briefer, and final orientation for interaction with the Christian symbol of divine suffering. In one sense, this chapter initiates that interaction, since it provides a hypothetical overview of the symbol's structure. In another sense, however, this chapter retains its orienting character, in that it does not yet *fully* begin to interpret actual Christian attestations to divine suffering. Rather, in this chapter, I offer an overview of the symbol's structure as a hypothesis that I will demonstrate throughout all three volumes of this work. The present chapter serves, then, as the first stage of transition from the more abstract considerations in the two previous chapters to the more concrete analyses that follow.

This chapter completes the orientations for interaction with the Christian symbol of divine suffering. Nevertheless, in part two of this book, I take two additional steps along the path from the abstract to the concrete by identification and interpretation of this symbol's two principal presuppositions, the identification and elaboration of which display the two major conditions of possibility for divine suffering in this particular Christian vision of God. Since the five chapters of part two actually engage the Christian symbol of divine suffering at the level of presuppositions, I have not included them in part one with its more abstract, orienting character. Because the following chapters do elaborate the basic *presuppositions* of the Christian symbol of divine suffering, however, they do not fully engage the concrete considerations of the symbol itself and remain somewhat abstract as well. Here, however, I submit only a brief survey of the symbol's hypothetical structure, which will prepare the way for an exposition of the symbol's presuppositions in the five chapters of part two.

My procedure follows the order of knowing, rather than the order of being. Even though the presuppositions constitute attestations to the conditions of possibility for divine suffering at all, I derive those presuppositions epistemologically from the symbol of divine suffering itself. I approach these presuppositions on the basis of another scholastic axiom: "*nemo dat quod non habet*," or "no one gives what one does not have." My procedure, therefore, moves from an investigation of the result to that which effected it: from the symbol itself to its presuppositions. Nonetheless, I have granted the priority for consideration, even if only in a preliminary fashion, to that which first comes into view, the symbol itself.

I began chapter 1 by delimiting the inquiry of this project to one fundamental question: What are the structure and dynamics of the Christian symbol of divine suffering? I more fully amplified that question in the following way: What are the various modes of God's suffering, and how are they both distinct from, as well as related to, one another, in the broader Christian symbol of divine suffering?

Chapter 2 identified an obscuration of the different modes of divine suffering in Christian attestations to the suffering of God. A text from Third Isaiah illustrates such obscurities in a pre-Christian text, a text that later Christian attestations to divine suffering often used:

> In all their affliction he was afflicted, and the angel of his presence saved them; in his love and in his pity he redeemed them; he lifted them up and carried them all the days of old. But they rebelled and grieved his holy Spirit; therefore he turned to be their enemy, and himself fought against them.[1]

Although the prophet attributes suffering to God, this text suggests different forms or modes of divine suffering. The prophet, however, does not clearly distinguish those forms of divine suffering from one another. God's affliction, pity, and grief all appear in this text, but not in such ways as to remain distinct from one another. Because of that

---

1. Isa 63:9–10 RSV (Revised Standard Version).

problem in many testimonies to divine suffering, in both those found
in Christian scriptures and those found in subsequent Christian traditions, I sought in chapter 2 an answer to the following question: What
obscures the distinctions between the various modes of God's suffering
in the testimonies to the suffering of God? In chapter 2, I claimed that
the obscuration results from an inability to perceive *distinct occasions*
for those various modes of divine suffering. Therefore, another question
arose in that connection: How may one distinguish the various types or
modes of divine suffering from one another, in order to examine their
inter-relatedness more carefully, in the face of the obscuration of their
distinctive characteristics by the indistinct *occasions* for the various
modes of divine suffering? In order to answer this second question, I
proposed *to distinguish between the various occasions* for divine suffering. This line of approach, however, generated a third major question:
How may one distinguish between the various occasions to which God
responds in various modes of suffering? To answer that question, in
chapter 2, I also developed a *distinction between essential or unfaulted
finitude and faulted finitude,* through the grid of which to interpret the
various Christian attestations to divine suffering.

As a consequence of my previous line of inquiry, in chapter 2, I
formulated a method for examining Christian *attestations* to divine
suffering, by which to distinguish the indistinct *occasions* of divine suffering from one another.[2] By fixing the grid of the distinction between
essential and faulted finitude upon attestations to divine suffering, *three
principal occasions for divine suffering* appeared distinctly in those testimonies: (1) faulted human finitude (human evil or sin); (2) the suffering of faulted human finitude (the misery of human sin); and (3) the
suffering of unfaulted, authentic, or essential finitude (the affliction of
authentic human life).

---

2. I have examined some of the following attestations from the Christian scriptures through this anthropological principle. Although I have included texts from the
first Christian canon, they remain Christian attestations to divine suffering insofar as
these Jewish scriptures, also the first Christian scriptures, became documents that the
earliest Christian communities appropriated in their religious and theological thought
and activity: see Gen 6:5–6; Exod 2:23–25; 3:7–8; Judg 2:18; 10:16; 1 Sam 15:11; Ps
78:40–41; Isa 63:7–10; Jer 4:19–22; 31:30; Ezek 6:9; Hos 11:1; Amos 5:1–2; Acts 20:28;
Rom 8:22–27; 1 Cor 1:18–31; Eph 4:30.

Exhibiting the Symbol's Structure

When the creaturely occasions for divine suffering appear distinct from one another (in attestations to divine suffering), immediately the divine responses to those occasions distinguish themselves from one another. Consequently, *three principal modes or types of divine suffering* emerge from their previous lack of distinction. I characterize these three modes of divine suffering or three divine wounds most formally as follows: (1) God *suffers because of* faulted human finitude; (2) God *suffers for* faulted and suffering human finitude in the misery of its sin and evil; and (3) God *suffers with* unfaulted, essential, or authentic human finitude.[3]

Based upon my previous summation of the initial encounter with attestations to divine suffering, I submit the following hypothesis in answer to the guiding question that I have formulated for this study. *Three primary moments or types of divine suffering constitute the fundamental structure of the Christian symbol of divine suffering, moments of God's suffering characterized as the free responses of divine love (within the conditions that God has established for the divine self with respect to the relations between the divine creator and the creation) to the three basic creaturely occasions for divine suffering.* Three propositions more fully display the greater specificities and complexities in the basic threefold structure of this Christian symbol, of these three divine wounds.[4]

- First, the God whose life is love grieves, as occasioned by the inauthentic actualization of the divine image in human being as love,

---

3. Several theologians of divine suffering also already identify this basic structure or, at least, central elements of it: Bushnell, *Vicarious Sacrifice*, 1:223; Fretheim, *Suffering of God*, 107–48; Hall, *Gospel of the Divine Sacrifice*, 111–13, 176, 196; Harrington, *Tears of God*; Hughes, *What Is the Atonement*, 76–77, 102, 141, 162; Moltmann, *Trinity and the Kingdom*, 60; Ohlrich, *Suffering God*, 70–104; Peacocke, *Theology for a Scientific Age*, 126–27; Tymms, *Christian Idea of the Atonement*, 311–29. Several theologians partially discern this symbol's structure as well: see Alves, *A Theology of Human Hope*, 118–19; Baker, "Christological Symbol of God's Suffering," 100–1; E. Beecher, *Concord of Ages*, 68–69; Hodgson, "Incarnation," 378; Lee, *God Suffers for Us*; Morris, "Anthropopathy," 545–56; Mullins, *Christian Religion in its Doctrinal Expression*, 238; Park, *Wounded Heart of God*, 111–27; Relton, *Studies in Christian Doctrine*, 82; Wolf, *No Cross, No Crown*, 197.

4. Chapters 4–8 identify, describe, and analyze the conditions of possibility for the relationships between creator and creature that God has established, as presuppositions in the Christian symbol of divine suffering. These five chapters in part two of this book construct concrete transitions to the analyses of the actual Christian symbol of divine suffering that occur in volumes two and three of this work.

a creaturely love that *both* estranges itself from God, others, and itself *and* hurls itself into the hopelessness of all human efforts to overcome this triple alienation.

- Second, the God whose life is love sacrifices the divine self, as occasioned by the misery of the beloved human's inauthentic actualization of itself as love, in God's desire and effort *both* to re-create the possibility to actualize authentically the divine image in human being as love for humans who have estranged themselves from God, others, and self *and* to restore in humans a hopefulness for the ultimate completion of this triple reconciliation.

- Third, the God whose life is love suffers affliction, as occasioned by God's desire and effort *both* to participate in the afflicted authentic actualizations of human life as love in humans who share genuine community with God *and* to generate in them the hopefulness of their ultimate participation in God, communion with others, and integration as selves.

In the three previous propositions reside all of the structural levels, in condensed forms, that I previously proposed to illuminate. Thus, Christian attestations to divine suffering disclose the three principal moments that constitute the basic structure of the Christian symbol of divine suffering: *divine grief, divine self-sacrifice*, and *divine affliction*. A structure within each of these moments of divine suffering also exhibits itself as the relationship between a creaturely occasion and a divine response. Thus, the occasions for each of the previous moments in divine suffering constitute essential components in this symbol: *human sin or evil, the misery of human sin*, and *human affliction*. Furthermore, the supporting presuppositions, even though not explicitly evident, begin to indicate themselves: (1) the creator as the God whose life is love, and (2) the human creature as the image of the God whose life is love. While I actually begin my exposition of this Christian symbol in the second volume of this work, in part two (chapters 4–8) of this book, I develop my exposition of the supporting structure of this symbol or its presuppositions.

Questioning the Symbol's Structure

In the present chapter, however, I provide no further analysis of the symbol's actual structure. Nevertheless, several general questions emerge about the hypothetical structure that I have identified previously and, therefore, require answers before analyzing, in the remaining chapters of this book, the presuppositions of this symbol.

Definitive Structure?

With a first group of questions, I consider the adequacy of the hypothetical structure that I have proposed as the Christian symbol of divine suffering. In the previously-identified hypothetical structure of the Christian symbol of divine suffering, does the claim that this is *the* structure of that symbol also imply that one will always discern this particular structure within every Christian attestation to divine suffering? Is my claim that this is *the* basic structure of this symbol a definitive claim? Another way of probing the heart of this issue inquires as follows: Why should I choose this particular structure of the symbol as the most adequate one and not a different structure?

As I have tried to show already in my discussion of method, I refuse to absolutize the claim that my hypothetical reconstruction of this symbol is *the* definitive interpretation. First, among the multitudes of Christian attestations to divine suffering, many testimonies do not exhibit the basic structure that I have previously identified and proposed. Nevertheless, second, on the basis of the richest attestations to divine suffering (wherein that structure does exhibit itself), on the basis of conformity to the basic symbol-system of the Christian faith, on the basis of the criterion for this analysis (that God most fully discloses the divine self as love in Jesus Christ), and on the basis of deductions from incomplete testimonies to the structures that numerous testimonies to divine suffering consistently imply (or within the rationality or logic of this particular symbol-system), my reconstruction of this symbol appears as more relatively adequate than most if not all other versions of this symbol. Third, however, the choice of another criterion from among the available options within the inter-textuality of the derivative Christian fact (such as, for example, *retributive justice* as the central metaphor for God) would yield a significantly different hypothesis about Christian attestations to divine suffering as the most adequate

Christian reconstruction of that symbol, as one may perceive in certain Christian interpretations of this symbol.[5]

Nonetheless, while I aim to present the most adequate account of structure and dynamism in the Christian symbol of divine suffering, I hope that additional studies of this symbol will display flaws, inaccuracies, and inconsistencies that continue to distort my own interpretations and reconstruction. Hence, I answer the question, as to the rationale for choosing this particular configuration of the symbol's structure, through the very specific analyses and arguments in following chapters and volumes, as I test the hypothetical structure of the Christian symbol of divine suffering that I have proposed.

Point of Commencement?

Through a second group of questions, I consider my rationale for this particular configuration of the symbol's structure. Why does this particular configuration of the symbol's structure begin with the mode of divine suffering that results from the rupture or alienation between God and the human? Why does this analysis of the symbol not commence,

5. For example, some Calvinist theologies commonly choose *retributive justice* as the central metaphor for God. "The Trinitarian holds that the Son of God is true and very God, and that when he voluntarily becomes the sinner's substitute for atoning purposes, it is very God himself who satisfies God's justice. The penalty is not inflicted upon a mere creature whom God made from nothing, and who is one of countless millions, but it is inflicted upon the incarnate Creator himself.... The doctrine of vicarious atonement, consequently, implies that in God there exist simultaneously both wrath and compassion. . . . Justice is necessary in its exercise, but mercy is optional. Here, the compassion and benevolent love of God propitiates the wrath and holy justice of God" (Shedd, *Dogmatic Theology*, 384, 401, 402). "Had rebel man been forgiven without satisfaction, the purity of divine justice must have been tarnished forever more. . . . Divine justice could not pardon mortal sin without adequate satisfaction.... Nor could it receive satisfaction in any coin save that of suffering.... The second person of the Trinity voluntarily became the vicarious Sufferer for the redeemed.... The suffering of its Creator was the price to be paid for the redemption of a lost world.... The Parent of the universe so loved our fallen race that, for their salvation, he awakened the sword of divine justice to smite his Other Self; his Other Self, moved by pity known only in the pavilion of the Godhead, freely bared his filial heart to the descending stroke, which naught but Omnipotence could have endured" (G. Griffin, *Sufferings of Christ*, 22, 49, 49–50, 50, 102, 186; the first edition of Griffin's book appeared in 1845). These two examples quite clearly point to an alternative central metaphor from which a Christian notion of divine suffering has been, and again may be, developed. Although both of these theologians link divine love or compassion to God's effort to satisfy divine justice, still divine love continues to serve divine justice and not the reverse.

rather, with the mode of divine suffering that unfaulted or essential human suffering occasions, experiences of suffering wherein human evil has not yet alienated the human from God?

In order to answer the second group of questions, I first must acknowledge that raising those questions became possible only upon the basis of the anthropological principle that I developed in chapter 2. That principle contains the distinction between faulted finitude and essential finitude, a distinction that, in itself, remains an abstraction never present in actual human experience. Thus, the anthropological principle transfers some degree of that abstraction to the attestations to divine suffering upon which it overlays the grid of its distinction. As a result, the primary moments of divine suffering, as rendered by that distinction, as abstracted from one another, always remain distinct from one another in principle, but never separate from one another in actual Christian attestations to divine suffering. Therefore, with this ordering of the moments in divine suffering, I have attempted to represent adequately both the abstract and the concrete aspects of this symbol.

I have given priority in my representation of the various moments in the symbol's structure, however, to the most concrete. In these studies, I take my point of departure from that moment within attestations to divine suffering which attests to faulted human finitude. My analysis commences, therefore, by interpreting testimonies to the ambiguity in the human experience of divine suffering, testimonies that run parallel to contemporary human experience—experience of a finitude that evil has fragmented or distorted. This remains, nevertheless, my preference for a point of commencement, rather than a full engagement with the situational or contextual pole in a fully correlative constructive theological effort. Each structural moment of this symbol is a concrete moment. I could begin this analysis with either of the three principal moments in divine suffering. The three forms of God's suffering integrate with one another in such ways that together they form a sort of triangle, at either point of which (divine grief, divine self-sacrifice, or divine affliction) one might embark on the journey toward an interpretation of the whole symbol. To some extent, then, my particular configuration of this symbol's structural moments indicates a preference for that which remains *de facto* the case, rather than for that which becomes *de iure* the case.

I conclude this preliminary elaboration of the hypothetical structure of the Christian symbol of divine suffering, then, with a brief statement about the place in this larger study wherein my interpretations of each one of the three primary modes or moments of divine suffering occur. As I have mentioned several times, this first volume of my work, *Divine Vulnerability and Creation*, examines the two major presuppositions that identify the conditions of possibility for divine suffering of any kind. The second volume, *Evil and Divine Suffering*, will examine the encounter between the vulnerable God and human sin and its consequences, which involves an exposition of the first two divine wounds: *divine grief* and *divine self-sacrifice*. The third volume, *Divine Suffering and Tragic Reality*, therefore, develops an interpretation of the third divine wound: *divine affliction*.

Presuppositions *of the* Christian
Symbol *of* Divine Suffering

I dedicate part two to my mother, step-father,
and the memory of my father,
with ever-deepening love and gratitude
for their biological and social contributions
to God's gift of life to me:

Billie Faye Hughes Pool
(1926–)

Roger Lee Pool
(1934–)

Wilson Corley Mauldin
(1917–1984)

Introduction to Part Two:
Conditions of Possibility for Divine Suffering

IN PART TWO, THE MOST COMPLEX TRANSITIONAL STEPS EMERGE IN THE movement of this study into the more concrete analyses of this Christian symbol. In the chapters that follow, I will examine this symbol's two principal presuppositions, both of which taken together supply part two of this book with its title: Presuppositions of the Christian Symbol of Divine Suffering. Nevertheless, a moment of abstraction remains. I have drawn these two presuppositions from testimonies to divine suffering in which they remain embedded as the conditions of possibility for divine suffering.

Although I have spoken previously of two symbolic presuppositions in the Christian symbol of divine suffering, I have construed them as two interdependent components of one fundamental presupposition. Again, I state the most general features of these two components in the following way. *First, God is the creator whose life is love; second, God has created the human in the image of the God whose life is love.* Obviously, then, in an analysis of this twofold symbolic presupposition, an interpreter can understand properly neither one of the two components without understanding the other component simultaneously.[1]

Furthermore, discourse about either aspect of this symbol's twofold presupposition at least implies the other aspect. This feature discloses a dialectical character in the relationships of these two presuppositions to one another. My general representation of the two presuppositions, as a dialectic between the divine creator and the human image of the

---

1. In his enlightening study of attestations to God's suffering in the first Christian canon, Terence Fretheim carefully identifies aspects of these two basic presuppositions from an exegetical point of view in the chapters that precede his analyses of the three principal moments in divine suffering: "Chapter 3: God and World: Basic Perspectives"; "Chapter 4: God and World: Foreknowledge"; "Chapter 5: God and World: Presence and Power"; and "Chapter 6: God in Human Form" (Fretheim, *Suffering of God*, 34–106).

creator, discloses the analogical character of their relationships as well. Thus, throughout my exposition of these two presuppositions, I will make more explicit the very close and intricate associations between dialectical and analogical discourse in attestations to divine suffering.

In addition, the second presupposition of this symbol, the human as created in the image of the God whose life is love, encompasses a twofold content itself: (1) the human created in the image of God as the steward of the world; and (2) the world, universe, or cosmos as both the created condition of possibility for human reality and yet the responsibility of that very humanity.

In some respects, this twofold presupposition expresses nothing significantly different from its counterparts in the dominant traditions of classical Christian theism, at least not on the surface. When described as the twofold presupposition for the Christian symbol of divine suffering, however, the fundamental distinctiveness of this twofold presupposition rapidly expresses itself. The qualifications of these conditions for divine suffering as a twofold presupposition for the Christian symbol of divine suffering both radically distinguish the twofold presupposition from its related formulations in classical Christian theism and establish it as a viable, though dissident, alternative Christian formulation. The distinctiveness of this twofold presupposition will appear through my interpretations of each element within its constitution.

Because of the complexity of this twofold presupposition, I have divided the second part of this first volume of studies into two major divisions. In division one, I develop an exposition of the first presupposition of the Christian symbol of divine suffering in two chapters: chapter 4 elaborates the characteristics of the divine life as love, while chapter 5 analyzes the actualization of the divine love in God's activity as creator. Division two develops an interpretation of the second presupposition of divine suffering, the creaturely counterpart to God as love, in three chapters: chapter 6 examines the characteristics of the human in terms of the image of God as love; chapter 7 interprets the beloved human's actualization of the *imago Dei* in terms of the *imitatio Dei* as love; and chapter 8 briefly describes the contours of the relationship between the larger cosmos or world and the human as the image of God.

Thus, the five chapters that follow examine the structure and dynamism of both presuppositions. As already apparent from my brief formulations of these presuppositions, they possess parallel structures relative to their analogical features. Moreover, because of the intimate dialectical relationships between these two presuppositions, speaking of either presupposition always implies the other presupposition. Consequently, even though I have abstracted the two presuppositions from one another in order to clarify the distinctive features of both presuppositions, in my interpretations of each presupposition a running dialectic with the other presupposition always appears.

Divine Lover:

Self-limiting Divine Creator

Introduction to Division One:

Divine Life and Creative Activitiy

THE CONFLUENCE OF TWO POWERFUL CONFESSIONAL STREAMS FORM
the first presupposition within the Christian symbol of divine suffering:
(1) an attestation to God as creator—principally, although not exclusively, upon the basis of testimonies from the first Christian canon; and
(2) an attestation to God as love—again, principally, although not exclusively, upon the basis of attestations within the second Christian canon
to God's self-disclosure in the event of Jesus the Christ.[1] As these two
streams of piety have flowed together, and have confessed a confidence
in the first conditions of possibility for divine suffering, the first presupposition has taken the following form. *The God whose life is love limits
the divine self in God's creative activity; or, as the creator who is love, God
limits the divine self as God creates.*

As this presupposition stands, it describes divine action or volition. Yet, behind that action, providing the condition of possibility for
its actualization (at least abstractly), lies the being, character, actuality,

---

1. Admittedly, for both streams of piety, testimonies abound in both Christian canons, even though their principal loci appear as stated. For references to God as creator,
also see the following texts: Gen 1:1—2:25; 14:19, 22; Job 9:5–13; 26:6–14; 38:1—39:30;
Pss 8:1–9; 19:1–6; 24:1–2; 74:12–17; 89:5–14, 47; 104:1–35; Prov 3:19–20; 8:22–31;
14:31; 20:12; Isa 27:1; 42:5; 43:1; 44:24–28; 51:9–17; 54:5–6; Jer 5:22; 2 Macc 7:23, 28.
With reference to God as love, see Johannine testimonies, as the clearest examples (e.g.,
1 John 4:8, 16). Also see my discussion of the criteriological principle for these studies
in chapter 2. In this connection, I refer again to Goitein's argument for the meaning
of the divine name, "Yahweh" (see Exod 3:14; 33:19; 34:6–7), as "the One who loves
passionately and helps those that worship Him, while, at the same time, demanding exclusive devotion to Himself" (Goitein, "YHWH the Passionate," 1–9; cf., Perry, "Jahweh,
the God of Love"). By beginning here, I share the following conviction with David
Tracy: "I believe, in sum, that a distinctively Christian systematic theological language
would, in fact, prove to be trinitarian, yet a trinitarian language that would follow from
the central metaphor 'God is Love' (not the "psychological analogy" of Thomas et al.)"
(Tracy, *Analogical Imagination*, 443).

and life of God. Thus, acquiring an adequate picture of the twofold structure in this first presupposition requires an understanding of both that which the Christian symbol of divine suffering presupposes about God's being or life as love and how this symbol presupposes that God actualizes the divine being or life as creator. Although in principle at least one must admit the inseparable unity of divine being and action (as most Christian traditions have tried to show), in a sense, this first presupposition implies other aspects about God's nature that radically alter the meaning, as construed in classical Christian thought, of the unity between God's being and action.[2] Nevertheless, methodologically, I have abstracted divine being or life and activity from one another: first, in order to clarify the way in which humans experience the divine being as love, as well as to characterize the dimensions of divine love; and, second, in order to identify the characteristics of God's actualization of divine being in creative activity.

Thus, in division one of part two, I examine this first presupposition in two major stages. In the first stage (chapter 4), I extrapolate the symbol's understanding of divine being as love from divine activity, in order to disclose the condition of possibility for the actualization of divine being as love in creation. Despite the problems, I acknowledge the circularity involved in this exercise. In the second stage (chapter 5), by expositing the actualization of divine being as love in creative activity, I gradually display the condition of possibility in divine creative activity for divine suffering.

2. See Dietrich Bonhoeffer's still relevant discussion of the relationship between divine act and divine being in the Christian concept of revelation (Bonhoeffer, *Act and Being*, 77–151). Bonhoeffer attempts to develop an ontology of revelation that avoids the pitfalls of both the classical Christian concept of God as pure act and idealistic epistemology.

4

Divine Lover:

Divine Life As Love

Introduction: Divine Life as Love

THIS CHAPTER CONSTITUTES THE FIRST STAGE IN MY ANALYSES OF THE first presupposition of the Christian symbol of divine suffering. I repeat my formulation of this presupposition: *The God whose life is love limits the divine self in God's creative activity; or, as the creator who is love, God limits the divine self as God creates.* This first stage of my analysis works on the basis of an abstraction of divine life or being from divine activity, in order to clarify the characteristic ways in which this symbol envisions the actualization of divine love in divine creative activity. In the present chapter, therefore, I examine the divine life as love, from which divine creative activity itself originates.

Thus, the study that follows first develops an epistemology through which to identify the material dimensions of divine love that serve as the ground of divine activity. I then analyze the characteristics of the material dimensions of divine love that I have discovered by employing this epistemology. From the results of my study of the material dimensions of divine love, I derive additional structural or formal characteristics of the divine life, which finally yield the first condition of possibility for divine suffering in the divine life or being.

Epistemology of Divine Life as Love

The Christian symbol of divine suffering, in most major versions of this symbol, arises principally from one basic attestation: "ὁ θεὸς

ἀγάπη ἐστίν"; "God is love."[1] Witnesses to the disclosure of God in
Jesus of Nazareth produce this startling attestation. Jesus, as the Christ,
expressed God's love, was God's love-in-act toward humanity and the
entire creation. The becoming-human of God decisively made present
God's love for creation in creaturely particularity.[2]

Thus, when the Christian symbol of divine suffering presupposes
that God's being or life is love, it also presupposes that creation originates from that source. As love, God's being or life both effects divine
creative activity and affects the character of creation. God as reconciler
in Jesus the Christ, however, discloses the definitive clue about God's
being, life, or character.

For many years, numerous theologians have discerned that which
they have described as a "soteriological understanding of the Creator,"
in the piety expressed by many traditions from the first Christian canon.[3] As Rolf Knierim so thoroughly and more recently demonstrated,

1. 1 John 4:8, 16. Rudolf Bultmann argued that these texts do not propose a definition of God any more than do either "God is light" (1 John 1:5) or "God is Spirit"
(John 4:24) (Bultmann, *Johannine Epistles*, 16, 66). Nevertheless, because on the basis of
biblical testimonies generations of theologians have believed that humans perceive the
divine character or nature through God's activities and because these same theologians,
also on the basis of biblical testimonies, have believed that the supreme act of divine
self-disclosure occurred in the life, teachings, death, and resurrection of Jesus as Christ,
many theologians of divine suffering consider this bold statement to define God's essence. By contrast, however, Gustaf Aulén, one of Bultmann's own contemporaries and
a theologian of divine suffering, organizes his interpretation of the Christian doctrine
of God around this central metaphor. "Nothing more decisive can be stated about the
Christian conception of God than the affirmation: 'God is love' " (Aulén, *Faith of the
Christian Church*, 112).

2. In this connection, then, I assume a task that resembles the theological task as
succinctly defined by Eberhard Jüngel. "To think God as love is the task of theology.
And in doing so, it must accomplish two things. It must, on the one hand, do justice
to the essence of love, which as a predicate of God may not contradict what people
experience as love. And on the other hand, it must do justice to the being of God which
remains so distinctive from the event of *human* love that 'God' does not become a su-
perfluous word" (Jüngel, *God as the Mystery of the World*, 315). Both my *approach* to
accomplishing that task and the theological *content* that my analysis yields, however,
differ dramatically from Jüngel's approach and results.

3. For example, von Rad, *Old Testament Theology*, 1:138. See the following application of this trajectory in biblical theology to constructive theology: "As the faith of
ancient Israel witnesses, the God understood as creator of all things has been encountered first as a redemptive power in *human* life and society: 'He who brought us out of
Egypt' is the maker of heaven and earth" (Howe, "God's Power and God's Personhood,"
42–43).

however, the older and more predominant viewpoint assumes that the conservators and transmitters of Israel's traditions produced narratives about creation as etiological explanations of Israel's history (a purpose that the creation traditions may have certainly, although not exclusively, fulfilled), rather than that Israel understood the purpose of its history to refer to, as well as to actualize, the meaning of creation.[4] For example, in Deutero-Isaiah, the prophet announces Israel's salvation from exile in Babylon, using the term גָּאַל (gaàl) rather than the term פָּדָה (padá). The latter term refers to a redemption that occurs in business relationships. The former term, specific to family law, refers to redemption of one person by another person because of a previously established kinship bond, a bond that provides the one person with both the right and the duty to redeem the other person. Trito-Isaiah refers to God with the former term as the "redeemer" of Israel, but couples it with the appellation of "father" for God.[5] This redeemer-relationship, furthermore, indicates a previous kinship relation: a relationship that Deutero-Isaiah characterizes as the relationship between divine creator and creature. Because God cares about God's creation, or on the basis of that divine concern, God redeems creation when it experiences need.[6] Hence, even though the first Christian canon may most often postulate divine creative activity on the basis of divine redemptive activity, those scriptures understand the divine creator as more than simply an etiological explanation of Israel's soteriological history. Israel's understanding of God as redeemer presupposes an understanding of God as creator. Following Knierim's insight, then, I describe Israel's understanding of the divine creator as a soteriological concept of the divine creator, qualified by the claim that this concept only represents Israel's epistemological enrichment and clarification of the divine identity that it already presupposed.[7]

4. Knierim, "Cosmos and History in Israel's Theology," 69.

5. Isa 63:16.

6. Isa 43:1, 7; 44:2; 54:5. See Tryggve N. D. Mettinger's concise interpretation of the relationship between God as creator and God as redeemer in Deutero-Isaiah (Mettinger, *In Search of God*, 158–74).

7. Thus, Knierim touches the heart of the issue, when he formulates the fundamental questions that his claim raises. "Israel's soteriology undoubtedly preceded and eventually expanded into its protology. But does this fact mean that its protology has to stand in the service of its soteriology? Or does it mean that lastly, her soteriology came to stand in the service of her protology?" (Knierim, "Cosmos and History in Israel's Theology," 70).

Similarly, as an epistemological assessment only, the Christian symbol of divine suffering presupposes a soteriological concept of the divine creator. To describe God as love within the divine self remains an abstraction, since humans discover the divine being as love only through God's actualization of the divine being toward creation. Thus, although from the world-order one may discern the *presence* of God (according to some traditions within both the first and second Christian canons), only God's particular self-revelation establishes and clarifies the *identity* of that divine presence. Thus, the world-order itself epistemologically obscures the divine identity.[8] As a consequence, for the Christian symbol of divine suffering, although humans discover the divine creator's identity through God's identity as savior in Jesus the Christ, the symbol of God as creator does not only serve the symbol of God as savior. Rather, as I will show, the symbol of God as savior identifies and fulfills the meaning of the symbol of God as creator. In this case, then, God as savior in Jesus of Nazareth identifies God the creator as a God with the being of love.

The attestation that God as creator discloses the divine self as love through Jesus of Nazareth does not significantly differ from the confessions of many other Christian traditions. Nevertheless, the Christian symbol of divine suffering presupposes a radically different meaning in its understanding of the divine being as love, a meaning that one may perceive in God's relationship to the creation, not so much from God's self-relatedness. Humans have no access to, and do not come to know the divine being as love from (even though most fully disclosed in Jesus of Nazareth), the inner-trinitarian relationship of love between

---

8. In this connection, Knierim referred to the book of Job as an attestation to epistemological obscurity within the world-order, although the book of Job seems to emphasize creation's chaotic and destructive aspects, rather than to emphasize the epistemological obscurity caused by human sin to which the apostle Paul, for example, attested (e.g., Rom 1:18–32) in the second Christian canon (Knierim, "Cosmos and History in Israel's Theology," 89–93). Similarly, see 1 John 3:16; 4:10–11. In these texts, the initiative of divine love on behalf of lost humanity discloses the reality of authentic love (as directed to both God and the human) and establishes such love as the *telos* of genuine human life—in order to know oneself as truly of God. In Christian protology, increasing epistemological obscurity in the world-order results from human sin. Thus, as Langdon Gilkey so carefully demonstrated, in the order of knowing, or epistemologically, salvation precedes creation; salvation reveals, however, that, in the order of being or ontologically, creation precedes salvation (Gilkey, *Maker of Heaven and Earth*, 269–85).

divine parent and divine child—however deeply Jesus' piety and death express such love. Rather, God's being as love discloses itself through Jesus of Nazareth, as the Christ-event re-presents God's love for God's beloved, though estranged, creation.[9] Hence, to describe God's being as love abstracts an understanding of the character of God's being from the dynamics of the relationship between divine creator and creation as portrayed in the event of Jesus the Christ.

Material Dimensions of Divine Life as Love

In spite of the thorny problems that it creates, an examination of God's relationship to the creation—as focused in the divine activity in Jesus as Christ—discloses the characteristics or dimensions of love in God's being or life. Thus, on the basis of the dimensions of love in God's being, perceived through the relationship between God as creator and creatures, the characteristics of the first presupposition appear. As I have already stated, on the basis of the criterion of God's self-disclosure as love in Jesus as Christ, Christian attestations to divine suffering describe divine being or life as love. Analyzing the event of Jesus as Christ, then, inasmuch as this event represents divine response to the human situation, yields a threefold structure that characterizes the divine being as love.

Agapic Dimension of Divine Life

The evangelists of the second Christian canon narrate the history of Jesus the Christ as God's gift of the divine self for human beings. The life, teachings, and death of Jesus, in their various portrayals in the ca-

9. The most adequate Christian attestations to divine suffering diverge rather sharply from the forms of trinitarianism that many theologians espouse. For example, because "what happened on the cross was an event between God and God," God the lover grieves over the death of the beloved divine son there (Moltmann, *Crucified God*, 244–45; also see, idem, *Trinity and the Kingdom*, 61–96). Following an insightful analysis of human love, Jüngel describes God's being as love, because God is both lover (in the person of God the Father) and beloved (in the person of God the Son), and because the divine parent sends the divine son to a certain death on the cross; he refuses, however, to describe *human being* as love on that basis (Jüngel, *God as the Mystery of the World*, 326–30; idem, "What Does It Mean to Say, 'God Is Love,'" 305–6). In the perspectives of both Moltmann and Jüngel, the cross remains an event between God and God, even though it happens for the sake of the world. This position, however, implicitly de-values the creature's place in relation to God.

nonical gospels, represent the divine offer of a new or restored relationship with humans who are presently estranged from God.[10]

According to various versions of the Christian story, Jesus' teachings and actions (in his communion with outcast and unrighteous people in his social world) repeatedly offer this gift. Finally, in the death of Jesus, God lavishly bestows that gift: the divine self-sacrifice on behalf of an utterly needy humanity. God offers divine resources to humans who, having estranged themselves from God, neither deserve divine assistance nor can restore that relationship with their own resources alone. Thus, the Christ-event initially discloses the character of divine action therein as God's forgiving, self-transcending, or self-renouncing action for the sake of the estranged and needy yet beloved human.[11] God relinquishes the claim for retributive justice, or even some kind of recovery of divine honor, in favor of an attempt to reconcile with God's beloved creaturely companion. Now, drawing from the event of Jesus as Christ in terms of its initial character, I can illuminate a first dimension of God's being as love. I have named this first dimension of the threefold structure with a well-known Greek term for love: ἀγαπή (*agapé*). The Hebrew word, אהב (*aheb*), used for God's electing love, illumines *agapé's* deeper connotations.[12] Since the agapic dimension of divine love appears in the Christ-event, it initially appears as the most prominent dimension of God's being as love, given the soteriological character of the event of Jesus as Christ as God's self-giving for the estranged yet still beloved human. The divine love that operated in the experience of Jesus as Christ displays God's way or method for recovering estranged yet beloved humanity. Without this divine effort, no human desire or effort to return to God could overcome the rupture and the rift that human infidelity to God had produced. Consequently, the agapic dimension of God's being as love possesses a self-sacrificial dynamic as the heart of its character.

Creativity characterizes this dimension of divine love, in the sense that God endeavors through the event of Jesus as Christ to re-create or to re-store authentic human being or life to that for which God origi-

---

10. John 3:16; Rom 5:1–11. Numerous biblical passages support this prevalent motif, the point so pervades both canons of Christian scriptures.

11. John 1:1–5, 9–14; Phil 2:5–11; Heb 1:1–4.

12. See Norman Snaith's discussion of this term: Snaith, *Distinctive Ideas of the Old Testament*, 131–42.

nally intended it. As creative, God freely offers, without compulsion or necessity, the divine self in love to the estranged other. The love that God actualized in the Christ-event, however, in no way re-creates or restores all value in the human for and to whom God offers it. Nonetheless, the estranged yet beloved human, no matter how distorted or alienated from God, retains value for God, if for no other reason than because the human, as well as the remainder of the cosmos, remains *God's* creation. In this respect, then, the Christian symbol of divine suffering does not attribute some sort of value-indifference to God. For God, the estranged human remains worthy of recovery. Furthermore, this dimension of divine love re-establishes the possibility of communion with God, because due to sin such humanity has lost its ability to re-establish community on its own. Even though estranged from God, the human, as a creature that God created for community with Godself, retains a religious dimension that the human can never obliterate, despite the extent of the human's distortion and obscuration of that dimension. Nevertheless, the human cannot reverse its obscuration and distortion of that dimension through which God intended for the human to relate to the divine self. Hence, God's agapic activity indicates a divine motivation behind this self-sacrificial love as well as a divine purpose or goal before it.[13]

13. My construal of divine agapic love sharply contrasts with Anders Nygren's construal of divine love as only *agapé*. In his proposal, this dimension of God's love completely defines *divine* love. Nygren describes divine love as "spontaneous and 'unmotivated,'" "indifferent to value," "value creating," and "the initiator of fellowship with God" (Nygren, *Agape and Eros*, 75–81). Inasmuch as my construal of the agapic dimension in God's love stands largely as an antithesis to Nygren's analysis of divine love, my own interpretation agrees more with Paul Tillich's understanding of divine love. Tillich describes *divine* love on the basis of an analogy to his ontological analysis of *human* love. For him, in every life-process, the unbroken unity between the trends toward separation and reunion defines the ontological nature of love. Thus, when describing divine being as love, one thereby predicates of God the unity of the two trends in every life-process. Divine love, however, as Tillich defines it in relation to his ontological analysis of love, differs from all other forms of love (including "*eros*," "*philia*," and "*libido*,"); at this point, Tillich's conception closely resembles Nygren's construal of love. Tillich, like Nygren, describes divine love as *agapé*. Also like Nygren, for Tillich, love contains these central characteristics: (1) it unconditionally affirms the other person apart from any positive or negative values within that other person; (2) God offers this love universally, neither excluding nor preferring anyone; (3) divine love accepts, with forgiveness, the other person in the face of that person's resistance and rejection; and (4) divine love acts to realize the other person's personal fulfillment. Unlike Nygren, however, Tillich can envision *that* the other three forms of love can "contribute to the symbolization of the divine love," but cannot describe *how* that contribution might

Erotic Dimension of Divine Life

Further exploration of this event in Jesus as Christ (divine self-giving for the human in its self-made need), by inquiring about its source, origin, or motivation, discloses God's desire to recover an estranged lover, child, or partner, God's longing to reconcile and to reunite with one who has betrayed the divine love. Drawing from the event of Jesus Christ a second time, in terms of its motivation, illuminates a second dimension in God's being as love.

I designate this second dimension of divine being with a second well-known Greek term for love: ἔρως (eros). Divine love's agapic dimension points behind or beneath itself to the dimension of love in God that activates and motivates divine agapic love. I have described the motivating or activating dimension in divine love as the erotic dimension, ἔρως θεοῦ, insofar as that description refers to God's longing

---

look, since, like Nygren again, for Tillich "the basic and only adequate symbol is *agape*" (Tillich, *Systematic Theology*, 1:279, 280, 281; cf. Irwin, *Eros toward the World*, 8–17). Jüngel developed a description of God's being as love that more adequately accounts for the dimensions of divine love on the basis of an analogy with his own ontological analysis of human love. He perceives both agapic and erotic structures within the divine being, but dilutes the strength of his analogical effort by distilling the meaning of divine love from the trinitarian relationship between the divine father and the divine son (Jüngel, *God as the Mystery of the World*, 314–30). E. Y. Mullins identified several biblical forms of love, three of which roughly correspond to the three dimensions that I have identified, although he described them with somewhat different terminology: "the love of *benevolence*" is love in ". . . the form of good will toward all creatures, regardless of moral character" (ἀγάπη); "the love of *affection*" is "a relation of special intimacy between God's love and its object" (ἔρως); and "the love of compassion" is God's love "when its object is in distress" (φιλία) (Mullins, *Christian Religion in Its Doctrinal Expression*, 239). Sallie McFague proposed even fuller and more adequate models of divine love that incorporate *agapé*, *eros*, and *philia*. She did not, however, systematically integrate these models with one another—thus, of course, remaining consistent with her genre of "metaphorical theology." My analysis of divine love's agapic dimension corresponds quite closely to, though operating much more systematically than, her analysis of *agapé*. Later in this section, I will develop that claim more carefully. For now, however, particularly at one point her analysis joins my proposal in diverging sharply from Nygren's classic description of *agapé*. When McFague stressed that God intends for all creation to flourish, she quickly and helpfully made the following distinction: such divine love for *all* creation intends to emphasize God's impartiality and inclusiveness, not God's disinterestedness; for God exhibits the most intense interest in the creation. God's love is never detached, unconcerned, or perfunctory (McFague, *Models of God*, 101–9). Also, see Edward Vacek's and Timothy Jackson's excellent and similar studies of the self-sacrificial character of divine agapic love (Vacek, *Love, Human and Divine*, 179–88; Jackson, *Priority of Love*, 136–69).

or desire for return of, restoration of, or reunion with, God's estranged lover.[14] This second dimension of divine love, although not perhaps immediately noticeable due to the potency of God's active agapic presence, nevertheless, functions foundationally for that first or agapic dimension of divine love. Driven by divine erotic love, God loves agapically.

In my description of God's motivating love as the erotic dimension of divine being, I acknowledge points of divergence from as well as points of convergence with classical understandings of ἔρως.[15] Loving erotically, God perceives value in the estranged human, but finds God's self estranged from that beloved other, due to the human's betrayal and rejection of divine love. Hence, even though God discerns value in the other whom God seeks, God knows the distortion and estrangement that suffuses and surrounds the beloved other and for which the created other remains responsible. Furthermore, the Christian symbol of divine

14. Many texts in Christian scriptures attest to God's erotic love: as examples, see Jer 31:20; Hos 11:1–4, 8; Luke 15:1–32). Yahweh's desire to recover Israel (described by both Jeremiah and Hosea as a wayward child), to restore or to renew the relationship that the deceit of Yahweh's child has distorted, resembles God's desire, in the presence and proclamation of Jesus, to recover sinners (as represented by the tax collectors and sinners in the Lucan gospel). In Luke 15, the parables of the lost sheep, the lost coin, and the father's love vividly portray the divine desire that drives each of these God-metaphors to search for and to retrieve that which they had lost. Divine desire, thirst, hunger, or longing for the lost and alienated beloved one motivates the divine search that divine self-sacrifice exemplifies. Some theologians characterize divine desire or the erotic dimension of divine being as divine appetite (B. Lee, "Appetite of God," 369–84).

15. Plato narrated a myth through which he communicated the classic conception. Eros was conceived at a feast of the gods, a celebration on Aphrodite's birthday. One of the guests, the god Poros or Plenty, had partaken too heavily of the intoxicating divine nectar and went into Zeus's garden where he fell asleep. After the feast, in her habit of taking advantage of such occasions, Penia or Poverty came to beg. Considering her own difficult situation, she lay down with Poros and there conceived a child—Eros. Eros became a follower of Aphrodite: because of his conception on her birthday, because of her beauty, and because of his love for the beautiful in all things. Eros embodies qualities from both of his parents. He is poor and always in distress like his mother. Like his father, Eros always plots against the fair and the good, is bold, enterprising, strong, a mighty hunter, keen in the pursuit of wisdom, and fertile in resources. Thus, Eros, neither mortal nor immortal, never wanting and never wealthy, always stands between ignorance and knowledge (Plato, *Symposium*, 203). Again, in his classic study of Christian love, Nygren characterized *eros* as (1) acquisitive love, (2) the human way to God, and (3) egocentric love (Nygren, *Agape and Eros*, 175–81). Nygren's interpretation of *eros*, however, confirms the accuracy of Nietzsche's judgment: "Christianity gave Eros poison to drink; he did not die of it, certainly, but degenerated to Vice" (Nietzsche, *Beyond Good and Evil*, 99 [168]).

suffering does not describe God's desire for the created other's value as the yearning of an inferior (in this case, God) for a superior value (the human). Nevertheless, in spite of the other's fault or betrayal, God still highly valorizes that creaturely other. God highly values the other because of that which the other remains as God's creature. Human fault does not eradicate the value with which God as creator has endowed the creature, so that God can value the beloved creature, both agapically in spite of sin and erotically because of its created goodness, without affirming the negative value in human betrayal of divine love.

The created other's fault, in its self-estrangement from God, produces, then, a lack or need in God. This need does not remove from God any characteristics of deity; the cessation of authentic love from the created other does not detract from the deity of God, making God less than divine. God remains free in divine erotic love as well. God needs the created other only in the sense that God loves the other because, as created, God has defined the other as good and valuable in itself.[16] Therefore, in God's active erotic love, God seeks to acquire that in which God no longer participates, a reciprocal relationship of love with the created other. God neither produced this need nor desired it for the divine self. The actions of God's other occasioned this divine need. A number of Christian traditions discern this erotic dimension in divine love, even though those traditions also sometimes qualify divine erotic love in order to conform to the orthodoxy of classical Christian theism. Some of those dissident traditions, describe this dimension of divine love as divine "yearning" (a divine zealousness for the creatures that God sustains, a unifying drive, a power that attempts to draw all things as good back into union with the Good), or as "the thirst of God": a divine yearning or thirst that persists in God as long as the created other remains in need because of self-estrangement from God. Other Christian traditions describe this dynamism as the divine longing to possess that which God has lost: *the estranged yet still beloved human.*[17]

16. This position differs slightly from the position which claims that God needs the other simply because God has chosen to depend upon the created other (e.g., Fiddes, *Creative Suffering of God*, 71–76).

17. Pseudo-Dionysius, *The Divine Names*, 4.12–17; Julian of Norwich, *Revelations of Divine Love*, 31, 75; cf., McFague, *Models of God*, 130–36. McFague developed a concept of divine *eros* that resembles my proposed construal. H. Martensen helpfully described this lack in God as a "superfluity" in creation, not "a blind hunger and thirst after existence," but "the inexhaustible riches of that liberty which cannot but will to reveal itself"

   In this divine desire for the created other, God not only desires to fulfill a divine need; in God's erotic love, God also seeks the created other's greater good. Thus, for the Christian symbol of divine suffering, its attestation to divine erotic love does not portray God's love as egocentric. God desires the created other, then, for that other's sake as well.[18] The divine ἔρως refers fundamentally to God's desire, longing, or yearning for the created other to live in, with, and from God as God lives in, with, and from God's own self: God's thirst or hunger for the beloved human to become and to do all that the human might be and might accomplish according to its purpose as God's creature.[19]

(Martensen, *Christian Dogmatics*, 114). Mullins understood this dimension of divine love as the desire of God's love "to possess its objects" (Mullins, *Christian Religion in its Doctrinal Expression*, 237). William Newton Clarke identified divine love's erotic dimension, when he described it as "God's desire" and "yearning impulse" both to give the divine self to God's creatures and to possess them for spiritual communion with Godself (Clarke, *Outline of Christian Theology*, 95, 97, 98). While I agree with so much of Edward Vacek's insightful analyses of love, his description and assessment of *eros*, primarily as a result of his basic definition of this form of love, do not permit the more complex dialectical relationships between erotic, agapic, and philial forms of love that my own analyses identify and attempt to describe. Vacek defines erotic love as one form of self-love, the other form being agapic self-love. According to Vacek, for erotic love, "the immediate object is something other than ourselves, which we love as a way of loving ourselves," the love ". . . of another for our own sake," or "love for other persons or things not for their sakes, but *for the lover's sake*" (Vacek, *Love, Human and Divine*, 240, 247). In other respects, however, Vacek does not allow this still one-sided definition of erotic love entirely to relieve the creative dialectical dynamism in the three forms of love. For example, in describing divine erotic love, Vacek says that "God wants our fulfillment for ourselves; but, as one involved with us, God also wants our fulfillment for God's relational self. . . . once God has decided to redeem, God the Redeemer needs to be needed" (Vacek, *Love, Human and Divine*, 257).

   18. Paul Avis described the desire, in divine *eros*, for the creature's good as "agapistic eros" or "erotic agape." For Avis, divine *eros* indicates divine vulnerability ". . . to being hurt by his human creatures," a divine capacity that ". . . contrasts strikingly with a strong element in the Hellenized Christian tradition" (Avis, *Eros and the Sacred*, 135, 137). See my brief discussion at the end of chapter 5 of transitive and reflexive divine vulnerability. The Christian symbol of divine suffering attests to both transitive and reflexive aspects in all three dimensions of divine love. Even though Avis limited his study to divine *eros*, his interpretation harmonizes with my interpretation of divine *eros* in this symbol. As related to divine suffering, this first appears as a presupposition in the broader category of divine vulnerability with its transitive and reflexive capacities.

   19. Dorner, *System of Christian Doctrine*, 2:25; Mullins, *Christian Religion in Its Doctrinal Expression*, 236; Varillon, *Humility and Suffering of God*, 164, 171; Weatherhead, *Why Do Men Suffer?*, 45; Oden, *Living God*, 1:119–22.

Philial Dimension of Divine Life

Probing more deeply into attestations to Jesus as the Christ, by inquiring into the goal or purpose of God's self-giving, one discerns the relationship both that God has lost and that God hopes and seeks to recover. The Christian symbol of divine suffering construes the relationship that God hopes to renew as the relationship between friends (never, of course, in the sense that humans either possess complete equality with God or become gods themselves), a relationship nonetheless of reciprocity, mutuality, partnership, and solidarity.[20]

Drawing a third disclosure from the event of Jesus as Christ, here in terms of its purpose or goal, unveils a third dimension of God's being or life as love. The second dimension, divine erotic love, points beyond the divine self to the desired object, goal, or purpose (τέλος) of divine presence in Jesus as Christ; thus, divine erotic love elicits the operation of divine agapic love. In erotic love, God desires to realize this third dimension of love in relation to an alienated humanity as well as to love agapically in order to realize this aim. Through agapic love, God exercises the divine method by which to establish the possibility of realizing this goal. I have designated the third dimension of divine love, then, with a third well-known Greek term for love: φιλία (*philia*). The predominant Hebrew term for God's covenant-love, חֶסֶד (*hesed*), significantly

---

20. Once again, Christian scriptures extensively attest to this third aspect of divine love. In the first Christian canon, a precursor to the emphasis in the second Christian canon upon God as friend appears in Yahweh's covenant-making and covenant-renewals with Israel: as examples, see Exod 19:1–8; Deut 4:1—26:19; 27:1—30:20; Josh 24:1–27. Although Israel's covenants imitate ancient Near Eastern suzerainty treaties (thus, relationships between superiors and subordinates), Yahweh enjoins mutual responsibilities upon both parties to the covenant; they pledge mutual trust and trustworthiness to one another. Furthermore, Yahweh's description of Israel as a "kingdom of priests" implies a mutual task or vision. Matt 11:19 describes Jesus as the "friend of tax collectors and sinners." Mark 16:20, though probably a later addition to the gospel, remembers proclamation as a task at which Jesus and the disciples worked together. Luke 15:11–32, the parable of the father's love, amply illustrates this philial dimension in divine love, when the father lovingly and joyfully welcomes the returning wayward son into full participation in the family. The father does not receive the son back as a subordinate or a servant. In the Johannine evangelist's more radical and powerful depiction of the Christ, Jesus shifts the status of the disciples from servants to friends (John 15:1–27). Sometimes, leaders who clearly thought of themselves as co-workers with God in the divine purposes and tasks of reconciliation even addressed the Pauline communities (1 Cor 3:9; 2 Cor 6:1).

resembles and enriches this symbol's construal of divine *philia*.[21] Divine actualization of philial love toward the estranged human indicates the goal of divine love, the object of God's longing, and the purpose for divine self-giving. As a concept, divine philial love represents the richness of the community that God seeks, creates, and promotes. I have described that goal, object, or purpose toward which God moves as the actualization and fulfillment of divine philial love, wherein God realizes a loving reciprocity, wholeness, health, completion, welfare, well-being, peace, and justice, or develops a mutuality or friendship, with God's beloved in a joyful union, a reality known in Hebrew as שָׁלֹם (*shalom*).[22]

Often, theologians refuse to attribute this dimension of love to God, because, for many Christian scholars, it connotes a relationship between equals, a preferential or exclusive relationship, one in which like seeks like, an individualistic and even egocentric relationship.[23] From the standpoint of that objection, then, authentic divine love would connote only a relationship between a superior and a subordinate, a relationship of indifference or non-preference, a relationship in which God seeks the

21. Cf. Snaith, *Distinctive Ideas of the Old Testament*, 94–130.

22. In his study of this Hebraic concept in relation to divine presence, John I. Durham ascribed this broad spectrum of meanings to the term "*shalom*" (Durham, "שָׁלֹם and the Presence of God," 272–93).

23. Aristotle constructed the classic model of friendship-love or φιλία (Aristotle, *Nichomachean Ethics*, 8.1–14; 9.1–12). Again, Nygren's construal of divine *agapé* excludes this philial dimension of divine love. Moltmann even, in some of his earlier work, declares that, "for the crucified Christ, the principle of fellowship is fellowship with those who are different, and solidarity with those who have become alien and have been made different. Its power is not friendship, the love for what is similar and beautiful (*philia*), but creative love for what is different, alien and ugly (*agapé*)" (Moltmann, *Crucified God*, 28). In those statements, Moltmann assumes the validity of the Aristotelian definition of friendship. In his later work, Moltmann speaks more favorably of God as the divine friend who freely offers friendship to the creatures. Still, Moltmann maintains a distinction between God's love in the Trinity as that of like for like and God's love for humanity as that of fellowship with those who are different. The real problem with his perspective revolves around his concept of friendship as the relation of like to like (Moltmann, *Trinity and the Kingdom*, 56, 58). By contrast, in Edward Vacek's theology of love, as the central thesis of his book, he claims "that communion or philia is the foundation and goal of Christian life." Elaborating the meaning of this thesis, he says, "[i]ndeed all human love finds its culmination and ultimate goal in a community of solidarity with and in God" (Vacek, *Love, Human and Divine*, 280, 281). Vacek identifies and elaborates a series of philial characteristics that resemble the results of my analysis of divine *philia*, in his discussion of human friendship with God (Vacek, *Love, Human and Divine*, 133–49).

dissimilar or the opposite, a strictly self-sacrificial and other-centered relationship. In this perspective, then, the tendency that opposed attestations to an erotic dimension in divine love also opposes attestations to a philial dimension in the divine life or being. Nevertheless, in this instance too, that purist tendency fails to account for other aspects of *philia* that Christians have predicated, and continue appropriately to predicate, of God.

God aims, as decisively depicted in the event of Jesus as Christ, to realize the divine-human friendship as offered and supported by the actualization of divine philial love. This goal defines the relationship that humans took from God and that God yearns to restore. Some Christian attestations to divine suffering identify this as the only appropriate foundation for a normative understanding of both divine and human love.[24] Unfortunately, such claims sometimes go too far in the opposite direction from the agapic purists. Still, insofar as the philial aspect of divine love expresses the zenith of God's relation to the creation, divine philial love does occupy a fundamental and necessary place in any Christian understanding of God's being or life as love. Given the self-made human condition of estrangement from and infidelity toward God, divine philial love can never realize itself, however, without the operation of divine agapic love.

Thus, on the basis of the Christ-event, a number of essential characteristics in this third dimension of divine love appear. In none of the characteristics that follow, however, does this symbol assume or claim an unqualified equality between God and the creature: the creature never becomes divine. Divine philial love always remains God's love. At least the following five pairs of related characteristics constitute the heart of this dimension in divine love.[25]

---

24. E.g., Post, "Inadequacy of Selflessness," 213; idem, *Theory of Agape*, 52–66. Despite the value of Post's proposal, he mistakenly claims that insights into mutual love between God and the human "can best be gleaned from Judaism" (Post, "Inadequacy of Selflessness," 215). Unfortunately, Post fails to examine thoroughly Christian traditions for the resources that already exist there and, in many cases, that existed prior to the work of Heschel upon whose work Post's proposal relies so heavily. Although Judaism does disclose many insights in this regard, many alternative Christian traditions have also developed these and related insights—often with quite self-conscious divergences from the traditions of divine love as exclusively agapic.

25. Besides deriving the core of these characteristics from resources in Christian scriptures, my analysis benefits from the helpful interpretations of some philial features

Divine philial love exhibits a *first pair of characteristics* in the tension between preferentiality and inclusiveness. On the one hand, divine philial love operates through divine freedom. God chooses friends, befriends those who have alienated themselves from the divine self. Nothing and no one requires or compels God to offer the divine self to a created though estranged other. On the other hand, God's *offer* of friendship denies itself to no one, but includes everyone and everything to which God communicates, and with which God shares, being. Divine philial love holds a depth and breadth vast enough to include in God's love all who differ from one another, despite any preferentiality involved in divine friendship.[26]

Divine philial love exhibits a *second pair of characteristics* in the tension between God's desire for self-disclosure and divine respect for creaturely alterity. On the one hand, divine philial love expresses the inmost depths of the divine heart, in terms of purposes, desires, and feelings. God offers the divine *self*, not so much *knowledge* about the divine self. Yet, on the other hand, this form of divine love respects the individuality, personality, and characteristics of the other to whom God offers the divine self. God refuses to overwhelm or to conquer the other with divine presence; God willingly endures the growth of depth and breadth, or its denial and refusal as the case may be, in relationships between God and creatures.

In trust and trustworthiness, God activates divine philial love's *third pair of characteristics*. Again, in the first characteristic, by disclosing the divine self's inmost depths, God's love expresses complete trust in the other with whom God desires to realize philial community. This implies that God risks the divine self on the one whom God desires. God exercises faith in the creature. Then, in the second characteristic, divine philial love declares total divine trustworthiness, loyalty, fidelity, or faithfulness to the friend of God, despite any human threat to betray

---

in notable Christian attestations to divine suffering: as examples, King, *Reconstruction in Theology*, 200–26; D. Williams, *Spirit and the Forms of Love*, 111–29; McFague, *Models of God*, 157–80.

26. Vincent Brümmer has developed the logic of divine love similarly, emphasizing the freedom that genuine love requires, even for God: "... the claim that God's love does not flow forth mechanically and that he loves us because he freely decides to do so, does not imply that God is fickle-minded like a finite person. On the contrary, unlike us, God does not suffer from weakness of will, and therefore always remains consistent and faithful to his own character" (Brümmer, *Model of Love*, 230).

God. God offers sustenance and companionship in this dimension of divine love.

Divine *philia's fourth pair of characteristics*, in the tension between interdependence and identity, relates closely to the previous pair. As a first characteristic, God's philial love allows itself to depend upon the creaturely other's love, establishing God and creation as interdependent, not ordaining an absolute creaturely dependence, thereby disclosing divine vulnerability. On the one hand, then, God's love opens itself to enrichment from the creature's love, making possible divine experience of joy and fulfillment from creaturely others. On the other hand, this divine dependence upon creaturely alterity opens the divine self to the possibility of diminishment as well. Without love from the creaturely other, though, something within the divine life remains unfulfilled. In the second characteristic, God's love maintains a divine identity, an identity that provides a center for both divine creator and creatures alike, despite the extent of any and all diminishment or enrichment of the divine life by creaturely alterity.

Divine *philia's fifth pair of characteristics*, as found within the tension between the divine pursuit of a common vision with creaturely alterity and divine persuasion of the creation toward that end, derives a more specific quality from the two previous pairs of characteristics. As a first characteristic of divine philial love, God offers divine interests, which radiate from the fundamental vision in the divine heart's inmost depths, to be shared with, or held in common by, the friends of God. This vast array of common interests centers around the divine desire to pursue or to seek the creation's best interests: including its reconciliation with God, its healing and health, and its reconciliation and harmony with all aspects of itself and creaturely others. As a second characteristic, God shares or offers this divine vision, with its many interests and concerns, yet never coerces God's partners, companions, or friends to assume this vision for themselves. Simply stated, God's philial love persuades and beckons the created companion into a common vision on the basis of an intimate relation, a constant association, and a gentle presence, not by coercion.

Mutual interdependence characterizes the three dimensions of divine love. Although this feature appears within the Christian symbol of divine suffering as a περιχώρησις, or mutual interpenetration, of divine love's three dimensions, this symbol refuses to identify any single dimension of God's being or life with only one of the three members in the Christian doctrine of the divine Trinity. All three dimensions in divine love define the life of each member in the divine Trinity.

These three dimensions of divine love do not oppose one another. Divine love reduces itself neither to one type of love (for example, ἀγάπη) nor to two types of love (ἔρως and ἀγάπη).[27] Three dimensions of the divine being as love always disclose themselves in divine activity. Furthermore, in terms of divine reconciliation with the human, although the agapic dimension appears to predominate, divine philial love represents the divine goal for the divine-human relationship. In the sense that God envisions this as the goal for presently-alienated humans, philial love remains the ideal of divine love. Divine philial love, however, does not exist apart from the other two dimensions of divine love. Because of their mutual interdependence, therefore, neither of these forms or dimensions of love commands a higher position than either of the others.

Formal Dimensions in Divine Life as Love

Finally, the threefold structure of divine being as love, as disclosed through the Christ-event, implies at least three formal dimensions or structures of the divine life: *temporality, possibility,* and *mutability* in divine being as love.[28] These characteristics, although here included to some extent as such, do not merely represent addenda to this threefold structure of divine being. Rather, these additional characteristics qualify the structures of divine being as love.

27. Although still working within much of the classical Christian paradigm, one theologian of divine suffering, E. L. Strong, perceived aspects of this insight. "[God's] justice and mercy are merely different aspects of [God's] love. God's justice means that because He is perfect love, therefore He is utterly opposed to sin always. His mercy means that He is always loving to sinners, wishing and striving for their highest good, in spite of all that they do against Him" (E. Strong, *Lectures on the Incarnation of God*, 59).

28. Similarly, Langdon Gilkey identified three central changes in modern and contemporary understandings of the traditional Christian symbol of God that the "rapprochement between the modern consciousness and the traditional symbol of God" has influenced and produced: (1) divine self-limitation; (2) divine temporality; and (3) divine mutability (see Gilkey, *Reaping the Whirlwind*, 306–10; idem, *Through the Tempest*, 81–85).

Temporality of Divine Life as Love

First, according to the Christian symbol of divine suffering, through its actualization in Jesus' life, divine love discloses a temporal structure within the divine life. In the history of Jesus, God actualizes agapic love in the present, upon the basis of, or as motivated by, a past actualization of divine erotic love, in order to make possible an actualization of divine philial love in the future.[29] Obviously, in various ways, each form of divine love has relationships to all three temporal moments. Nonetheless, in Jesus of Nazareth, those relationships appear most emphatically, initially at least, as related previously. Temporarily setting aside this issue, however, I note here, in a preliminary way, only that divine life as love discloses temporal structures that constitute the divine being. This insight does not necessarily imply a finite deity. This symbol only presupposes that divine everlastingness possesses a temporal structure. Although God does not either originate or terminate, God does have, nevertheless, past and future as well as present moments of temporality. The following study will include analyses of the peculiar temporality in each moment of divine suffering. Consequently, I have postponed my fuller elaboration of divine temporality until I can examine it in less abstract terms.

29. Martin Heidegger noted the following: "Wenn die Ewigkeit *Gottes* sich philosophisch 'konstruieren' ließe, dann dürfte sie nur als ursprünglichere und 'unendliche' Zeitlichkeit" (Heidegger, *Sein und Zeit*, 427 n. 1); "If God's eternity can be 'construed' philosophically, then it may be understood only as a more primordial temporality which is 'infinite' " (Heidegger, *Being and Time*, 499 n. xiii). See Schubert Ogden's insightful interpretation of Heidegger's note on divine temporality (Ogden, *Reality of God and Other Essays*, 144–63). In the early nineteenth century, one North-American theologian argued for a doctrine of divine immutability that he modified by his awareness of divine temporality; for this theologian, divine temporality disclosed itself through human discernment that God experiences successive perceptions, volitions, and affections (Jones, "Immutability of God Considered with Reference to Prayer," 566). Edgar Sheffield Brightman found evidence for divine temporality in (1) the human self's temporal character, (2) the world's temporal and evolutionary processes, (3) human history's reality and value, (4) the idea of progress, and (5) morality as the task of the good life (Brightman, "Temporalist View of God," 544–55). Other numerous and helpful discussions of divine temporality and related characteristics abound: see Barth, *Church Dogmatics*, 2.1: 608–40; Varillon, *Humility and Suffering of God*, 57; Gilkey, *Reaping the Whirlwind*, 308–9; idem, *Message and Existence*, 87–107; Placher, *Narratives of a Vulnerable God*, 27–52; Clarke and Long, eds., *God and Temporality*; Felt, "Temporality of Divine Freedom," 252–62; Schilling, *God and Human Anguish*, 237–39; Heron, "Time of God," 231–39; O'Donnell, "Trinity and Temporality."

Possibility in Divine Life as Love

Second, and upon the basis of my brief note on divine temporality, divine being as love discloses itself in terms of possibility as well as in terms of actuality. At the very least, the future possibility of divine-human friendship appears upon the basis of the philial dimension in divine love. Also, in that regard, even though God loved erotically in the past, it remains actualizable for the future in a variety of ways: for example, in response to further human self-estrangement from God.

Mutability in Divine Life as Love

Furthermore, the threefold structure of divine being yields a third major characteristic. Both because of divine temporal movement in divine love, and because of divine actualization of possibilities for God's own self, divine love implies mutability or changeability as a fundamental dimension of the divine life.[30] This claim in no way implies that, or necessitates the conclusion that, God is finite or in any way loses deity; in that sense, then, God does not change, but remains divine. Nevertheless, as God risks the divine self on the creation, divine mutability implies both that the creation can enrich God through the divine-human friend-

---

30. Some Christian theologians attempt to recover, although not always consistently or convincingly, traditions of divine mutability from both patristic and mystical Christian theologians such as Tertullian, Novatian, Arnobius, Lactantius, and Meister Eckhart (e.g., Hallman, "Mutability of God," 373–93; idem, *Descent of God*; Loeschen, "God Who Becomes," 405–22; Duclow, " 'My Suffering Is God': Meister Eckhart's Book of Divine Consolation," 570–86; cf. Dodds, *Unchanging God of Love*; idem, "Thomas Aquinas, Human Suffering, and the Unchanging God of Love," 330–44). One Christian theologian of divine suffering finds that petitionary prayer presupposes divine mutability: "For God to change does not mean that he becomes another, or even that he gives himself up, but that he descends and enters into the distress and depth of human existence" (Eibach, "Prayer and Conceptions of God," 66; also see, idem, "Die Sprache leidender Menschen und der Wandel des Gottesbildes," 53–58). Thus, the Christian symbol of divine suffering, at this point especially, openly contradicts the dogmatic and theological traditions of orthodox Christianities, as represented, for example, in Augustine's theology (Augustine, *Confessiones*, 12.11.11; 12.15.18; 13.8.9; 13.16.19, in *Corpus Christianorum*, vol. 27, *Sancti Augustini Opera*, 221–22, 224–25, 245–46, 252). Accordingly, another theologian of divine suffering, Catherine Mowry LaCugna, notes, with most theologians of divine suffering, that "God's immutability is God's fidelity, both to be God and to be God-for-us. God remains eternally faithful to the Covenant made with Israel. God's self-given name, YHWH, speaks of God's promise always to be with Israel. For Christians, Jesus Christ is the definitive and fully personal sign of God's everlasting fidelity to-be-with-us" (LaCugna, *God For Us*, 301–2).

ship and that the creation can deny to God that enrichment by human refusal of divine philial overtures. One way or the other, the creation makes a difference in the divine life; God does not remain, as the classic Christian theistic tradition has held for centuries, *id ipsum et id ipsum*, or "the selfsame."[31]

Divine Humility: Condition of Possibility for Divine Creative Activity

In my extrapolation of divine being from divine activity, I perceive one more major characteristic, a characteristic that suffuses all three dimensions of divine love: *divine humility*. Through the entire history of Jesus from Nazareth, one can observe this trait.[32] In the event of Jesus as Christ, God most decisively discloses the divine humility by seeking the estranged though beloved human. In the Christ-event, then, God most fully displays the divine humility that characterizes divine life. As such a divine reality, divine humility establishes the condition of possibility for God's creative activity as self-sacrificial divine activity.

All three dimensions of divine love exhibit divine humility. In divine agapic love, divine humility evinces itself most clearly, since therein God relinquishes the right to deny forgiveness to the offender. God renounces a retributive justice that would fulfill vengeful divine motivations. Instead, God offers mercy to the one who has betrayed the divine love. In divine erotic love, divine humility discloses itself as the desire for the other for the sake of the other as well as for God's own self. God's desire does not selfishly grasp for the other in order exclusively to enhance divine selfhood. Also, philial divine love exhibits divine humility as God's offer of reciprocity to the human, rather than as the demand for subservience, obedience, or submission from human alterity. God refuses both to coerce creaturely alterity into proper interdependence with God and to impose divine purposes for the creation upon the creature from whom God desires free response to the divine offer.[33]

---

31. See, for example, Augustine, *Confessionem*, 12.7.7 (Chadwick, 249).

32. For example, see one biblical paradigm for understanding divine humility through the entire Christ-event in Phil 2:5–11.

33. See Varillon's informative and somewhat parallel analysis of divine humility (Varillon, *Humility and Suffering of God*, 1–121).

In addition, then, divine humility operates dramatically within the divine life itself. Each dimension of God as love yields itself to the other dimensions in order to realize the divine purpose, rather than becoming absolutes in themselves. For this reason, paradoxically, divine agapic love does not completely define the divine life. When divine philial love fails, when the human injures or terminates the divine-human friendship, divine philial love yields to the operation of the erotic dimension in divine being as the movement toward divine agapic love. When divine erotic love exercises its potential, it yields to the operation of divine agapic love, as the means or movement toward realizing divine philial love once again. When divine agapic love fulfills its function, it yields the place of privilege to philial love in the divine life. Thus, as Varillon perceives, according to this Christian symbol, God continues to efface or to renounce the divine self even for the sake of the divine self.[34] Through my analysis of God's being or life as love, the crucial and central characteristic of divine humility discloses itself as the condition of possibility for the self-sacrificial actualization of divine being or life in creative activity.

34. Ibid., 82, 90. This insight provides resources to interpret the Christian symbol of the Trinity, although development of such an interpretation remains partially implicit in my studies here. This does not imply a construal of the three divine loves, however, as the three *members* of the divine Trinity.

5

Divine Lover:

Divine Life As Love in Creation

Introduction: Actualizing Divine Life as Love in God's Creative Activity

I NOW SHIFT FROM CONSIDERING GOD'S BEING AND ACTIVITY, AS methodologically abstracted from one another, to discussing divine love's actualization in God's creative activity.[1] Previously, I have surveyed characteristics and dimensions of God's being as love through attestations to divine activity in the history of Jesus the Nazarene. The present chapter examines the character of God's creative activity, as determined by the divine being, in order to disclose the meaning of the first presupposition for the Christian symbol of divine suffering as well as to illumine the basis upon which to analyze this symbol's second presupposition. Thus, I proceed in this chapter on the basis of the following question: *What does it mean to claim that a God whose being is love creates?*

Before I can offer an answer to the procedural question of this chapter, though, another series of questions requires attention. *Must a God whose being is love create? Does God create from necessity? Does the divine being or some external reality and power constrain God to create?* More specifically, does God *freely produce* creation (a claim that perhaps implies an arbitrary divine freedom), or does creation *necessarily emanate* from God as the growth or overflow of divine life (a

1. One theologian of divine suffering understands creation as "the first and external manifestation of the empathetic self-communication of God to participate and communion with us, whose very existence is determined by His will to be for us" (J. Lee, *God Suffers for Us,* 47).

claim that perhaps implies an organic process but not necessarily divine personality).[2] This series of questions arises from a dilemma that numerous Christian theologians have posed: If God is love, as I have previously described the divine being, then God has no choice but to create an other to whom the divine desires to relate in love.[3] Both this dilemma and its question to my analysis link themselves to issues of necessity for God: either a necessity within the divine being over which God's will exerts no control or a necessity outside the divine life with which God must struggle in order to accomplish the divine purposes by creating and within creation.[4] From the perspective of that dilemma, to satisfy the eternity of divine being as love, then, God eternally requires another to whom God relates or can relate in love. Thus, from such a viewpoint, creation itself is everlasting.

2. John Macquarrie described this dilemma and attempted to combine the models (Macquarrie, *Principles of Christian Theology*, 200–5; also see idem, *In Search of Deity*, 177–79).

3. Some theologians describe this necessity as God's limitation by the divine being, or as "the holy limitedness of God, God's incapacity to be other than a caring presence" (Howe, "God's Power and God's Personhood," 49). Also, on God's limitation by the divine nature or being, see the following works: DeWolf, *A Theology of the Living Church*, 107–8; J. Williams, "Divine Limitation," 253–66; and A. Strong, "God's Self-Limitations," 521–32.

4. These issues organically link themselves to two other related ancient viewpoints that some contemporary theologians also hold in various forms: (1) the co-eternity of God and the creation; and (2) God's creation of the world from some sort of pre-existent matter. Some theologians describe the latter as "necessity," "the errant cause," "the nurse of all becoming," "the receptacle," "the recipient," or "space," as everlasting, indestructible, the situation for all that becomes. Analogically, Plato compared this *pre-existent principle* to a mother; Plato compared *being*, as the eternal model, to a father, while comparing *becoming* to an offspring of the union between the two parents (Plato, *Timaeus*, 47–53). Ancient Near Eastern myths depicted creation as a battle between a chaos-monster (a serpent or dragon) and a creator god. Ancient Israel adopted this metaphor (among others) and allusions to it to describe Yahweh's creation of the world as well: see Exod 15:1–27; Job 3:8; 40:15—41:34; Ps 74:12–17; Isa 51:9–11; Hab 3:1–19. The great sufferer, Job, reversed this metaphor, summoning Leviathan to reinstate chaos, as a protest or revolt against the disordered creation of his own experience (Perdue, "Job's Assault on Creation," 295–315; similarly, Mettinger, *In Search of God*, 175–200). Many modern and contemporary theologies formulate more recent versions of the Platonic paradigm in relation to these two viewpoints, versions in which to some degree either an internal or an external necessity for God remains (see Rolt, *World's Redemption*, 81–89, 107–8, 119; Whitehead, *Process and Reality*; Brightman, *Problem of God*, 107–38; idem, *Philosophy of Religion*, 305–41; Bertocci, *Introduction to the Philosophy of Religion*, 389–468).

Orthodox Christian responses, both from theologies that attribute suffering to God and from theologies that refuse to attribute suffering to God, have denied that any kind of internal or external necessities can affect or constrain God's will.[5] Thus, in this regard, the orthodox Christian symbol of creation has refused both the concept of the creation's eternity and the concept of a pre-existent or eternal matter (chaos) from which God fashioned the creation.[6] Following this path, the Christian symbol of divine suffering presupposes that nothing either internal or external to God compels God to create. God creates only upon the basis of divine choice, as God actualizes that choice from the divine being as love. Hence, when God does choose to create, then God cannot relate arbitrarily to the creation, without contradicting the character of the divine being or life as love, even though God retains the freedom to violate the chosen divine character of love. Later, in my exposition of this symbol, this question emerges again in another form: Must God behave agapically, or must God forgive, sacrificing something of the divine self or claims for the other? In both cases, the present one and the one to follow in other parts of this project, God actualizes the divine life as love with grace. Nothing obligates God to forgive or to love sacrificially; if God chooses to forgive, however, God cannot relate arbitrarily to the object of divine forgiveness without contradicting God's freely-chosen fundamental character. Although I have not addressed every complexity in this question about necessity in divine creative activity, I have identified the parameters by which the Christian symbol of divine suffering, at this juncture at least, follows orthodox Christian attestations to the grace in God's free choices both to create and to re-create. On the basis of the humility in divine being as love, then, God creates. For this symbol, divine humility supplies the condition of possibility for God's self-sacrificial creative activity.

5. See Stott, "God on the Gallows," 28; Aquinas, *Summa Theologica*, Ia, q. 19, a. 1. Thomas helpfully distinguished between two types of necessity for God. (1) He described that which God wills about the divine self as an *absolute necessity*. (2) He called that which God wills apart from the divine self a *suppositional necessity*, that is, necessary because God willed it and, therefore, God cannot un-will it, since God cannot do so without change; but it was not necessary that God will it originally.

6. Again, Thomas Aquinas forcefully delivered these refusals (Aquinas, *Summa Theologica*, Ia, q. 44, a. 2; q. 45, a. 1; q. 46, a. 1, a. 2). Also see idem, *Sermon-Conferences of St. Thomas Aquinas on the Apostles' Creed*, 38–41.

Now, I return to my procedural question: What does it mean to claim that a God whose being is love creates? In an attempt to answer this question, I distinguish three aspects of God's creative activity from one another, within each of which the threefold structure of divine being as love characterizes that creative activity. God's being as love, therefore, radically affects the character of divine creative activity and, thereby, radically revises the classic Christian symbol of God as creator.

Once again, given the characteristics of creation as experienced, testimonies to divine suffering first announce divine self-limitation as the principal basis upon which to understand God's suffering.[7] Christian theologians of divine suffering often discern two types of divine self-limitation. Following attestations to divine suffering, I have described these types as constitutional and volitional divine self-limitations.[8] Examining these two types of divine self-limitation discloses a third

---

7. Langdon Gilkey criticized eschatological theologies, because their concept of God determines all creaturely history from the future, just as classical Christian theism's God had done from eternity, thus not genuinely addressing the problems of theodicy, human freedom, and the future's goodness. According to Gilkey, "these issues can be resolved only" with "an explicitly ontological doctrine of the self-limitation in every present of the divine power in relation to the freedom of the creature" (Gilkey, *Reaping the Whirlwind*, 235). Even otherwise quite Reformed, fundamentalist, North-American theologians have developed various versions of divine self-limitation as the presupposition to God's creative and re-creative activities (e.g., Erickson, *Word Became Flesh*, 607–12).

8. Numerous theologians identify these two types of divine self-limitation: see A. Strong, *Christ in Creation and Ethical Monism*, 88–90; idem, "God's Self-Limitations," 521–32; Gore, *Belief in God*, 115–18. Harold DeWolf identified three forms of divine self-limitation, though one could classify the latter two of these as constitutional and the former as volitional. He called them God's voluntary limitation, limitation by God's rational nature, and limitation by God's own being (DeWolf, *Theology of the Living Church*, 105–8). Henry Maldwyn Hughes developed notions of both *constitutional* (Hughes, *Christian Idea of God*, 152) and *volitional* (idem, *What Is the Atonement*, 91–92) divine self-limitation. Virginia Mollenkott perceived volitional divine self-limitation in the biblical narratives about Adam and Eve (Gen 1:26–28) as "caretakers of the world and cocreators of society" (Mollenkott, *Divine Feminine*, 77). Nonetheless, some theologians of divine suffering (for example, Marcel Sarot) regard the concept of divine self-limitation (as God's exercise of power to limit divine power) as nonsense. Marcel Sarot, however, replaces this notion with the idea of divine self-restraint: "God can resolve that he will not use His power in a certain way during a certain time, but He cannot limit His power" (Sarot, "Omnipotence and Self-limitation," 183). One must question, however, the very meaningfulness of Sarot's criticism of divine self-limitation, since self-restraint of any kind requires the exercise of the will or power.

phenomenon, that which serves as the final condition of possibility for divine suffering: *divine vulnerability*.

Constitutional Divine Self-Limitation

The concept of constitutional divine self-limitation describes the limits that divine being or life places upon the character of divine activity.[9] The Christian symbol of divine suffering presupposes that divine perfection limits divine actions to those that remain congruent or consistent with divine being as love. In God's self-constitution, God limits Godself to the logic or rationality of love as *caritas*, to the values and praxis of love in that love's freedom, and to the divine Trinity as love. Divine action does not (although God retains the freedom or capacity to do so)

9. The concept of constitutional divine self-limitation solicits support from scriptural attestations to divine fidelity or constancy, the confidence that God will not deny the divine self (e.g., 2 Tim 2:13). Thus, although God remains capable of doing so, God does not change the divine character and will not, therefore, contradict Godself. Some theologians tie this biblical theme, most often connected to divine relationality or to the divine creator's covenant with creation, to the classical philosophical concept of immutability. Christian traditions that have been influenced by this philosophical idea also affirm the immutability of divine being. These Christian traditions, by far the dominant ones historically, also support their perspectives with biblical authority (see the key texts: Mal 3:6; Heb 13:8; and Jas 1:17). The commitment of these dominant Christian traditions to the classical philosophical concept of divine immutability also motivates their appeals to biblical declarations that Yahweh does not repent (Num 23:19; 1 Sam 15:29). Through Platonic, Neoplatonic, and Aristotelian philosophies, this ontological conceptuality soon supplanted the relational and covenantal understanding of God's unchangeableness. In contrast to the philosophical concept of divine immutability, theologians of divine suffering affirm a notion of divine mutability that, nevertheless, emphasizes the fidelity of God to divine being; in other words, God's being will always remain divine, and yet God *chooses* not to contradict the divine self-actualization of that divine being (e.g., Hughes, *Christian Idea of God* , 152). Hence, Christian theologians of divine suffering often formulate the notion of constitutional divine self-limitation. "God's action must be limited by His character as Rational and Love. Moreover it follows from this, that the created order cannot attain two contradictory ends at the same time. It cannot, for example, be both a sphere in which free spirits are at liberty to seek good and attain fellowship with God, and also a sphere in which no mistakes are possible and every hardship and disaster is eliminated" (Matthews, *God in Christian Thought and Experience*, 236; similarly, Peacocke, *Theology for a Scientific Age*, 121–23). "That through bringing the universe into being God has subjected Himself to certain limitations is generally recognized. It is agreed, too, that His omnipotence does not mean that He can do absolutely anything, such as changing the past, but that He can do such things as are in harmony with His own Nature and Will" (Hughes, *Christian Idea of God*, 150).

contradict the character of divine being as chosen and actualized by the divine self, without undermining or negating that specifically chosen divine character.[10] Nonetheless, God freely chooses the character of the divine being. Constitutional divine self-limitation simply reaffirms the constancy or fidelity of God to the divine self or to the character of divine self-actualization. God's action remains faithful to God's being, in that God's action actualizes that being and chooses to do nothing to contradict it. Thus, *constitutional* divine self-limitation provides the basis upon which God exercises *volitional* divine self-limitation in creative activity. In this form of divine self-limitation, God principally limits the divine self reflexively or for God's own sake.

Volitional Divine Self-Limitation

According to the Christian symbol of divine suffering, when creating, God limits the divine self in two stages. In the first stage, God *withdraws, constricts, contracts,* or *retracts* the divine self in order to allow a region of possibility to appear within God, within the divine *all-in-all,* in order to allow creation to possess a reality distinct from God. In the second stage, when God creates the creature, God endows the creature with being and life analogous to God's own life or being, in order to provide the creature with genuine alterity, with the capacity to relate to God as God relates; thereby, God *restricts* the divine self.[11]

Both stages of God's self-limiting creative activity, consequently, entail negative and positive moments. Their negative moments consist in their limitation of the divine self. Nevertheless, the positive moments consist in divine creation of a creature who exists as truly other-than-yet-like-God and, thereby, who can potentially enrich the divine life through the proper use of this divine gift as well. In this sense, Kyle Pasewark helpfully described divine power as "the communication of

10. According to Vincent Brümmer, the essentialist tradition in Christian theology holds that, "since it belongs to God's essential nature to be good and faithful, it is 'logically' impossible for him ever to let us down." Brümmer understands this as a flawed perspective, one which ". . . takes God's love for us to be the result of an 'ontological' determinism." Brümmer, to the contrary, argues that ". . . it is incoherent to try to avoid the risk involved in loving God by denying God the ability to reject us or become unfaithful to us. We cannot thus avoid the conclusion that faith involves a leap" (Brümmer, *Model of Love*, 229, 230).

11. Moltmann also identified the two stages of volitional divine self-limitation (Moltmann, *Trinity and the Kingdom*, 110).

efficacy." "The life and power of God are constituted in the benefits they provide the faithful, that is, the power of believers, which in turn emerges in the profit and power provided for the neighbor. Power of this kind can be described as a 'communication of efficacy'"[12] Thus, in light of God's possible enrichment through this volitional divine self-limitation, God also continues paradoxically to operate omnipotently, communicating efficacy to creaturely alterity. Nonetheless, God does not communicate efficacy without also establishing at least the possibility for the negative operation of power in creaturely freedom, an operation of power that can negate the purposes for which God communicates such power—both for creaturely alterity and for God. Of course, such concepts of divine self-limitation also implicitly distinguish between inauthentic and authentic operations of power. Moreover, both stages arise principally from the constitutional divine self-limitation of divine humility in the agapic dimension of the divine life or being.

At this point in my analysis, two central elements emerge, elements that attestations to divine suffering depict as aspects of a birthing process, aspects metaphorically ascribed to God in such attestations. I have described the first element in the divine birthing process as God's creation *of* nothing (*creatio nihili*) or *divine self-retraction*, the first stage of volitional divine self-limitation. I have described the second element, with traditional terminology, as divine creation *out of* nothing (*creatio ex nihilo*) or *divine self-restriction*, the second stage of volitional divine self-limitation: within the metaphor, as the birth of the creation from the womb of divine possibilities into the dwelling prepared for crea-

12. Pasewark, *Theology of Power*, 198. Unfortunately, Pasewark did not perceive the operation of power in the negative operation of divine self-limitation. He misunderstood consistent concepts of divine self-limitation. According to Pasewark (mistakenly citing Langdon Gilkey as a proponent of this concept), such positions hold that ". . . any claim that God is omnipotent, in light of God's creation of something other than God, is senseless" (Pasewark, *Theology of Power*, 200). Consistent attestations to divine self-limitation, however, construe God's creation of a genuine other (although not always in Pasewark's language) as an operation of divine omnipotence in which God does communicate efficacy to creaturely alterity. Although consistent theologies of divine self-limitation already eschew concepts of divine power as domination, theologians espousing notions of divine self-limitation will benefit by considering carefully Pasewark's critical proposal. Nonetheless, Pasewark's own language about divine power often betrays its similarity to the language used by theologians of divine self-limitation: for example, "God's omnipotence is defined by production of power that is not God, rather than by God's sovereignty" (Pasewark, *Theology of Power*, 201).

turely alterity. I will examine and clarify their relationships to, as well as
their differences from, one another in the following analyses.

Divine Self-Retraction: Creatio Nihili

For the Christian symbol of divine suffering, in the first stage of volitional divine self-limitation, divine self-retraction, God limits the divine
self by moving from being the *all-in-all* to giving birth to, or to creating,
a nothing, a space from which God has withdrawn in order to allow the
creation to come into being. In this act, God actualizes self-sacrificially
the divine being as love.

DIVINE ALL-IN-ALL

The Christian symbol of divine suffering confidently affirms that, before
God created, God was in some sense *all-in-all*. One may recognize such
confidence even in the theology of the apostle Paul, when he declares
that, ultimately, even Christ will be subjected to God who had subjected
all things to Christ, so that "God may be all in all."[13] Identifying and
stating the assumption in Pauline piety adds clarity to his claim: Christ
became subject to God, so that God might become *all-in-all*, as God had
been both before the creation and before the eruption of sin through
and into creation's goodness. The Christian symbol of divine suffering
assumes that God was *all-in-all* before the creation.

DIVINE CREATION OF NOTHING

Many attestations to divine suffering announce a divine act prior to
God's creation of anything, a divine act that established the condition of
possibility for the emergence of something other than God through divine creative activity. God, the *all-in-all*, cannot create a creature distinct

---

13. 1 Cor 15:28 NAS. Some theologians question the extent to which God can ever
become *all-in-all* again after the fact of creation, without the total dissolution or disap-
pearance of creation. So long as creation persists in any form, God is not *all-in-all* in
the most absolute sense. Nicolas Berdyaev rejected the notion of God as *the all-in-all*, as
part of the conceptual network of God as "master," "absolute monarch," "the Absolute,"
the cause that determines everything, the dominator, or "*pantokrator*"; Berdyaev correctly detected within this orthodox conceptual network "a pantheism which enslaves
man" (Berdyaev, *Slavery and Freedom*, 82, 83, 85, 89, 90). Hence, the Christian symbol of
divine suffering highly qualifies any eschatological understanding of God as *all-in-all*,
in terms of the *reality* of the creation's eschatological alterity.

from the divine self, until in some sense God provides a place or space, wherein that creature can truly become an other-than-God. Therefore, since God precedes creation as the *all-in-all*, God must in some sense withdraw the divine self in order for such an opening to appear. In this divine self-retraction, then, God creates a nothing inside the divine self, pulling back the divine self and, therefore, setting a limit upon the *all-in-all*. This nothing does not actively challenge God's being. Rather, it becomes a nurturing space within God. Thus, one more adequately describes the non-being that this nothing represents as a relative non-being, a nothingness of possibilities or potential. This nothing resembles a room or crib that God prepares for the not yet born or delivered infant of the pregnant divine mother.[14]

This moment in the concept of volitional divine self-limitation discloses a genuinely speculative logic in the first presupposition for the Christian symbol of divine suffering. Nonetheless, many attestations to divine suffering understand this conceptual moment as a mediating

---

14. One can trace this conceptuality to its origin in the Jewish theology of third-century Midrashic writings and thirteenth-century Kabbalistic mystical writings. The conceptuality originates in the central image of "*tsimtsum*," variously translated as "concentration," "contraction," "retreat," or "withdrawal" (see Kuhn, *Gottes Selbsterniedrigung in der Theologie der Rabbinen*, 47–60; Scholem, *Major Trends in Jewish Mysticism*, 260–63). Contemporary Jewish thinkers endeavor to retrieve this notion, both as a modern and as a post-holocaust theological resource: as examples, see Rosenzweig, *Star of Redemption*, 1–90; Cohen, *Tremendum*, 89–91; Jonas, "Concept of God after Auschwitz: A Jewish Voice," 7–12; idem, "Is Faith Still Possible," 18. This conceptuality has affinities with some of the concepts in the mystical writings of Jacob Boehme and Meister Eckhart. Thus, a number of Christian theologians have retrieved elements from those sources as well: see Schelling, *Ages of the World*; Berdyaev *Destiny of Man*, chapter 2; idem, *The Divine and the Human*, chapters 1 and 2; idem, *Freedom and the Spirit*, chapters 5 and 6. In this connection, I also mention Paul Tillich's work, though relations in his thought to those mystical traditions become slightly more problematic. More recently, Christian theologies have begun to appropriate the Jewish concept of *tsimtsum* more directly: see Moltmann, *Trinity and the Kingdom*, 27–30, 59, 108–11; and Fritz, "A Midrash: The Self-Limitation of God," 704–5. Another Christian theologian expressed a similar view, although I have found no evidence that he relies directly upon Jewish or mystical Christian thought for it: "God has parted with his privilege of sole and only existence, in order that he may give room for other things and other beings; but this limitation is no derogation to his greatness, because it is *self*-limitation" (A. Strong, "God's Self-Limitations," 524). In some ways, the creation of this nothing also compares to fertilization of the womb. This analogy weakens, however, because in this metaphor the creation, as the child in the divine womb, must be born into, as well as from, the space or the divine nothing that God has prepared for the new child.

theological entailment between the symbol of God as the *all-in-all* and the symbol of God as divine sufferer.

At this juncture, however, the Christian symbol of divine suffering distinguishes divine self-retraction from two other related Christian understandings of God as both creator and sufferer. On the one hand, some testimonies to divine suffering construe creation as the result of tragedy within the divine life. On the other hand, some expressions of this symbol presuppose that creation originates from a divine struggle to overcome another pre-existent reality or principle.

To the contrary, first, according to relatively more adequate attestations, the Christian symbol of divine suffering does not construe creation as originating from some sort of a pre-creative divine tragedy. Some Christian witnesses to divine suffering posit a struggle within the divine life through which God generates the creation.[15] No opposition within God, however, generates created reality in the most adequate Christian attestations to divine suffering. The creation does not result from divine emanations, emanations that yield a creature that in some sense remains divine though created. Thus, the Christian symbol of divine suffering reaffirms (and reinterprets) the orthodox Christian formulas: *non de Deo* and *de nihilo* or *ex nihilo*.[16] The most adequate

15. From perspectives within the first and older Christian canon, "God is not a melancholy being who could find within himself the occasion for being dissatisfied or bitter" (Gerstenberger and Schrage, *Suffering*, 100). The concept of creation's origin in an internal divine struggle has affinities with ancient forms of Valentinian Gnosticism, wherein a crisis within the *pleroma* of the divine being causes suffering there and leads to the world's creation, as part of the salvific process necessitated by the divine tragedy (Jonas, *Gnostic Religion*, 174–205). One can find Christian versions of similar viewpoints in theologies that theologians base upon the concept of the *Ungrund* as developed by Jacob Boehme: see Boehme, *Six Theosophic Points and Other Writings*, 1–37; Schelling, *Philosophical Inquiries into the Nature of Human Freedom*; Tillich, *Construction of the History of Religion in Schelling's Positive Philosophy*, 54–76; Berdyaev, "Introductory Essay: Unground and Freedom," v–xxxvii; idem, *Destiny of Man*, 23–25; idem, *The Divine and the Human*, 50–58; Elmore, "Theme of the Suffering of God in the Thought of Nicholas Berdyaev, Charles Hartshorne, and Reinhold Niebuhr," 17–71; Hartshorne, "Whitehead and Berdyaev," 71–84. When Tillich joined the doctrines of creation and fall to one another, as well as when he described the divine life as the eternal conquest of non-being, he approached a doctrine similar to that of the Gnostic divine tragedy that generates creation (Tillich, *Systematic Theology*, 1:186–89, 235–89). Also see Tillich's related analysis of the demonic: Tillich, *Interpretation of History*, 77–122; also see, Hartshorne, "Tillich and the Other Great Tradition," 245–59.

16. "Not from God" and "out of nothing" (Augustine, *De nuptiis et concupiscentia*, 2.28.48; *Confessiones*, 12.7.7; 12.8.8; 12.22.31; 13.33.48; *De civitate dei*, 12.1, 8; 14.11,

Christian testimonies to divine suffering perceive creation's origin in the divine desire to confer the gift of being upon a genuine other, in such a way that, though the other differs from God, God has endowed the other, nevertheless, with a being like the divine being.[17] The nothing that God creates, though in God, is not God; rather, this created nothing constitutes that space in which the actual other-than-God might be created in such a way as to possess a distinctiveness, a creatureliness that one cannot identify as or equate with God.

Second, neither does the Christian symbol of divine suffering depict this divine self-retraction, or divine *creatio nihili*, as a pre-creative divine struggle with some form of pre-existent matter or mythical chaos-monster. The nothing of divine self-retraction remains a reality that divine action institutes. No other ultimate competitor, either personal or impersonal, stands against God. God alone limits the divine self and does that first in the sense of divine self-retraction. Even if one conceived this nothing of potentiality as some form of matter, then God would also have created it as such and it would, therefore, not stand against God as a negative factor that God must conquer or with which God must contend in order to remain fully divine. Nevertheless, the formula *non ex materia sed ex nihilo* implies the divine creation *of* this nothing of potentiality, as the denial of a pre-existent matter with which God had to struggle in order to create. Hence, this concept does not represent an ultimate dualism or pluralism. Everything that exists, including the nothing from which God creates, originates from God.[18]

13; 15.21; *De fide et symbolo*, 2; *De natura boni contra Manichæos*, 1). Also see Gilkey's interpretation and revision of this aspect of protology in Christian theology (Gilkey, *Through the Tempest*, 89–100).

17. Gilkey, *Maker of Heaven and Earth*, 58–66.

18. Jon Levenson attempted to demonstrate that ancient Israel's faith closely followed the faith of her ancient Near Eastern neighbors about creation: Israel's protology espoused the idea that Yahweh had defeated forces that had interrupted a "benevolent and life-sustaining order" and, as their conqueror, God has restored that order; but Israel's ancient creation-theology expressed nothing like the idea of *creatio ex nihilo*. Thus, theologians cannot legitimately use Gen 1:1—2:3 to support that idea (Levenson, *Creation and the Persistence of Evil*, 12, 47, 121). On the other side, some theologians defend the position that "even the remnants of ancient mythologies, such as the struggle with Behemoth or Leviathan, that are alluded to in various biblical passages apparently relate tensions generated by the Creation process itself rather than precosmogonic conflicts." Furthermore, some scholars who hold this position contend that, within the Bible, "God stands *beyond* the universe." Moreover, "[m]ythical descriptions in ancient

DIVINE WOMB

The Christian symbol of divine suffering continues to presuppose the metaphor of the divine womb. Legal, prophetic, and sapiential texts from the first Christian canon employ this metaphor. When Yahweh, speaking to Israel, describes the divine self as "the Rock that begot you" and "the God who gave you birth," the Deuteronomist metaphorically presupposes that God had first conceived the people of God within the divine womb. This motif appears as well in Deutero-Isaiah, when Yahweh agonizes over human failure to fulfill the divine purposes. "I have kept silent for a long time, I have kept still and restrained Myself. Now like a woman in labor I will groan, I will both gasp and pant." Sapiential texts metaphorically presuppose the same images, not only of God's people but of the entire creation, when Yahweh questions Job from the whirlwind. "Has the rain a father? Or who has begotten the drops of dew? From whose womb has come the ice? And the frost of

---

sources, however, regarded the gods as standing *within* the cosmos; hence, there was an organic link between theogony and cosmogony, a link eliminated in the biblical account. Discussions concerning divine nature or precosmogonic action therefore were irrelevant for earlier layers of Jewish cosmogony" (Idel, *Kabbalah: New Perspectives*, 113). Miguel de Unamuno advanced a view similar to that of Levenson, when he declared that the "brute matter" around God limits the divine self and human beings; God seeks liberation for the divine self, as well as liberation for human beings, from that binding reality (Unamuno, *Tragic Sense of Life in Man and Nations*, 227). Also, one Christian process theologian expressed a similar perspective, in his contention that the world-process may frustrate rather than fulfill creatures and, therefore, limit the divine life (Baker, "Christological Symbol of God's Suffering," 101). Even though some biblical testimonies to God as creator retain elements of testimonies to a pre-creative divine struggle, many Christian traditions (as well as some Jewish traditions) continue vehemently to resist this idea with the concept of *creatio ex nihilo*. Gilkey thoroughly analyzes this concept's meaning, as held by orthodox Christian communities throughout the centuries, in relation to the present discussion of an ultimate dualism or pluralism: Gilkey, *Maker of Heaven and Earth*, 44–58. The poet and artist, William Blake, also depicted a rather Gnostic view of creation as error, in which Elohim (in his judicial mode) struggles with matter in order to create humans to be judged (see, for example, his painting, "Elohim Creating Adam," in *Paintings of William Blake*, 12). In this connection, Blake illustrated the above claim with these words from his notebook: "I will not Flatter them Error is Created Truth is Eternal Error or Creation will be Burned Up & then & not till then Truth or Eternity will appear It is Burnt up the Moment Men cease to behold it I assert for My self that I do not behold the Outward Creation & that to me it is hindrance & not Action it is as the Dirt upon my feet No part of Me" (Blake, *Complete Poetry and Prose of William Blake*, "A Vision of the Last Judgment," 565).

heaven, who has given it birth?"[19] The problems for God began when the child, released from the divine womb into the larger world that God had prepared for it, actualized possibilities that thwarted the divine mother's purposes and threatened her child. At this stage in my exposition of this symbol, however, the divine womb remains pregnant, not yet delivering the child that God has conceived. The divine mother delivers the child in the second moment or stage of divine self-limitation, divine self-restriction, and places the child in the nurturing, yet risk-filled, nothing of possibilities or relative non-being.

ACTUALIZING DIVINE LIFE AS LOVE IN CREATION OF NOTHING

Within this first stage of divine self-limitation, God has actualized all three dimensions of divine love. First, God has actualized the erotic dimension of divine love both as God's desire for an other-than-God to emerge from nothing, to exist, and as God's effort to initiate the process to establish the conditions for the other's origination. God actualizes the first dimension of divine being as one who envisions an other who may become partner, companion, or friend, even though created. Second,

19. Deut 32:18; Isa 42:14; Job 38:28–29 NAS. Also see Isa 49:15; Job 38:8–10. According to Mayer I. Gruber, the Hebrew scriptures often compare Yahweh to a father, while only rarely comparing Yahweh to a mother. Nevertheless, according to Gruber, such attestations make explicit a very important implication that appears throughout the Hebrew scriptures: Yahweh ". . . is neither specifically male nor specifically female" (M. Gruber, *Motherhood of God and Other Studies*, 3, 8). The newer Christian scriptures also describe humans as "being then offspring of God" (Acts 17:28–29 NAS) and announce the need for humans to be "born of the Spirit" (John 3:1–9 NAS). Arthur Peacocke suggested the conception of an embryo within a female's womb as a model with which to describe God as creator (Peacocke, *Intimations of Reality*, 64). Feminist theologians have contributed most significantly to the return of the symbol of divine motherhood to Christian theology: as examples, see Johnson, *She Who Is*, 100–3, 170–87; Case-Winters, *God's Power*, 201–32. On God as a mother giving birth to the world and God's people, see, Mollenkott, *Divine Feminine*, 15–19; cf. Rae and Marie-Day, *Created in Her Image*, 105–18. See McFague's concept of God as mother, in terms of God the creator. She helpfully employed this model to aid in the critique, on the one hand, of an absolute distinction between God and creation and, on the other hand, of the hierarchicalization of creation upon the basis of the dualism between spirit and matter (McFague, *Models of God*, 97–123). Ruether's notion of "God/ess as Matrix" also holds importance for this discussion, even though she rightly suspects parental models of God as symbols that can perpetuate "spiritual infantilism" (Ruether, *Sexism and God-Talk*, 68–71). In connection with spiritual birth, Julian of Norwich applies to Jesus the image of the mother giving birth to and nursing the child (Julian of Norwich, *Showings*, 60–61).

God has actualized divine agapic love in God's withdrawal or retraction, God's opening of a space within Godself, that which is not God yet within God, in order to allow for an other the space to realize its own creaturely alterity. Hence, divine self-retraction (though operating with and even expanding omnipotence, omniscience, and omnipresence) begins also to limit God's power, knowledge, and presence. This divine self-retraction activates the self-sacrificial dimension of the divine life. Third, God has loved philially at least partially in divine self-retraction, since, in that movement, God has provided the fundamental condition for the appearance of one who will be genuinely other-than-God though like God.

As the desire for mutuality, divine erotic love establishes the ἀρχή or *primordium*, even motivation, for divine agapic love. Divine agapic love functions as the *modus* to reach the τέλος or *locus* of mutuality in the actualization of divine philial love.

Although here I will not fully elaborate a concept of the divine Trinity, for the Christian symbol of divine suffering, creation remains a trinitarian activity. Hence, upon the basis of the identification of Jesus as Christ with God in the symbol of the becoming-human of the divine Logos, the Christian symbol of divine suffering declares that God, most fully disclosed as love in the event of Jesus as Christ, has created on the basis of that love through the divine Logos. Thus, even in the first stage of volitional divine self-limitation, the divine Logos acts to restrict the divine self and to open up a nothing or relative non-being within God.[20] In this way, the divine Trinity actualizes divine being as love in creative activity.

Divine Self-Restriction: Creatio ex Nihilo

I have described the second stage of volitional divine self-limitation in creation as divine self-restriction. God enacts this stage of volitional

---

20. A variety of Christian scriptures attest to this aspect of christological protology in the symbol: John 1:3; Col 1:16–17; Heb 1:2; cf. Phil 2:5–11. To some extent, God reverses, or at least modifies, the limitation of God by the divine Logos in creation, through the limitation of the divine Logos when the divine Logos becomes human. Thus, however speculative one may regard such a concept to be, one can demonstrate (in light of the entire history produced by God and creation) a genuine reciprocity within the divine Trinity that eliminates the threats posed by the subordinationistic tendencies of most orthodox christologies.

divine self-limitation on the basis of the first stage wherein God has opened up a space within the divine *all-in-all*.

Divine Creation from Nothing

Here the Christian symbol of divine suffering rejoins the classic, or orthodox, Christian traditions through its fidelity to the symbol of *creatio ex nihilo*. The nothing from which God creates, even though a nothing of possibilities for the creature, still represents that environment from which God has evacuated the divine self in some sense, in order to allow creaturely alterity to exist, in order to summon into being that which is other than the divine self. This nothing remains, however, that which God has created and that for which God has established certain limits as finite. The nothing that God has created does not constitute another ultimate reality that might threaten Godself. Rather, it represents both a space in which a genuine other-than-God can appear and that in which God might actualize divine possibilities toward and with creaturely alterity. [21]

Thus, the symbol of *creatio ex nihilo* expresses, both for orthodox Christian thought and for Christian affirmations of divine suffering, a conviction with several implications. First, God did not create from some kind of pre-existent material: *non ex materia sed ex nihilo*.[22] Such a position at least would imply some form of ultimate dualism and would render God finite in some sense. Second, creation did not emanate from God because of an internal divine struggle: *non de Deo*. An inner divine conflict has not resulted in an infusion of the creation with a tragic quality. God has produced the creation (even with its tragic features and dimensions) through the freedom of divine love. Moreover, in relation to this implication, God fashions created reality as God's work not as God's body.[23] God remains distinct from the world: in that way, created

21. See Gerhard May's excellent study of the symbol's early Christian development in the context of the challenges from gnostic and philosophical protological doctrines (May, *Creatio Ex Nihilo*).

22. Miguel de Unamuno understood God to be limited by the brute matter around God (Unamuno, *Tragic Sense of Life*, 227). C. E. Rolt, relying on a Platonic ontology, understood the order of the universe to originate from chaos or brute necessity through the attractive power of God's omnipotent, yet passive, love (Rolt, *World's Redemption*, 72, 75, 81–82).

23. Vernon Storr reiterated this orthodox point (Storr, *Problem of the Cross*, 119). See also Gilkey's excellent discussion of the formula: "non de Deo et non ex materia

reality can truly remain other-than-God, even when possessing features of resemblance to God. Along this path, the symbol attempts to avoid the dangers of pantheism. Third, in the creative act, God does something unique, something new; God produces the creation from nothing that has previously existed. God institutes finite reality, and finite reality can fashion but never establish something that has its source in something other than itself. Creatures create only from raw materials that God has supplied, including the relative non-being of possibility that occurs as freedom in its various forms throughout creaturely reality. Fourth, because God created finite reality, nothing that exists can be evil in itself. Rather, as genuine love (*caritas*), God communicates this goodness to creation. Fifth, and finally, God's creative act fashions a reality that God has endowed with purposefulness, meaning, and intelligibility, because it arises from the will and wisdom of divine love.[24]

DIVINE DESIRE FOR CREATION

God's creation from nothing implies God's desire for that which is other than God, God's desire for an alterity that remains distinct from the divine self, not a divine emanation or semi-creaturely extension of the divine self. God desires, however, not only that something different than God exists. God desires a creation with which God might also share communion, reciprocity, mutuality, solidarity, even friendship.[25] God

sed ex nihilo" (Gilkey, "Creation, Being and Nonbeing," 226–41; also in, Gilkey, *Through the Tempest*, 89–100). Many feminist and process theologians construe creation as the body of God: see McFague, *Models of God*, 69–78; idem, *Body of God*; Jantzen, *God's World, God's Body*; idem, "On Worshipping an Embodied God," 511–19. This topic has generated a new series of debates about divine corporeality as well: see Taliaferro, "Incorporeality of God," 179–88; Jantzen, "Reply to Taliaferro," 189–92). Marcel Sarot, a theologian of divine suffering, even argued that the concept of divine passibility implies at least some form of divine corporeality (Sarot, *God, Passibility and Corporeality*).

24. See Gilkey's thorough discussion of the meaning expressed by the Christian symbol of *creatio ex nihilo*: Gilkey, *Maker of Heaven and Earth*, 44–58.

25. Numerous theologians, some of whom diverge widely from one another on many other points, express the intuition that God desires free creatures, at least implying the reciprocity of love between the human and God: as examples, see Berdyaev, *Slavery and Freedom*, 84; Brunner, *Dogmatics*, 1: 254; Carr, *Transforming Grace*, 150; Dorner, "Dogmatic Discussion of the Doctrine of the Immutability of God," 132; idem, *System of Christian Doctrine*, 2:21, 25; Gilkey, *Maker of Heaven and Earth*, 277; Hall, *God and Human Suffering*, 70; Martensen, *Christian Dogmatics*, 114, 169; Moltmann, *Trinity and the Kingdom*, 106; Mullins, *Christian Religion in Its Doctrinal Expression*, 236; Post, "Inadequacy of Selflessness," 219; Simon, *Reconciliation by Incarnation*, 148;

seeks, as the end, goal, or purpose of creation, a deep and rich life of love between divine creator and creation. Thus, God desires a reality other than yet like God. This divine desire, then, implies God's preference for creatures with being that resembles the divine being. God desires creatures, and in this sense God desires finitude to come into existence, to stand forth from the relative non-being. God desires, however, to endow creation's finite character with the being of love. Such being implies freedom. The omission of freedom dissolves the possibility of love.

God created finite reality in order to fulfill this divine desire. Since God has established a finite reality that can actualize this divine desire as well, God has chosen to glorify or to fulfill the divine longing or purpose only in the nature, life, and destiny of humanity and in the existence, growth, and purpose of the cosmos as a whole, only where the creature can return to God the active response of authentic love.[26] Mirror-like creatures, however, do not simply reflect God's love upon the divine self. God desires creation for its own sake as well; creation originates in such a way that it genuinely actualizes alterity alongside the divine alterity.[27]

DIVINE GIFT OF CREATURELY LOVE

As love, God creates a reality with the capacity to relate as God relates without being either divine or a divine extension. As a result, in the creative act, God endows the creature with both an ontological dependence upon and an ontological separation from God.[28] The creature depends ontologically upon God, because it has received itself as a gift from God; God has given being to the creature and remains its empowering source. In addition, God has endowed creaturely being with

Storr, *Problem of the Cross*, 115; Varillon, *Humility and Suffering of God*, 57, 164, 171; Ward, *Rational Theology and the Creativity of God*, 67–88.

26. Caird, *Fundamental Ideas of Christianity*, 1:155; Brunner, *Dogmatics*, 1:20.

27. Thus, in spite of emphases upon divine freedom in creative activity, many of the best thinkers from very different traditions refuse to conceive God's creative activity as a divine egotism or extreme self-love: see Dorner, *System of Christian Doctrine* 2:25; Pseudo-Dionysius, *Divine Names*, 4.10; Varillon, *Humility and Suffering of God*, 164. Also see Phyllis Trible's superb exegesis of the erotic dimension of love in creation (Gen 2:4–24), under the heading "Eros Created" (Trible, *God and the Rhetoric of Sexuality*, 75–105).

28. See Gilkey's distinction between ontological dependence upon and ontological separation from God (Gilkey, *Maker of Heaven and Earth*, 277–78).

the character of divine being, has fashioned the creation in the divine image; hence, creation depends upon God for both its existence and the character of its existence. The character of creation's reality becomes the link between creation's ontological dependence upon God and creation's ontological separation from God. The creature experiences an ontological separation from God, because God has supplied the creature with the potential to develop the capacity to actualize its being as authentic love. Paradoxically, though, the capacity of love, with its central characteristic of freedom, comes to the creation from beyond itself, from God. The creation's ontological dependence upon God, then, produces the creature's need for God, a need that elicits love for God from the creation. Correspondingly, creation's ontological separation from God establishes the possibility for creation's response of authentic love to God.[29] Such a possibility, however, implies a negative side as well: the possibility both for the creation's refusal to love God authentically and for the creation's corresponding false love of itself or some other aspect of finite reality in place of God.

God has ordered the creation in terms of the capacity that God has given to each aspect or entity of finitude to actualize its being as love. As a result, at least during the present period of the creation's development or evolution and within the current range of human understanding, humans embody the greatest capacity for fulfilling this divine hope. In this capacity, however, both promise and threat reside. That ambiguity exemplifies the enormous risk that God has taken in creating creatures in the divine image. By endowing the creature with the being of love, God has created a reality with the capacity, not only for authentically loving God and the creation, but also with the capacity for freely loving only itself, rejecting God's love, and refusing to love God or the rest of

---

29. Dorner, speaking against the concept of divine self-limitation, viewed God's creation of beings, whom God had destined freely to actualize themselves, as the supreme disclosure of "the omnipotent causality of God," since God's creative power would lessen if God did not create such creatures (Dorner, "Dogmatic Discussion of the Doctrine of the Immutability of God," 128, 129). Dorner's argument resembled Pasewark's position at this point (see Pasewark, *Theology of Power*, 197–207), in both perspective and weakness. Dorner, however, used an argument against the concept of divine self-limitation that also resembles the argument which those who develop concepts of divine self-limitation often employ: to the effect that, if God cannot limit the divine self by creating others with a freedom that resembles the divine freedom, then God is not omnipotent.

creation authentically in return.[30] The first Christian canon's emphasis upon covenant approximates, points toward, or foreshadows this understanding of God as a seeker of mutuality in divine creative activity. I will more fully elaborate the features of creation as the image of God, or creation's part in this covenant, in my exposition of the second presupposition in the Christian symbol of divine suffering. I will more fully elaborate the covenantal aspects of creation from the divine side later in the present chapter as divine risk.

DIVINE RESPONSIBILITY FOR THE POSSIBILITY OF EVIL

God produced a creation with divine likeness, a creation with capacity to actualize its being as love either authentically or in-authentically: either loving God in return or refusing God's love and falsely loving itself, everything else, and even God. Nothing coerced God's creative activity, neither something distinct from though co-eternal with God nor some internal divine conflict. In creating, God actualized certain possibilities and refused to actualize others. God created a reality other than the divine self, a reality with the capacity to choose even that which God has chosen not to bring into being. God alone retains the responsibility, therefore, for the *possibility* that the creature might choose against the divine creator. Love, however, cannot be love, if it is coerced. To be love, love must be free. Love, then, implies the freedom to choose the object of love, to choose one's lover whether or not one is the beloved

---

30. Numerous theologians who develop various versions of divine suffering identify the creation's relative autonomy, particularly the creation's human components, as a fundamental dimension in this symbol's twofold presupposition: see von Balthasar, *von Balthasar Reader*, 199; Brunner, *Dogmatics*, 1:251, 254; Carr, *Transforming Grace*, 150, 152; Clark, "Doctrine of a Finite God," 43; C. D'Arcy, "Love and Omnipotence," 44; Dorner, *System of Christian Doctrine*, 2:21, 25; Fiddes, *Creative Suffering of God*, 33, 35; Forsyth, *Person and Place of Jesus Christ*, 314; Gilkey, *Reaping the Whirlwind*, 249; Gore, *Belief in God*, 116; Hall, *God and Human Suffering*, 70; MacGregor, *He Who Lets Us Be*, 19, 98, 141–43; Macintosh, *Theology as an Empirical Science*, 183; Martensen, *Christian Dogmatics*, 114; Simon, *Reconciliation by Incarnation*, 299–300; Storr, *Problem of the Cross*, 115; Streeter, *God and the Struggle for Existence*, 167; A. Strong, *Christ in Creation and Ethical Monism*, 90; Varillon, *Humility and Suffering of God*, 67, 68, 90, 91, 93; and D. White, *Forgiveness and Suffering*, 84. Scriptural attestations to this insight into the relationship between divine creator and creation, especially as disclosed through Jesus of Nazareth, led Karl Barth to his own creative formulation of the doctrines of creation and covenant in terms of one another: "creation as the external basis of the covenant" and "the covenant as the internal basis of creation" (Barth, *Church Dogmatics*, 3.1: 94–228, 228–329; cf., Varillon, *Humility and Suffering of God*, 57).

of the chosen other. Only the choice against authentic love for God, the choice of another lover rather than God, actualizes creaturely being falsely. For the Christian symbol of divine suffering, the negative actualization of creaturely being, the refusal of God's love and the replacement of the divine lover with another lover, actualizes *evil*. When the creature chooses in this way, that which God had chosen to remain only a possible reality has become an actual reality. Consequently, the most theologically-consistent Christian testimonies to divine suffering conceive of God as responsible for the *possibility* or *potentiality* of evil.[31] This possibility constitutes a real possibility, even though a possibility that God has chosen both not to will for the divine self and not to desire for creatures. God chooses to love creation authentically, but God gives the creation the choice, the possibility, between loving God properly and loving God improperly. The creation's negative response actualizes possibilities that God has not authorized as legitimate ones. Those destructive possibilities, as not-yet-being, do not possess the same status as the nothing that God has created from which to summon creation. Rather, the negative possibilities of creaturely life threaten to oppose God's purposes for the creation.

---

31. Karl Barth developed the most consistent and comprehensive understanding of this position in his concept of evil as "the reality of nothingness" (Barth, *Church Dogmatics*, 3.3:289–368). Martensen similarly understood evil: "but evil is just that possibility which ought to have remained a possibility forever" (Martensen, *Christian Dogmatics*, 159). C. E. Rolt as early as 1913, however, already proposed a concept of evil almost identical to the concept that Barth would later develop. Barth's writings on nothingness appear strikingly similar to Rolt's discourse on evil, even though Rolt elaborates his concept of evil from an avowedly Platonic ontological framework. "Evil is there not because God has created it, but precisely because He has refused to create it; not because He allows it, but precisely because He does not allow it. Evil exists precisely because He commands it not to exist; and thus it depends for its existence on His command and yet He is not its creator" (Rolt, *World's Redemption*, 125). Numerous theologians describe divine responsibility for the possibility of evil, based upon the self-limitation of God in the creation of finite freedom: see C. D'Arcy, "Love and Omnipotence," 44; Brasnett, *Suffering of the Impassible God*, 5; Cowburn, *Shadows and the Dark*, 75–81; W. Farley, *Tragic Vision and Divine Compassion*, 98, 107; Gilkey, *Reaping the Whirlwind*, 281; H. Robinson, *Redemption and Revelation in the Actuality of History*, 267. Charles Gore implied this view, when he argued that God submitted to the misuse of creaturely powers. Gore cited two important biblical texts to support this view: Isa 43:24 ("but thou hast made me to serve with thy sins, thou hast wearied me with thine iniquities"), and Ps 78:61 ("and delivered his strength into captivity, and his glory into the enemy's hand") (Gore, *Belief in God*, 115–16).

Here an important distinction requires identification and elaboration. According to this symbol, God has created certain negative actualities as part of creation's finitude.[32] Because God has created them, these negative aspects in the creation are good; God does not create evil. Thus, the Christian symbol of divine suffering does not construe those features as *natural* evil. Although these negative elements in creation can and do generate suffering, God has not actualized evil by creating them. As a result, one more properly describes creation's negative features and dynamics as *tragic* and as responsible for tragedy. Nonetheless, according to this symbol, one cannot legitimately construe as evil either these aspects or the suffering that they cause. The concept of *natural* evil contradicts the concepts of a good God and a good creation.

Thus, only because God grants to the creation a being in the divine image, does God open the divine self, the creation, and God's purposes for it, to the possibility of evil. The negative actualization of creaturely being can thwart God's activity and purposes. Divine self-restriction

32. I have discussed this distinction in connection with "the anthropological principle" in chapter 2. This view of finitude *as tragic*, although *not as evil* in any natural sense, appears first with the advent of modernity. Most Christian traditions, prior to modernity, understood the creaturely limits of finitude (weakness, old age, illness, affliction, loss of physical and mental capacities, death, etc.) as the results of sin, and therefore as evil, yet not as part of the original, and therefore good or perfect, creation (e.g., Augustine, *City of God*, 13.1, 3, 20). Martin Luther believed that, prior to sin, Adam and Eve had perfect health, perfect knowledge of all other creatures, eyesight better than the eagle's, greater strength than lions and bears possessed (as well as the gentleness to handle those same creatures like puppies), no lust, no fear of anything (not even of the serpent); furthermore, Luther believed that, as originally created, the natural world was far superior to its condition after the fact of sin: no thorns or thistles, a brighter sun, purer waters, more fertile fields, and even more fruitful trees. Consequently, the appearance of sin produced all human weaknesses and ills; furthermore, sin corrupted the natural world and all other creatures as well; finally, death became a reality for the world, whereas prior to sin death was not a reality (Martin Luther, *Lectures on Genesis*, 1:26). Even in contemporary theology, this older view still prevails within more traditional Christian communities (e.g., Amundsen, "Developing Role of Suffering in Salvation History," 12–25). Following the lead of modernity, and against much of the classical Christian tradition (including the Protestant reformers and the Protestant orthodoxies that their work eventually yielded), a growing number of theologians also elaborate a concept of tragic reality that resembles the concept that I have found within the Christian symbol of divine suffering, an interpretation of finitude's negative aspects that does not construe them as evil or as the result of human sin: as examples, see E. Farley, *Good and Evil*, 29, 40–46, 56–62, 72–75, 89–96, 109–13, 117–18, 121–24, 137–38, 143–44, 253–54, 270–72; and Sands, *Escape from Paradise*. I analyze the region of the tragic as the occasion for the third divine wound in volume three of this study.

in the face of finite freedom additionally implies, however, that God's purposes can, may, and will be retarded or thwarted by aspects of finite reality that have no intention of refusing the divine love and actualizing themselves falsely: rather, by the tragic features, aspects, or dimension of creation. Lack of knowledge, abilities, strength, time, and so forth, the very things that define creaturely reality as finite, can contribute to the limitations that God has placed upon the divine self by endowing the creation with a being that resembles the divine existence and life.[33]

Divine Trust, Venture, and Risk in Creation

In the divine gift of finite being as an analogue to the divine being of love, God offers the divine self in love to the creature and desires the creature's genuine responding love. God trusts the creature, has faith in the creation; and God faithfully commits divine love to the creature without measure. God invites the creature, then, reciprocally to actualize its being of love as trust of and faithfulness toward God. Hence, with the notion of covenant, God founds the relationship between divine creator and creaturely reality. This divine comportment not only indicates God's desire for a creature who voluntarily seeks interdependence with God. The divine attitude also indicates that God seeks interdependence with the creature for God's sake, though not on the basis of a divine need that God must fill outside the divine self in order to complete God's deity in some way. By creating finite reality with being that resembles divine being, then, God has renounced divine aseity in the absolute sense and has announced and inaugurated the interdependence of divine creator and creaturely reality.[34]

Divine trust exposes, therefore, both divine creator and creation to risk.[35] God takes a risk, of course, with a double possibility: either,

33. Few theologians perceive this aspect of divine self-limitation, since most of them concentrate upon how the creature's freedom *intentionally* accomplishes this. Nevertheless, divine self-limitation inheres in the very constitution of finite reality, entirely apart from freedom's place in it (e.g., Weatherhead, *Why Do Men Suffer*, 27). God's creation of the tragic region of reality, as distinct from a good creation that has turned evil, discloses other facets of divine self-limitation as well. See volume three of this study.

34. Fiddes, *Creative Suffering of God*, 56; Fretheim, *Suffering of God*, 58; Varillon, *Humility and Suffering of God*, 51, 53, 57. Some theologians have held the similar position, though one not fully consistent, that, by creating, God limits the divine ἀπάθεια, thereby becoming passible (e.g., Hodgson, "Incarnation," 376–78).

35. Balthasar, *von Balthasar Reader*, 199; Brasnett, *Suffering of the Impassible God*,

on the one hand, a risk that might bring joy, accomplishment, mutuality, reciprocity, community, and solidarity; or, on the other hand, a risk
that might bring sorrow, failure, egocentricity, isolation, and alienation.
God's risk may either enrich or diminish the divine life.[36] For the divine creator, God's venture entails the possibility that the creature will
thwart God's purposes for the creation, the possibility that God's love
will not receive the beloved's reciprocal love, the possibility that God's
faith will extend itself for nothing, the possibility that God's venture will
ultimately fail.[37] For the creation, the divine venture entails the possibility that creatures will ultimately deny their essential or authentic nature
as created for genuine loving communion with God and, in the various
forms of their false self-loves, ultimately destroy themselves. Thus, in

---

6, 62; D'Arcy, "Love and Omnipotence," 56, 64; Fiddes, *Creative Suffering of God*, 56;
Fretheim, *Suffering of God*, 74–78; Hall, *God and Human Suffering*, 70–71; MacGregor,
He Who Lets Us Be, 136; Macquarrie, *Principles of Christian Theology*, 200, 234;
Martensen, *Christian Dogmatics*, 170; Post, "Inadequacy of Selflessness," 219–20; D.
Williams, *Demonic and the Divine*, 33–43; Varillon, *Humility and Suffering of God*, 91,
164.

36. Brasnett, *Suffering of the Impassible God*, 85; Coldman, "Self-limitation of God,"
45–47.

37. This symbol implies such a possibility, indeed, if, for God, "the history of the
Universe is the history of a Great Adventure" (C. D'Arcy, "Love and Omnipotence,"
60). Some Christian theologians argue that God would not have imposed limitations
upon the divine self, if creatures could or would ultimately thwart the divine purposes.
Thus, even though that position sometimes admits divine self-limitation, it fails to consider the implication of possible divine failure. In spite of the negative actualizations
of creaturely freedom, if one asserts that God will still fulfill the divine purposes as
God had originally conceived them, then the whole course of history will have had
no real effect upon God; nonetheless, according to the previous view, if things do not
proceed as God has planned for them to proceed, then God will manipulate rather
than circumvent the established procedures in order to attain the divinely-desired and
proper results. In the more traditional view, because God already resides within the
creation and exercises all divine energies there, divine intervention would implicitly
entail at least God's self-confessed failure. Several theologians advocate this position: as
examples, see C. D'Arcy, "Love and Omnipotence," 64; and Weatherhead, *Why Do Men
Suffer*, 27, 34, 35. In a related discussion about divine repentance in the first Christian
scriptures, Fretheim notes that divine repentance implies a "genuinely open" future for
God. "The future is not blocked out in advance. What happens within the relationship
has a *direct* bearing on the shape of Israel's life in the world, and indeed the life of all,
for God's repentance is available to the entire world. Moreover, it has a direct bearing
on the future of God himself, how God will respond within the relationship and the
extent to which God's activity is marked by success or failure" (Fretheim, "Repentance
of God," 65).

order to provide the creation with divine love's advantage and its implicit freedom, God has placed the divine self at a disadvantage.[38]

As I noted previously, however, God's risk involves the limitations of finite reality as well as the freedom with which God has endowed creation. God's adventure of faith, therefore, has created nature as well as freedom, cosmos as well as history. Thus, divine risk includes the venture that God has taken with the world of nature by endowing it with a developmental or evolutionary character. Theologies of divine suffering repeatedly identify divine risk in the creation of freedom and history or the "arena of essential ambiguity."[39] In God's creation of the cosmos or nature as the house of history, that God also exposes the divine self as well as the creation to risk, testimonies to divine suffering have perceived less often.[40] Nevertheless, many Christian attestations to divine suffering acknowledge divine self-limitations that God has risked in the creation, in terms of the natural processes that science observes and describes as evolution.[41]

DIVINE ATTRIBUTES AND CREATION

Christian testimonies to divine suffering often consider the impact of divine self-limitation upon the traditional divine attributes. In light of

38. Brabant, "God and Time," 353.

39. Gilkey, *Reaping the Whirlwind*, 281.

40. Process theologies and their precursors perceive this implication of divine self-restriction in the creation (e.g., Whitehead, *Process and Reality*).

41. A variety of theologians share this perspective: see Coldman, "Self-limitation of God," 41–42; MacGregor, *He Who Lets Us Be*, 77; Peacocke, *Theology for a Scientific Age*, 123–24; Simon, *Reconciliation by Incarnation*, 280–82; Storr, *Problem of the Cross*, 120; Studdert-Kennedy, *Hardest Part*, 24–27; Weatherhead, *Why Do Men Suffer*, 47; see also, McWilliams, "Kenotic God and the Problem of Evil," 15–27; another version of his essay appears also as a chapter, "Geddes MacGregor: God as Kenotic Being," in McWilliams, *Passion of God*, 73–95). Other theologians much more radically conceive God's creation kenotically, but perceive that divine protological *kenosis* as total. God totally empties the divine self, in order to allow the creation to come into being with complete freedom and without any interference or direction by God; thus, *kenosis* "is not an *attribute* (however important it may be) of God, but the fundamental *nature* of God" (Abe, "Kenotic God and Dynamic Svunyata," 16; Vanstone, *Risk of Love*, 59, 60). Christian theologies of divine suffering generally do not adopt the most radical forms of *divine protological kenosis*, principally due to their shared conviction that such a position suggests pantheistic tendencies. Some theologians reject *total* divine protological *kenosis* upon other logical grounds: e.g., that God must remain "a cause producing an effect that does not exhaust the cause" (Brabant, "God and Time," 353).

various aspects of divine self-restriction, the Christian symbol of divine suffering portrays the divine attributes much differently than the dominant Christian traditions have usually construed them.[42] Hence, for the Christian symbol of divine suffering, divine self-limitations significantly alter the divine attributes.

I commence this consideration of divine self-restriction's effects upon the divine attributes, by briefly describing the condition of possibility for the illimitability of all divine attributes. God's capacity for self-limitation inscribes the definitive mark of God's infinite perfection upon every divine attribute: *unless God also possesses the capacity to limit the divine self in the operation of any attribute, then God cannot be unlimited in any of those respects.*[43] Attestations to divine suffering largely understand the self-restrictions that God has imposed upon the divine attributes in relation to creation as the implications of creaturely freedom. Theologians of divine suffering often analogously postulate this position, to a significant degree, on the basis of a phrase that an ancient Christ-hymn contains and that the newer Christian scriptures preserve. This hymn declares about Christ that, when taking human form, "he emptied himself," "ἑαυτὸν ἐκένωσεν."[44] Thus, theologians of divine suffering understand divine *soteriological kenosis*, as represented

42. From another perspective, God is finite either in power, knowledge, or both at once (James, *Essays in Radical Empiricism and a Pluralistic Universe*, 311). The viewpoint persists, however, even among some of those who proclaim a suffering God, that God does not limit Godself at all. Rather, this perspective claims that God's attributes, instead of being divinely self-limited, operate in their incomparable manner; but this perspective defines those attributes much differently than classical Christian theism defines them. This perspective, however, almost always equates divine self-limitation with some sort of finite deity (e.g., Rolt, *World's Redemption*, 60). Because Rolt opposes the concept of a finite deity, though, he also opposes the notion of a self-limiting deity. Nonetheless, some who strongly oppose any conception of a finite deity also espouse some conception of God as self-limiting (e.g., McCreary, "Finite God," 435).

43. Several theologians of divine suffering hold this viewpoint: see Mullins, *Christian Religion in its Doctrinal Expression*, 183; F. Robinson, *Self-Limitation of The Word of God*, 16). P. T. Forsyth argued similarly, when he reversed Calvin's principle, from "*finitum non capax infiniti*" to "*infinitum capax finiti*": "if the finite lies beyond the infinite and outside it then the infinite is reduced to be but a larger finite; the infinite can only remain so if it have the power of the finite as well" (Forsyth, *Person and Place of Jesus Christ*, 309).

44. Phil 2:7.

in this Christ-hymn, as the second major movement of a divine *kenosis* that began in God's creative activity, in a divine *protological kenosis*.[45]

Although divine protological *kenosis* remains an epistemological inference from divine soteriological *kenosis*, the first stage of *kenosis* affects the divine attributes in much the same way as the second stage does; the effects of divine creative activity upon the divine attributes resemble the effects of divine soteriological activity upon the divine attributes. Some differences will appear, however, when I examine divine soteriological *kenosis* in volume two of this study. The question for soteriological *kenosis*, however, remains the same for protological *kenosis*: How did God accomplish this divine protological *kenosis*, or divine self-restriction as I have described it here, in reference to the divine attributes; how did divine protological *kenosis* affect the divine attributes? On the one hand, has God *renounced the use* of the divine attributes in creation (analogously to the way in which the Giessen school described the renunciation of divine attributes by the incarnate Logos)? On the other hand, has God merely *concealed* the operation of the divine attributes in creation (analogously to the way in which the Tübingen school described the concealment of the divine attributes by the incarnate Logos)?[46]

45. For example, the following statement succinctly and accurately expresses this perspective: "the κένωσις, which reaches its paradoxical climax in the Cross of Christ, began with the Creation of the world" (Brunner, *Dogmatics*, 2:20). Other examples of the emphasis upon God's self-limitation as creator, or protological *kenosis* (as an implication of soteriological *kenosis*), appear more frequently since the nineteenth century. See the following examples: Coldman, "Self-Limitation of God," 44; Davison, "God and the World: A Theodicy," 15–16; Dawe, *Form of a Servant*, 191–200.

46. See the helpful discussions of kenotic christology in the following studies: Dawe, *Form of a Servant*; Kasper, *God of Jesus Christ*, 189–97. Forsyth distinguished his own version of kenotic christology from both *kenosis* as renunciation of use and *kenosis* as concealment. He described the *kenosis* of the attributes "as the retraction of their mode of being from actual to potential. . . . The attributes of God, like omniscience, are not destroyed when they are reduced to a potentiality. They are only concentrated. The self-reduction, or self-retraction, of God might be a better phrase than the self-emptying" (Forsyth, *Person and Place of Jesus Christ*, 308). His position, however, differs only slightly, if at all, from a concept of *kenosis* as the renunciation of use. If a capacity exists, yet remains unused or unexercised, then it becomes potential but not actual. Forsyth's language shifts the concepts from personal to ontological categories, but leaves the position virtually unchanged. Furthermore, a self-reduction differs substantially from a concentration of attributes.

Largely upon the previous basis, then, testimonies to divine suffering construe the divine attributes. Christian attestations to divine suffering generally consider God's limitation of three principal attributes, those usually designated as the relative attributes: omnipresence, omniscience, and omnipotence. Although a more thorough treatment requires an examination of other divine attributes as well, in this study I will examine only these three central examples.

1. *Divine presence* first submits to divine self-limitation. God, as the divine *all-in-all*, so retracts the divine self that a space of nothing opens within God, a space in which God can create something other than God. Nevertheless, God's retraction of divine presence as the *all-in-all* does not leave a nihilistic vacuum. God moves within this nothing, this space for the creation; thus, in the act of creating, God remains present. Hence, in created reality, God becomes present, first, in a structural sense, as the "principle of the possibility of existence" for all that comes into being.[47] The creation involves both space and time. Thus, when God produced creaturely space and time, the divine self became structurally present in all of creation's space and time. For this reason, the concept of God's everlastingness closely adheres to this understanding of divine presence. From this conviction, arose the prophetic pronouncement from Yahweh's mouth: "'Do I not fill the heavens and the earth?'"[48] Hence, God's presence in its spatial character pervades all reality in a general, even in a quasi-physical, sense. Yet, God has restricted this divine omnipresence in order to allow other, creaturely presences to become fully themselves. Here, then, due to divine respect for creaturely alterity or otherness, God humbly hides the divine self—thus, the invisibility of God.[49] God's limitation of divine presence preserves creation's independence, preventing a divine absorption of all things into God. Such a position avoids pantheism as well as theistic determinism. For this symbol, however, God extends the divine presence beyond the most general and structural sense, without which extension such a position resembles deism. As a result, testimonies to divine suffering announce a second kind of divine presence, one that I have described as *modes of divine presence within creation*: within animate and inanimate, sentient

---

47. Fretheim, *Suffering of God*, 61; Brunner, *Dogmatics*, 1:261.

48. Jer 23:24 NAS. See also, Job 38—41; Ps 139:1–16; Amos 9:2–6.

49. Varillon, *Suffering and Humility of God*, 48.

and non-sentient, or human and non-human beings. This indicates a third kind of divine presence as well, different intensifications of divine presence within both individual and social human experience. The first Christian canon attests variously to differing intensities of divine presence: God's presence accompanying the people during their journeys (in the exodus and in exiles); God's presence dwelling among the people at certain places, thus, accommodating the human need for stability (in the temple in Jerusalem); or God's more particular presence in theophanies (in the pillar of cloud and as various divine messengers in human form).[50] A fourth kind of divine presence occurs as a consequence of the third type or mode. Because of human freedom, and although God desires to be as persuasively present as possible, God is not present to the same extent in all persons. Humans (as both individuals and groups) may, if they refuse authentic love to God, distance themselves from the most intimate divine presence.[51] Even though in each of these kinds of divine presence God remains significantly present, the divine presence refrains from the immediacy of the *all-in-all*, due to divine respect for creaturely alterity.

2. *Divine knowledge* next submits itself to divine self-limitation. In divine self-restriction toward creation, God also places limits upon divine knowledge. Once again, Christian witnesses to divine suffering confess divine omniscience with the classic traditions, but do so in light of divine self-restriction.[52] Thus, God knows everything that can be known according to the conditions that God has placed upon God's cognitive activity. God's knowing, like the divine presence, operates in different modes. God first experiences a structural or general knowledge of creation.[53] In this form, God knows everything that can be known about the creation, especially since God fashioned everything that exists. Thus, God knows all past realities, both actualities and pos-

50. Fretheim, *Suffering of God*, 60–65, 79–106.

51. F. Robinson, *Self-Limitation of the Word of God*, 27–28; Brunner, *Dogmatics*, 1:258. In volume two, in my examination of the second divine wound, I will discuss God's most concrete historical presence in the event of Jesus Christ. In volume three, which consitutes my study of the third divine wound, my exposition will examine this symbol's witness to God's most universal historical presence as the indwelling Holy Spirit.

52. Theologians base the traditional doctrine upon biblical texts such as Ps 139:1–6.

53. Brunner, *Dogmatics*, 1:262.

sibilities. God also knows every actuality of present reality. Because both the divine life and creaturely reality possess temporal structures, however, God knows future reality only as possibility and never as actuality. Perhaps God knows all future possibilities, and even knows the probability for the actualization of every possibility and for all of their combinations. Since they have not yet occurred, though, even for God as everlasting, God cannot yet know any future possibility as an actuality.[54] This symbol construes such a divine self-limitation as a constitutional divine self-limitation, then, due to divine life's temporal structure. Nevertheless, had God created something *absolutely or wholly other* than God, without a freedom that resembles divine freedom, then God would foreknow completely all that would happen. Whereas God has introduced freedom into the created other, however, God has introduced an infinite variable, one that implies God's willingness to await creaturely decisions and actions before knowing them as actualities. Of course, this also means that God's knowledge increases. Hence, the temporal structures of both divine and created being not only constitutionally limit God's knowledge of creation. God volitionally limits or restricts

54. Dorner, "Dogmatic Discussion of the Doctrine of the Immutability of God," 134; Gilkey, *Reaping the Whirlwind*, 308–9; B. Lee, "Helplessness of God," 333–34; Macintosh, *Theology as an Empirical Science*, 184; Martensen, *Christian Dogmatics*, 95; F. Robinson, *Self-Limitation of the Word of God*, 24–25; Simon, *Reconciliation by Incarnation*, 285–87. The first Christian canon also supplies resources for conceptualizing the limitations in divine knowledge of the future. Prophetic utterances attribute a "Divine Perhaps" to God's speech, in order to indicate divine uncertainty in regard to future human responses to God's love and care (e.g., Ezek 12:1–3; Jer 26:2–3; 36:3, 7; 51:8; Isa 47:12), even though, given God's thorough knowledge of Israel's past and present, God knows the greatest probable responses (e.g., Pss 11:4; 33:13; 94:9–11). Also, the presence of conditional statements that certain texts attributed to divine speech indicates a biblical confidence that God will not decide upon a course of action, until God knows for certain the response of the people to the divine proposals (see Jer 7:5; 22:4–5; 26:4–6). Fretheim described another important aspect of this biblical tendency as "Divine Consultation," where God consults with prophetic leaders (Gen 18:7–22 [Abraham]; Exod 32:7–14 [Moses; cf. Deut 9:13–29]; Num 14:11–20 [Moses and Aaron]; 1 Sam 15 [Samuel]; Amos 3:7; 7:1–6; Jer 18:20; cf. Jer 15:11). Fretheim also described one final example of the limitation in God's knowledge of the future as the "Divine Question." Biblical writers attribute questions to God that relate both to the divine decision-making process in the future (see the following examples: Hos 6:4; [cf. Hos 11:8a]; Jer 5:7, 9; [cf. Jer 5:29; 9:7, 9]) and to divine inquiry into the past for an explanation of Israel's behavior (Jer 2:31; 8:5, 19c; [cf. Jer 2:14b; 30:6]; Isa 5:4; 50:2). See Fretheim's insightful formulations of these categories (Fretheim, *Suffering of God*, 45–59).

divine knowledge and does so out of respect for the independence, for the genuine alterity, of creation. Yet, God's knowledge of creation, even as volitionally conditioned by Godself, necessarily holds all things together as the divine creation. Furthermore, this symbol construes God's knowledge as divine wisdom, in that divine knowledge enables God to work in the best ways possible to attempt a realization of divine purposes for creation. Thus, a second mode of divine knowledge appears. Just as God becomes present in different ways to different aspects of creation, so too God knows, and knows about, creation's various aspects in different ways. God's knowledge of persons includes much more than every minute detail about the sub-atomic, atomic, molecular, chemical, physical, biological, emotional, and spiritual dimensions of their lives. Such divine knowledge serves God's desire for deeper knowledge of the human creation. God desires a relationship of complete mutual love with the human creation. This experience involves the most intimate divine knowledge.[55] Nevertheless, because of the capacity for freedom within human life as love, humans can refuse God's love and to love God properly in return. Correspondingly, then, human response limits the divine knowledge, the divine love. This limitation, however, God enables with the divine gift of freedom to the creature. Hence, at least potentially, God limits this intimate form of divine knowledge. God exercises this divine self-restriction, though, on the basis of divine respect for the creature's genuine alterity. God refuses to freeze human and creaturely liberty even by divine knowledge of creation.[56]

3. By the *divine power*, God limits both divine presence and divine knowledge. Yet, through this third attribute, by virtue of its ability to limit the other attributes, God submits divine power itself to limitation as well. Nevertheless, nothing external to God limits divine power, except inasmuch as God has set limits for the divine self (by sharing power) that open God to limitations from creatures. For the Christian symbol of divine suffering, two types of divine power appear in this connection.

First, even though God limits divine power in order to allow the possibility of an other's coming-to-be, this in no way implies that the

---

55. 2 Tim 2:19 attests that God knows those who belong to God. Divine knowing in this sense means God's love for the creation (Brunner, *Dogmatics*, 1:263) as well as the human's corresponding love for God.

56. Varillon, *Humility and Suffering of God*, 63–64.

creation comes into existence through its own power since God no longer prevents it from doing so. Rather, God intentionally brings the creation into existence and does so with the divine power. The universe, as experienced and known, moves, changes, develops, decays, disintegrates, reintegrates, and renews itself on the basis of the power that it receives from God in its various intensities and levels. In this sense, the Christian symbol of divine suffering depicts God as the source and basis of all quasi-physical power.[57] Were God to withdraw the divine power at the basis of creation, the creation could not sustain itself. Hence, in this first type of divine power, God shares a quasi-physical power with the creation: the power of energy, strength, and so forth, necessary for the creation to actualize its genuine alterity. According to this symbol, certainly, God places certain limits upon creation, certain constants within the cosmos. Thus, the creation operates through its power within these parameters, however great or small the parameters. God's power, always greater, sustains or grounds creaturely power in this sense; and, yet, divine power never violates that shared power with divine domination. Hence, God's power always remains a power in relation, a relation the limits of which God has established.[58] One additional facet distinguishes this first sense of divine power from divine power as *potestas*

57. Numerous biblical examples principally attest to this understanding of divine power: see Gen 18:14; and Jer 32:17, 27.

58. Both Brunner and Martensen seem to imbue their understandings of divine power with this sense, when they describe God's omnipotence as God's power "over all." They certainly refuse to define divine omnipotence as "*potestas absoluta.*" Yet, neither one of them reduces divine power to moral power alone (Brunner, *Dogmatics*, 1:249–50; Martensen, *Christian Dogmatics*, 95). Geddes MacGregor similarly noted that the Christian scriptures do not attest to an abstract notion of divine omnipotence as the "ability to do anything whatsoever," but rather refer to God both as the one who exercises sufficient power to accomplish the divine purposes and as the one who always *exercises* power over all things instead of simply *possessing* omnipotence. He made this point with brief studies of the Hebrew name for God, *El Shaddai* (the one who suffices), and the designation, from the newer Christian canon, of God as "παντοκράτωρ" ("ruler over all"). In other words, for God, power exists as power-in-relation. Nonetheless, according to MacGregor, Christian scriptures indicate that conditions neither created nor approved by God often limit God. "I hope only that the notion of a God whose power is limited by conditions that he neither creates nor approves, will not, whether accepted or rejected by Christian opinion, be glibly condemned as heterodox. If it be heterodox, both Testaments may be in the same condemnation" (MacGregor, "Does Scripture Limit the Power of God," 386). Daniel Migliore similarly holds that God exercises "self-limiting power" in creative activity (Migliore, *Power of God*, 95).

absoluta. God freely refuses any power that contradicts God's being as authentic love. I recall, in this connection, my previous discussion of divine constitutional self-limitation.

Thus, a link appears with a second type of divine power. While some attestations to divine suffering often deny or overlook the first type of divine power, almost all of those testimonies agree upon the nature of this second type of divine power: the utter power of divine love, sometimes described as God's moral power.[59] One cannot adequately describe the divine power of love, however, even though conceived not as brute force or domination, only as an attraction or a "lure." When described only as a lure before or an attraction to the creature, attestations to divine suffering too closely, perhaps exclusively in the extreme forms of this perspective, identify divine power as love with *aesthetic* categories and too distantly distinguish divine power as love from *volitional* and *moral* categories.[60] Hence, in this second sense, divine power actively engages the creation: persuading, participating, pursuing, always offering itself to and for the other. God's power as love never passively abides in its beauty, no matter how deep its sorrow from rejection might become. Yet, even this type of divine power is not illimitable. In the actualization of God's being as love, God limits the divine self. Thus, in the face of the creaturely freedom that God has granted, divine being as love risks being unfulfilled and, therefore, injured due to the creature's refusal both to receive the divine love and to return genuine love to God, others, and self. This limits the divine ability to fulfill completely the destiny of both the creation (including humanity) and the divine self; and this limit the creature places upon God through the freedom that God has given. The relation of this second type of divine power to the first type holds the place of utmost importance in this discussion. For, divine love, as God's constitutional self-limitation, limits the divine

59. B. H. Streeter reduced divine power to moral goodness exclusively (Streeter, "Suffering of God," 610). Although Edward Beecher did not argue for such a reduction, and even though he could refer to God's *physical* power, for Beecher, God's moral power is illimitable while God's physical power is not (E. Beecher, *Concord of Ages*, 150).

60. C. E. Rolt developed this viewpoint. Rolt clearly and intentionally fashioned a modern Christian Platonism, a dangerous construction most often intentionally avoided by those who espouse a doctrine of divine suffering. In Rolt's system, God's suffering finally and only means divine *patience.* Hence, God's power is always the "attraction of love" (Rolt, *World's Redemption*, 15, 27, 84, 87, 112). Tillich also described divine love as luring or attracting the human to reunion (Tillich, *Systematic Theology*, 1:283).

quasi-physical power, as the reality that guides it, as the region, nature, and norm of divine quasi-physical power.[61]

Moreover, the strength of divine power remains its ability to limit itself. Paradoxically, God would not be unlimited, if God were unable to set limits upon the divine self, beyond even constitutional divine self-limitations.[62] God does not make the divine self impotent; but God does restrict the divine self from exercising divine power as control over or domination of creaturely freedoms.[63] As a consequence, although only a very small part of God's entire creation, human freedom holds an extremely important place in creation in relation to divine power. God shares power with the human, both quasi-physical and moral powers. In considering these two types of power separately, I abstract them from one another for the purpose of distinguishing dimensions in divine power. In reality, however, although one may distinguish these two types of power, one cannot finally separate the one from the other. Thus, for this symbol, God endows human reality with, and thereby shares, power, both the power to love (which involves the freedom to love God either authentically or in-authentically) and the quasi-physical power to actualize human being in doing, actively embodying love as a responsible being (of course, the human may actualize that being either negatively or positively as well).[64] Because of human freedom, and the divinely-shared power that it implies, just as God's presence intensifies

61. Dorner, *System of Christian Doctrine*, 2:24; Forsyth, *Person and Place of Jesus Christ*, 313. Although Kasper did not distinguish between the quasi-physical and moral powers of God, he clearly perceived a connection between the two forms of divine power. "God need not strip himself of his omnipotence in order to reveal his love. On the contrary, it requires omnipotence to be able to surrender oneself and give oneself away; and it requires omnipotence to be able to take oneself back in the giving and to preserve the independence and freedom of the recipient. Only an almighty love can give itself wholly to the other and be a helpless love" (Kasper, *God of Jesus Christ*, 194–95).

62. F. Robinson, *Self-Limitation of the Word of God*, 16.

63. Moltmann goes too far by describing creation as God's "lowering of himself into his own impotence" (Moltmann, *Trinity and the Kingdom*, 110). O. C. Quick claims that, although God is ultimately and absolutely impassible, God becomes externally or relatively passible when God creates free agents; thus, Quick's notion of God's creative act resembles my description of volitional divine self-limitation (see Quick, *Doctrines of the Creed*, 184–86).

64. Some theologians understand this as a divine delegation of responsibility to humans (Bertocci, *The Person God Is*, 150). Also, feminist theology emphasizes that "God's power is *in humans* as embodied human agents" (Carr, *Transforming Grace*, 152).

to greater or lesser degrees due to either human reception or human rejection of God, the human reception or rejection of divine love also enhances or restricts God's ability to do certain things and to act in particular cases.[65]

ACTUALIZING DIVINE LIFE AS LOVE IN CREATION FROM NOTHING

Through the divine *creatio ex nihilo*, divine being as love has actualized itself. In divine desire for creation, God actualized divine erotic love. This divine desire motivated God to retract within the *all-in-all* in order to create the space in which genuine creaturely alterity might exist. Thus, in this second stage of volitional divine self-limitation, God loved erotically. God's desire began to realize its goal. God granted to an *other* a being that resembles divine being. Nevertheless, divine desire for creaturely alterity only actualized itself through its gift of creaturely love, through the gift of a being that remains similar to divine being. In this sense, God relinquished a portion of the divine self, a part of the *all-in-all*, in order to grant the kind of being to an other-than-God that God requires for such an other to relate to God as God relates—through the freedom of love. In this regard, God's sacrifice involved creating, and thereby becoming responsible for, the possibility of evil. Thus, through this divine risk or venture, God actualized divine agapic love. Finally, inasmuch as the divine creator brought creaturely alterity into existence, God began to realize the philial dimension of divine life. God has brought into being the creation through which and in which the reciprocal freedom of love might return to God. Yet, this divine desire, once a divine possibility that God has now actualized in a divine mutuality with the creation, initiates a grand venture for God, an extreme divine risk: *the vulnerability of God.*

Divine Vulnerability: Condition of Possibility for Divine Suffering

Hence, upon the basis of God's self-actualization as caritative love in creative activity through both constitutional and volitional divine self-limitations, the Christian symbol of divine suffering depicts God as

65. See discussions of this point by Fretheim, a perspective developed almost exclusively on the basis of resources from the first Christian canon (Fretheim, *Suffering of God*, 72–78).

vulnerable.[66] Because God has limited the divine self through both the nature of God as love and divine creative activity, God stands before the creation as the divine other in whose image God has analogously created the creature. Paradoxically, only a creature with being that resembles divine being could realize genuine alterity before God. If the creature's being is not love (with its heart of freedom), then the creature represents only a cognitive, volitional, and emotional extension of the divine self. By endowing the creation with such a gift, however, God accepts a great risk. Divine love, a love that seeks reciprocal love from its beloved—the creation—then opens itself to rejection as well as to reciprocity and mutuality. With the possibility of such rejection, therefore, arises the possibility of divine pain, sorrow, and suffering.[67]

66. Christian testimonies to divine suffering traditionally utilize the concept of "divine passibility," as the antithesis to the concept of "divine impassibility," to express the presupposition of the Christian symbol of divine suffering that I have described as divine vulnerability. O. C. Quick, for example, developed concepts both of God's "external passibility" (or "the capacity to be acted upon by something from without") and God's "sensational passibility" (or "liability to those feelings of pleasure and pain, and more especially those of pain, which are caused within a conscious being by the action of some other being upon it") as products of God's self-limitation in the divine creation of others (Quick, *Doctrines of the Creed*, 184, 185). Also, contemporary discussions of divine vulnerability still contend with the residual effects of Hellenistic ontological forms of the two-natures christology. For example, guided by the thought that ". . . it is precisely God's utter transcendence of and autonomy from the world that explains his universal and intimate involvement with every finite reality and event," William J. Hill concluded with the following points: "first, that God remains immutable and impassible in his own intrinsic godhead, so that his genuine love for creatures cannot entail suffering within divinity as such; but secondly, that God does choose to enter personally and relationally into the heart of mankind's [*sic*] suffering in his transcendentally free and loving response to it." Hill allowed the whisper in classical theism's ontologies to grow louder still: "God truly suffers, not (as Moltmann would have it) in his very deity, but in and through his humanity which is one with the humanity of all men and women. . . . What all of this amounts to is a genuine Christian panentheism, wherein God who lies beyond suffering in his divinity, chooses freely to suffer as man [*sic*] for mankind [*sic*]" (Hill, "Does Divine Love Entail Suffering in God," 56, 68, 69).

67. God also opens the divine self to the possibility of joyous enrichment through the creature's faithful return of love to God. The first creation account in the Book of Genesis suggests that divine joy, pleasure, enrichment, and perhaps even surprise, come to God from the creation (Gen 1:4, 10, 12, 18, 21, 25, 31). Arthur Peacocke argued that humans can make sense of the divine creator's intention to create the "rich multiformity of entities, structures, and processes in the natural world" only "if we say that *God has joy and delight in creation*. We have a hint of this in the satisfaction attributed to God as Creator in the first chapter of Genesis" (Peacocke, *Theology for a Scientific Age*, 114).

God's volitional self-limitation in the creation exposes the divine wound-ability. The act of creating does not cause suffering for God in the most extreme meanings of suffering.[68] The act of creating, however, does expose divine vulnerability, in that creation supplies the condition of possibility for God's experience of woundedness. Finally, only upon this basis, does this symbol properly ascribe any kind of suffering to God. By bringing into existence an other, God opens the divine love, the divine being, to the possibility of injury by the one whom God desires to know as companion, partner, and friend.[69] This symbol does not associ-

68. This claim, however, requires a brief qualification. In light of God's creation of both creaturely freedom and tragic existence (that is, God's production of the possibility of evil's appearance, through human freedom; the definite future actuality of a non-evil suffering and ambiguity, through tragic aspects of creation; and further ambiguities through the intersection of these two realities), the possible operations of these created realities, at least implicitly, must have caused God some sorrow (perhaps even guilt?) in divine creative activity.

69. Fretheim's careful analyses of theophanies in human form from the first Christian canon yield rich resources upon the basis of which to describe divine vulnerability as the condition of possibility for divine suffering. After describing the common elements to many theophanies, Fretheim discussed how the central elements of these divine appearances expose God's vulnerability. As one common feature, God gives the assurance of a continuing divine presence. God's vulnerability discloses itself, in that human rejection "can effectively push God back into less intensified and less desired forms of presence." Fretheim described another common feature as a word to the recipient upon which each particular appearance focuses. God's word becomes vulnerable, because it faces the possibility of abuse or misuse. Fretheim identified the divine name as a third common element that exposes divine vulnerability. In God's protection of the name's holiness (Exod 20:7; Deut 5:11; Lev 19:12), God shows concern for the divine future, since God places the name at the disposal of those to whom God communicates it. Humans also can abuse, misuse, or dishonor this name (Fretheim, *Suffering of God*, 97–101). Others also locate the source of divine vulnerability in divine creative activity: see Koyama, "Hand Painfully Open," 42; Peacocke, *Theology for a Scientific Age*, 123–24; Williams, "Vulnerable and the Invulnerable God," 27–30; idem, *Spirit and the Forms of Love*, 123–29; idem, *Demonic and the Divine*, 34–43, 56–61, 66–67, 70–71; also see, McWilliams, "Daniel Day Williams' Vulnerable and Invulnerable God," 73–79; idem, *Passion of God*, 119–46; Placher, *Narratives of a Vulnerable God*, 3–26. Vanstone also agreed that God's creative activity exposes the divine vulnerability; he described divine vulnerability, however, as "the susceptibility of God" (Vanstone, *Risk of Love*, 66–67). Victor Ryssel translates the letter of Gregory Thaumaturgus to Theopompus (concerning divine passibility and impassibility) into German as "*die Leidensunfähigkeit und Leidensfähigkeit Gottes*" (Ryssel, *Gregorius Thaumaturgus: Sein Leben und seine Schriften*, 71–99). The English translator of Seeberg's massive history of Christian doctrine rendered Seeberg's reference to Ryssel's translation of Gregory's work as "the susceptibility and unsusceptibility of God to suffering" (Seeberg, *Text-Book of the History of Doctrines*, 1:171). Charles Beecher, Edward Beecher's brother,

ate such vulnerability with the weaknesses that some scholars attribute to finite deities. Rather, God's voluntary openness discloses the greater divine strengths: only a love that can be wounded can heal. Precisely the vast reaches and infinite sensitivity of divine love disclose the enormous divine capacity for suffering.

Divine vulnerability, however, contains a dual capacity. On the one hand, God possesses a sensibility that can experience wounds on behalf of the divine self. I have designated this type of vulnerability as *reflexive divine vulnerability*. God has the capacity to suffer for the divine self. On the other hand, God can be wounded on behalf of creaturely others and their needs. This second capacity, I have correlatively designated as *transitive divine vulnerability*. Roughly speaking, testimonies to divine suffering depict these two capacities as the divine capacity of pain for the divine self, in the first instance, and as God's capacity for sympathy toward and solidarity with the other, in the second instance.[70] Both ca-

---

also argued for God's possibility of, or "liability to," suffering; he similarly described it as God's "susceptibility of heart" or "susceptibility to pain" (C. Beecher, *Redeemer and Redeemed*, 262, 264, 270). Dorner described God's creation of free creatures for the purpose of reciprocity of love between God and human as divine self-exposure "to the creature's possible opposition and defiance" (Dorner, "Dogmatic Discussion of the Doctrine of the Immutability of God," 133). Others also have discussed divine vulnerability on the basis of divine love and in the encounter of two freedoms: see Avis, *Eros and the Sacred*, 135–37; Boff, *Passion of Christ, Passion of the World*, 114; Brümmer, "Moral Sensitivity and the Free Will Defence," 96–97; idem, *Speaking of a Personal God*, 139–45; idem, *Model of Love*, 223–32; Kasper, *God of Jesus Christ*, 196; Lucas, *Freedom and Grace*; idem, "Foreknowledge and the Vulnerability of God," 119–28). Jüngel develops a concept related to divine vulnerability, divine perishability (Jüngel, *God as the Mystery of the World*, 184–225). One may more properly construe this notion, however, in terms of the much broader notion, divine vulnerability, since divine perishability relates principally to the death of Jesus on the cross—the divine event of suffering that I will later treat as derivative from a prior divine wound. Although remaining within the classic Christian theistic paradigm, Angelus Silesius poetically discerns divine vulnerability as well (Angelus Silesius, *Cherubinic Wanderer*, 4.52).

70. An emphasis upon divine sensibility directs attention to the pain that God experiences in and for the divine life itself. Taken too far, however, this understanding of divine vulnerability can become a theological sentimentalism in light of a pathetic divine self-pity. Although he seemed to avoid its extremes, Edward Beecher's viewpoint certainly exhibited this tendency at times (E. Beecher, *Concord of Ages*, 119–21, 132). On the other hand, a simplistic emphasis upon divine sympathy that excludes God's suffering for the divine self seems to strip from divine life the necessary precondition of any divine sympathy for creaturely alterity (e.g., Buckham, *Humanity of God*, 154). I borrow the linguistic distinction between the terms "reflexive" and "transitive" from Abraham Heschel, who distinguished between reflexive concern as *self-directed* or self-

pacities, however, constitute divine vulnerability. These two capacities require one another. Without reflexive divine vulnerability, or the ability to experience pain for the divine self, God would not possess the capacity to suffer from, for, and with creaturely alterity. Without transitive divine vulnerability, or the capacity to suffer from, for, and with creaturely alterity, God would not possess the capacity to suffer from, with, and for the divine self in its needs. Thus, divine vulnerability in all of its mystery and complexity becomes visible with the advent of the cosmos that God has created in the divine image.

---

centered and transitive concern as *other-directed*. God, according to Heschel, exercises only transitive concern (Heschel, *Prophets*, 2:5–6; idem, *Man Is Not Alone*, 136–39; idem, "Divine Pathos," 62). I apply both of these terms to divine vulnerability, however, because the Christian symbol of divine suffering attests to a pain within God that results from the divine loss of God's beloved creature. Yet, this divine loss produces not only divine sorrow over a wasted creature (or transitive suffering), but also divine pain because of a loss to the divine self (or reflexive suffering) of that with which God chose to make the divine self at least somewhat interdependent. To a certain extent, Heschel's refusal to ascribe reflexive concern to God seems to ignore this point, even though Heschel's own insight implies it: "*God is in need of man*" (Heschel, *Man Is Not Alone*, 25, 241f.; idem, *God in Search of Man*, 413). Heschel's position may also reflect the influence of Christian neo-orthodox theologies on his theology of divine pathos (see Merkle, "Heschel's Theology of Divine Pathos," 151–65; Berkovits, "Dr. A. J. Heschel's Theology of Pathos," 67–104).

Beloved Human:

Imago Dei *and* Imitatio Dei *As Love*

Introduction to Division Two:

Human Life As Image and Imitation of God

MY ANALYSIS OF THIS SYMBOL'S FIRST PRESUPPOSITION DISCLOSED the implicit character of the second presupposition in the first presupposition. As a consequence, that disclosure requires an analysis of the second and implied presupposition, in order to comprehend as satisfactorily as possible even the first presupposition. Having begun with an analysis of this second presupposition would have required the same procedure in reverse. The elegant and fertile dialectical network between this symbol's first and second presuppositions, as a result, begins to appear in all of its complexity through the present exposition. Although herein I continue to *treat* these two presuppositions *distinctly* from one another, I also continue to understand both presuppositions as two interdependent aspects of one fundamental presupposition and, thus, *never separate* from one another. I have acknowledged the necessity of this awareness through the repeated, although partial and indirect (*actu exercito*), appearances of this second presupposition in chapters 4 and 5. In the following analyses of chapters 6, 7, and 8, I will examine more intentionally and directly (*actu signato*), as well as more fully and systematically, the various strands in previous appearances of this second presupposition. Here, thus, in connection with this symbol's second presupposition, the first presupposition will also repeatedly although partially reappear as well.

Two powerful and rich streams of piety and their mutual transformations of one another, both flowing originally from the Christian scriptures, also form this second presupposition: (1) the attestation to God's creation of human reality in the divine image; and (2) the confession that God conforms faithful human beings to Jesus as Christ, the perfect image of God.[1] As with the first presupposition, however,

---

1. The first Christian canon preserves the first attestation, although only in the book of Genesis: see Gen 1:26, 27; 5:1, 3; 9:6). Furthermore, this motif appears only in the

the first stream of piety yields a more general representation of the symbol, while the second stream yields a most specific representation of the symbol, one that maintains its locus in the criterion of the criteriological principle for these studies. I repeat the criterion of the criteriological principle that guides my study and that I identified in chapter 2: *God most fully discloses the divine self as love in Jesus as the Christ.* Nevertheless, this second presupposition requires an account of the interaction between both streams of piety for its most adequate exposition. The second presupposition of the Christian symbol of divine suffering, then, takes the following form: *God has created the human in God's own image, the God whose being or life is love; or, more precisely, God has created human being, through the actualization of the divine being as love in God's self-limiting creative activity, in the image of God with the being or life of love.*

As this presupposition stands, it describes human being without reference to human action. As formulated, this presupposition further abstracts essential or structural human being from actual human existence with its experience of both tragic ambiguities and evil. This presupposition does not appear strictly through an analysis of actual human experience. Previously, I abstracted divine being and activity from one another, in order to clarify the ways in which divine creative activity actualized itself as love, while acknowledging the artificial character of such an abstraction. In reality, divine being and activity are never separate from one another. Similarly, even though in my present study of the human as the image of God I have also abstracted human being and its actualization from one another, in reality they do not exist apart from one another; human activity is human being's actualization and human being is always human activity.[2] In this respect (that is, in terms of the relationship between act and being), then, God has cre-

---

Priestly source (P) among this book's several source documents. The second Christian canon records the second attestation, in several of its documents: Rom 8:28–30; 1 Cor 15:45–50; 2 Cor 3:18; 4:4, 6, 10–11; Phil 2:5–8; Col 1:15; 3:9–11; and Heb 1:3.

2. This point resembles significantly Paul Ricoeur's philosophical ontology, particularly his description of being-in-act or the becoming-real of freedom: see Ricoeur, *Freedom and Nature*, 334; idem, *Political and Social Essays*, 32. Bernard Lee developed this insight specifically with reference to divine suffering. "We are conditioned by our inheritance. We are pressured by our circumstances. Our freedom is never total, but it is always radical. The decisions we make *are* ourselves. We are not separate from our decisions. We are not makers of our decisions so much as our decisions are makers of us" (B. Lee, "Helplessness of God," 328).

ated creaturely existence in the divine image or analogously to God.[3] Thus, when represented in this way, one need not conceive creaturely existence in the image of God as only one of two opposing alternatives: as *either* substantial *or* relational understandings of the *imago Dei*.[4] In light of God's being or life as love, disclosed through divine activity (as the God who creates the human in the divine image), *being* need not oppose *acting* or relating. My analyses of this second presupposition demonstrate how this symbol's construal of the *imago Dei* can correct problems that inhere in both of the two traditionally-opposed interpretations of the *imago Dei*, while demonstrating how this symbol's construal of the human as the image of the God whose being is love requires both perspectives as components of a more holistic concept.

---

3. These discussions rely upon the meaning of the terms used in both Hebrew and Greek Christian scriptures. The Hebrew version of Gen 1:26 uses the following two key terms: *tselem* and *demuth*. The Greek translation of the Hebrew scriptures, the earliest Christian bible (the Septuagint or LXX), renders these terms respectively as εἰκών (*eikon*) and ὁμοίωσίς (*homoiosis*). The Latin Vulgate translates these two terms respectively as *imago* and *similitudo*. More recent biblical scholarship emphasizes that, on the one hand, *tselem* (a masculine noun) carries a material or plastic meaning; related to a verb-form meaning "to cut off," *tselem* means "something cut out" or shaped from some substance. This term still designates resemblance or similarity, but in the sense of material "copy." On the other hand, *demuth* (a feminine noun), also found elsewhere in masculine form and related to a verb that means to "be like" or "resemble," though it too may carry the material sense of *tselem*, when used as a parallelism, effectively softens the excessively material sense of *tselem* (Jacob, *Theology of the Old Testament*, 166–67; von Rad, *Genesis*, 57–58; Eichrodt, *Theology of the Old Testament*, 2:123; Wolff, *Anthropology of the Old Testament*, 161). *Eikon*, also used in the second Christian canon, carries a number of meanings, some of which significantly resemble the meanings of both *tselem* and *demuth*. These two terms have inspired careful distinctions in theological anthropologies from the times of the earliest Christian theologians: as an example, Irenaeus (born around 130 CE) established a distinction between the two terms which, in various forms, tended to dominate theological anthropologies with respect to the motif of the *imago Dei* at least until the time of Martin Luther. Peter Schwanz has supplied an excellent study of this symbol's early history (Schwanz, *Imago Dei als christologisch-anthropologisches Problem in der Geschichte der Alten Kirche von Paulus bis Clemens von Alexandrien*). David Cairns offered a more comprehensive historical survey that assessed some theological perspectives (Cairns, *Image of God in Man*). For systematic and problem-oriented approaches, older studies remain valuable: as examples, see Orr, *God's Image in Man and Its Defacement in the Light of Modern Denials*; and Berkouwer, *Man*.

4. Several theologians summarize this dichotomy between substantial and relational conceptions of the *imago Dei*: as examples, see Ramsey, *Basic Christian Ethics*, 249–64; and D. Hall, *Imaging God*, 88–112.

Therefore, the subsequent analyses follow the analytical structure that I employed upon the first presupposition: first, an examination of human being or life, the *imago Dei*, as distinct from its actualization, beginning with a description of both the epistemological source and the procedure of this analysis, while ending with an analysis of formal and material dimensions of human being as love; and second, a study of the actualization of human being, as the *imitatio Dei*, and its central relationship to Jesus' double-love command. A third portion of my analysis, however, prevents my exposition of this second presupposition from reflecting the exact symmetry that appears in my analyses of the first presupposition. I will also examine the place of the world (in both its natural and historical forms) as the source, context, co-creature, and responsibility of the human as *imago Dei*. Thus, in that analysis, I consider the entire creation's role in the second presupposition. Such considerations figure prominently in my interpretation of the relationship between divine suffering and tragic reality and experience in volume three of this work. With the third analysis of this second division of part two, I endeavor not to neglect the *three referents* of a religious symbol (the divine or ultimate reality, the human, or the world), the *presuppositions* of this particular Christian symbol, or the Christian *symbol* of divine suffering itself. Thus, I develop division two, "Beloved Human: *Imago Dei* and *Imitatio Dei* as Love," in three chapters: an exposition of the symbol's understanding of the beloved human whom God has created as *imago Dei*, with the being or life of love (chapter 6); an exposition of the symbol's notion of the beloved human that actualizes the *imago Dei* as love in terms of *imitatio Dei* or imitation of God (chapter 7); and an exposition of the human as part of the cosmos or world itself, rather than the world as only the context and resource for the human's life as *imago Dei* (chapter 8).

6

Beloved Human:
Imago Dei *As Love*

Introduction: Human Life as Love

This chapter develops the first half of an exposition of the second major presupposition of the Christian symbol of divine suffering. As I have mentioned already, most specifically, this presupposition takes the following form: *God has created human life or being, through the actualization of the divine being as love in God's self-limiting creative activity, in the image of God with the being or life of love.* Working on the basis of the abstraction of being or life from its actualization, this chapter will identify and analyze the formal and material structures of the human as the image of God, the *imago Dei* as love, or human being or life as love. As the first stage of my analysis of the human as love, I follow the same pattern that I employed in my analysis of divine life as love in chapter 4. I begin with a description of an epistemology of human life as love, which I derive from the Christian traditions of divine suffering themselves. Through that epistemology, the formal and material dimensions of the *imago Dei* as love will appear respectively and in that order. This chapter, therefore, constitutes an analysis of those dimensions of the *imago Dei* as love.

Epistemology of Human Life as Love

For the Christian symbol of divine suffering, not only does the event of Jesus as Christ disclose most fully, clearly, and decisively God's being as love. In addition, and just as importantly, the event of Jesus as Christ discloses most fully, clearly, and decisively authentic human being or life, human being's most authentic actualization of the human as *imago Dei* and the *imago Dei* as love. My analyses of the first presupposition addressed how the character of divine being in God's protological activity discloses itself through divine soteriological activity. Analogously, then, my present exposition focuses upon the character of the soteriological presence and activity of Jesus, as the epistemological key to the human's authentic actualization as *imago Dei* (in the human's original, created, essential, or authentic state), as abstracted from the human's sinful destruction, ambiguity, and distortion that requires God's salvific activity. In this connection, then, Christian attestations to divine suffering, basing their confessions upon scriptural attestations, understand Jesus the Christ as the perfect image of God.[1]

This Christian symbol's rationality or logic, then, operates in the following way. Since the being of God is love as disclosed in Jesus the Christ, and since this Christ is the perfect image of God, then, not only does the event of Jesus as Christ disclose God's being as love, but this decisive event most adequately and decisively discloses the image of God in human being to be love as well.[2]

---

1. Christian scriptures use this symbol most explicitly when they describe Christ as "the image of God" ("εἰκὼν τοῦ θεοῦ") (2 Cor 4:4) or "the image of the invisible God" ("εἰκὼν τοῦ θεοῦ τοῦ ἀοράτου") (Col 1:15). Christian scriptures less directly employ this symbol in other, yet related, terms: describing Christ as both in "the form of God" ("μορφῇ θεοῦ") (Phil 1:6) and "the very stamp (or "exact representation")" of his [God's] nature" ("χαρακτὴρ τῆς ὑποστάσεως αὐτοῦ") (Heb 1:3).

2. One may observe this logic about the nature of the *imago Dei*, for example, also in the theology of John Wesley, who sometimes speaks of God's suffering, although usually in connection with the crucifixion of Christ. "In this image of God was man made. 'God is love'; accordingly, man at his creation was full of love; which was the sole principle of all his tempers, thoughts, words, and actions. God is full of justice, mercy, and truth; so was man as he came from the hands of his Creator" (Wesley, *John Wesley's Theology*, 111). Because of his relational (rather than substantial) concept of the *imago Dei*, however, Wesley held that, through sin, humans lost the image of God, but that, through salvation by faith in Christ and the process of sanctification, God restores that image of love (Wynkoop, *Theology of Love*, 109–11). As a result, in the process of sanctification, Christian perfection consists of loving God with one's complete self and loving the neighbor as oneself (Wesley, *Plain Account of Christian Perfection*, 7, 11–14, 41–42, etc.). In a constructive theology, in which one would develop a mutually-critical correlational theology, one would need to consider the relationship of the process of evolution to the claim that God has created humanity in the *imago Dei* as love, assuming both the validity of evolutionary theory and the theological claim. Thus, the Christian theologian of divine suffering would need to address the question of the evolution of the *imago Dei* as love. Consider the following examples of this awareness

This entry into an understanding of the *imago Dei*, however, commences on the basis of three assumptions that the Christian symbol of
divine suffering holds: first, the reality of sin has obscured *knowledge
of the fact of, the nature of,* as well as *the authentic realization of the
nature of, the imago Dei*; second, only through the event of Jesus as
Christ, which dispels the obscurities by breaking the bondage of sin,
do humans acquire such knowledge; and, third, the character of that
acquired knowledge is not merely cognitive, but, rather, experiential as
humans receive divine love through Jesus as Christ. In spite of these
three assumptions, however, the Christian symbol of divine suffering
claims that humans have lost only the *knowledge* of the reality, of the
nature, and of the proper realization of the nature, of the *imago Dei*. In
its most coherent and consistent forms, this symbol does not declare the
total loss of the *imago Dei* from human life.

The second Christian canon announces the renewal and completion of the *imago Dei* in human life through Christ. God has predestined humans for conformity to the image of Christ. Christians should
put on a new nature in God's likeness. Christians have put on a new
nature that is being renewed in knowledge after the image of the divine creator. God presently transforms Christians into God's likeness.
Moreover, Christians shall finally bear the complete image of Christ,
the heavenly human.[3]

On the basis of such proclamation, some theologians claim that
the second Christian canon assumes both that God created humans in
the divine image and that human sin has obliterated that image. Thus,
only Christ can restore that image.[4] Such a judgment, however, largely
remains unjustifiable. The second Christian canon nowhere *explicitly* declares the loss or complete obliteration of the divine image from
human life. Nevertheless, many testimonies in the newer Christian

---

by theologians and theological ethicists: Kagawa, *Religion of Jesus and Love, the Law of
Life*, 49–81; Pope, *Evolution of Altruism and the Ordering of Love*, 99–160.

3. Rom 8:29; Eph 4:24; Col 3:10; 2 Cor 3:18; 1 Cor 15:49.

4. For example, see Kittel, "Metaphorical Use of Image in the NT." Also, Emil
Brunner distinguished between formal and material dimensions of the *imago Dei* in
human beings. On the basis of this distinction, Brunner claims that humans do not lose
the formal aspect of the image due to sin; but humans do forfeit the material aspect of
the *imago Dei*. Brunner based his argument on testimonies from the second Christian
canon to Christ as the image of God. Only through Christ does the human regain this
lost material sense of the *imago Dei* (Brunner, *Dogmatics*, 2:55–61).

scriptures *imply* the conviction that the human has lost the *imago Dei*. At this point, however, I question the validity of the tendency in the second Christian canon to indicate the loss of the *imago Dei* (if the newer Christian canon in fact demonstrates that tendency), insofar as that indication expresses a Gnostic or dualistic tendency, a tendency to deny the presence of goodness even in fallen humanity and, hence, to deny actual human experience, despite its ambiguities; such a tendency even over-rates human capacities, when assuming that the human can entirely obliterate the divine creator's work. Hence, texts from the *first* Christian canon offer alternatives to this tendency (or implicit conviction) within the *second* Christian canon, resources that one may properly employ as correctives to any such tendency. This epistemological move, however, more significantly affects my exposition of the actual character of the *imago Dei* in the next section than it affects the exposition of this section.

Here, however, I maintain a focus upon the disclosure of authentic human being or life in Jesus of Nazareth. Due to human sin, humans lost experiential knowledge both of human being created in the image of God and human being actualized properly or authentically (as *caritas*). Only through encounter with Christ do humans fully and most decisively experience God as love. As Brunner says, when Christian scriptures declare ". . . that God 'knows' anyone it means that he loves him."[5] In this knowledge of God through Jesus of Nazareth, humans discover again knowledge of themselves as God's image, of their own being as love. Thus, through Jesus of Nazareth, humans receive a threefold knowledge about the *imago Dei*: (1) that God has created humans in the image of God; (2) that, as that image, the nature of human life or being is love; and (3) that the human can properly (as *caritas*) or improperly (as *cupiditas*) actualize this *imago Dei*, this being of love. Hence, in light of Jesus' life and activity, then, I will display both formal and material dimensions of human being as love. On the basis of this christological source for the knowledge about the fact of, the nature of, and the proper actualization of the *imago Dei*, my analysis of the *imago Dei* as presupposed by the Christian symbol of divine suffering follows.

5. Brunner, *Dogmatics*, 1:263. Also, see the following canonical Christian texts: Exod 3:7–8; Jer 29:11; Matt 6:8; 2 Tim 2:19. For Brunner's negative point, see Matt 25:12; cf. Ps 18:44.

The Christian symbol of divine suffering assumes that the previ-ously-described threefold knowledge of the human as *imago Dei* sur-faces through human encounter with God in Jesus of Nazareth. That encounter, then, discloses both formal and material dimensions in the human as *imago Dei.*

Formal Dimensions of *Imago Dei* as Love

Encounter with Jesus of Nazareth discloses several formal dimensions of the *imago Dei*: the ineradicability or persistence of the *imago Dei*; totality and universality of the *imago Dei* in human life; *imago Dei* as similar to and representative of God; and differentiation of *imago Dei* from God or the limits of the *imago Dei.*

Persistence of Imago Dei

The first formal dimension, the persistence of the *imago Dei*, indicates this symbol's sublimity and boldness. Assuming the fullest and most authentic actualization of the *imago Dei*, in Jesus of Nazareth, witnesses to divine suffering claim that humanity has neither lost nor obliterated the image of God.[6] Humans have lost *only* the threefold *knowledge* of

6. According to the Christian symbol of divine suffering, not only does God's be-coming-human imply that human sin did not annihilate the *imago Dei* in the human; Christian scriptures themselves strongly imply that humans, although obscuring the *imago Dei* through its inauthentic actualization, did not eradicate this created reality. For example, the genealogy of the patriarchs, from Adam to Noah, implies that succes-sive human generations inherited the *imago Dei*—after the entrance of human sin into the story (Gen 5:3). Additionally, following the flood, God established a covenant with Noah and his descendents; in that context, God forbade humans to kill one another, because God had created humans in the divine image. Again, the priestly writer implies the presence of the *imago Dei* in humans, following human sin and divine judgment (Gen 9:6) (Eichrodt, *Theology of the Old Testament*, 2:129–30; von Rad, *Genesis*, 132–33; idem, *Old Testament Theology*, 1:147). Edmond Jacob developed a somewhat contradic-tory approach to this question: on the one hand, he stated that neither human sin nor divine judgment destroyed the image of God; on the other hand, he stated that, to remain an image of God, the human must maintain a proper relationship with God (Jacob, *Theology of the Old Testament*, 166, 171). In the second Christian canon, more ambiguity complicates the problem. The first related reference to this idea, and perhaps the widest sense of meaning to be identified with the symbol of the *imago Dei*, appears in the context of a Lucan sermon that the evangelist attributed to the apostle Paul; on the Areopagus, in Paul's address to the Athenians, he tells them to seek God, "for in Him we live and move and exist, as even some of your own poets have said, 'For we also are His offspring.' Being then the offspring of God, we ought not to think that the

that reality. With this claim, testimonies to divine suffering acknowledge
the enduring strength with which God has endowed creation, even the
creatures to whom God has given a freedom that resembles God's own
freedom, a freedom even to turn from God and the divine purposes for
creation. Moreover, according to this symbol, the possibility for God
to become a human creature through human creatures relies entirely
upon the persistence of the *imago Dei* in human life. Thus, through
Jesus of Nazareth, God-become-human, God displays to humans their
authentic creatureliness with God. The history of Jesus as the Christ
also discloses to humans that, even though they have not lost their being as *imago Dei*, nevertheless, humans have defaced, damaged, soiled,
defiled, misused, abused, distorted, or wrongly actualized the *imago Dei*

Divine Nature is like gold or silver or stone, an image formed by the art and thought of
man" (Acts 17:28–29 NAS). In the context of making an argument based upon the created order, concerning the reasons that women ought to cover their heads in worship,
the apostle Paul also claimed that a male ought not to cover his head, since he is "the
image and glory of God." Here, in spite of the problems with Paul's theological anthropology and hermeneutical rhetoric, Paul appealed to the original image of God that
remains implicit to all human beings (does he mean males only?) (1 Cor 11:7). Also,
in another text, the second Christian canon assumes that the image of God remains
in humans in spite of sin, for the human tongue both blesses God and curses humans
whom God fashioned in the divine likeness (ὁμοίωσιν) (Jas 3:9). Other texts from the
newer Christian canon seem to regard the image of God as lost or no longer present in
humans who have estranged themselves from God; hence, these texts may understand
salvation through Christ as the restoration of the divine image: see Col 3:10; Eph 4:24;
Rom 8:29. If these portions of the second Christian canon really support this latter and
most negative claim, then here one can legitimately use the priestly sources that the
book of Genesis preserves to unmask the (at least implicit) world-denying tendency of
those texts from the second Christian canon, in spite of their christological focus. This
inner-canonical conflict and critique in no way detracts from the continued affirmation
of the second Christian canon: that renewal or renovation of the wrongly actualized
imago Dei comes by divine grace through Jesus Christ. Many Christian testimonies
to divine suffering assume that humans have not lost the image of God, but rather
have distorted that image through its false actualization and, therefore, that God alone
can renew the *imago Dei* (Bulgakov, *Wisdom of God*, 121; Oden, *Living God*, 1:151–52;
Quick, *Doctrines of the Creed*, 51, 143; D. Smith, *Atonement in the Light of History and
the Modern Spirit*, 142, 150). Brunner discerned both formal and material aspects in the
imago Dei: he described the formal or essential structure of human nature as the fixity
of responsibility, or the necessity of human response to God, the aspect of the image
that the human cannot lose in spite of sin; he described the material aspect of human
nature as the human's authentic actualization of the formal aspect, in human reception of divine love and in human love's response to God, the aspect of the *imago Dei*
that the human can lose when the human no longer reflects the divine love (Brunner,
Dogmatics, 2:55–61; idem, *Man in Revolt*, 83–204).

as *cupiditas.* Consequently, only through divine action does the *imago Dei* recover the possibility of actualizing itself properly as *caritas.*[7]

Totality and Universality of Imago Dei

A second formal dimension of human being as the image of God, and one related to the heights of the previous characteristic, indicates the extent of this reality in human life: the totality and universality of *imago Dei.* Jesus of Nazareth, in his person, deeds, and teachings, through his entire life, most authentically actualized the *imago Dei.* In his actions toward others, Jesus assumed the totality and universality of the *imago Dei:* in his offers of the gospel, in his healing of lepers and the blind and the crippled, in his forgiveness of female prostitutes. The symbol of the *imago Dei* represents no single aspect, quality, or capacity in human life. The image of God defines the entire human creature: volitionally, affectively, and cognitively, but not in any single sense alone.[8] The image of God pervades the cognitive and emotional elements of human volition, the volitional and cognitive elements of human emotion, and the emotional and volitional elements of human cognition. In other words, the whole or total human being resembles the whole being of God.[9] Furthermore, God has created *all* humans in the image of God:

7. I reserve my considerations of this latter aspect, however, for discussion in my analysis of the second divine wound or structural moment in divine suffering in volume two of this study.

8. Eichrodt made this point when he claimed that God did not attach the *imago Dei* to human existence as something extra (Eichrodt, *Theology of the Old Testament,* 2:128–29). Jacob emphasized this as well when he described the human as representative of God on earth, in terms of both human physical being and spiritual functions (Jacob, *Theology of the Old Testament,* 168). Von Rad further emphasized that the two Hebrew terms at the basis of the symbol of the *imago Dei* refer to the whole human being, not only to human intellectual or spiritual capacities, but also "equally, if not first and foremost," to the splendor of the human bodily form and glory that God has given to the human (von Rad, *Old Testament Theology,* 1:144–45). As G. Ernest Wright and Reginald H. Fuller have expressed it, "in the Hebrew language, then, the phrase 'in the image of God' would be the simplest way to express the thought that the total being of man bears a likeness to the total being of God" (Wright and Fuller, *Book of the Acts of God,* 54). Systematic theologians build upon this biblical anthropology: as examples, see Bulgakov, *Wisdom of God,* 118; and Weber, *Foundations of Dogmatics,* 1:560–61.

9. Of course, such a perspective raises questions about the bodily, fleshly, or material aspects of human being. For the majority of Christian testimonies to divine suffering, however, God identifies with, but remains distinct (though not separate) from, that creation. Therefore, Christian testimonies to divine suffering only rarely conceive creation,

both genders; persons in every age group; persons of every color. God created the *imago Dei* as a universal quality in human reality, both individually and socially.[10] Thus, the image of God not only includes the

---

in any sense, as the "body of God" as in some contemporary viewpoints. See the following examples: McFague, *Models of God*, 69–78; idem, *Body of God*; Jantzen, *God's World, God's Body*. Such a position still too closely resembles pantheism for most Christian testimonies to divine suffering. Still, insofar as Jesus the Christ represents the perfect actualization of the *imago Dei*, and especially insofar as Christian traditions regard this Christ as both divine and human, then the theological symbol of the divine incarnation re-introduces the question of whether or not the human's bodily dimensions do actually participate as essential aspects of the human as *imago Dei*! In one sense, if a focus upon the body, as organically and completely interwoven with the remaining dimensions of human life, thereby truly confers a holistic quality upon the human rather than dividing the human into distinct faculties (as in most ancient anthropologies: e.g., body, soul, and spirit), then refusal of a place to the bodily dimension in discussions of the *imago Dei* returns to (or refuses to diverge from) the still prevalent traditional Christian (yet dualistic) concepts of the *imago Dei* as the power of reason, the human will, the mind, or some other distinctively so-called *spiritual* capacity or attribute. Somehow one must avoid both extremes: on the one hand, avoid describing the human body as one faculty of the *imago Dei* or, at least, avoid describing the human body so as to imply that the divine self also has a body; on the other hand, avoid describing the *imago Dei* with terminology that identifies it as some faculty attached to the body but in no way truly dependent on the body for its most authentic functioning, perhaps even degraded or prevented from its most authentic functioning by human bodily life. Especially in the activities of love (in all three of its major dimensions: agapic, erotic, and philial), as in all other human experience, the bodily dimension remains absolutely necessary for and definitive of human life! Modern and contemporary social, biological, socio-biological, medical, and physical sciences have contributed helpfully to dissolving the credibility of dualistic interpretations of human life: hence, the dissolution among theologians of dualistic interpretations of the *imago Dei*. This anthropological revolution has also inspired both the liberation of the Christian symbol of divine suffering from its domination by classical theism and the consequent production of numerous theologies of divine suffering. These theologies, in turn, with their discussions of passibility, and passibility's implicit relationships to creaturely (specifically human) bodily life, have reopened among Christian theologians the once long-settled question of divine corporeality: see, for example, Taliaferro, "Incorporeality of God," 179–88). One philosophical theologian of divine suffering, Marcel Sarot, carefully developed a concept of divine corporeality that remains compatible with a passible God (Sarot, *God, Passibility and Corporeality*).

10. The priestly writer (e.g., Gen 1:27) did not restrict the image of God to males (Eichrodt, *Theology of the Old Testament*, 2:126–27; Mettinger, *In Search of God*, 205). Apparently, this aspect of the symbol did not figure into the apostle Paul's use of the symbol in his treatment of problems at Corinth (1 Cor 11:7). John G. Gammie understood the image of God as a part of the priestly vision in which Israel posited the parity of male and female; and, although Israel allowed only the ordination of males according to priestly regulations, the symbol of the *imago Dei*, therefore, "furnishes

complete being of individual humans, but also designates every human and the human community as a whole.

Resemblance and Representation in Imago Dei

I have described a third formal dimension of *imago Dei*, one also related to this symbol's boldness, as the unique value or position that God has given to the human within the whole creation: resemblance and representation in the *imago Dei*. Two central characteristics constitute this dimension of the human as the image of God.

First, humans resemble God. Although humans always remain creatures, according to the symbol of the *imago Dei*, God has endowed the human creature with being that resembles divine life.[11] Thus, the Christian symbol of divine suffering, by presupposing the symbol of the *imago Dei*, emphasizes that God created humans, whom God created in the divine image, though "a little lower than God," *theomor-*

---

the foundation for a parity in ordination today." Furthermore, the Christian symbol of divine suffering most fully conceives the symbol of the *imago Dei* in light of the insight that the apostle Paul finally expressed: "There is neither Jew nor Greek, there is neither slave nor free man, there is neither male nor female; for you are all one in Christ Jesus" (Gal 3:28 NAS) (Gammie, *Holiness in Israel*, 43).

11. The priestly writer formulated this concisely: "And God created man in His own image, in the image of God He created him; male and female He created them" (Gen 1:27 NAS). Affirming the priestly theology, one psalmist described the human proximity to God: "What is man, that Thou dost take thought of him? And the son of man, that Thou dost care for him? Yet Thou hast made him a little lower than God, And dost crown him with glory and majesty!" (Ps 8:4–5 NAS). A point of controversy in this latter text concerns the translation of the term "*Elohim*," in verse 5b, as "ἄγγελοι" in the LXX and "angels" in the King James Version. Gen 1:27 contains the same Hebrew term, in the phrase that the King James Version translates as "image of God." Regarding Gen 1:27, von Rad saw in the use of the term *Elohim* an indication, by the writer, of Yahweh's resolve to associate the divine self with God's heavenly court, thereby hiding Godself in the court's plurality. Moreover, he understood Ps 8:5 to refer to angels, even though the psalm addresses Yahweh. Thus, because the psalm introduces "Elohim," instead of repeating "Yahweh," von Rad understood this example as an attempt to delineate the upper limit of the human creature's dignity (von Rad, *Old Testament Theology*, 1:145). Eichrodt concurred with von Rad on one important aspect of this issue, whatever the significance of the plural suffix in Gen 1:27 ("Let us make man in *our* image"): "the reference to creation as 'in our image' instead of 'in my image' is definitely aimed at avoiding an altogether too narrow connection with God's own form, and at changing the naively materialistic conception of earlier times into a more vaguely worded correspondence between the human and divine natures" (Eichrodt, *Theology of the Old Testament*, 2:124–25).

phically. This aspect of the *imago Dei* implies, astonishingly, that God is *not wholly other* than the human creation.[12] As a consequence, the

12. von Rad, *Old Testament Theology*, 1:145–46; Caillard, "The Suffering God: A Study in St. Paul," 580; Brasnett, *Suffering of the Impassible God*, 131. The Eastern Orthodox Catholic soteriological emphasis upon divinization or *theosis* also relies upon a strong doctrine of the *imago Dei*. Eastern Orthodoxy develops this doctrine, however, far more potently, by describing the human as "theandric" (God-human), by analogy to the "Prototype," Christ the God-Man. For example, "man's original mode of being is theandric" and, therefore, that becomes the human destiny in salvation (Bulgakov, *Wisdom of God*, 129, 130). Angelus Silesius attempted poetically to articulate something similar to this insight. "I am God's other Self, He can in me behold what from eternity was cast in His own mould." "Why God created us the image of His own? I say because He has simply no other one" (Angelus Silesius, *Cherubinic Wanderer*, 1.278; 5.239).

In the nineteenth century, Søren Kierkegaard significantly pioneered the notion of the "Wholly Other," with his insistence upon the "absolute difference between God and man" (Kierkegaard, *Concluding Unscientific Postscript*, 195). In 1917, Rudolf Otto published his phenomenological description of "the Holy," in which he described the concept of the "wholly other" ("*das 'Ganz andere'*") as "... that which is quite beyond the sphere of the usual, the intelligible, and the familiar, which therefore falls quite outside the limits of the 'canny,' and is contrasted with it, filling the mind with blank wonder and astonishment" (Otto, *Idea of the Holy*, 26). In his early thought, Karl Barth also emphatically described God as "Wholly Other" (around 1918, when the first edition of his commentary on the apostle Paul's epistle to the Roman Christians appeared). For example, speaking of sin, Barth said the following. "The distance between the incorruption, the pre-eminence and originality of God, and the corruption, the boundedness and relativity of men had been confused. Once the eye, which can perceive this distinction, has been blinded, there arises in the midst, between here and there, between us and the 'Wholly Other,' a mist or concoction of religion in which, by a whole series of skilful assimilations and mixings more or less strongly flavoured with sexuality, sometimes the behaviour of men or of animals is exalted to be an experience of God, sometimes the Being and Existence of God is 'enjoyed' as a human or animal experience" (Barth, *Epistle to the Romans*, 49–50). Each of the previous writers, Kierkegaard, Barth, and even Otto, in other writings qualified their stark interpretations of this concept. For example, observe the forcefulness with which Barth later attacked this notion. "We may believe that God can and must only be absolute in contrast to all that is relative, exalted in contrast to all that is lowly, active in contrast to all suffering, inviolable in contrast to all temptation, transcendent in contrast to all immanence, and therefore divine in contrast to everything human, in short that He can and must be only the 'Wholly Other.' But such beliefs are shown to be quite untenable, and corrupt and pagan, by the fact that God does in fact be and do this in Jesus Christ" (Barth, *Church Dogmatics*, 4.1:186). Paul Ricoeur, though more dialectically, even integrated something of this thought into his philosophy. "To be sure, I speak of the Wholly Other only insofar as it addresses itself to me; and the kerygma, the glad tidings, is precisely that it addresses itself to me and ceases to be the Wholly Other. Of an absolute Wholly Other I know nothing at all. But by its very manner of approaching, of coming, it shows itself to be Wholly Other than the *archê* and the *telos* which I can conceptualize in reflective

complaint (that all talk about divine suffering is anthropomorphic or anthropopathic) has often been misguided, because God's self-disclosure in Jesus of Nazareth also discloses authentic human being in the world. This formal dimension begins to display the material dimensions of the *imago Dei.* This development requires a brief assessment of the structural presence of freedom in human life. Precisely this affirmation by Christian testimonies to divine suffering, that God created in the human something analogous (as finite) to the divine freedom, establishes grounds to dissolve *classical theism's construal* of God's predestination of human life. Genuine human freedom (even when conceived as relative not absolute) entails an indeterminacy for human life, a requirement for the human's self-actualization of that which God has given.[13] Freedom defines the structural possibility for the actualization

thought. It shows itself as Wholly Other by annihilating its radical otherness" (Ricoeur, *Freud and Philosophy*, 525). Many Christian theologians of divine suffering, of course, seriously question the notion of God as "Wholly Other." For example, Henry Maldwyn Hughes wrote an entire chapter challenging this claim: "'The Wholly Other'?" (Hughes, *Christian Idea of God*, 58–79). Nevertheless, reaction to this concept came, not only from other theologians, but also from scholars of the Hebrew Bible and scholars of Ancient Near Eastern languages and civilizations as well. "God is in the heavens; God is far other than man. But it is entirely false to Old Testament thought to introduce into the statement that adverb favored in recent theological speculation and say that God is 'wholly' other. Israel's thinkers would have repudiated such an idea with indignation" (Irwin, *Intellectual Adventure of Ancient Man*, 263).

13. For John Calvin (one of the principal and most influential representatives of classical Christian theism), however, God has willed everything that happens—including, thereby, all specific human actions, the human fall into sin, and every human's ultimate destiny either to salvation or damnation (e.g., Calvin, *Institutes of the Christian Religion*, 1.16.3–9; 3.21.5; 3.23.2). This understanding of creation's process and history arises necessarily from Calvin's doctrine of God. In Calvin's theology, God as the eternal present experiences all aspects and events of creation's history as present realities; for God, no past or future exists (see Calvin, *Institutes of the Christian Religion*, 3.21.5). With this concept, Calvin elaborates one facet of divine immutability. God has predestined all events. If God were to alter this plan, then God's will would not remain immutable and, thus, God's perfection would be nullified (e.g., Calvin, *Institutes of the Christian Religion*, 1.7.12–14; 3.21.7–8). Calvin's concept of God, of course, has its roots in Augustine's theology. "Will you say that these things are false, which, with a strong voice, Truth tells me in my inner ear, concerning the very eternity of the Creator, that His substance is in no wise changed by time, nor that His will is separate from His substance? Wherefore, He willeth not one thing now, another anon, but once and for ever He willeth all things that He willeth; not again and again, nor now this, now that; nor willeth afterwards what He willeth not before, nor willeth not what before He willed. Because such a will is mutable, and no mutable thing is eternal; but our God is eternal. ...Moreover, all thought which is thus varied is mutable, and nothing mutable is eternal;

of human being as love. Without freedom, love is not possible, since love cannot be coerced and remain love. Nevertheless, the divine creator has *given* this freedom: in this sense, then, as paradoxical as it may appear, God destines the human to be free, to exercise freedom.[14]

Second, therefore, God has distinguished the human, though the human participates within the world of creatures as one of them and like them, from the remainder of created reality. Although God has *distinguished* humans from all other creatures, God has *not separated* them from the creation in which they participate. Nevertheless, God has granted to humans a unique status, not so much in terms of honor or privilege as in terms of functional responsibility.[15] The second aspect

---

but our God is eternal. . . . I find that my God, the eternal God, hath not made any creature by any new will, nor that His knowledge suffereth anything transitory" (Augustine, *Confessions*, 12.15.18, in *Select Library of the Nicene and Post-Nicene Fathers of the Christian Church*, 1:180; Augustine, *Confessiones*, 12.15.18, in *Corpus Christianorum: Series Latina*, 27:221–22). In light of such statements and following Gotthard Nygren's evaluation, Jaroslav Pelikan correctly notes that Augustine's concept of double predestination ". . . was an inescapable corollary of his view of God the Creator as the sovereign God of grace" (Pelikan, *Christian Tradition*, 1:298). Pelikan also examines this connection between divine immutability and double-predestination in the theology of the ninth-century Christian theologian, Gottschalk of Orbais (Pelikan, *Christian Tradition*, 3:84–86). Christian theologians of divine suffering acknowledge that testimony to a suffering God requires the dissolution of classical theism's construal of human freedom (e.g., Cooper, "Education for Suffering and the Shifting of the Catena," 29–30). Naturally, as I will later demonstrate, this shift affects classical Christian soteriologies, both Catholic and Protestant alike, as well. Pelagius, at least, perceived quite well this aspect of Christian anthropology, whatever conceptual problems he encountered elsewhere due to his position on human freedom. "Actually, of course, he [God] intended and commanded that we should do what is good. His only purpose in giving the capacity for evil was that we accomplish his will by our own will. Our ability to do evil is, therefore, itself a good. . . . Thus we have the freedom to choose or oppose, to accept or reject" (Pelagius, "Letter to Demetrias," 43 [¶3]).

14. Non-Christians and Christians alike perceive the paradox of this insight. "I am condemned to exist forever beyond my essence, beyond the causes and motives of my act. I am condemned to be free. This means that no limits to my freedom can be found except freedom itself or, if you prefer, that we are not free to cease being free" (Sartre, *Being and Nothingness*, 415). "We do not, however, cause our freedom, our capacity to decide and to shape. It, too, is given to us as a basic power that is ourselves, that is itself the basis for all we do or create. Nor is our freedom caused by the heavy pressure of the past, for then it would not be the freedom to reshape and even to transform the past. Further, we can no more escape this gift or burden of freedom than we can escape time and passage, or the past. As not caused either by itself or its world, freedom too, therefore, must have a ground beyond both" (Gilkey, *Message and Existence*, 80).

15. The priestly writer formulated this idea in the following way: "and God blessed

of the unique value with which God has endowed human creatures, as a result, relates the human's theomorphic being to its theomorphic function or activity. Once again, Jesus' history discloses this aspect of the unique axiological endowment from God. The Christian symbol of divine suffering depicts Jesus as the most authentic actualization and most perfect disclosure of the divine purpose for human being in creation. In the creation stories of the book of Genesis, God charges humans "to subdue" the earth and "to rule over" all the creatures upon and within it.[16] God qualifies this endowment as the function of *imago Dei*, not the function of a creature with complete independence from God.

Even a brief examination of the social world within which this symbol developed greatly clarifies the meaning of the concept, *imago Dei*. In the ancient Near East, rulers often erected statues of themselves in the geographical and political regions that they controlled. These statues announced a particular ruler's ownership of that region.[17] Similarly, according to the book of Genesis, God created humans as such representatives, beings in the divine image who proclaim the peculiar kind of government over and sustenance of creation that God exercises. In Jesus of Nazareth, the specificity of that divine presence and activity fully discloses itself as love. In that disclosure, the announcement of authentic divine love implies the inauthenticity of any other alternative definition of divine presence within as well as divine activity toward

them; and God said to them, 'Be fruitful and multiply, and fill the earth, and subdue it; and rule over the fish of the sea and over the birds of the sky, and over every living thing that moves on the earth'" (Gen 1:28 NAS). Again, the psalmist reiterated the priestly piety: "Thou dost make him to rule over the works of Thy hands; Thou hast put all things under his feet, All sheep and oxen, And also the beasts of the field, The birds of the heavens, and the fish of the sea, Whatever passes through the paths of the seas. O Lord, our Lord, How majestic is Thy name in all the earth!" (Ps 8:6–9 NAS).

16. In Gen 1:28, the two key Hebrew verbs, translated respectively as "to subdue" or "to bring into bondage" and "to rule over," both suggest the exercise of power through violence. In the first instance, the verb suggests trampling or treading down a path. The ancient Hebrews used this verb-form to refer both to the subjugation of countries, peoples, or slaves and to the rape of women (see Num 32:22, 29; 2 Sam 8:1; Neh 5:5; Esth 7:8). In the second instance, the verb also suggests treading and trampling (Joel 4:13) or dominating. The Hebrews often applied this verb-form to a king's rule (see Pss 72:8; 110:2; Isa 14:6; Ezek 34:4) (von Rad, *Old Testament Theology*, 1:146; Wolff, *Anthropology of the Old Testament*, 163).

17. For example, in the thirteenth century BCE, court artisans carved the image of Pharaoh Ramesses II into rock at the mouth of a river on the Mediterranean Sea north of Beirut (Wolff, *Anthropology of the Old Testament*, 160).

the world. Thus, in Jesus as Christ, God refuses domination and oppression as forms of divine responsiveness to and relationality toward the creation as a whole and to all creatures in their particularities. God has desired this limit, furthermore, for the *imago Dei*, the divine representative on earth: God identifies domination, abuse, oppression, exploitation, and degradation as inauthentic modes of actualizing the *imago Dei*. In this sense, then, by illuminating the truths in the creation story, Jesus' history as Christ extends this understanding of the *imago Dei*. Even that earlier testimony, however, implied responsible human stewardship of the earth, despite the ideological infiltration of distortions from the social world at the time of that testimony. God communicated that stewardship to, and required it from, all humans, not only one class, one social stratum, one gender, or one race of humans. Thus, the earth's stewardship belongs equally to all humans: a stewardship that no humans should usurp from other humans or shirk for themselves. Also, according to the Christian symbol of divine suffering, humans should not exercise this function to deny meaningful life either to other non-human creatures or to any of the others whom God has created in the image of God. Humans, through the disclosure of authentically-actualized humanity in Jesus of Nazareth, discover that God has granted to them, and has required them to exercise authentically, a representative function between the world and God, in a way that resembles the representational presence and activity that Jesus of Nazareth exercised.[18]

18. This appears principally to motivate usages of the notion of the mediator, despite this concept's participation in a hierarchical understanding of the relationship between divine creator and creation (e.g., Heb 1:3–14; 2:9–18). In one respect, a priestly piety, such as that expressed in Gen 1:27–28, may seem to remain utterly, irretrievably, and dangerously anthropocentric, especially in a world where humans have initiated efforts to de-center themselves for the sake of the entire ecosphere in which they form only a small and very interdependent part. No one can deny, as Langdon Gilkey emphasized almost fifty years ago (Gilkey, *Maker of Heaven and Earth*, 117–62), that the scientific and technological development of the Western world arose from the central affirmation of the world's goodness in the Christian symbol of creation. One might add, however, that the extreme anthropocentricity that has developed at the expense of the global ecosystem (e.g., taking little or no care to prevent pollution, extinction of other species of life, etc.) may also originate from the anthropocentricity in the symbol of the *imago Dei*—one central component of the Christian symbol of creation. The historian, Lynn White, Jr., similarly criticized the Christian conception of love for its own contributions to the world's contemporary ecological crises. In one essay, he identified scriptural warrants for three human attitudes toward the natural world: the first warrant (based upon Gen 1:26–28) views the human as the *absolute ruler* over the rest of creation; the

In one sense, this symbol seems to espouse an extreme anthropocentricity: humans at the pinnacle of a created order, dominating everything below themselves. Because humans *re-present* the divine creator in some sense, however, God has granted to them their lives in order to function with authentic love toward all created realities and, thereby, to fulfill the divine creator's purposes for the creation as a whole. Therefore, the symbol of *imago Dei* promotes a radical theocentricity. Inauthentic actualization of the *imago Dei*, human sin, converts the theocentricity that God intended into the demonic, a radical anthropocentricity, as a betrayal of divine trust—a risk, nevertheless, that God willingly has assumed. *Hence, the image of God, as a symbol, declares* (in spite of its bold

---

second warrant (based on Gen 2:15) views the human as a *trustee*, for whom the rest of creation becomes the human's responsibility to tend and to protect; and the third warrant (based upon Ps 96:11–13 and Dan 3:57–90 [the *Benedicite*, found in the Septuagint or LXX only, having been removed from Protestant bibles because the Hebrew bible did not contain it]) views the human as a *comrade* of the rest of nature. He argued against the human as absolute ruler simply because of the damage that the human's arbitrariness in that role inflicted upon the environment. White also argued against the human as trustee, because of the reality of sin. The human cannot be trusted, due to extreme human self-concern. Thus, White argued for the third scripturally-warrantable attitude. Such an attitude, however, must purge Christian ethics of all prudential motivations: the human must care for creatures both in terms of the needs for their own particular well-being and in terms of how they and other creatures relate. Thus, humans must exercise a sort of "spiritual comity" toward all other creatures, at the core of which is "courtesy." Such an attitude necessarily requires, as White realistically acknowledged, a balancing of the rights of all creatures (L. White, "Future of Compassion," 99–109; also see idem, "Historical Roots of the Ecological Crisis," 1203–7). White developed his position, however, from something of a blind spot. Precisely because humans become responsible (and have the power) to balance creaturely rights (if they did not, then humans would always promote their own rights over the rights of all other creatures; humans have that kind of power, even if it is an ignorant and a dangerous power), since humans make such decisions about their own rights and those of other creatures, even this third, and definitely more adequate, attitude reflects a strong sense of trusteeship for (and, perhaps, even a bit of rulership over) the creation as a whole. Thus, White neither fully de-throned or purged anthropocentricity even from this third attitude. Therefore, I hope to dispel an illusion about the critique leveled against anthropocentricity. In human attempts to prevent the breakdown of the ecosphere that defines planet earth, reside both the human self-interest to preserve the conditions of possibility for human life and, derivatively perhaps, the interest to preserve the conditions necessary to sustain other forms of life as well. Such efforts never fully constitute purely altruistic motives in favor of the non-human, non-sentient, and even non-living others that both constitute nature itself and inhabit this planet. In the anthropology that the Christian symbol of divine suffering depicts, however, God has created possibilities for legitimate forms of self-interest—analogous to God's own self-interests.

claim that humans are like God) *that humans are not God*; humans re-present God; yet, God has not authorized them to thwart or to modify the divine aims for creation, even though God has endowed them with the capacity to do so.

Differentiation in Imago Dei

A fourth formal dimension in the image of God, then, indicates this symbol's humility: the differentiation that appears in the *imago Dei*. To state the obvious, the human, as *imago Dei*, is not God. The previous dimension signaled the appearance of this humility in its final claim that the human re-presents God. A representative, while *analogically* announcing another's *presence*, also *literally* declares that other's *absence*. Thus, human resemblance to God implies and requires human differentiation from God. Although in Christian piety a significant difference persists between Jesus as the Christ and all other human beings (at least, in terms of the central Christian attestations to Christ's deity), in the presence and activity of the Nazarene Christ, the previous paradox about human being as *imago Dei* discloses itself—yet, in the most intensified form. Even though according to this symbol Christ is divine, Jesus is also other-than-God as human. Christ, then, stands before both God and humanity as representative. Therefore, Jesus of Nazareth discloses *the* authentic actualization of human being. Thus, while the *imago Dei* in the human creature permanently persists despite its misuse and distortion, nevertheless, as created it also indicates the human's limits before God. Humans, though possessing a being in God's image, are truly other-than-God as well. Hence, while Christ discloses identity, likeness, similarity, or resemblance between the human and God, so too Christ discloses dissimilarity, unlikeness, or difference as well. This symbol signifies human dissimilarity from as well as similarity to God; in a sense, then, metaphor characterizes human being.[19] Only a

19. Wolff, *Anthropology of the Old Testament*, 161. With this point, I intensify Langdon Gilkey's insight (an insight that follows Tillich, of course): ". . . that potentially every creature is a symbol, and even more that it is itself only as a symbol" (Gilkey, *Through the Tempest*, 55). Karl Barth discerned this paradox as well. "He is the image of God in the fact that he is man. For the meaning and purpose of God at his creation were as follows. He willed the existence of a being which in all its non-deity and therefore its differentiation can be a real partner; which is capable of action and responsibility in relation to Him; to which His own divine form of life is not alien; which in a creaturely repetition, as a copy and imitation, can be a bearer of this form of life. Man was

genuine other can represent someone else, no matter how similar to one another the two individuals might be. Difference, otherness, or alterity also supplies the condition for similarity, just as similarity, resemblance, or identity provides the condition for difference. More specifically, only when God grants to the creature a being that resembles divine being does the God whose being is love create a genuine other-than-God both to whom God can relate in love and who can in turn relate to God with genuine love. Only a creature whose being is love can become a genuine other-than-God to whom God can relate in love. Love becomes love only if the lover can freely choose the beloved. This symbol prevents, therefore, the complete identification of the human with God and prohibits any kind of monism or pantheism. At the same time and on that basis, however, the symbol elicits the confidence that genuine love appears, persists, and is found again and again between God and the human. At this point, the formal dimensions of the *imago Dei* begin to disclose the material dimensions of the *imago Dei* in this second, although fundamental, presupposition.

Material Dimensions of *Imago Dei* as Love

Christian scriptures explicitly state very little about the material character of the *imago Dei*. Here again, however, the christological criterion of the Christian symbol of divine suffering most fully enables an exposition of this second presupposition. Not an analysis of human being, rather, an exposition of the divine being in light of Jesus' history, exhibits the material character of the *imago Dei*. For this reason, some Christian theologians of divine suffering describe human being

---

created as this being. But the divine form of life, repeated in the man created by Him, consists in that which is the obvious aim of the 'Let us.' In God's own being and sphere there is a counterpart: a genuine but harmonious self-encounter and self-discovery; a free co-existence and co-operation; an open confrontation and reciprocity. Man is the repetition of this divine form of life; its copy and reflection.... In this way He wills and creates man as a partner who is capable of entering into covenant-relationship with Himself—for all the disparity in and therefore the differentiation between man as a creature and his Creator" (Barth, *Church Dogmatics*, 3.1:184, 185; cf. Westermann, *Elements of Old Testament Theology*, 97–98). Emil Brunner developed a similar anthropology. "The first effect of this Being of God 'for us' is the Creation; this therefore is both the manifestation of His Nature and the revelation and the work of His Love: the gracious, kindly Creation of the Lord who in Himself is Perfect, who desires to have an 'other' alongside of Himself, and to have communion with him, who wishes to impart Himself to him" (Brunner, *Dogmatics*, 1:193).

as theandric or theomorphic. That the *imago Dei* is love constitutes the unstated conclusion in the logic of the two following claims in the piety that has produced this symbol: (1) that Jesus of Nazareth most fully discloses divine being as love; and, (2) that God created human being in the divine image. In this sense, as Max Scheler said, prior to the human's life as "an *ens cogitans* or an *ens volens*," the human "is an *ens amans*": indeed, love "awakens both knowledge and volition."[20]

As problematic as it may appear to describe human being as love, the two following qualifications at least partially dispel the controversy that this affirmation generates. First, the distinction between human being and human action remains an abstraction from actual experience; hence, human being as experienced always occurs as being-in-act, an *ens actu*. Second, when according to its own rationality or logic the Christian symbol of divine suffering describes human being as love, this symbol assumes that humans actualize their being either positively or negatively: *either* toward God and in fulfillment of the divine purposes as *caritas or* away from God toward other penultimate objects (as extensions of absolute human self-love) and in frustration of the divine purposes as *cupiditas*.[21]

20. Scheler, "*Ordo Amoris*," 110–11. In connection with his citations of Matt 5:45 and 1 John 4:19, Brunner concluded similarly. "It is the Love which God gives which streams back to Him as a return of love from man, that love which is to make man like God, that self-giving love which has no other reason than that it is love itself, ... The man who has been created to be like God is one who has been created in love, and for love" (Brunner, *Dogmatics*, 1:193). "The life originally given to man is being in the love of God. This gift, not merely a divine task, is prior to our empirical sinful existence" (Brunner, *Man in Revolt*, 104). Otto Weber similarly understood the *imago Dei*. "Whoever loves God acts in responsive 'analogy' to God's activity (see 1 John 4:19). To put it another way, man is in the 'image of God' in his predetermination to be one who loves. But he cannot love God without seeing his 'neighbor' as destined to be a co-partner in God's covenant and to love him as such" (Weber, *Foundations of Dogmatics*, 1:574). Also, Daniel Day Williams, a theologian of divine suffering, more clearly and consistently than anyone else, espoused and developed an interpretation of *imago Dei* as love. "The image of God is reflected in every aspect of man's being, not as a special entity but as the meaning of the life of man in its essential integrity. But surely this can be most clearly grasped if we say that love is the meaning of the *imago dei*. . . . This thesis that the *imago dei* is the form of creation for life fulfilled in love gives us our basis for the interpretation of sin. The root of sin is failure to realize life in love. The cleft in man which results from sin is more than the loss of a supernatural endowment. It is disorder in the roots of his being. It is the disaster resulting from twisted, impotent or perverted love" (D. Williams, *Spirit and the Forms of Love*, 134).

21. In this respect, such an understanding of human being reflects an Augustinian pattern: "Accordingly, two cities have been formed by two loves: the earthly by the love

Nevertheless, whether actualized positively or negatively, human life actualizes itself as love. Human being persists as the image of God. Following Augustine, I have designated the negative actualization of human being as *cupiditas* or *concupiscence* (ultimately an absolutization of *amor sui* or self-love), while the positive actualization of human being I have designated as *caritas* (contrastingly, then, *amor Dei* or love for God).[22] In the negative mode of the human's life or effort to be, the human actualizes itself as un-ordered love (*dilectio inordinata*), with its focus upon the world or upon itself through the world's objects. In the positive mode of human life, the human actualizes itself as ordered love (*dilectio ordinata*), with its focus upon God and upon all other

of self, even to the contempt of God; the heavenly by the love of God, even to the contempt of self. The former, in a word, glories in itself, the latter in the Lord. For the one seeks glory from men; but the greatest glory of the other is God, the witness of conscience. The one lifts up its head in its own glory; the other says to its God, 'Thou art my glory, and the lifter up of mine head' (Ps 3:3). In the one, the princes and the nations it subdues are ruled by the love of ruling; in the other, the princes and the subjects serve one another in love, the latter obeying, while the former take thought for all. The one delights in its own strength, represented in the persons of its rulers; the other says to its God, 'I will love Thee, O Lord, my strength' (Ps 18:1)" (Augustine, *City of God*, 14.28, in *Select Library of the Nicene and Post-Nicene Fathers of the Christian Church*, 2:282–83). As far as I can tell, although Augustine does not describe human being as love, clearly for Augustine humans actualize their lives either in love for God or in love of self (in its many forms); humans actualize their lives as love either authentically (as *caritas*) or inauthentically (as *cupiditas*). For Augustine, when humans properly order love, a proper self-love appears. Martin Luther's critique of self-love in all of its forms helps to clarify this point; but I will examine this point more closely in following discussions of the double-love command.

22. Even though the basic metaphors differ, the orientations that Augustinian categories express significantly resemble the basic Pauline distinction between σάρξ (flesh) and πνεῦμα (spirit). Thus, I will use the terms "*caritas*" and "*cupiditas*" to denote the authentic and inauthentic orientations of human life or actualizations of human being as love. In no way does my use of this distinction imply a negative view of sexuality, anymore than the apostle Paul's use of the distinction between flesh and spirit implies a disparagement of the material world. Admittedly, the apostle Paul uses these two terms to express a variety of anthropological and theological concepts. One fundamental distinction, however, retains particular theological relevance in the present connection. The two sides of this distinction represent, in various places within the Pauline and Deutero-Pauline literature, two basic orientations, attitudes, or modes of existence (Ridderbos, *Paul*, 64–68). More specifically, however, Rudolf Bultmann noted that the phrases, "κατὰ σάρκα" ("according to the flesh") and "κατὰ πνεῦμα" ("according to the spirit") (e.g., Rom 8:1–10), as modifiers of verbs stamp a mode of being either as sinful, on the one hand, or as of God, on the other (Bultmann, *Theology of the New Testament*, 1:237, also especially 1:239–49).

things and persons through God.[23] Thus, in the second case, human being actualizes itself theocentrically. Moreover, although I will elaborate
these thoughts in the second volume of these studies, *Evil and Divine
Suffering*, here I describe the negative actualization of human life in love
as the entrance of sin—in the sense that humans distort and misuse this
human capacity for proper or authentic love.

Thus, again, whether human being as love actualizes itself positively or negatively, it displays a threefold ontological structure of love
that resembles the structure of love in the divine life. At this stage, I will
concentrate my analysis of this second presupposition upon the threefold structure of essential human being as it stands abstracted from
both its negative and its positive actualizations. This structure supplies
the condition of possibility for any actualizations of human being as
imago Dei whatsoever. In the following section, however, I will discuss
only the structure as the condition of possibilities for either positive or
negative actualizations of human being. I will discuss the negative actualization of human being and its consequences in the second volume
of this study.

Looking to the Christ's history once again yields love's same three
dimensions as ontologically constitutive of human reality. At this point,
however, I examine these three dimensions of love through the characteristics of creation or finitude, rather than through those of the divine creator's infinity. Nonetheless, love's dimensions in this threefold
structure still appear within human life as most authentically disclosed
through Jesus as Christ: agapic, erotic, and philial dimensions.

---

23. Augustine, *On Christian Doctrine*, 2.22–27. Note here that Augustine ordered
the loves in terms of enjoyment (*frui*) and use (*uti*). When one enjoys something in
love, one loves it for its own sake (*diligere propter se*). When one uses something in love,
one loves it for the sake of something else (*diligere propter aliud*). One can genuinely
enjoy only an eternal (and therefore unchangeable) object. Thus, only God, as the true
object of enjoyment, meets these criteria. Therefore, humans cannot legitimately enjoy
changeable and temporal things; humans should use changeable and temporal objects
for the sake of another—for the sake of their divine creator. Proper love, *caritas*, uses
the world (and the self) for the sake of God and enjoys God; improper love, *cupiditas*,
uses God for the sake of the world (and the self) and enjoys the world (and the self)
(Augustine, *City of God*, 11.25; 15.7). While Augustine made useful distinctions, his
Neoplatonic ontology differs radically from the ontology that the history of Jesus as
Christ implies.

Agapic Dimension of Human Life

Once again, in Jesus' humanity, the first, or at least the most immediately apparent, material dimension of the *imago Dei* discloses itself through Jesus' self-sacrificial activity. According to the testimonies of his earliest followers, through the resources of his relationship to God as creator and redeemer, Jesus consistently shared every finite resource of his own life: physical, spiritual, emotional, intellectual, and so forth. Jesus willingly sacrificed his time and surrendered his space in the world, in order to communicate the power and resources of God's love to those in need. For that reason, Jesus went to the poor, the lepers, the prostitutes, even to the most self-righteous persons.[24] Thus, Jesus sacrificed his place within the traditional society in which he lived. Jesus sacrificed propriety as understood by his powerful contemporaries. He willingly endured insults for his behavior, behavior that his society defined as unclean, shameful, or even blasphemous. Jesus sacrificed his religious respectability before the religious leadership of his day, in order to minister to those people with the greatest need. Ultimately, Jesus sacrificed his own life, rather than flee from those whom he loved, but who had made themselves his enemies. In his resistance to injustice, Jesus sacrificed his own claims upon justice for himself, rather than retaliate against his persecutors and oppressors. The history of Jesus' actions, therefore, opens a window into the human being of Jesus: first, explicitly into his humanity's agapic dimension.

I have described this dimension of human being with the Greek term ἀγάπη, a term that resembles the Hebrew word for election-love, אהב (*aheb*), as the self-renouncing or self-transcending ontological dimension of human being as love.[25] As finite, however, this dimension in the *imago Dei* contains inherent limitations because God has *created* it. This agapic structure of the *imago Dei* is neither absolute nor

---

24. Witness this paradox in Luke 14:1—15:32. Jesus dines at the home of a Pharisee. Jesus then associates with tax collectors and sinners, actions for which the Pharisees criticize him. When Jesus proclaims the table-communion in God's eschatological community in chapter 14 as well as through his parables (most notably that of the prodigal sons and father) in chapter 15, he implies that God seeks the sinner not the righteous person. Ironically and paradoxically, however, Jesus declares that, in light of their self-righteousness, religiously-elite humans sin most heinously!

25. See Norman Snaith's discussions of God's election-love: Snaith, *Distinctive Ideas of the Old Testament*, 131–42.

infinite. A human possesses limited capacities and resources, obviously exhaustible resources. The human can actualize its agapic dimension with reference either to God as the ultimate reality or to some aspect or feature of the creation as the ultimate reality. When humans actualize their lives in love of the penultimate as the ultimate (whether or not the object of their love is the world as a whole, some aspect of the world, other humans, or themselves), then the human actualizes its agapic love as *cupiditas*, or idolatrously. When humans sacrificially actualize themselves as love toward the world, other humans, or themselves as God's creation (as penultimate values with their source in the ultimate value), however, humans properly realize this first dimension of *imago Dei* as love.

The following question arises, then, for the Christian symbol of divine suffering: Can humans love God agapically? God has created the human first to be oriented (at least structurally) to God as creator; God has created the human with a second orientation, an orientation that depends upon the first, toward other humans and the remainder of creation. If one defines this first dimension of love as totally spontaneous, or as unmotivated by value or need, then of course humans cannot love God agapically.[26] If, however, as I have tried to show previously, with agapic love, God perceives value in estranged creatures, and sacrifices for those others who are in need and cannot help themselves, then one can legitimately describe as agapic love the human response to God as

26. Anders Nygren did precisely this. Nygren defined ἀγάπη, as God's love, in such a way that humans cannot possibly love agapically. Thus, for Nygren, God always remains *wholly other*, as the early Barth emphasized as well. "If Agape is a love as absolutely spontaneous and entirely unmotivated as the love manifested in the Cross of Jesus, then it is plain that the word Agape can no longer fittingly be used to denote man's attitude to God. In relation to God, man is never spontaneous; he is not an independent centre of activity. His giving of himself to God is never more than a response. At its best and highest, it is but a reflex of God's love, by which it is 'motivated.' Hence it is the very opposite of spontaneous and creative; it lacks all the essential marks of Agape. Man's devotion to God must therefore be given another name: not ἀγάπη, but πίστις" (Nygren, *Agape and Eros*, 125–26). Along these same lines, although with at least some attention to the erotic aspect of human faith, O. C. Quick made the following claim. "Man cannot will God's good, nor reciprocate towards God the agape which he receives.... We must, I think, say that the highest love of which man is capable strictly as a creature is the eros for God, and that this eros at every stage short of complete fulfillment is in a manner self-regarding.... But we can manifest God's agape within us towards one another" (Quick, *Doctrines of the Creed*, 57). Also, by radical and insightful contrast, cf. Vacek, *Love, Human and Divine*, 130–49, 188–90.

well as to sinful human neighbors—since God has created humans in the image of God. Although this question remains very important, its fuller consideration must await further discussion, in chapter 7, of human life's authentic actualization.

Here, however, I only acknowledge that God has constituted the human as *imago Dei* with an agapic dimension. Thus, the human, at the very least, can authentically actualize this self-sacrificial dimension toward both the creation and God.[27]

Erotic Dimension of Human Life

Jesus of Nazareth also discloses the second material dimension of human life as love. In Jesus' life, the erotic dimension of the *imago Dei* clearly appears.[28] The second Christian canon remains explicitly silent about sexuality in the life and activities of Jesus. Nevertheless, Jesus was clearly attracted to people, to women as well as to men. Often, the narratives about his encounters and exchanges with women, in several instances with women involved in prostitution or adultery, yield more striking disclosures of the divine presence and purposes for creation than some of his encounters with the men of his society. Jesus searched for the lost sheep, the prodigal daughters and sons, those who had

27. Numerous theologians of divine suffering have discerned this dimension of the *imago Dei*. For example, ". . . in the act of creation God confers in some way his own nature upon all his creatures. . . . The image of God is only more noticeable, because more fully developed, in a human being than in a canary or a turnip. . . . Self-emptying, the principle of the kenotic Being of God, is the law of life" (MacGregor, *He Who Lets Us Be*, 142, 183). "Our capacity for sacrifice is but an element in our likeness to God (Eph 5:2)" (Mullins, *Christian Religion in Its Doctrinal Expression*, 238). Again, "love has been written into the character of God and into the ethical duty of man; not only common love, but self-sacrificing love. . . . If love is the fundamental quality in God, it must be part of the constitution of humanity" (Rauschenbusch, *Theology for the Social Gospel*, 271, 273). "What is thus revealed to us is that the relation of love is the original form of being . . . the core of being is love: communion. . . . . He [Jesus] is in *kenosis* as Image of the Father, but it is of a *kenosis* that he is the image. He would not be in *kenosis* if the Father were not in it. . . . We are made in God's image, and our vocation is to be like him" (Varillon, *Humility and Suffering of God*, 80, 96, 97). Almost all of these theologians, however, reduce the *imago Dei* to this agapic structure or dimension alone. In this *reductive* respect, their interpretations of agapic love resemble Nygren's concept.

28. With her "feminist hermeneutic of erotic power," Rita Brock illuminated significantly this dimension of human love that the Marcan Jesus disclosed. Her suspicion of patriarchal distortions helps immensely to release the erotic within the narratives about Jesus (Brock, *Journeys by Heart*, 67).

marginalized themselves and whom their own societies had marginalized. In his attempt to draw humans to God through his ministry, Jesus most authentically exercised this erotic dimension of himself as *imago Dei*.[29] Correspondingly, Jesus' efforts to direct other humans to God did not always succeed. As a result, his desire to gather everyone into the community of God remained, quite significantly, unfulfilled.[30] Jesus also expressed sorrow over the loss through death of his close friend Lazarus.[31] Moreover, the struggle within Jesus, between his own drive to maintain and to preserve his own life, on the one hand, and his drive to embody his message and mission, on the other hand (two legitimate drives finally and tragically conflicting with one another), also reflects this erotic dimension in Jesus of Nazareth.[32] According to the testimonies of his earliest disciples, all of these instances in the life and ministry of Jesus indicate at least one fundamental factor for God-become-human: as finite, the time of Jesus was limited; death stalked Jesus too—whether or not his death arrived via the aging process or via murder by crucifixion. Thus, the drive toward completion, toward fulfillment of his life in relation to God and his own short time and space, promoted a tension in Jesus between his desire for agapic attestation to God for the sake of his enemies and his desire to preserve the life that he loved.

This dimension of the *imago Dei*, which also resembles the erotic structure of the divine life, constitutes ἔρως. The tension that Jesus experienced appears in every human, according to the rationality or logic of the Christian symbol of divine suffering. Here, as in my earlier dis-

29. John 3:14–16; 12:32. In the fourteenth century, the mystic, Julian of Norwich, carried the notion of Christ's desire for his people even farther: Christ's desire, his spiritual thirst, his loving longing, to have all humans integrated into him for his enjoyment endures until the Day of Judgment (Julian of Norwich, *Showings*, 31).

30. The Gospel of Luke includes two instances where Jesus bemoans Jerusalem's fate, a city that had killed the prophets and the messengers of God's new world whom God had sent to her. In the latter passage, Jesus weeps over this loss: Luke 13:34–35; 19:41–44; cf. Matt 23:37–38.

31. John 11:33–35. This experience, of course, principally manifests Jesus' relation to the tragic region of reality, a consideration that properly relates to my analyses of the third divine wound, an exposition that I have reserved for volume three of this study, *Divine Suffering and Tragic Reality*.

32. John 12:25–27. This conflict between two goods or values within Jesus of Nazareth also indicates, according to the Christian symbol of divine suffering, the created or essential character of the tragic region of reality even within human life.

cussions of the ἔρως θεοῦ, this erotic dimension of human being also implies a lack or a need. In God's case, divine desire implied the lack of nothing that God requires to complete deity itself; rather, divine desire communicates God's choice to become interdependent with genuine others. In the case of the *imago Dei*, human being's erotic dimension indicates an analogous possibility. In other words, one can describe the human's erotic dimension neither as peculiar to creatures nor as peculiar to humans alone. The presence of an erotic dimension in human life, in itself, does not function as part of the definition of finitude. To be finite is not necessarily to be filled with desire for completion as compared to an infinitude that is perfect and complete and, therefore, in need of nothing and untouched by any form of desire. Nevertheless, because the human is finite, the erotic dimension, like the human's agapic love, manifests an intensity in its drive to meet its needs due to the limits of its time and space. The limitations that define the human's finitude always circumscribe the human's infinite desire-to-be.[33]

One should not denigrate this erotic dimension in human life as something less glorious than the human's agapic love. Erotic human love is part of God's creation and, therefore, by the divine evaluation, good. The erotic dimension also serves both to preserve and to fulfill creation. Without it, agapic love would lead quickly to the creature's dissolution, as it would also by itself even for God.

If the human loves God erotically, according to the Christian symbol of divine suffering, does the human love God properly? Furthermore, does such human love accomplish anything for the human?[34] If, through this dimension of *imago Dei*, the human attempts to re-establish a relationship with God, a relationship that the human has distorted, then, according to the Christian symbol of divine suffering, the human loves God improperly and the human's erotic love does not effect the human's reconciliation with God. If, however, with its erotic love, the human endeavors to know God more fully upon the basis of first having been

33. See Ricoeur's philosophical analysis of this factor in human existence (as the constitutional basis for the appearance of evil in human life: "fallibility") (Ricoeur, *Fallible Man*).

34. Julian of Norwich understood desire or longing for God as necessary to draw humans to heaven (Julian of Norwich, *Showings*, 75). Gregory the Great similarly emphasized human desire for God. For Gregory, the increase in desire results in a certain possession of God, which yields peace in the midst of suffering (Leclercq, *Love of Learning and the Desire for God*, 40).

known by God, through the divine efforts to overcome estrangement, then the human loves God properly and the human's erotic love deepens the communion or intimacy between God and the human, in the same way that such desire strengthens and deepens human friendships. With this disclosure, then, my analysis approaches the third material dimension of the *imago Dei*.

Philial Dimension of Human Life

By examining Christian attestations to Jesus' history once again, the third material dimension of human being as love also appears. In his interaction with people, Jesus consistently attempted, with the word and deed of divine grace, to liberate people from all forms of oppression. In so doing, he offered to them hope, dignity, respect, love, and solidarity in their plights, in short, mutuality, reciprocity, companionship, or friendship. Jesus raised others to stand with him; he did not raise them to become his subordinates; he did not liberate them to ingratiate them. This radical, even subversive, divine presence in human life, according to one story in the Gospel of John, Jesus succinctly formulated in a declaration to his disciples: "you are my friends. . . . No longer do I call you slaves."[35] The unity and identity that Jesus shared with the divine creator, Jesus disclosed to and shared with his disciples. By no means does this imply that Jesus led his disciples to consider themselves divine like God the creator. Jesus never erased *the line*, nor obscured it, between God as creator and the creation. He did alter and redefine forever, nonetheless, *the distance* between the two; Jesus re-presented God's offer to the creation of intimate mutuality and reciprocity. Jesus actualized this philial dimension of his life with God and humans.

I have designated this third dimension of human being as love by the Greek term with which I have already denominated the third dimension in divine love: φιλία, also similar to the Hebrew term for covenant-love, חֶסֶד (*hesed*).[36] By creating human being as *imago Dei*, then, God has constituted human life with a philial dimension as well. Through this dimension, the human envisions as its goal the web of companionship, mutuality, reciprocity, and solidarity with others. This

35. John 15:14–15.

36. See Snaith's discussions of divine covenant-love: Snaith, *Distinctive Ideas of the Old Testament*, 94–130.

aspect of human life, as *imago Dei*, contains the possibility for human actualization in relation to the human self, all created others, and God.[37]

For the Christian symbol of divine suffering, however, can philial love genuinely appear between the human and God, between creature and divine creator? On the basis of many testimonies from Christian scriptures and traditions, the Christian symbol of divine suffering answers affirmatively. This symbol relies significantly upon biblical understandings of *covenant* in order to develop this insight. Clearly, ancient Israel modeled its predominant understanding of covenants between Yahweh and the people upon agreements between kings and peasants, upon the suzerainty or vassal treaties of the ancient Near East.[38] The first Christian canon, however, contains two main types of covenants, both of which have analogues in the ancient Near East: (1) *the vassal treaty*, like those forcefully contracted by the Hittites with the nations that they had conquered; and (2) *the parity treaty*, like the treaty contracted between the two rulers, Hattusilis III and Rameses II.[39] Nevertheless, for Israel, even most of the parity-covenants occurred between conquering empires and smaller conquered kingdoms. As a result, ancient Israel described the relationships that developed between the entities in such socio-political models in extremely hierarchical and dualistic terms: su-

---

37. "To come into friendship with God is really to share his life; but the very life of God is love, self-giving, pouring himself out into the life of his creatures. To share his life, therefore, is necessarily to enter into like loving relations to all men" (King, *Reconstruction in Theology*, 208). Edward Vacek's analyses of philial love for God, as "cooperative friendship with God" (Vacek, *Love, Human and Divine*, 133–40), more closely resemble my description, with its emphasis on mutuality and reciprocity between God and the human.

38. The covenants between God and Noah (Gen 6:18; 9:8–17) and between God and the patriarchs (Gen 15 and 17) quite possibly do not conform to this widespread judgment. For assessments of the central issues in these discussions, see the following works: McCarthy, *Treaty and Covenant*; Mendenhall, "Covenant Forms in Israelite Tradition," 50–76; Muilenberg, "Form and Structure of the Covenantal Formulations," 357–60; Also see my previous consideration of this point with reference to divine philial love.

39. The Hebrew scriptures contain two different sub-types of the vassal treaty: (1) the human-to-human sphere, for example, between the Israelites and the Gibeonites (Josh 9—10); and (2) the divine-to-human sphere, for example, between Yahweh and Israel at Sinai (Exod 19—24). The parity treaty-form appears strictly within the human-to-human sphere: for example, the treaty between Israel and the Phoenicians began between David and Hiram (1 Kgs 5:1).

perior/subordinate, father/son, lord/servant, master/slave, and so forth. The use of such models, of course, often resulted in the structuring of analogous relationships between God (superior, father, lord, master) and the human (subordinate, child, servant, slave). At least according to the Johannine tradition, however, Jesus re-framed the divine-human relationship in terms of a friendship model. The Christian symbol of divine suffering conceives this emphasis in Jesus' theology as a move from the superior/subordinate-, father/child-, or lord/servant-model to a modified parity-model based upon friendship: modified because it remains a relationship between God (infinite, creator) and human (finite, creature). Thus, however small, a trajectory appears within the second Christian canon, even if not a fully developed theology, that begins to travel beyond hierarchical, patriarchal, and dualistic metaphors. Hence, one may discern at least traces of inferential testimonies to God as friend. Because God has fashioned human being as *imago Dei*, then, I also detect the five pairs of characteristics that I previously uncovered in the philial dimension of divine being (within their creaturely limitations) in human philial love as well.

I formulate the *first pair of characteristics* in a way that resembles my formulation of a correlative pair disclosed in the divine life. On the one hand, this final dimension of human being establishes the possibility for choosing the objects with whom to actualize this love. Humans possess the freedom to choose whom to love in this deepest way. Humans can refuse God's offer and, thereby, refuse such mutuality to God. Hence, humans can refuse this love to others and can refuse to accept such love from others. On the other hand, however, the second characteristic of this pair implies the possibility of offering such love to everyone whom the human encounters. Given the conditions of finitude, however, no human can actually offer such love to every creature. Nor can any human expect, when he or she makes such offers, either that others will accept each offer or that mutuality, solidarity, and community will necessarily result from the offer.

The *second pair of characteristics* in the philial dimension of human life also exhibits qualities that resemble the qualities of divine philial love. On the one hand, this dimension of human being includes the capacity to offer, not only some common experiences or knowledge, but also one's whole self to the other. To God, this offer means that God will experience the whole of each life offered in love to God. For the human who responds with love to God's offer of love, this response to God means that the human can or may experience the divine self to the capacity available to creatures or the finite. On the other hand, this dimension includes the capacity to respect the individuality, uniqueness, or alterity of the other, whether the other is divine creator or another creature. In other words, in the human's offer of itself, this form of love does not coerce or overwhelm the other with the self's presence. This human capacity does not seek fusion with the other, but rather genuine communion.

A *third pair of characteristics* lies more deeply within the mystery and radicality of the philial dimension of human reality. On the one hand, this dimension of human life holds the capacity for trusting the other. Offering oneself to another involves the risk of at least an initial rejection and possibly, if the other receives the offer, at most later betrayal. This is the capacity to place one's faith or trust in another. Certainly, this characteristic accurately describes the human's relation to God. This situation occurs, however, also in the human's relationships with other humans. All conditions of finitude conspire to deepen the difficulties and complexities here: for example, limited time, space, knowledge, physical and mental endurance. On the other hand, the matching characteristic involves the capacity for trustworthiness, loyalty, or fidelity to the other to whom one has submitted this offer; such an offer entails risk for the one sought in such love. While setting intentional human misuse of this capacity aside for the moment, still all of finitude's conditions conspire to prevent this capacity's full exercise in relation both to creatures and to God.[40]

A *fourth pair of characteristics* emerges from the previous pair of characteristics. On the one hand, the philial dimension contains the capacity for depending upon the other with this love. This capacity for dependence involves a willingness to draw strength from another person, one who remains distinct from one's own self: ultimately from God, but penultimately also from other humans, other creatures, and the creation as a whole. This capacity for dependence, or rather interdependence, signifies that, without the other, the one has refused genuine fulfillment. On the other hand, this mutual interdependence remains possible, only because the philial dimension maintains the self's identity through the

40. Again, this signals the appearance of creation's tragic region, as tragic reality and experience manifest themselves in undistorted or non-sinful human experience.

self's refusal of absorption by the other. Through this aspect of human life, the human can benefit and grow from the other precisely because of difference from the other, because of the other's alterity.

A *fifth pair of characteristics* follows from the previous pair. On the one hand, this dimension of human being involves the human's capacity for sharing its fundamental vision, for sharing its inmost interests, from within the heart of the human's being. Yet, on the other hand, as before, this also means that the human can express this fundamental vision only as an offer. This characteristic implies that the human can refuse to coerce or to overwhelm the other with its own vision. This respect for the other also implies an openness to disclosure from and transformation by the other's vision as well.

Once again, however, these three dimensions of love depend mutually upon one another.[41] Thus, for example, often Christian theologians construe ἀγάπη as the highest form of human love, precisely because of its self-transcending or self-sacrificial capacities. If the human were to convert all love to this one form, however, the human would lose or annihilate itself. Also, the human can actualize this first dimension of love as well in order to fulfill and to justify self-destructive tendencies, in the guise of serving higher ends or values connected with a genuine other, rather than truly serving the other. In this sense, the human would actualize the agapic dimension with a self-centered τέλος or termination. One wonders, then, how often and how authentically many Christian martyrs have realized this agapic dimension throughout Christian history.[42] As a result then, ἔρως, the second dimension of human being,

41. With my analysis of the dialectical relationships between these three dimensions of love, I have attempted to heed the caution that Jüngel expressed about the relationship between what he called the "eros-structure of love" and the "agape-structure of love": ". . . one should be very careful that one does not establish these different forms as opposing alternatives" (Jüngel, *God as the Mystery of the World*, 318). I have pursued farther than Jüngel, however, the analysis of love's dialectical structures in the Christian symbol of divine suffering, through my analysis of human being's philial dimension.

42. Perhaps Ignatius of Antioch (ca. 35—ca. 107 CE) represents one of the most notable examples of this point. See his epistle to the church in Rome. "Pray, then, do not seek to confer any greater favour upon me than that I be sacrificed to God, while the altar is still prepared; that, being gathered together in love, ye may sing praise to the Father, through Christ Jesus, that God has deemed me, the bishop of Syria, to become a martyr in behalf of His own precious sufferings, so as to pass from the world to God, that I may rise again to Him. . . . Entreat the Lord for me, that by these instruments I may be found a sacrifice to God. . . . May I enjoy the wild beasts that are prepared for

serves to protect, to promote, and to preserve the *imago Dei*. Hence, this dimension of human being checks, to some degree at least, the tyranny of ἀγάπη. Like the first dimension of human being, however, the human can actualize ἔρως in such a way that purely self-serving motives, goals, and norms would subordinate the higher values, in the service of which the human can actualize its agapic love. Thus, the agapic dimension of human being serves, at least to some extent, to curb the inauthentic realization of ἔρως. Without the third dimension of human being, however, the other two dimensions constantly struggle against one another: on the one hand, under the guise of the absolutization of the other, the agapic dimension (as enacted through an absolutization of the self as concupiscence) apparently exalts the self through its own self-destruction; on the other hand, however, under the pretension of self-absolutization, the erotic dimension destroys the self through its apparent self-exaltation. Consequently, the third material dimension of *imago Dei*, the philial dimension of human being, proposes the proper goal for the actualization of both erotic and agapic loves. With φιλία as the goal, thus, ἔρως defines the drive toward this proper goal: an end in mutuality, not in concupiscent ἔρως. In like manner, ἀγάπη functions as the mode of access, the method, to reach the goal of φιλία, instead of becoming concupiscent ἀγάπη. Thus, the philial dimension inhibits the absolutization of either self or created other. Even this third dimension of human being, however, holds the capacity to become concupiscent φιλία, without its dialectical relationships to the other two material dimensions of *imago Dei*. The agapic dimension supplies the possibility for preventing the use of mutuality as a purely self-serving reality. The erotic dimension of human being supplies the possibility for prevention of the self's loss in the other. Thus, ἀγάπη preserves the other's alterity or difference, while ἔρως preserves the self's ipseity or

---

me. . . . Let fire and the cross; let the crowds of wild beasts; let breakings, tearings, and separations of bones; let cutting off of members; let bruising to pieces of the whole body; and let the very torment of the devil come upon me: only let me attain to Jesus Christ. . . . Permit me to be an imitator of the passion of my God" (Ignatius, *Epistle to the Romans*, 2, 4, 5, 6 [74–76]).

identity. The proper realization of φιλία (mutuality, solidarity, companionship, and community) requires the authenticity of both the erotic and agapic dimensions of human life.[43]

43. In this symbol's anthropology, its dialectic between *agapé*, *eros*, and *philia* supplies symbolic resources for a Christian theological ethic. In a theological ethic that one might construct upon its basis, this anthropology suggests a dialectic between teleological and deontological concerns with reference to the neighbor, the world, God, and the self. From a philosophical perspective, Paul Ricoeur dialectically inscribed a deontological moment within a broader teleological ethic, in a form that resembles the dialectic that this symbol's anthropology suggests (see Ricoeur, *Oneself as Another*, 169–296). Also, Bonnie J. Miller-McLemore demonstrated an awareness of this dialectic in the moral life (e.g., in terms of "duties *and* benefits as two intransigent elements in moral discourse") in her theological analysis of death and its relation to sin (Miller-McLemore, *Death, Sin and the Moral Life*, 182).

7

Beloved Human:
Imitatio Dei *As Love*

Introduction: Actualizing Human Life as Love

IN MOVING FROM THE DISTINCTION BETWEEN HUMAN BEING AND HU-
man action to their union, through the present consideration of human
being's actualization, I note again the abstract character of this distinction: human being always remains, and one can examine it empirically
only as, *ens actu*, being-in-act. Also, the insights that this abstraction
discloses about this symbol's anthropological presupposition refer to
aspects of *essential* human being.

So far, my analyses have identified both formally and materially
the structural characteristics of human being in this anthropological
presupposition of the Christian symbol of divine suffering, characteristics of authentic human being or human being considered apart from
estrangement and alienation from God. As a result, both the preceding study in chapter 6 and the analysis of this present chapter examine
this symbol's vision of human life from the standpoint of the unfaulted
creation and, in that sense, in a way abstracted from actual human
experience—riddled as it is by the presence of both evil and tragic reality in their various forms. Thus, I have exercised a dual abstraction: first
the abstraction of human being from its own actualization (analyses
of which occurred in chapter 6); and, second, the abstraction of essential human being from existential human being (analyses of which
will occur in volume two of this work). Nevertheless, I have gathered
insights about essential or authentic human finitude or creaturehood
by examining God's reconciling activity in the history of Jesus as Christ.
Therefore, methodologically, I have discerned the features of essential

or authentic human life by reading in reverse the anthropological component of this symbol's story. Consequently, according to the Christian
symbol of divine suffering, the characteristics of essential human being
disclose themselves through the authentic human life that Jesus' teachings, ministry, deeds, death, and resurrection themselves depict.[1]

1. The *imitatio-Dei* motif, although best known perhaps through several notable
works of medieval piety, originates from both canons of the Christian scriptures, though
from the second Christian canon most explicitly. In medieval piety, Christians literally
attempted to reproduce the life of Jesus in their lives as *imitatio Dei* via *imitatio Christi*:
see, as examples, the lives and works of both Bernard of Clairvaux and Francis of Assisi.
Bernard conceived the imitation of God more along the lines of a "conformity" to God
by which the soul married the Word of God (Bernard of Clairvaux, *On the Song of Songs*,
83.1.2, 3). Other notable and influential medieval examples include *On the Imitation of
Christ* by Thomas à Kempis and *Theologica Germanica*. The issues that concern both
the presence and the extent of the *imitatio-Dei* motif in Christian scriptures have divided scholarly opinion. On the one hand, for example, Wilhelm Michaelis defended
the position that the notion of imitation, in general, is foreign to the Jewish scriptures,
or the first Christian canon, and that in those texts the thought of an *imitatio-Dei*, in
particular, is wholly absent; he claimed that Rabbis first introduced this idea into the
Hebrew scriptures as a development of the idea of the divine likeness (Michaelis, "μιμέ
ομαι, μιμητής, συμμιμητής," 663). On the other hand, Edmond Jacob, in his extended
discussion of "The Imitation of God, The Principle of the Moral and Spiritual Life,"
contended the opposite about the anthropology of the first Christian canon: "If man's
nature can be defined by the theme of the image of God, his function can be qualified
as an imitation of God" (Jacob, *Theology of the Old Testament*, 173). One cannot deny,
however, the presence of imitation-*terminology* in the second Christian canon, even if
one finds, as Michaelis claimed, such language only in Pauline and Deutero-Pauline
epistles. See the following examples: "I exhort you therefore, be imitators (μιμηταί) of
me" (1 Cor 4:16 NAS); "Be imitators (μιμηταί) of me, just as I also am of Christ" (1 Cor
11:1 NAS); "You also became imitators (μιμηταί) of us and of the Lord, having received
the word in much tribulation with the joy of the Holy Spirit, so that you became an
example (τύπον) to all the believers in Macedonia and in Achaia" (1 Thess 1:6–7 NAS);
"For you, brethren, became imitators (μιμηταί) of the churches of God in Christ Jesus
that are in Judea" (1 Thess 2:14 NAS); "For you yourselves know how you ought to follow
our example (μιμεῖσθαι)" (2 Thess 3:7 NAS); "Brethren, join in following my example
(Συμμιμηταί)" (Phil 3:17 NAS); "Therefore be imitators of God (μιμηταὶ τοῦ θεοῦ), as
beloved children" (Eph 5:1 NAS). Although this explicit terminology exists, scholars still
disagree: Does the presence of this terminology mean imitation in the strictest sense of
imitating the behavior of another person; or does it mean something like obedience?
On the one hand, again, Michaelis concluded that, not only does this terminology and
motif appear only in Paul's epistles, but in no way does the "call for an *imitatio Christi*"
find support "in the statements of Paul" (Michaelis, "μιμέομαι, μιμητής, συμμιμητής,"
666, 672–73). Nevertheless, on the other hand, Werner Georg Kümmel found both that
the terminology in Paul's writings recommends a notion of the *imitatio Christi* and that
the concept draws broader support from the gospels themselves (Kümmel, *Theology of
the New Testament*, 44, 166). Perhaps Michaelis resisted this motif so strongly because

Dialectic between *Imago Dei* and *Imitatio Dei*

In light of the previous considerations, then, this relationship between human being and its actualization also requires a description of the relationship between *imago Dei* and *imitatio Dei*, before I proceed with the more specific analyses of the *imitatio-Dei* motif. Once again, my analysis operates by examining God's reconciling activity in Jesus as Christ. Hence, although that method will yield the meaning of the *imitatio-Dei* motif according to the Christian symbol of divine suffering, the characteristics of that motif display the authentic actualization of the *imago Dei* in the world.

This dialectic between the *imago Dei* and the *imitatio Dei* resembles the symbolic framework in the Pauline distinction between the *indicative* and the *imperative* within the Christian's life. On the one hand, the Pauline and the Deutero-Pauline epistles represent the Christian's life as a gift or work of God in Christ through the Holy Spirit (*the indicative*, that which comes from God and that which Christians have already become because of God's work and through no efforts of their own): the old selves of Christians have been crucified with Christ; Christ has set them free from the law of sin and of death; they have become new persons created by and existing in Christ; God works in them both willing and working for the divine good pleasure; they have been created in the likeness of God in the truth's righteousness and holiness; they have died and their lives have been hidden with Christ.[2] Yet, on the other hand, Pauline theologies clearly perceive the active side of the Christian's life in which Christians must actualize this indicative, this gift of their new being (*the imperative*, that call from God for Christians to enact that for which God has enabled them): they must not allow sin to control their lives; they must kill the deeds of the flesh; they must put on the Lord Jesus Christ; they must walk after the Spirit; they must work out

---

he so thoroughly understood its meaning only in terms of its medieval expressions. He refused this symbol a scriptural basis, it seems, because this symbol for him implied a "pattern to be copied," "examples to be emulated," or "models to whom one is to become similar or equal by imitation" (Michaelis, "μιμέομαι, μιμητής, συμμιμητής," 667, 669). Most importantly, however, the concept of God that Michaelis held crucially required his resistance to this symbol: for example, when he refuted the use of Eph 5:1 as support for the notion of an *imitatio Dei*, he emphasized that the text maintains "the distance between God and man" (Michaelis, "μιμέομαι, μιμητής, συμμιμητής," 671). In this example, one senses the inhospitable presence of the *Wholly Other* once again.

2. Rom 6:6; 8:2; Galatians 3:28; Phil 2:13; Eph 2:15; 4:24; Col 3:3.

their own salvation with fear and trembling; they have put off the old selves and have put on the new selves; they should lay aside all of the practices of the old selves and put on the activities of the new selves with their hearts of compassion and love.[3] Without doubt, Pauline and Deutero-Pauline writings plainly declare that the imperative or the active side of the Christian's life arises completely from the indicative or the passive side. The imperative forms the conclusion to the indicative. Still, one cannot properly describe the imperative as optional; rather, the indicative, as the presupposition, requires the imperative in the life of Christ's disciple. Both require one another: the imperative depends for its possibility upon the indicative; the indicative exists in reality only upon the condition of the imperative's actualization.[4]

If the Pauline dialectic between indicative and imperative represents the dominant symbolic framework for understanding the origin and reality of authentic human existence in the second Christian canon, then that dialectic enables a proper recovery of the dialectic between *imago Dei* and *imitatio Dei* in this second presupposition of the Christian symbol of divine suffering. Even in the first Christian canon, the *imitatio-Dei* motif requires as its premise the *imago Dei*. Therefore, when the Christian symbol of divine suffering depicts the *imago Dei* as human nature or being, correspondingly it depicts the *imitatio Dei* as human function or actualization.[5] Hence, my previous brief description of the Pauline dialectic between indicative and imperative in human life helps to illustrate the relationship between *imago Dei* and *imitatio Dei*

3. Rom 6:12; 8:13; 13:14; Gal 5:16, 25; Phil 2:12; Eph 4:22, 24; Col 3:8–14.

4. See the discussion by Ridderbos of this dialectic between the indicative and imperative in human life (Ridderbos, *Paul*, 253–58). Martin Luther stressed this distinction in his lectures on Rom 9:1—16:27 from the summer of 1516, even though he did so in admittedly Aristotelian categories. "It is of no value for a tree to grow green and produce blossoms, unless it also bears fruit from the blossom. Therefore many die in the blossom stage. For just as there are five stages in the case of the things of nature: nonbeing, becoming, being, action, being acted upon, that is, privation, matter, form, operation, passion, according to Aristotle, so also with the Spirit: nonbeing is a thing without a name and a man in his sins; becoming is justification; being is righteousness; action is doing and living righteously; being acted upon is to be made perfect and complete" (Luther, *Lectures on Romans: Glosses and Scholia*, 434).

5. For example, texts from the first Christian canon assume the human's capacity for *imitatio Dei*: "You shall be holy, for I the Lord your God am holy" (Lev 19:2 NAS; cf. Lev 11:44). For two different expositions of these ideas, see the following works: Fromm, *You Shall Be as Gods*, 53; Jacob, *Theology of the Old Testament*, 173.

in the Christian symbol of divine suffering. This symbol first construes *imago Dei* as the divine gift of existence or being that resembles the life or being of God. Second, then, this symbol construes *imitatio Dei* as the actualization of that being. Thus, *imago Dei* becomes the condition of the very possibility for *imitatio Dei*. The image of God, however, only verifies its reality as the imitation of God; the *imago Dei* exists only upon the condition of its actualization as *imitatio Dei*. In this sense, then, one cannot properly describe the image of God as a human "task" that God requires, something optional that "appears in the course of history," "a kind of life which must first be attained."[6] The *imago Dei* is never *in fieri*, never in the process of becoming constituted by human actions. Rather, the *imago Dei* is already *in facto esse*, already constituted and completely in being. The *imago Dei* constitutes human being, defines human being. Nonetheless, the *authentic* realization of the *imago Dei* does constitute a task, is *in fieri*, may be understood as something optional that does appear in the course of history; this is the proper *imitatio Dei*. Of course, since in either of two directions humans can actualize their being as love, these two directions become two possibilities for the imitation of God as the actualization of *imago Dei*; and, therefore, this notion implies possibilities for both an inauthentic or a counterfeit (as *cupiditas*) and an authentic or a genuine (as *caritas*) *imitatio Dei*. Human actualization of the *imago Dei* along either trajectory, however, depends entirely upon the prior divine gift of that reality. Consequently, as astutely, boldly, and piously discerned during the patristic period, and as later assumed by theologians of divine suffering, by the divine will the human *can* imitate God and *can do so authentically*.[7]

6. Hermann, *Systematic Theology*, 90. Similarly, describing the human created in the image of God, John Caird said: ". . . it is to be considered that what this idea points to is not the *initial* or *original*, but the *ideal* perfection of man's nature. . . . It is human nature interpreted, not by what it immediately or actually is, but by what it is capable of becoming. . . . But whilst thus the ideal perfection of man's nature, which is expressed in the phrase, 'image of God,' is to be looked for, not at the outset, but at the final stage of the spiritual life, there is a sense in which it belongs to the original constitution of man's nature" (Caird, *Fundamental Ideas of Christianity*, 1:169, 176). For Caird, however, this image of God, though present from the beginning and therefore an essential dimension of human being's constitution, represents a principle, a "self-realizing idea" from which the whole human historical and spiritual life originates. One easily tastes the subtle Hegelian flavor of this tidbit.

7. "For God loved mankind for whose sake he made the world, to whom he subjected all things which are in the earth, to whom he gave reason, to whom he gave mind, on

Thus, while in one sense God does not invite the imitation of God as a human task, in another sense God does offer such an invitation. The *imitatio Dei* does not represent God's demand for humans to become by their own efforts that which they are not yet; rather, the *imitatio Dei* symbolizes the actualization of that potential with which God has already constituted humans. In the first sense of its inauthentic actualization (as *cupiditas*), *imitatio Dei* depicts the human effort of *preparing for* a not-yet-available divine grace; in the second sense of its authentic actualization (as *caritas*), however, *imitatio Dei* depicts the human activity of *living from* a prior divine grace. However humans choose to

---

whom alone he enjoined that they should look upward to him, whom he made in his own image, to whom he sent his only-begotten Son, to whom he promised the kingdom in heaven,—and he will give it to them who loved him. And when you have this full knowledge, with what joy do you think that you will be filled, or how greatly will you love him who thus first loved you? But by your love you will imitate the example of his goodness (ἀγαπήσας δὲ μιμητὴς ἔση αὐτοῦ τῆς χρηστότητος). And do not wonder that it is possible for man to be the imitator of God (μιμητὴς ἄνθρωπος γενέσωαι θεοῦ); it is possible when he will. . . . But whoever takes up the burden of his neighbour, and wishes to help another, who is worse off in that in which he is the stronger, and by ministering to those in need the things which he has received and holds from God becomes a god to those who receive them,—this man is an imitator of God (οὗτος μιμητὴς τοῦ θεοῦ)" (*Epistle to Diognetus*, 10.2–4, 6). Protestant theologians of *grace*, such as Anders Nygren, have often criticized the paradigmatic medieval work by Thomas à Kempis as oriented toward works rather than grace: "Even in His death on the Cross, Christ is regarded by the Mediaeval mystics primarily as 'exemplum.' . . . —but, be it noted, only in the Cross which *we*, as we follow Christ, bear" (Nygren, *Agape and Eros*, 664). Even so, à Kempis's work reflects a strong grounding of the imitation-motif in a prior divine grace: "O Lord my God, who hast created me after Thine own image and likeness, grant me this Grace, which Thou hast shewed to be so great and so necessary to salvation; that I may overcome my most evil nature, which draweth me to sin and to perdition. . . . neither can I resist the passions thereof, unless Thy most holy Grace fervently infused into my heart do assist me. . . . O Lord Jesus, forasmuch as Thy life was strict and despised by the world, grant me grace to imitate Thee, though with the world's contempt" (Thomas à Kempis, *Of the Imitation of Christ*, 3.55, 56). See the following mid-nineteenth-century conception of this faith. "As once a general, when his soldiers refused to perform some servile but indispensable work, shamed and excited them by working himself, so God, when his creatures shrunk from salutary and indispensable suffering, undertook to restore tone to the universe by suffering himself. . . . Indeed, this is that glory which he regards as peculiar and preëminent in himself, and which he proposes as the highest standard of perfection for the imitation of his creatures" (E. Beecher, *Concord of Ages*, 98, 155). See also the following from one of many early twentieth-century examples of this confidence: ". . . it is always possible for any individual to fulfil his destiny and to achieve the divine ideal for him. Such possibility of attainment follows from the fact that God never wills that man should accomplish the impossible" (Brasnett, *Suffering of the Impassible God*, 111).

actualize the image of God, that actualization remains the imitation of God: even though it can appear as either an authentic *imitatio Dei* or an inauthentic *imitatio Dei*. Notwithstanding the two possible directions of its actualization, this chapter considers only the essential (and, therefore, the authentic) characteristics of *imitatio Dei*.[8]

Imitatio Dei via Imitatio Christi

I introduce here an additional epistemological interlude. I have consistently examined the two presuppositions in the Christian symbol of divine suffering through testimonies to the history of Jesus. Attestations to that event identify both the divine being (and then the divine creative activity) and human being to be constituted as love. I have followed this procedure because human sin has obscured both the divine character and essential human being, according to testimonies to divine suffering. Hence, from the standpoint of the *Christian* symbol of divine suffering, decisive, trustworthy, and transformative knowledge of both God and the human remains basically unavailable without its divine disclosure through Jesus as Christ. Thus, even though (as seen in my analysis of *imitatio Dei*) this motif or symbol represents authentic or essential human creaturehood prior to the appearance of sin or human alienation from God (as the presupposition of, even the condition of possibility for, human alienation), humans can only know most fully the characteristics of this actualization of the *imago Dei* (as also the second presupposition of this symbol) through the event of Jesus as Christ. As a result, then, the Christian symbol of divine suffering epistemologically conceives this second aspect of the second presupposition as the imi-

---

8. "The Biblical commandment of the love of our neighbor, both in the Old and in the New Testament, springs from the proclamation of the divine generous love which comes first.... In the message of the Bible the gift comes first and the task second. Thus only where the commandment is understood as coming second does the rational principle of respect for human persons become the religious commandment of the love of our neighbour. For only there can love be understood as the love which gives, and man as the neighbour who needs this love" (Brunner, *Dogmatics*, 1:198). Bulgakov, writing upon the basis of the patristic distinction between the *image* of God and the *likeness* of God, said that they ". . . are related to each other as something *given*, implanted by God, and something *imposed* upon man, the task he is called upon to fulfill in his creative freedom. The realization of this task is a painful process full of temptations and demanding effort, but at the same time it is the royal road, an effort wherein *man can imitate God*" (Bulgakov, *Wisdom of God*, 121).

tation of God through the imitation of Christ. Therefore, the event of Jesus as Christ will once more, prior to my exposition of the dynamism in the *imitatio Dei*, elucidate, ever so briefly, the key to the operation of this God-given human capacity.

Certainly, resources from the first Christian canon abound for developing a concept of *imitatio Dei*, without recourse to the idea of an *imitatio Christi* either from the second Christian canon or from the Christian traditions that derived from that canon.[9] Yet, for the Christian symbol of divine suffering, the *imitatio Christi* most adequately and most concretely yields the *imitatio Dei*. Certainly, at many points, notions of the imitation of God from both the first and second Christian canons work reciprocally upon one another toward this symbol's correction and clarification. Still, the criterion of the criteriological principle, that *God discloses the divine self as love most fully and decisively in the life of Jesus as Christ*, determines the final form of this symbol's meaning.

Taking this epistemological point of departure, of course, does not resolve every problem that relates to the *imitatio Dei*. A return to the initial question of this symbol's validity by its detractors, however, enables the recovery of an additional important dimension of this symbol. For those who deny that Christian scriptures hold resources for this symbol, the following question focuses the issue. Does being a disciple of Jesus mean following the teachings and commands of Jesus, rather

---

9. Numerous elements from both religious and secular life in ancient Israel support this claim: (1) the exercise of faith in God, thus seeing things as God sees them in security and with confidence (therefore with knowledge, trust, and active obedience); (2) faithfulness or love (*hesed*) shown to other human beings; (3) the pursuit of righteous or holy life because Yahweh possesses this life perfectly (Lev 11:44; 19:2; Ps 145:17); (4) the human expression of joy (Ecc 2:26; 8:15; 9:7; 11:9ff; Lev 23:40; Num 10:10; Deut 12:7; 14:26; 16:11) like that of Yahweh (Job 38:7; Prov 8:22–31; also cf. Gen 1 and Ps 104:31); (5) the union of human will with divine will in prayer; (6) the expression of love (*hesed*) at the ritual level through sacrifice; (7) the human observance of the Sabbath day, during which humans rest like God had rested after creating; (8) the expression of conjugal love like that between Yahweh and Israel; (9) human work like that of the divine creator (Eccl 9:10); and (10) the exercise of love (*hesed*) toward those in need (e.g., Jacob, *Theology of the Old Testament*, 173–77). Of course, as previously noted, scholars disagree about whether or not the first Christian canon suggests an *imitatio-Dei* motif. Furthermore, as von Rad noted, even though often viewed as patterns of pious behavior in relation to God, the lives of the patriarchs often supply examples of deep moral ambiguity. Thus, to construe the patriarchs completely as patterns or models creates more problems for the idea of imitation than it provides biblical testimony for its support (von Rad, *Old Testament Theology*, 1:175, n. 16).

than following his example or the pattern of his behavior? Quite often, those who pose the question in this way quite clearly communicate that the second Christian canon has already chosen between *obedience* and *emulation* in relation to Jesus, in favor of obedience.[10] Is discipleship in this sense, then, singularly *obedience*?

In order to answer the previous question, one may take the following approach. If one must obey Jesus' teachings, then the teachings must represent real possibilities, possibilities that humans possess the capacity to actualize. In this connection, therefore, the historical actuality of Jesus, his real presence, and his living of the teachings that he espoused, become necessary for the follower of Jesus as Christ also.[11] Without both Jesus' historical life and his fulfillment of the teachings that he delivered to his disciples, those teachings remain only unrealizable ideals of the imagination: impractical values and, thus, so thoroughly susceptible to the powers of the world that they appear to ignore the harsher realities of life. Thus, with the following thesis, I extend this insight: if Jesus has already realized the teachings that he has delivered for his disciples to follow, then the dichotomy between obedience and emulation or imitation dissolves. If one has obeyed the teachings and commands of Jesus, then one also has emulated or imitated his example or the pattern of his life. According to the canonical gospels, on more than one occasion, Jesus referred to his own conduct as an example, particularly his actions as a servant of others.[12] In addition, Jesus challenged his followers to imitate God in several respects, although not in that exact terminology: for example, "be merciful, just as your Father is merciful"; "therefore you are to be perfect, as your heavenly Father is perfect."[13]

10. Michaelis, "μιμέομαι, μιμητής, συμμιμητής," 667, 669, 672–73.

11. Langdon Gilkey argued similarly: ". . . these ideals represent not only 'possibilities,' rather, as we have stressed, in him—in a genuinely historical figure—this authenticity or perfection was itself actual, realized, historical. That is, Christianity begins with and is dependent on an *actual* historical founder, a concrete person, one who really lived and who lived *in some such way* as we have described—else it be a faith merely offering us noble but unrealized ideals, a new vision, a new law—but one which no one has yet fulfilled. . . . unless he was actually loving, committed, self-giving, serene, in a word, 'authentic,' all this remains merely a hope, an impossible possibility. And also, let us note, if he be not actual, the important confidence that God loved the world in him remains merely an idea, a wish and in fact now a dubious one" (Gilkey, "Meaning of Jesus the Christ," 197; also in, idem, *Through the Tempest*, 104).

12. E.g., Luke 22:27.

13. Luke 6:36; Matt 5:48 NAS. Kümmel made this point (Kümmel, *Theology of the New Testament*, 49).

Here, then, an important derivative question emerges. What must the disciple imitate from the event of Jesus as Christ, in order authentically or properly to actualize the *imitatio Dei*? Formulated more simply, this question assumes another form. Must the disciple imitate everything in Jesus' life? Must the disciple reproduce the stages in Jesus' life: for example, must the disciple, to demonstrate her or his piety, literally carry a wooden cross or suffer martyrdom? Motivation for such behavior, of course, becomes important for this kind of imitation. *Why* should anyone imitate Jesus' life? What does it *mean* to imitate the life of Jesus? In many cases, historically at least, agents intended for such behavior to make themselves more worthy of God's grace.[14] This form of the imitation-motif, however, in no way resembles the challenges that Jesus issued. For example, even though Martin Luther exhorted his readers toward a version of the *imitatio Christi*, he entirely rejected, as one can see throughout his writings, any sense of this motif as works that might prepare a person for divine grace.[15] Furthermore, even though John Calvin also taught a version of the *imitatio-Christi* motif, he followed Luther in rejecting it as in any sense preparatory for divine grace. Moreover, according to Calvin, Jesus did many things that he did not require his disciples to do: Jesus fasted forty days once as his preparation for a certain task, not to inspire its imitation. Hence, for Calvin, Christian zeal requires also a certain kind of discernment and then a certain kind of discrimination in its expression.[16] Instead, Jesus

14. Nygren correctly perceived that, for much medieval imitation-mysticism (e.g., that of Thomas à Kempis), medieval Christians expected salvation from the cross that they carried as followers of Jesus, not so much from the work done by Christ upon his own cross—rather by their work in bearing their own crosses! Thus, medieval theologies of the *imitatio Christi* primarily regarded Jesus, in his death by crucifixion, as an *exemplum* (Nygren, *Agape and Eros*, 664).

15. Luther called the Christian to give herself as a Christ to her neighbors just as Christ offered himself for others, and to ". . . become as it were a Christ to the other that we may be Christs to one another and Christ may be the same in all, that is, that we may be truly Christians" (Luther, "Freedom of a Christian," 367–68).

16. Calvin wrote positively about the imitation-motif (Calvin, *Institutes of the Christian Religion*, 4.17.40), even though he, like Luther before him, tended to construe Christian life more in the Pauline terms of becoming conformed to Christ (Calvin, *Institutes of the Christian Religion*, 3.8.1). When Calvin discussed things that Jesus did which Jesus never intended as examples for emulation, Calvin legitimately criticized the abuses of medieval passion-mysticism (Calvin, *Institutes of the Christian Religion*, 4.12.20; 4.19.29). Paul Tillich also resisted the *imitatio-Christi* motif (Tillich, *Systematic Theology*, 2:122–23).

intended for the disciple's imitation to issue from the love that the sinner had freely received from God.

As an aside, and as preparation for later discussions, at least the two following historical factors affect many approaches to the *imitatio-Dei* and *imitatio-Christi* motifs. First, legalistic and literalistic understandings of the *imitatio-Christi* motif have contributed to the demise of its exposition and practice since the Protestant reformations of the sixteenth century. In addition, second, because for most Christians Christ has functioned as the unearthly Lord with unequaled power, majesty, and authority, the idea of imitation also has become inconceivable for many Christians.[17] The majority of Christians simply can neither identify with nor begin to imitate an omnipotent emperor. Thus, even where the *imitatio-Christi* motif found expression in Christian history, it remained a minor symbol; add to that its legalistic understanding as seen in medieval passion-mysticism, and authentic theological and praxiological interpretations of its meaning became rarer still.

The question, however, persists. For the Christian symbol of divine suffering, what in Jesus' life must the disciple imitate? If this motif or symbol does not include the accoutrements of first-century Palestine (for example, the food and drink of Jesus, the clothing of Jesus, particular religious and ethical practices and attitudes peculiar to his culture), then what claims the disciple's imitation in the life of Jesus for this symbol? The answer to this question, although available, makes the task of the *imitatio Christi* no less difficult.

Imitation of Christ entails an imitation of the *types or kinds* of activities, actions, attitudes, thoughts, and words that Jesus expressed or actualized, in which God most fully discloses the divine self as love. Hence, in such authentic actualizations of human being as love, the human always responds to divine grace and never pleads or searches for a yet-to-be-offered mercy. Furthermore, this answer appears most concretely in the double-love command of Jesus to his disciples: to love God with one's whole self and to love one's neighbor as another who is like oneself. In that command, not only did Jesus summarize the entire teaching from his community's scriptures, even the entire divine revelation, "the law and the prophets." Jesus had already lived and displayed

---

17. Hall, *Imaging God*, 187.

the realities of that dual command in his own life. [18] When I distinguish between Jesus' being and activity, I apply the anthropological abstraction to his life for analytical purposes. In reality, however, even with this abstraction, I acknowledge the indissoluble fusion of being and act in his life. Hence, on the one hand, from the human being of Jesus, arose his teachings and actions; or, on the other hand, through his teachings and actions, Jesus authentically actualized his human being.

Thus, according to the Christian symbol of divine suffering, God not only actualized divine love toward creation through the life of Jesus; but also, as an essential dimension in that divine activity, the life of Jesus establishes for humans the authentic pattern by which to actualize human being as love. Although God re-creates human life on the basis of divine initiative alone, with no human encouragement other than receptive response (the indicative), God provides a pattern, an example, or a measure of that to which the final product of that re-creation should conform (the imperative). Consequently, in the proper realization of human being as love, divine and human energies cooperate to attain the divine goal.

Attestations to Jesus as the Christ, therefore, enable the transition from the divine purposes for the human creature (as *imago Dei*) to the actualization of human being as love (as *imitatio Dei*). Jesus' history produced this body of testimony, this memory of the Christian community. Yet, this testimony, this witness to that historical reality, does not immediately or automatically translate itself into concrete historical actualities in the contemporary disciple's life when the disciple hears or reads it. An experience of this historical event (and its corresponding claim upon the human for the authentic actualization of her or his life), through the testimony of Christian scriptures and tradition, reaches the human at a pre-moral level; as the apostle Paul said it, ". . . do not be conformed to this world, but be transformed by the renewing of your mind, that you may prove what the will of God is, that which is good and acceptable and perfect."[19] Thus, initially, the human will does not

18. See the contexts for this double-love command in the well-known narratives in the Synoptic Gospels: Matt 22:34–49; Mark 12:28–34; and Luke 10:25–29.

19. Rom 12:2 NAS. One Deutero-Pauline source also states this imperatively, so that, even though God accomplishes it in human beings through Christ (e.g., as the apostle Paul says in 2 Cor 4:16), God gives humans the responsibility to actualize it (Eph 4:23). Christian scriptures illustrate the paradox of this divine-human coopera-

play the key role here in the human's encounter with the Christ, whether in the original event of the Christ or in later memories of it. Rather, the human imagination, as the vehicle of divine grace and love to the human and the initial vehicle, at least, of human reception and response to God, functions centrally in this meeting with Jesus as Christ. This insight does not prevent or paralyze human religious and moral experience or response, the authentic actualization of human being as love. Instead, through the organ of the imagination, God offers authentic possibilities to humans; here, the Christian symbol of divine suffering insists again on the necessity of the previous historical actualization of these possibilities in Jesus of Nazareth.[20] Without Jesus' historical actu-

---

tion: e.g., one teacher admonishes the Christians in Colossae (1) to put on new selves (2) which were being renewed according to a true knowledge in the image of their divine creator (Col 3:10).

20. Kierkegaard discerned the central role of the picture or vision of Christ and the correspondingly central—at least initially central—role of the human imagination: "every man possesses in a greater or less degree a talent which is called imagination, the power which is the first condition determining what a man will turn out to be; for the second condition is the will, which in the final resort is decisive" (Kierkegaard, *Training In Christianity*, 185). Walter Robert Matthews also perceived the imagination's key role. "The imagination is the link between intellect, emotion, and will. The will is set in motion through the imagination, and through the same means an emotional state is translated into action. The power of the imagination to 'make real' to the self what is already real in the outer world is one of its functions which is overlooked by those who agree with Bishop Butler that it is a 'delusive faculty'" (Matthews, *God in Christian Thought and Experience*, 230). As Ricoeur emphasized, the imagination "... is the organ of a veritable ontological exploration" (Ricoeur, "Language of Faith," 231). Ricoeur wrote similarly about Jesus' language: "... these limit expressions open up a problematic space not so much for the will as for the imagination. Do we not too often think that a decision is demanded of us when perhaps what is first required is to let a field of previously unconsidered possibilities appear to us? Would not the function of this type of discourse be, after having totally disoriented us, to make us take up again the path of a concrete ethic, but an ethic that is more mobile, more attentive to breaking points? And does not it first appeal to the imagination ... to explore the new and the possible in the order of the ethical space?" (Ricoeur, "Problem of the Foundation of Moral Philosophy," 192). Also see his development of these insights in his concept of "threefold mimesis." In Ricoeur's theory, the practical field's *prefiguration* in human experience encounters the practical field's *configuration* in texts through reading, thereby generating the practical field's *refiguration* for human experience (Ricoeur, *Time and Narrative*, 1:52–86). For the Christian symbol of divine suffering, the *imitatio Dei* becomes crucial, as in Edward Beecher's work. For him, God as a sufferer provides "the standard of human perfection." According to Beecher, "[God] regards his own character as more glorious, he is conscious of a higher and more divine power, from the very fact that he can and does suffer for the good of his creation. Indeed, this is that glory which he regards as

ality, Christian testimonies to divine suffering claim, such possibilities remain impossible possibilities for actual humanity. Thus, Jesus' life and teachings constitute, not only the event wherein God overcomes an alienation from God to which humans have enslaved themselves although from which they cannot liberate themselves, but also a pattern, an example, a model by which humans can measure the authentic actualization of the human being that God has created. In this sense, then, even though the living Christ makes the historical Christ present for, with, and to the believer, God also provides a picture that always invites the viewer to envision possible vistas far beyond the viewer's present experience.

Hence, this epistemological interlude identifies the imitation of Christ as the window through which humans may visualize the imitation of God. The way in which this process occurs further complicates the use of this portal. The human imagination, as the vehicle of reception and initial response, plays a central role in the actualization of human being as love, thus in the *imitatio Dei*.

Dynamism in *Imitatio Dei*

In light of my previous epistemological interlude, I now unfold the essential dynamism of the *imitatio Dei* (or human being's actualization as love). As I indicated previously, according to this symbol, humans may actualize themselves as love either authentically or inauthentically, as *caritas* or *cupiditas*.[21]

---

peculiar and preëminent in himself, and which he proposes as the highest standard of perfection for the imitation of his creatures" (E. Beecher, *Concord of Ages*, vii, 98, 103, 155). Also, in this regard, cf. William Schweiker's masterful problematization of the categories of imitation and mimesis for contemporary theology and ethics: Schweiker, *Mimetic Reflections*.

21. The theological anthropology and its corresponding theological ethic, along with their foundational metaphor of God as love, that the Christian symbol of divine suffering presupposes originate from a basic conviction that a large number of theologians of divine suffering hold: *the notion of love serves in various ways as the unifying theme or motif of the scriptures in the second or newer Christian canon.* To the contrary, however, Richard Hays argues that "love cannot serve as the focal image for the synthetic task of New Testament ethics" for three reasons. First, according to Hays, a number of major texts (he cites, as examples, the Gospel of Mark, the Acts of the Apostles, the Epistle to the Hebrews, and the Revelation) in the second Christian canon do not include love as "a central thematic emphasis." Second, Hayes claims that "love" does not constitute a "focal image," but serves as "an interpretation of an image," the

Caritas Trajectory

Because God has created human being in the image of God, humans actualize their being in love; in this, as in the exercise of their freedom (an essential component of human being), they have no choice; God destines humans to actualize themselves as love either authentically or inauthentically. Thus, in the actualization of the *imago Dei* as the *imitatio Dei*, the imitation of God may assume either authentic or inauthentic forms; human life engages either the *caritas* trajectory or the *cupiditas* trajectory of the *imitatio Dei*. Strictly speaking, however, one cannot properly describe human *cupiditas* as the imitation of God; rather, as *cupiditas*, the human counterfeits the *imitatio Dei*. In this section, consequently, I examine only human life as love in its authentic or essential dynamics, not in its aberrations as *cupiditas*. I will consider the symbol's construal of human life as *cupiditas* in volume two of these studies, *Evil*

---

cross of Christ. Third, following the lead of Stanley Hauerwas, Hays says, because the term, "love," "has become debased in popular discourse," the term "has lost its power of discrimination, having become a cover for all manner of vapid self-indulgence" (Hays, *Moral Vision of the New Testament*, 200–3). All three reasons that Hays offers, however, manifest serious weaknesses. One may legitimately question his invocation of at least two of the texts that he has chosen as so-called major witnesses in the second Christian canon (the Epistle to the Hebrews and the Revelation). Although one might dispute his claims about each of his textual examples on various grounds, his other reasons manifest even greater weaknesses. In reference to his second reason, one must simply say that the various narratives of the gospels as well as the remaining documents of the newer Christian canon themselves constitute in various ways *interpretations* of the event of the Christ as focused in the death of Jesus on the cross. Love becomes no less a unifying theme (even if not an "image" in the sense with which Hays has defined it) because it interprets the cross of Christ. Moreover, Hays has disqualified the theme of love as a candidate for a unifying motif in advance, by establishing a criterion that, by definition, does not allow the consideration of love as a theme. Finally, and most importantly, the last reason that Hays offers represents the weakest element of his argument. Because a concept has experienced debasement in popular discourse does not authorize ignoring the centrality of its presence in an exposition of the unifying themes or motifs (or "images") in the Christian scriptures (if that represents the goal of an analysis of the texts), especially given its prominence in so many texts of the second Christian canon (notably the Gospel of Matthew itself, which Hays treats quite inadequately, although he does acknowledge that the double-love command functions as a "hermeneutical filter" for the community to which the evangelist has addressed the gospel: Hayes, *Moral Vision of the New Testament*, 101). Most importantly, though, if one eliminates themes as unifying images on the basis of their distortion or debasement in popular contemporary culture, then Hays should also disqualify all of the central focal images that he actually chose as the heart of his moral vision of the New Testament: community, cross, and new creation have all experienced similar distortions in popular culture.

and Divine Suffering, through my analyses of the occasions for the first and second divine wounds.

Subjects of Love in Imitatio Dei

To display the deeper dynamism in the *imitatio Dei* requires an examination of the order of love or the subjects of human life as *caritas*. A study of the double-love command (often called the "great commandment" of Jesus) helps to identify this *ordo amoris*.

DOUBLE-LOVE COMMAND OF JESUS

I have condensed this dual command as follows: *love your God with your entire self and your neighbor as yourself*.[22] For Jesus, these two commands did not require human duties in two separate regions of human experience: on the one hand, in religious experience (the first command) and, on the other hand, in moral experience (the second command). According to the canonical gospels, Jesus indicates repeatedly that authentic love for God expresses itself not only in prayer and worship, but also toward and with humans in need: whether need for material necessities of life, emotional resources, spiritual sustenance through either affirmation or confrontation, forgiveness, or for something else. For Jesus, these two summaries of the entire divine revelation intimately intersect with one another, so that humans love God in the

---

22. In this form, all three Synoptic Gospels attest to the dual love-command: see Matt 22:34–40; Mark 12:28–34; Luke 10:25–29. The Gospel of Mark contextualizes this commandment within a "scholastic dialogue" between Jesus and a scribe, a dialogue in which Jesus praises the scribe's understanding. Both the Gospel of Matthew and the Gospel of Luke contextualize the dual command of love within a "controversy dialogue," through which, by the scene's conclusion, both evangelists have imputed to the questioner the motive of "tempting" Jesus. The Lucan gospel, with the lawyer's inquiry into the identity of the neighbor about whom Jesus had spoken, links this teaching to the parable of the good Samaritan; this setting, however, probably does not represent the original framework of this parable. The Gospel of Matthew, with this dual command, summarizes the entire teaching of "the law" and "the prophets," or the entire divine revelation. Furthermore, in the Gospel of Matthew, Jesus formulates this dual command with two texts from the Pentateuch. The first command (a quotation of Deut 6:5) originates from the *Shema* (the Jewish creed, which consists of three biblical texts: Deut 6:4–9; 11:13–21; Num 15:37–41); in the Gospel of Mark, Jesus quotes the "Hear O Israel" from Deut 6:4, while both the Gospel of Matthew and the Gospel of Luke omit this part of the text. Jesus takes the second command from the holiness code (Lev 19:18, 34) (see Bultmann, *History of the Synoptic Tradition*, 22–23, 51).

human other and the human other in God as well.[23] In addition, Pauline theology proclaimed both love for God (e.g., Rom 8:28; 1 Cor 2:9; 8:3; Eph 6:24 [Christ]) and love for neighbor; but, most often, when the apostle Paul calls for fulfillment of *the law* through love, he refers to love for neighbor. Paul principally describes love for God as *faith*. Thus, he formulated the dialectical relationships between love for God and love for neighbor as "faith working through love" (Gal 5:6).[24] Furthermore,

23. One theologian of divine suffering forcefully expressed this. "There is no divine pity, no sympathy, no love in human society, according to the gospel, save as it is mediated by human hearts. . . . We attain to the consciousness of the Eternal sympathy through the sympathy of good men. . . . The Infinite tenderness comes in but one way, through man to man" (Gordon, *New Epoch for Faith*, 151). In an eschatological parable, Jesus supplies his disciples with a praxiological epistemology for salvific certainty, one based upon the exercise of love toward those in need. Furthermore, and most strikingly, Jesus declares that, by serving persons in such dire straits (hunger, thirst, alienation from community, nakedness, illness, and imprisonment), disciples also serve him; and, he further insists upon such loving service, not only because he has commanded his disciples to love those who have such needs, but also, and most amazingly, because Jesus as Christ identifies himself as that marginalized humanity—and because that humanity also represents the people of God; as long as God's creatures have need, God in Christ remains in need (Matt 25:31–46)! H. Richard Niebuhr developed concepts on the basis of the intimate tie between the two love-commands of Jesus. First, Niebuhr's understanding of faith as a fundamental personal attitude or action illustrates this. Faith is "the attitude and action of confidence in, and fidelity to, certain realities as the sources of value and the objects of loyalty. This personal attitude or action is ambivalent; it involves reference to the value that attaches to the self and to the value toward which the self is directed. On the one hand it is trust in that which gives value to the self; on the other hand it is loyalty to what the self values" (Niebuhr, *Radical Monotheism and Western Culture*, 16). Toward God, Niebuhr characterized these two sides of faith as "universal faith assurance" and "universal loyalty." In his understanding of faith as universal loyalty, Niebuhr insightfully acknowledged the intimate union between the two love-commands of Jesus: "such universal loyalty . . . is loyalty to all existents as bound together by a loyalty that is not only resident in them but transcends them" (Niebuhr, *Radical Monotheism and Western Culture*, 33–34). He similarly stated this elsewhere. "Responsibility affirms: 'God is acting in all actions upon you. So respond to all actions upon you as to respond to his action'" (Niebuhr, *Responsible Self*, 126).

24. Nevertheless, although the apostle Paul only seldom wrote explicitly about love for God, "in a certain sense this can be called accidental since for Paul, too, love for God was the fundamental principle of true religion." Furthermore, as noted in the double-love command of Jesus, ". . . love for God shows itself in particular in love for one's neighbor. There is here a double commandment, but no double love" (Ridderbos, *Paul*, 299). Many theologians have understood faith and love, according to their interpretations of Pauline theology, as quite distinct from one another, the first receptive of divine love and the second active in giving that love to other human beings: thus, for these theologians, because the human cannot love God spontaneously and without motiva-

Jesus restricted the application of this love for one's neighbor neither to Israel, neither to the community of disciples, neither to the righteous, nor to one's friends, acquaintances, or family members. For Jesus, the category of the *neighbor* extended even to include repeatedly-offensive friends, fellow disciples, or even one's own enemies.[25]

In addition, although Jesus communicated about the reality of love through a dual *command*, nevertheless, these two imperatives *describe* authentic human being and its authentic actualization as life.[26] They *do*

---

tion (since the human always loves God as a response to divine love), Paul seldom speaks about the believer's love for God (e.g., Nygren, *Agape and Eros*, 123–33; also see, Furnish, *Theology and Ethics in Paul*, 203). "The content of the new obedience, in the epistles of Paul too, finds its most central and fundamental expression in love. . . . Just as faith can be called the mode of existence of the new life, so also can love. . . . 'To be rooted in Christ' can also be described as 'to be rooted in love' (cf. Col 2:7 and Eph 3:17) . . . . Love is mentioned together with faith and hope as the real heart and content of the Christian life. . . . Love therefore explains what it means to be in Christ, to be in the Spirit, to be in the faith" (Ridderbos, *Paul*, 293). See, for example, the following Pauline and Deutero-Pauline texts: 1 Cor 13:13; 1 Thess 1:3; Col 1:4; Gal 5:5ff.; cf. 1 Tim 6:11; 2 Tim 3:10; Titus 2:2.

25. For example, according to the first Christian canon, Jesus taught that God prescribes no limits to the number of times (seventy times seven) that a person who has been wronged must unilaterally forgive the offending person (Matt 18:21–22; Luke 17:3–4); in the previous connection, also see the parable of the unforgiving and ungrateful servant who, although his own master had forgiven him of vast debts, had exacted the most severe punishment upon his own servant for lesser debts (Matt 18:23–34). On the love of enemies, also see the following texts: Matt 5:38–48; Luke 6:27–36. Also see, in the Gospel of Luke, Jesus' parable of the good Samaritan, in which Jesus extends the meaning of *neighbor* to include even the despised person; this parable, as a matter of fact, does not answer the lawyer's question ("And who is my neighbor?"); rather, through this parable, Jesus shows the lawyer what it means to act in a neighborly way in any circumstance. Thus, indirectly, Jesus identifies the neighbor and, therefore, who is to be loved: the one present and the one in need (Luke 10:29–37)! Many other texts from the second Christian canon also encourage forgiveness of enemies, even though on the basis of a variety of motives: as examples, see Matt 5:7, 39–48; 6:12; 6:14–15; Mark 11:25; Luke 6:27–37; 11:4; Rom 12:14, 17, 19, 21; 1 Cor 4:12–13; Eph 4:32; Col 3:13; Phlm 10, 18; 1 Pet 3:9. This teaching even appears to a limited extent in the first Christian canon: see Exod 23:4–5; Prov 19:11; 24:17, 29; 25:21–22; and Eccl 7:21.

26. Tillich, *Systematic Theology*, 1:125. The apostle Paul also developed this position in more theological categories. One can identify a Pauline ontology of love. Paul personified love; but clearly, for him, the believer actualizes the qualities that Paul attributes to love (1 Cor 13:1–13). Human being, though, *is* this new reality (and, by implication at least, now humans have become that which God originally created them to be) only because of God's prior love for the human in the person of Christ and with the gift of the Holy Spirit (the gift of love) (Gal 2:20). Through the Holy Spirit, God has poured love into previously-alienated human hearts (Rom 5:5). Thus, although believers fulfill

not prescribe a certain set of actions to perform. As commands, they summarize "the law and the prophets" only insofar as they describe authentic human life, human love as God designed it.[27] Thus, these two commands describe humans as they love authentically, as they realize lives of *caritas*. In the canonical gospels, then, Jesus assumed the real human capacity for fulfilling or keeping this dual command. These commands do refer, however, to an authentic human existence, in relation to both God and the creation, that never realizes itself (neither from the beginning at creation nor especially after the entrance of human sin) without God's prior creation or re-creation of its possibility and never through some capacity that humans can develop on their own. Humans love authentically only because God has first (both in creation and in re-creation) loved the entire creation![28] For human life vitiated by sin, however, Jesus' summary both reminds humans of their failure to love authentically and invites them to renewal through himself as Christ who enables them again to do so.

Moreover, the human can experience this authentic life as a reality through a dialectical, praxiological epistemology. Two criteria enable human awareness of authentic human love or human life as *caritas*: as

---

the law for Paul through *loving the neighbor* (Rom 13:8–10; Gal 5:13–14), believers accomplish this responsibility only through the enabling love of God, through their re-creation by God's Spirit. For Paul, then, "the believer *is* 'love'; he has been made love in his resurrection to newness of life in Christ. . . . As a new man in Christ, the believer *is* love; that is the total meaning of his life and the reason why his obedience is the yielding of his whole life to God" (Furnish, *Theology and Ethics in Paul*, 199, 200).

27. For the Matthean Christ, at the very least, this dual-command becomes a canon-within-the-canon of the sacred scriptures in his own Jewish religious tradition. Thus, for the Christian symbol of divine suffering, joined with the fundamental claim that "God is love" and the corresponding claim of the *imago Dei* as love, according to Jesus, the dual-command of love becomes the guide to disciples for the realization of the authentic *imitatio Dei*. Moreover, also according to the Gospel of Matthew, Jesus provided for the disciples and their community this dual-command of love as a hermeneutical key for the interpretation of scripture. See my own work to develop a contemporary Christian hermeneutic of love on this basis: Pool, "*Non Intratur in Veritatem Nisi per Charitatem*," 159–88; idem, "Toward a Christian Hermeneutic of Love: Problem and Possibility," 257–83; and, idem, "No Entrance into Truth Except through Love," 629–66. I have considered and invoked this hermeneutic, although less rigorously, in the context of other studies: see Pool, "Baptist Infidelity to the Principle of Religious Liberty," 17–18 n. 15; idem, "God's Wounds," 60–61 n. 12, 187–211; idem, "Chief Article of Faith," 65–69, 97 n. 77; idem, "Christ, Conscience, Canon, Community," 429–34; idem, *Against Returning to Egypt*, 92.

28. 1 John 4:19.

the first criterion, the human can know that she loves God when the human keeps the divine commandment (to love one's neighbor); as the second criterion, the human can know that she loves the neighbor, if she loves God (by keeping the divine commandment).[29]

LOVE'S DIRECTIONALITY AND SEQUENTIALITY IN IMITATIO DEI

One further inquiry into the double-love command discloses two aspects of authentic human life as love, two aspects that hold significance for the dynamism of the *imitatio Dei*. First, this analysis identifies the *subjects or relationships* in human-life-as-*caritas*: the *directionality* of *caritative* love. Furthermore, this consideration of the double-love command also discloses the *proper ordering of those subjects or relationships* in human-life-as-*caritas*: the *sequentiality* of *caritative* love.

The Christian symbol of divine suffering depicts the heart of Jesus' teaching as his summary of divine revelation in the two imperatives: (1) love your God with all of your being and (2) love your neighbor as another who is like yourself. Hence, these two imperatives identify *explicitly* two subjects in the authentic human life, two directions that the trajectory of *caritas* follows: the human *will* love both God and the human neighbor and *should* love them authentically. In addition, however, for this symbol, the second imperative identifies *implicitly* a third subject of human *caritas*, a third direction that the trajectory of *caritas* follows: the human *will* love his or her own self and *should* do so authentically. This Christian symbol even suggests, on the basis of the second imperative's implication, an implicit fourth subject in the directionality of love's actualization: *divine self-love*.[30]

29. Johannine theology most notably depicts this: see 1 John 2:3–6; 5:1–2; also see John 14:15, 21–24, 28, 31. I have previously identified this epistemology in Matt 25. For a humanity re-created through God's action in the Christ-event, Jesus not only overcomes human alienation from God, by opening the possibility of renewal for humans and by offering to them divine forgiveness, but he also becomes the paradigm or model against which humans can check, measure, or test knowledge and experience of actual human love. In this sense, even though here I have examined the beginning from the end, the event of Jesus as Christ becomes the test of the criteria.

30. For example, Tillich said, "It has been said that man's love of God is the love with which God loves himself. This is an expression of the truth that God is a subject even where he seems to be an object. It points directly to a divine self-love and indirectly, by analogy, to a divinely demanded human self-love.... Without separation from one's self, self-love is impossible.... The divine life is the divine self-love. Through the separation *within* himself God loves himself. And through separation from himself (in creaturely

Interpreting "As Yourself" in the Second Command

Christian interpreters have developed inferences, and resultant speculations, about both divine and human self-loves principally upon the basis of the second command as formulated in the Greek language of the second Christian canon. In this command, as I noted previously, Jesus quoted Lev 19:18b. The writers of the canonical Christian gospels, writing in Greek, quoted faithfully from the Septuagint translation of the Hebrew version of this text. In the Greek of that command, the syntax emphasizes the verb (love) in the command. Thus, one should *love* one's neighbor as one *loves* (implicitly) one's own self. The Hebrew of Lev 19:18b, however, supplies a more ambiguous construction.[31] In the Hebrew, the question revolves around whether one should regard the phrase "as yourself" either as an *adverbial phrase* (as traditionally thought), and therefore modifying the verb "love," or as an *adjectival phrase* that modifies the noun "neighbor." More recent studies have uncovered significant linguistic support for the second (the adjectival) rendering of that Hebrew linguistic construction. As a consequence, however, a quite significant shift of meaning results. In the traditional Christian interpretation of this Hebrew phrase, the "as yourself" in its adverbial sense conveys the following meaning: love your neighbor as you already *love* yourself. In the adjectival sense of the "as yourself," however, the meaning's emphasis shifts to the noun (neighbor): love your neighbor as *another person* (also implicit) who resembles yourself.[32]

---

freedom) God fulfils his love of himself—primarily because he loves that which is estranged from himself" (Tillich, *Systematic Theology*, 1:282). To accept Tillich's definition of love, then, requires acceptance of the notion of divine self-love. Nevertheless, a twofold problem arises from this development of the traditional Christian viewpoint: first, a separation *within* God, of the sort that God must overcome in order to fulfill the divine self, tends to bifurcate the divine being into gods; second, although God creates that which is separate *from* the divine self in the creation, separation and otherness, or alterity as such, need not necessarily imply estrangement! In my analyses of the different moments in divine suffering, various expressions of divine self-love certainly appear. I have previously identified the basis for such moments of reflexive divine suffering through my previous brief description of reflexive divine vulnerability.

31. See the Hebrew version of Lev 19:18b. Here discussion and research revolve around the phrase that scholars most often translate, following the Septuagint (and, therefore, the second Christian canon), as "you shall love your neighbor as yourself" (New American Standard). Some translate the phrase, on the basis of more recent research, as "you shall love your neighbor as a man like yourself" (New English Bible).

32. The discussion about, and research into, the Hebrew form of Lev 19:18b has become quite complex. Scholars translate the problematic syntax of this passage from

At least two reasons recommend the adjectival interpretation of the "as yourself" in Lev 19:18b. This explanation, then, requires me temporarily to suspend my examination of the other subjects of human *caritas*.

First, within the second Christian canon, various teachings of Jesus have always produced some dissonance with the traditional interpretation of self-love that the second command implies. For example, consider the hyperbolic teachings of Jesus: (1) those who love their parents more than Jesus are not his disciples; (2) those who do not hate their families cannot be Jesus' disciples; (3) those who desire to follow Jesus must deny their own selves; (4) those who do not hate even their own lives cannot be Jesus' disciples; (5) those who do not carry their own crosses cannot be his disciples; (6) those who have found their lives, seek to keep their lives, or seek to save their lives, shall lose them; (7) but those who lose their lives for Jesus' sake will find and preserve them.[33] These teachings, whatever their hyperbolic value or extent, nevertheless at least seriously modify, though they do not eliminate altogether,

---

at least three major hermeneutical perspectives. The first interpretation, of course, supports the traditional translation with its emphasis upon the verb: "you shall love your neighbor like you *love* yourself." A second major interpretation, the one that my previous analysis construes as most relatively adequate, supports a translation with its emphasis upon the subject of love: "you shall love your neighbor as *another person* like yourself" (e.g., Ehrlich, *Randglossen zur hebräischen Bibel*, 2:65; Ullendorff, "Thought Categories in the Hebrew Bible," 273–88; Muraoka, "Syntactic Problem in Lev. XIX. 18b," 291–97). Martin Buber also seemed to favor this second interpretation of the command to love the neighbor. "The Bible does not directly enjoin the love of man, but by using the dative puts it rather in the form of an *act* of love (Lev 19:18, 34). I must act lovingly toward my *rea*, my 'companion' (usually translated 'my neighbour'), that is toward every man with whom I deal in the course of my life, including the *ger*, the 'stranger' or 'sojourner'; I must bestow the favours of love on him, I must treat him with love as one who is 'like unto me'" (Buber, *Eclipse of God*, 57). Also see the correspondence between Ullendorff and C. H. Dodd concerning whether or not the texts from the second Christian canon should be made to conform to the meaning of the Hebrew in the New English Bible (*Times Literary Supplement* [1 January 1971; 15 January 1971]). There Dodd refused this proposal, because one cannot dispute this command's meaning in the Greek from the second Christian canon. A third interpretation of the ambiguous Hebrew syntax in Lev 19:18b yields an even more complex translation: "you shall *love* your neighbor '*as if he were yourself*'" (emphasis mine). In this third viewpoint, the interpreter attempts to emphasize "... *both* the nearness of the neighbor and the quality of the love" (Derrett, "'Love Thy Neighbor as a Man Like Thyself,'" 55–56).

33. Matt 10:37–39; 16:25; Mark 8:34–35; Luke 14:26–27; 17:33; John 12:25. In addition, the apostolic church sometimes regarded self-love as opposed to love for God. For example, see the Deutero-Pauline opposition between "lovers of self" ("φίλαυτοι") and "lovers of God" ("φιλόθεοι") (2 Tim 3:2–7).

every understanding of self-love that Jesus' second command implies. Consequently, the adjectival meaning of the "as yourself" in the Hebrew version of Lev 19:18b illuminates connections between the double-love command and other teachings of Jesus, instead of exposing their disharmony with one another. Traditions from the first Christian canon in their Hebrew forms, then, helpfully correct the newer Christian canon and the scriptures (the Septuagint) from which the writers of the newer Christian canon quoted. Upon the basis of this clarification from the Hebrew scriptures of Jesus' double-love command, Jesus' remaining major teachings on love no longer appear to contradict that command. Also, the remaining teachings of Jesus about love consistently corroborate the adjectival interpretation of the second command's Hebraic form.

A second reason that recommends the adjectival interpretation of the "as yourself" in Jesus' command to love one's neighbor rests upon the correspondence between this interpretation of the command and Jesus' actions, at least as attested by the canonical gospels. According to the canonical gospels, Jesus consistently denied himself in order to perform his ministry in all of its forms: teaching, healing, and friendship. Jesus did not exercise self-denial simply to gain some eternal reward. God had not ejected Jesus from heaven until Jesus fulfilled some self-denying task. Rather, God voluntarily became human in the world, surrendering glory as God alone to live as an apparently insignificant human and then to die an ignoble death, in order to establish the possibility for reconciliation of humans with the divine lover and friend.[34] God's becoming-human, therefore, disclosed within God a divine self-denial for the sake of creation. Thus, the adjectival meaning of the "as yourself" in the double-love command more properly corresponds even with the overall character of attestations to Jesus' history, as it also did with Jesus' teachings. What does this interpretation mean, then, both for the directionality and for the sequentiality of human life as *caritative* love?

Directionality of Love

In order to answer the previous question, I will first examine the directionality in human life as *caritas*. Two subjects of the *imitatio Dei*

---

34. John 1:1–5; 2 Cor 5:19; Phil 2:5–11; Col 1:15–17; 2:9–10; Heb 1:1–14.

immediately appear: God and the creaturely neighbor. Human being dialectically actualizes itself as love in relation to these two subjects. As well as loving both creatures and the divine creator as others with value in themselves, humans also love God through their love for the neighbor, and humans love the neighbor through their love for God. Furthermore, one does not love the neighbor like one *loves* oneself; rather, one loves the neighbor because the neighbor *resembles oneself*, constitutes *a creature like one's own self*. Therefore, God has created and loves that creature in the same way that God has loved the one to whom God has issued this claim. Rather than eliminating every form of self-love, whatever the character and extent of that self-love, this claim entirely transforms self-love. Rather than being able to love the neighbor because one first loves oneself, one loves the neighbor because one has first been loved by the human neighbor and the divine other.[35] In Jesus' teaching, then, one must turn from self-love as the basis from which to love the neighbor, in order to love genuinely the neighbor as an other. If self-love were the basis for loving the neighbor, then any love for neighbor would not be love of a genuine other, but rather love of some aspect of one's own self in the other and, therefore, a love of the *same*, of one's ipseity or identity, in the other. Jesus' teaching, consequently, leads to a more radical conclusion about self-love. Because only a self lost for the sake of following the Christ truly finds itself and gains life, only through the love for the neighbor as a genuine other, as an other that God created and first loved, can humans discover their genuine humanity and, therefore, authentically love themselves. Authentic self-love, then, depends upon love for the other; authentic love for the other never depends first upon authentic self-love. Paradoxically, though, because one has first encountered the other in and through God—both the divine other and the human other—that authentic self-love arises simultaneously with love both for God and for neighbor.[36]

35. 1 John 4:10–11.

36. Thus, if I may apply a text somewhat poetically, "he who gets wisdom loves his own soul" (Prov 19:8a NAS). Martin Buber developed a similar view about the discovery of the self through the other: "Through the Thou a man becomes I" (Buber, *I and Thou*, 28).

Sequentiality of Love

The previous interpretation, then, transforms an assessment of the sequentiality in human life as *caritas*. Furthermore, even though one may perceive an ordering of the subjects in the actualization of the genuine *imitatio Dei*, this order differs dramatically from the order that classical Christian traditions developed. Classical Christian traditions developed the *ordo amoris* on the basis of Neoplatonic ontologies. These traditions discerned four objects of love: that which is above the human self (God); the human self (the soul); that which is on a level with the human self (other human souls); and that which is beneath the human self (the self's body). Thus, on the basis of this dualistic, hierarchical, and even patriarchal axiological framework, classical Christian traditions developed the order of love: as the object of eternal enjoyment, one loves God only for God's sake; as an object of use, one loves the self or soul also for God's sake, since the soul may participate in the enjoyment of God; one loves other human souls, also as objects of use, also for God's sake, since they may have communion with other souls in the enjoyment of God; the body, however, although also an object of use, appears last in the *ordo amoris*, since it cannot share in the enjoyment of God. Obviously, my description of the classical Christian *ordo amoris* omits numerous other nuances that I cannot examine here.[37] Nonetheless, the Christian symbol of divine suffering attests to a significantly different sequentiality in human life as *caritas*, even beyond this symbol's refusal of Neoplatonic frameworks. Even though an order of authentic love (in relation to its three subjects) appears in my previous discussions, this *ordo amoris* only appears abstractly. I represent this sequentiality serially as follows: love for God, love for neighbor, and human self-love. Nevertheless, these loves, even when authentically actualized, never appear separately from one another in actual experience and never in this serialized and abstracted way. Rather, as problematic as it remains both to express and to conceive in this way, this sequentiality appears simultaneously. The dialectic that emerges among these three subjects in my

37. The works of Augustine of Hippo and Thomas Aquinas represent some of the major sources for this classical Christian order of love: see Augustine, *On Christian Doctrine*, 1.22–35; and Thomas Aquinas, *Summa Theologica*, IIaIIae, qq 25–26. Also, see Stephen Pope's brief but careful analysis of the order of love in the theology of Thomas Aquinas (Pope, *Evolution of Altruism*, 50–76) for an indication of the complexity and nuances in this tradition.

previous analysis of the double-love command discloses this insight. Hence, rather than a hierarchy of relationships, a sort of spherical web of relationships, with God as the ground of them all in the core of that sphere, depicts the sequentiality in human life as *caritas* or in genuine *imitatio Dei*.

Human Life as Caritas

Finally, I arrive at the point in which various factors in human life as *caritas* converge, the point at which my analysis displays the full complexity in the *imitatio Dei*. As a first step, and also as a reminder, I qualify this final stage as an analysis of *authentic* human love, as an exposition of the *imitatio Dei* as *caritas*. I commence an interpretation of human life as *cupiditas* only in volume two, *Evil and Divine Suffering*, as the occasion of the first divine wound. Thus, as *caritas*, human being, through its three dimensions (erotic, philial, and agapic), actualizes itself in relation to the three subjects or in three directions (toward God, neighbor, and self). In a sense, then, because love is not a substance (though human being is love), love is *the between*, that which constitutes *the relationship between* the human and God, *between* the human and its neighbor, *between* the human and herself. Human life as *caritas*, *imago Dei* expressed as genuine *imitatio Dei*, discloses the human as relationality and responsibility. Without the others, both God and creatures, a human will not exist. Moreover, not in itself does the human exist; the human exists in the relational space between God and other creatures, between self and neighbor, and between the human and itself.[38] In that which follows, I schematically examine human life as *caritas*. The two dialectics that I have described previously generate this dynamism: (1) the dialectic between the three subjects in *love's sequentiality* (God, neighbor, and self); and (2) the dialectic between *love's three dimensions* in the human as well as in God (erotic, philial, and agapic).

---

38. H. Richard Niebuhr articulated a similar position. "The interrelations of self, companion and God are so intricate that no member of this triad exists in his true nature without the others, nor can he be known or loved without the others.... God's love of self and neighbor, neighbor's love of God and self, self's love of God and neighbor are so closely interrelated that none of the relations exists without the others" (Niebuhr, Williams, and Gustafson, *Purpose of the Church and its Ministry*, 34). In my expositions of the anthropological and creaturely referents in every moment of the Christian symbol of divine suffering, I attempt to identify the implications of this claim.

HUMAN LIFE AS CARITAS TOWARD GOD

Because the human actualizes authentic human life as *caritas*, human life as God created it to be, the human always actualizes its love toward God along this trajectory as response to God's prior love (in the divine creation, gift, and sustenance of human life in the world and through the world), as grateful responsiveness to divine protological grace. In the human's authentic exercise of philial, erotic, and agapic loves, then, the human exists in a situation of mutuality, reciprocity, communion, participation, and solidarity with God, the remainder of creation, and itself.

Philial Caritas toward God

In its authentic relationship with God, therefore, the human's philial love predominates. Philial love defines the reality that the tension between erotic and agapic dimensions in human being creates.

First, the human self authentically actualizes its philial love directly toward God. The self responds with trust and trustworthiness to God's fidelity and trust toward the human self. Completeness, wholeness, and peace characterize this relationship: in God, the creature discovers the meaning of its creaturely being; and, through the creature, God continues to enrich the actualities of divine experience. In the predominating relationship of divine-human friendship, the human endeavors to sustain and support the mutuality, the community, the solidarity between the human and God. Hence, human life as authentic love exhibits faithfulness or fidelity: φιλία in Greek, or חֶסֶד (*hesed*) in Hebrew. Every characteristic that appeared earlier through my analysis of the human's philial dimension enters into the dynamic of this foundational relationship. Only upon the basis of this divine-human community of friendship, however, does the human properly relate to the rest of creation, with a love that resembles God's love for the entire creation. Furthermore, the human's erotic and agapic dimensions conspire as well to maintain and deepen this authentic relationship of love.

Second, the human self authentically actualizes the imitatio Dei in the philial love that the self mediates to God through its love for neighbors or created others. This divine-human community makes itself real via the creaturely community through which it has originated and through which it transmits itself anew to each new individual and to each succeeding generation. In addition, such community includes the non-human creatures as well. Without this real creaturely community, the divine-human community would not exist. Hence, the self actualizes its philial dimension in relation to God through the creaturely community as well. The human loves God philially, through its philial love of that which God also loves. This love of creatures, however, does not elevate penultimate realities to the status of ultimacy. The Christian symbol of divine suffering never depicts the creature as God (with the possible exception of its christological claims). Therefore, this understanding does not reduce all love for God to love for creatures. The divine-human community persists even though it becomes a distorted and abused creaturely community and despite the breakdown of creaturely community. Rather, humans also love God indirectly, through their philial love toward all other creatures that God has created and loves. Such human attempts to engender community express mercy and justice as analogous to divine mercy and justice. Hence, the notion of "neighbor" becomes a symbol by which to understand, not only other human beings, but also all other non-human creatures. Such love offers, seeks to engender, and desires to sustain mutuality and reciprocity. This claim also implies that the self loves neighbors also for their own sakes as well as for the sake of God their creator, because neighbors are genuine others and God loves them as such. This foundation, as I will show more fully in subsequent studies, makes possible even the human's love for its enemies.

Third, the human authentically realizes the imitatio Dei in the philial love that it mediates to God through its philial self-love. Because the human discovers itself in relation to the other, the human can love itself philially. Although highly problematic, for several reasons, this concept communicates legitimate significance. The human self possesses a self-transcending capacity by which the human can valorize the other more highly than itself. As a note, the agapic dimension holds the key to this capacity of self-transcendence. Nevertheless, because the human possesses this capacity, the human can experience and perceive itself as a created other that resembles all created others. Therefore, the self can then actualize its philial love toward itself for its own sake, as a creature also similarly valorized by God. In so doing, the self also expresses philial love to God indirectly, insofar as the human self has first loved God as the ultimate reality in and for God's sake.

This relationship of community, solidarity, mutual fidelity, reciprocity, and friendship constitutes the normal, genuine, authentic, or essential relationship between God and the human. The Hebrew term *"shalom"* fully expresses both the extent and the richness that this dimension of human life as *caritas* between God and human reality engenders. This philial reality assumes its form, not only directly in the love that God and the human share, but also indirectly through both neighbor-love and self-love.

Erotic Caritas toward God

Fulfillment of the philial relationship or community, however, does not imply *stasis*. This community of friendship does not represent the state of *rest* as conceived in classical Christian theism's concept of heaven. No matter how complete, no matter how perfect, no matter how authentic the actualization of creaturely life (in this case human being), human life always holds potentiality and possibility for growth, change, and development; *stasis* finds no place even in the divine life.

First, the human authentically actualizes its erotic love directly toward God. Hence, always active, even within the predominance of the philial relationship, through its erotic love, the human strives to know the divine lover and friend more deeply as well as to understand that knowledge more completely. God as the ultimate reality, as infinite creator, as loving mystery, always remains far more than creatures have experienced and can experience, as well as far more than the human self has known or may know about that human experience of God. In addition, because God embraces growth and enrichment, no creature ever can possibly exhaust the wealth of the divine life. Because the human is the image of God (and, therefore, constituted as a genuine other-than-God even though like God), even God continues to develop the relationship between God and the human from the divine side and for God's sake as well. Once again, however, such human love for God operates on a dual basis: first, the divine other has always already loved human alterity into being; and, second, the divine lover and friend has always already sought more fully to know the beloved human. Consequently, this symbol does not categorize human erotic *caritas* as *works* (as contrasted with faith). Authentic erotic love enriches or deepens the mutuality or reciprocity of divine-human friendship. Although through its erotic love the human desires love from and inclusion by God, the human also desires its own fulfillment or satisfaction with the knowledge and the enjoyment of that love.

Second, however, the human self truly actualizes its erotic dimension through the authentic erotic love that it mediates to God in its authentic erotic love for the neighbor. Here also, by extension, the term "neighbor" refers to the entire creation. The human most completely loves God through the neighbor by desiring for that creaturely other its participation in the divine-human community of friendship, for there the neighbor can most authentically actualize its own life. Still, through its erotic love as human life's preservative and enriching drive, the human endeavors to deepen its own community with God, as well as with other creatures for their own sakes, through those created others. Nevertheless, the human's agapic dimension prevents its erotic love from absorbing created others and from using God solely for the self's own sake: in both cases, such self-love would tend to deify the human self.

Third, the human indirectly actualizes its authentic erotic love for God through its authentic erotic self-love. In its self-expression as human desire for the divine other, as ἔρως, the human therefore preserves its own otherness and attempts to fulfill its own needs, even in its effort to know more fully its divine lover and friend and to do so through created others as well. In this material dimension of human life, human erotic love for God through human erotic self-love (though indirect here also) more clearly discloses itself. Here the human self perceives itself as an other whom God desires for the human's own sake. Thus, the human legitimately seeks to promote itself, through its erotic love for itself, in order to love that which God loves (the human, in this case) and, in so doing, to love God erotically through this authentic human erotic self-love.

Agapic Caritas toward God

Self-transcendence and self-sacrifice characterize the foundational capacities of agapic human life. This dimension of human love enables the human to exercise self-abnegation for God and God's purposes, on the basis of the human's fidelity to the community between divine creator and creatures. Due to that faithfulness, the human desires to build and to sustain the breadth and depth of that community. Only through human faithfulness to that authentic divine-human relationship does the human's agapic dimension actualize itself authentically.

First, the human authentically actualizes its agapic love directly toward the divine other. The human's authentic agapic love restrains any tendency toward human self-absolutization through the human's erotic love. Actualized toward God, the human's agapic love prevents the human from elevating any created other to the status of ultimate reality; it prevents, most basically, the elevation of the human self to divine status. Thus, because the human trusts the divine wisdom, love, and strength, human life can authentically actualize itself agapically in relation to the divine other, in such situations where human self-sacrifice (from the most minor to the most extreme degrees) becomes necessary in order to accomplish God's purposes for other aspects of the creation or for the divine life itself. Nevertheless, in its agapic love for God, the human always responds to a prior divine agapic love for creation. Thus, the *imago Dei* actualizes itself in its agapic love for God as *imitatio Dei*.

Second, the human also mediates to God an agapic love through the self's agapic love for neighbor. The human actualizes itself as love indirectly toward God, when the human sacrifices itself in order to preserve and promote other aspects of creaturely being. Naturally, such efforts become problematic, simply because the human always preserves or promotes some aspects of creation at the expense of other aspects: in this case, for example, the preservation or enrichment of at least one human or some other creature at the expense of the self-abnegating human. In this human love, which resembles the divine activity (and, therefore, authentic imitation of God), the human loves God in the human's agapic love for created others; in human self-abnegation, the self fulfills a divine love for those others as well. Nevertheless, even though the human's love of neighbor for the neighbor's own sake may also express itself in such love, the human's authentic erotic love restrains the human's agapic love from any absolutization or deification of the created other, from elevating the created other or neighbor to the status of ultimacy. Furthermore, the human's agapic dimension actualizes itself in relation to God through the human's agapic love for the neighbor, also in order to fulfill human reciprocity and mutuality to God; thereby, the agapic love operates in order to preserve and promote community between the divine creator and the creation.

Third, human agapic love toward God also actualizes itself indirectly through agapic self-love. With the notion of agapic self-love, however, more difficult problems come to the surface. Can the self sacrifice itself in love for God through a self-sacrificial love of itself? For the Christian symbol of divine suffering, the human can sacrifice or transcend its whole self, or even aspects of itself, in order to become most fully that for which God has created the human. When the human exercises such agapic self-love, then the human has indirectly actualized its agapic love for God through agapic self-love, for the self has sacrificed aspects of itself in order to contribute to the realization of the divine purposes for itself. Paradoxically, the human also actualizes its erotic love in such an operation, in its *desire* to promote the agapic love for God through agapic self-love. This, in turn, deepens the authentic divine-human community of friendship, through the human's imitation of God's self-sacrificial and self-transcending love toward creation.

HUMAN LIFE AS CARITAS TOWARD NEIGHBOR

The human also authentically actualizes the three material dimensions of its life as love in relation to the creaturely neighbor. In human life as *caritas* for neighbor, all three material dimensions of the *imago Dei* dialectically relate to one another in a manner that resembles their relationships to one another in love for God.

Philial Caritas toward Neighbor

The human's philial love realizes the essential or authentic relationship between the human self and its neighbor, between humans and all created others. This relationship of love, like that between the human and God, establishes itself as a relationship of community, solidarity, mutuality, reciprocity, fidelity, trustworthiness, and wholeness or peace (*shalom*). As such, the human self's philial love for neighbor deepens and preserves itself through both erotic and agapic human loves as well.

First, through its direct authentic philial love for God, the human mediates its philial love toward the neighbor. Through the divine-human community of friendship, the human experiences the genuine meaning and nature of the neighbor, of *all created others as neighbors.*[39]

---

39. See Sallie McFague's excellent insights into Christian love for the larger creation: McFague, *Super, Natural Christians*, especially 91–178.

Previously, with regard to the proper human love for God, I have described how, for the Christian symbol of divine suffering, the human indirectly actualizes its authentic philial love toward God through its direct philial love for neighbor. At this point, then, the other side of this dialectic appears. The human indirectly realizes its proper philial love for neighbor, love that sustains and deepens community, solidarity, justice, mutuality, fidelity, and so forth, through the human's authentic and direct actualization of its philial love for God.

Second, the human properly actualizes its philial love for neighbor directly, because of the neighbor's value in itself. Through love for the neighbor in God, the human discerns the neighbor as a genuine other. Paradoxically, God, though the creator of all creaturely others, endows all creatures with an alterity that God values precisely because of that otherness in itself. God has created nothing that one can designate as an extension of the divine self. The creation is other-than-God, even though and precisely because God has created the human as *imago Dei.* Through that alterity, God established the condition for community between the divine self and creation. Without that otherness, no community, no divine friendship with creation would have been possible. As a consequence, the human most deeply loves the neighbor philially when the human self promotes, preserves, sustains, and develops the philial relationship between God and neighbor.[40] This dimension of love for

---

40. I will re-emphasize this point in reference to both erotic and agapic loves for neighbor. Perhaps the Gospel of Matthew supplies one of the most poignant testimonies to the unity of these two commandments in one of Jesus' eschatological parables. There Jesus identifies love for Christ with love for needy and distressed humans. Those who fail to minister to humans in distress also fail to love God: in this case, the Christ who is present in afflicted humans (Matt 25:31–46). A second testimony from a Johannine text most explicitly announces the unity of love for God with love for neighbor (even though the author of this text perceived neighbors as other members of the Christian community or "brothers"): "If some one says, 'I love God,' and hates his brother, he is a liar; for the one who does not love his brother whom he has seen, cannot love God whom he has not seen. And this commandment we have from Him, that the one who loves God should love his brother also" (1 John 4:20–21 NAS). Augustine stressed this point: proper love for neighbor urges the neighbor to love God with her or his whole person (Augustine, *On Christian Doctrine*, 1.22.21). Gene Outka also discussed this call as the encouragement toward "conscious life in relation to God" (Outka, *Agape*, 263). Stephen Post argued strongly for a renewal of this neglected theme in contemporary discussions of neighbor-love (Post, "Purpose of Neighbor-Love," 181–93). From a similar perspective, see Karl Rahner's discussions of the radical union of the love commands; in particular, see his understanding of this union in relation to his notion of

neighbor mediates between the two great commandments as formulated by Jesus. Thus, in a manner analogous to the divine activity, the
human loves the neighbor as a genuine other, precisely because of that
otherness. Hence, the human can deepen and sustain the fundamental human relationship of love—friendship—in the various creaturely
communities: the religious, the natural, the familial, the political, and
so forth.

*Third, through its authentic and immediate or direct philial self-love,
the human mediates philial love to the neighbor.* Through the disclosure
of creaturely alterity in its relationships with God, the human self discovers its own otherness as well. Through the human's promotion of
mutuality, solidarity, mercy, and justice toward itself within community,
the human supports, preserves, and promotes its actualization of human
being as friendship toward all created others. For, again paradoxically,
the human promotes its identity with its neighbor. This human similarity to all created others corresponds to their creaturely characteristics.
In a sense, then, because God has created all creatures, they share an
equality with one another. The human's preservation of this equality
for the sake of equality itself, discerned through the human's authentic
philial love for itself, actualizes human philial love toward the neighbor
as well.

Erotic Caritas toward Neighbor

The human's authentic erotic love for neighbor sustains and deepens
the essential and authentic relationship that the human expresses in and
through its philial love for neighbor. The erotic dimension of human life
accomplishes this principally while preserving and promoting the self's
interests, although the human self's erotic love first focuses upon God
and then upon neighbor.

*First, the human actualizes its authentic erotic love indirectly to-
ward the neighbor through its authentic and direct erotic love for God.*
At this point, the dialectical correlate of the indirect erotic love for God
through the direct erotic love for neighbor appears. Through a direct
erotic love for God, the human desires to deepen the community of
friendship between itself and God. Through this direct erotic love to-

---

"anonymous Christianity" (Rahner, "Reflections on the Unity of the Love of Neighbour
and the Love of God," 231–49).

ward God, the human, therefore, indirectly loves the neighbor. Only from human fidelity to the mutuality within the divine-human community does the human's erotic love arise, a drive that can deepen this philial love. Because that community includes the neighbor, then, the human indirectly loves the neighbor in its direct erotic love for God. Without the erotic drive to deepen that divine-human community, the human's erotic love would seek to use and ultimately to absorb creaturely others. In its authentic and indirect erotic love for the neighbor through its direct erotic love for God, however, the human indirectly desires the best for its creaturely neighbors.

Second, the human directly loves the neighbor erotically because the neighbor, whether human or non-human, possesses value in itself. Although God created the neighbor, God has endowed it, as a creature, with genuine alterity. Thus, the human, in its direct erotic love for the neighbor, can desire the neighbor for human community, solidarity, mutuality, reciprocity, or friendship without simultaneously absorbing the neighbor, without loving only those aspects of itself that it perceives in the neighbor or those aspects of the neighbor that it perceives in itself. The human expresses the most proper and deepest form of its direct erotic neighbor-love in its desire for the neighbor to love God and to discover therein its own authentic actualization.[41] The neighbor possesses value in itself as God's creation; paradoxically, however, because God created the neighbor with genuine alterity, the self loves the other for the other's own sake, since even God loves the neighbor for its own sake. In this respect, then, erotic love for the neighbor in itself means the self's desire for the neighbor's authentic life. Consequently, such neighbor-love erotically actualizes the authentic *imitatio Dei.*

Third, the human also properly actualizes an indirect erotic love for neighbor through its direct erotic self-love. From this erotic relationship, a dialectical correlate emerges that will appear later in my analysis of human self-love: the human mediates erotic love toward itself through its direct erotic love for neighbor. At this stage, however, my focus remains

---

41. This implication, in the rationality of the Christian symbol of divine suffering, raises many issues about the competing claims of other religious traditions, the history of missionary impulses in various Christian and other religious communities and their relationships to political and cultural and religious colonialisms, imperialisms, inter-religious dialogue, and religious pluralism. See David Ray Griffin's recent argument for the validity of his process-theological perspective, while still affirming the truth of other religious traditions: D. Griffin, "Religious Pluralism," 3–38.

upon indirect erotic neighbor-love through the human's immediate erotic self-love. In this respect, because the human seeks to preserve, promote, and develop its own life (as a creature that God has constituted to do so), indirectly the human loves the neighbor as a created other like itself; operation of the human's erotic self-love yields at least an implicit acknowledgement of the similarity, the identification, the region of *the same*, that both neighbor and self share. As such, erotic neighbor-love, even mediated through direct erotic self-love, then endeavors to preserve, promote, and develop the life of creaturely alterity. Here, then, human philial love motivates this erotic love for neighbor that the human mediates through direct erotic self-love. Moreover, the human's agapic love inhibits the drive of human erotic love to absorb the other into the self.

Agapic Caritas toward Neighbor

Human agapic love for neighbor resembles human agapic love for God. In this relationship, however, the human principally transcends itself and sacrifices itself for *created others* rather than mainly for the divine creator.

First, however, through the human's direct agapic love for God, the human mediates indirectly an agapic love to the neighbor. This aspect of human agapic neighbor-love discloses the second part of the dialectic that I introduced previously. In my analysis of human agapic love for God, I have described an indirect human agapic love for God through the human's immediate agapic love for neighbor. In the present relationship, however, through a direct agapic love for God, the human mediates an agapic love to the neighbor. By transcending or sacrificing the self for God's purposes or calling, in order to deepen the community between God and God's creatures, in order to imitate the divine self-retraction and self-restriction for the sake of the divine other, the human indirectly loves the neighbor agapically as well. The divine creator has constituted all created others as participants within the community of God and the creation. Thus, any human self-transcendence or self-sacrifice that the human enacts on behalf of God and God's purposes expresses human agapic, even though indirect, love for the neighbor.

Second, in proper agapic love for neighbor, the human agapically loves the neighbor for the neighbor's own sake and, therefore, loves the neighbor directly. Through the human's agapic love toward the neighbor, the human affirms the neighbor's genuine otherness or alterity. The neighbor's alterity always represents the condition of possibility for community. This symbol, then, describes the heart of human agapic love for neighbor as the human's willingness to deny itself for the sake of created others, to exercise self-abnegation in order to protect, preserve, or promote the authentic existence of those creaturely others (the definitive component of which is the neighbor's genuine alterity). Neighbors attain their most complete authenticity, however, only when they love God authentically and discover, as their purpose within that relationship, the actualization of their lives in a proper *imitatio Dei.* Thus, the human that sacrifices itself, so that the other might at least acquire the possibility for loving God, also most deeply exercises agapic love on behalf of the neighbor. Any human absolutization of this agapic dimension of the *imago Dei* for the neighbor, of course, idolizes creaturely alterity as well. Both other dimensions of human life, however, when properly actualized, inhibit this tendency. The human's philial love checks its advance, because to lose oneself in any other, but especially in the created other, would dissolve community by fusing the necessary plurality of its alterity into a monism. The human's erotic love inhibits the advance of the self's tendency toward an absolutization of created others, through its promotion of the self's individuality and uniqueness, as an essential dimension to the community of friendship toward which it drives and which it seeks to sustain when attained. The human's proper agapic neighbor-love for the neighbor's own sake, nevertheless, requires a prior authentic orientation in love for God.

Third, through its direct agapic self-love, the human also mediates an agapic love to its neighbor. The problematic of self-love enters again into the human's agapic neighbor-love. This aspect of human love for the neighbor corresponds dialectically to the agapic self-love that the human mediates to itself through its direct agapic love for the neighbor. I will consider, however, that pole of the dialectic later. The human's self-transcendence and self-sacrifice of its whole self or, more often, of an aspect or aspects of itself (such as time, space, resources, perhaps even values of a penultimate nature), in order for the self to affirm and promote the alterity and value of either God, created others, or both, promotes and preserves thereby the self's own authentic life as a participant within the community of God and created others, while also actualizing the agapic dimension of its own life. Paradoxically, while negating itself through various degrees of self-sacrifice, the human genuinely affirms an essential dimension of its own life. Through this human agapic self-love, the human indirectly actualizes its agapic love for the neighbor. Thus, in its authentic agapic self-love, the human preserves, promotes, and deepens the life of the neighbor as well.

HUMAN LIFE AS CARITAS TOWARD SELF

As shown in my previous expositions of human love for both God and neighbor, self-love has appeared within each of the three structures of love that the self actualizes toward these two subjects. Although the second command of the double-love command does not imply that the human should love the neighbor like it *loves* itself, this command does construe the neighbor as a *created other like the human subject* of the command. Thus, the second command truly implies that the self perceives itself as an other with an intrinsic value of its own, a value to protect, preserve, promote, nourish, enrich, and develop as well. Nevertheless, only through the other (first, the divine other and, second, the created other) does the human self discover its authentic self, the authentic actualization of itself as *imago Dei* via *imitatio Dei*.[42] In that which follows, then, I will analyze self-love in terms of all three material dimensions of the *imago Dei* as actualized through the web of relationships that the various dialectics of the preceding analyses have already exhibited.

Philial Caritas toward Self

The human actualizes its philial love for itself, because this dimension of its life represents the goal, the aim, the τέλος, of the relationships between God, neighbor, and self. Again, this dimension of human life

---

42. Luther also rejected the interpretation that identifies an implied command to love oneself in the second command. He held, however, that the "as yourself" refers to the sinful self-love with which the human already loves itself. Nevertheless, the insight that he derived from this command regarding self-love closely resembles the point that I make here. As Luther developed this point, he appears thoroughly to refuse any notion of self-love. On the contrary, however, his position clearly allows for a legitimate concept of self-love. "But true love for yourself is hatred of yourself. . . . Therefore he who hates himself and loves his neighbor, this person truly loves himself. For he loves himself outside of himself, thus he loves himself purely as long as he loves himself in his neighbor" (Luther, *Lectures on Romans*, 512, 513).

actualizes itself as community, solidarity, mutuality, reciprocity, and wholeness or peace (*shalom*). As with each of the other dimensions in human being, so too conceiving the human's philial love toward itself immediately appears problematic. The human's proper actualization of this dimension represents the human's authentic and essential relationships to God, the neighbor, and itself. The human, however, actualizes philial self-love only after it has discovered itself through its love for both God and created others.

First, therefore, through its direct philial love for God, the human mediates an indirect philial love to itself. This relational dynamic, in conjunction with its previously analyzed polar correlate, completes yet another dialectic. My analysis of its correlate indicated that the human mediated an indirect philial love toward God, through its direct philial self-love. Through authentic human responsiveness to God, human fidelity to God, reciprocity and solidarity with the divine life and purposes, in short through the human maintenance and development of the community of friendship between God and created others, the human thereby actualizes its philial love for itself as a member of that community, as a beneficiary of that completeness, welfare, peace, wholeness (*shalom*). In this case, however, the self loves itself philially only indirectly.

Second, the human similarly mediates a philial love toward itself through its direct philial love for neighbor. A polar correlate from my previous analyses, in conjunction with this present dynamic, completes another dialectic. I formulated that correlate as follows: the human mediates philial love to the neighbor through its direct philial love for itself. At this stage of my analysis, however, through its direct philial love for neighbor, the human self mediates philial love to itself. Again, self-love that the human actualizes through the other always remains indirect, perhaps even unperceived as such. The human's philial love for the neighbor promotes and preserves the completeness of the philial community on behalf of the created other. Such demonstration of love for the neighbor, however, solicits and encourages from the neighbor a similar mutuality. In the philial community, through the philial dimension in human life, equality and partnership between the members of that community sustain and deepen the community. Thus, without the mutual exchange between self and others, between ipseity and alterity, no community arises or sustains itself. Hence, the human, on the basis of its philial love, rightfully expects a corresponding reciprocity from the neighbor. In this manner, then, the human loves itself philially through its philial love for neighbor.

Third, the human loves itself directly, therefore, with a philial love. On the basis of its discovery of the conditions that the community of friendship requires, through its philial love for God and neighbor, the human loves itself with philial love indirectly. The human legitimately perceives itself as a created other with an intrinsic value of its own because of that alterity; and, therefore, the human legitimately and lovingly promotes its equality, its own right to mutuality and reciprocity from the others in the community of friendship, directly loving itself with a philial love.

Erotic Caritas toward Self

Human erotic love desires, and drives toward or endeavors to realize, the essential or authentic actualization of human being as love, the proper actualization of *imago Dei* via *imitatio Dei*. Again, however, the human actualizes its erotic love for itself only after its erotic love for both God and neighbor.

First, through its direct erotic love for God, the human mediates an erotic love to itself. The dynamism of this relationship correlates to a dynamism that appeared earlier. There the human indirectly expressed its erotic love for God through its direct erotic love for itself. Briefly, human erotic love for God designates the human response to the divine gift of being and community, the human response to God's desire both to share the mutuality or fidelity within that community of peace (*shalom*) and to extend or to enrich that community of friendship between divine creator and creation; as response, however, in its direct erotic love for God, the human actively seeks the divine for the sake of God who initiates the relationship. In this erotic love for God, the human perceives its identity in God, even perceives its similarity and likeness to God. Thus, the self seeks fuller participation in its likeness for the sake of the philial community that God has envisioned and engendered. Through this direct erotic love for God, the human loves itself indirectly. In the self's desire to seek God, to respond by receiving (not *taking* or *possessing*, which characterizes the temptation of the human's erotic love) God, the human seeks its own most authentic actualization, although the human realizes this genuine life indirectly through its direct erotic love for God and the divine purposes.

Second, therefore, the human also mediates an erotic love to itself through its direct erotic love for neighbor. A previously analyzed correlate also forms a dialectic in conjunction with this aspect of human love's dynamism. In the previous correlate, the human actualized its mediated erotic love for neighbor through its direct erotic self-love. In the present correlate, in an immediate erotic neighbor-love, human discovery of the created other's sameness or similarity, of its identity with that other, attracts self to neighbor. The human desire to invite the neighbor into the community of friendship—*either* initially *or* more deeply and fully—follows the self's attraction to neighbor. Through that direct erotic love for the neighbor, the human mediates an erotic love to itself, since the human enriches itself through participation with neighbor in philial community. Indeed, the neighbor always discloses itself as more than *the same*, more than resemblance or similarity, more than *that with which the self can identify.* Thus, the neighbor's alterity enriches and deepens the community of friendship. In doing so, the neighbor deepens the self's life as well. Thus, the human exercises its erotic love for itself indirectly through a direct erotic love of neighbor.

Third, the human loves itself erotically for its own sake, because it possesses an intrinsic value. Without the human self's alterity, its uniqueness, no community appears or originates. Thus, in the human's erotic love of itself for its own sake, the human promotes, preserves, deepens, and develops its own life, and does so legitimately since God constitutes the human as an other precisely with that alterity as a goal.

Agapic Caritas toward Self

As I have often stated in the preceding analyses, human agapic love contains the capacity for self-transcendence, self-sacrifice, and self-abnegation. Of the three dimensions in human being as *imago Dei*, this agapic dimension becomes most problematic to describe as authentic self-love. Philial love promotes equality between self and neighbor. Erotic love promotes uniqueness and alterity, the distinction of self from neighbor. Agapic love, however, negates the self in favor of the other, whether created other or divine other. Nevertheless, as I have indicated to some extent already, even though paradoxical, the human loves itself agapically. Once again, however, authentic agapic self-love occurs only after and through the human's agapic love for both God and neighbor.

First, then, the human mediates an agapic love to itself through its direct agapic love for God. This dynamic also completes a dialectic that the dynamic mentioned earlier in a similar connection has already introduced. In the previous analysis, the human indirectly loves God agapically through its unmediated agapic love for itself. There the focus remained principally upon God. Even at this point, however, God remains the primary reality. In its direct authentic agapic love for God, the human surrenders aspects of itself, or even its whole self, in order to promote the divine life, presence, and purposes. In the self's direct agapic love for God, the human transcends self-interest, concern for its own uniqueness and partnership or community with God, in order to enhance, protect, or promote the greater divine interests and purposes. Paradoxically, however, with its direct agapic love for God, the human actualizes its agapic love for its own self, since the human actualizes an essential dimension of itself, a dimension that the inhibition of any self-absolutizing tendencies in the human's erotic love requires. Thereby, the human's agapic love makes community possible, with its interest in others—both creatures and divine creator. In addition, the human indirectly loves itself agapically through its direct agapic love for God, when the human gives up, or transcends, certain aspects of itself that inhibit or distort the most complete mutuality and reciprocity with God. Not only does the human directly love God agapically in such a situation, but the human indirectly loves itself agapically. Human self-sacrifice in the promotion of divine values demonstrates indirectly (since the human represents a value to God) the human's self-sacrificial love on behalf of itself.

The human, second, mediates an agapic love to itself through its direct agapic love for the neighbor. This dynamic moment completes the final dialectic in my analysis. The previous correlate to the present pole in the dialectic took the following form: the human mediates an agapic love to the neighbor through its direct agapic love for itself. At this stage, the dynamic at work greatly resembles the previous dynamic in the mediated agapic self-love through the direct agapic love for God. Self-abnegation for the neighbor's sake indirectly returns this agapic love to the human self. The human self, in its sacrifice to promote the neighbor's life, benefits through the construction, expansion, and preservation of the community of friendship, mutuality, solidarity, and peace. Furthermore, through this self-abnegation for the creaturely other, the human actualizes the fullness of its most authentic self. Also, in such a community of mutuality and reciprocity, the self, through this aspect of the imitation of God, indirectly loves itself agapically by encouraging and activating agapic love for itself from the creaturely others who also participate in the philial community.

Third, and finally, the human directly loves itself agapically for its own sake. In its capacity for self-transcendence, the human perceives itself as an other like all creaturely others. The human loves itself legitimately, then, because God created the human as an other with precisely that alterity as a goal; God did not produce creatures only to extend or solely to enrich the divine self. Thus, the human self may, in its own best interest as a creaturely other, sacrifice those aspects of itself that prevent or inhibit the complete actualization of its authentic alterity. The human self may also discern the necessity toward that greater end, at some singular point in the course of its existence, to sacrifice its whole life in order to authenticate, and thereby to affirm, its whole previous course of life and the values in which it has invested its ultimate loyalty or fidelity.

With the previous analyses, I have proposed a sketch of the material dimensions in the human's authentic or essential actualization in the image of the God who is love. Augustine most succinctly summarizes the enormous openness and risk of human love's authentic realization in his radical though profound homiletic pronouncement: "Dilige, et quod vis fac."[43]

---

43. Translate this as, "love, and do what you wish" (Augustine, *Tractatus in epistolam Joannis*, 7.8). Of course, the order of love and the supporting ontology that Augustine proposed differ significantly from those that my own analyses have identified in the Christian symbol of divine suffering.

8

Human Life As *Caritas* and the Cosmos

Introduction: Role of the Cosmos for Human Life

As stated in chapter 2, every religious symbol expresses, either explicitly or implicitly, a threefold referentiality: (1) reference to some notion of ultimate reality, the sacred, or God; (2) reference to a concept of the human; and (3) reference to a specific vision of the world. The Christian symbol of divine suffering naturally exhibits that threefold referentiality in both the explicit symbol and its twofold presupposition. Thus, in these two primary presuppositions, the human and God do not relate to one another in some sort of vacuum. The human (ὁ ἄνθρωπος) and God (ὁ θεός) relate to one another in and through the world (ὁ κόσμος); in addition, however, both the human and God relate to cosmos. Moreover, the cosmos, in its own ways, relates to both God and the human.

Although I have briefly identified these connections at numerous points throughout the preceding chapters, without a direct exposition (however abbreviated and incomplete) of this third referent, the cosmos, I could not adequately prepare to examine several important aspects of and challenges from the Christian symbol of divine suffering: those studies, of course, will appear especially in the two subsequent volumes, as they address specifically the relationships of divine suffering to both evil and tragic reality respectively. This present chapter entails, therefore, three limited considerations: first an inquiry into the cosmos as the ground and context of the dynamic relationships between the human and God; second, an inquiry into the cosmos as the responsibility of the *imago Dei*; and, third, upon the basis of the two preceding analyses, an exposition of the world's basic dimensions.[1]

Cosmos as Human Ground and Context?

Strictly speaking, the cosmos neither serves as the ground of nor merely contextualizes the human creature. On the one hand, God serves as the ground of both the cosmos and the human. Yet, in one sense, even though God ultimately underlies all reality as its ultimate ground, including human reality, the Christian symbol of divine suffering describes the world or cosmos as the human's penultimate ground. On the other hand, the cosmos always constitutes more than the backdrop, stage, or theater for both human life and interaction between God and humans.[2] Therefore, the human neither solely discovers itself *in* the cosmos as the human's context or base of operations, nor even simply conceives the cosmos as the human's source or ground; instead, the human discovers itself as an aspect *of* the cosmos as well.[3] The human creature represents

1. With the terms "world" and "cosmos," I refer to the whole creation, not simply to the planet Earth or its solar system.

2. In this connection, when internally consistent, Christian attestations to divine suffering avoid the metaphor for creation in Reformed Christian theology of the "*theatrum gloriae Dei*" (e.g., Calvin, *Institutes of the Christian Religion*, 1.5.8; 1.6.2; 2.6.1; Barth, *Dogmatics in Outline*, 50–58), precisely because such language trivializes, when it does not altogether negate, the genuine alterity that the divine creator communicates to creation. Although Calvin used this central metaphor to describe a theocentric creation, he also oscillated between a theocentric and an anthropocentric creation in which God has created the entire creation for the sake of humans and their salvation (Calvin, *Institutes of the Christian Religion*,1.14.22; 1.16.6). Although also using this metaphor to describe "the *goal* of creation," Karl Barth identified a "riddle of creation": that God has created a reality distinct from God with its own freedom (a genuine alterity) for which God has no intrinsic need (Barth, *Dogmatics in Outline*, 54, 58). Barth, thus, maintained a theocentric protology without eliminating the divine valorization of creaturely alterity in the way Calvin did.

3. Admittedly, the most well-known creation-traditions in the first Christian canon (Gen 1:1—2:4; 2:4–24) portray the human as the pinnacle of creation, while the rest of creation merely contextualizes the divine-human drama. In the first account of creation in Genesis, the priestly writer describes how God created all of the world before creating humans. Still, even there, the text distinguishes humans from the rest of the creation by the mode of creation: from the "let there be" about all other aspects of creation to the "let us make" about the human. In the second account of creation in Genesis, the Yahwistic writer more unashamedly claims that God created the entire creation to benefit "man": the garden in which God placed the "man" with its plants for nourishment (as context), the animals as "his" companions, and finally (when God

only a microscopic moment in the time and space of the entire creation or cosmos. One must, at least, note this factor in any adequate study of the *imago Dei*.

Even though I have attached my analysis of this symbol's presupposed cosmic referent to my analysis of human reality, and have appeared to promote a somewhat anthropocentric significance for the world thereby, the Christian symbol of divine suffering neither identifies nor construes the cosmos in that way. To the contrary, this symbol refuses to locate the creation as a whole around human being as the center. Insofar as humans find themselves within the world as the penultimate condition (although a derivative one) of possibility for their existence, and find themselves there only as a small part (though an extremely important and sometimes threatening part) of that world, then humans in one sense always remain somewhat cosmocentric: humans remain dependent upon both their greater context and the conditions of possibility for their existence at all (at least in a derivative sense) and, therefore, not only *in* but integrally part *of* that world. Thus, the Christian symbol of divine suffering holds within itself a latent critique of anthropocentric protologies. In one sense, the cosmos as the derivative context and penultimate ground for the presence and actualization of human life does function as the locale for human history. In another and more profound sense, however, the cosmos takes its own place as a participant or agent in these events, a significant factor with its own purposes, dynamics, and ends in the interactions between divine creator and creation as a whole.

Consequently, the preceding considerations require an answer to the following question: Has one most properly understood the worldhood of the cosmos, when conceiving it only as the penultimate ground or context of the human, as the locale of the divine-human interaction? From that which I have already indicated here, as well as in my preceding analyses of human love, the Christian symbol of divine suffering answers that question negatively. In one sense, the world penultimately functions as the ground from which the human grows; the world does contextualize the interaction between God and humans. After all,

---

finally understood the "man's" needs) woman as "his" companion. Thus, this second text (more, in fact, than in the first text), narrates a theological rationale for the human male's mastery over both non-human creatures and the human family that participates in both cosmic or natural and historical dimensions of the world.

humans actualize their relationships to God in this world, the space and time of the larger creation. In another sense, however, the world possesses an existence and a value of its own, quite independently from any human conferral of significance to it as the *theater* of a divine-human drama. The Christian symbol of divine suffering, then, conceives the human only as a very small component (however powerful this component may be or may have become) of the world's life and purposes in the interaction between the creation as a whole and the divine creator.[4]

Cosmos as Human Responsibility?

Christian traditions, with their emphasis upon the human as *imago Dei*, at their best have often depicted the cosmos as a vast storehouse of resources that God has placed at the disposal of humans, for wise use by humans to support and benefit their own existences. At their worst, these same traditions have justified the domination, abuse, and misuse of the world's resources.[5] Nevertheless, in either case, often, Christian traditions have depicted the world, in some sense, as the human's

4. Many contemporary theologians acknowledge this point in related theological projects (e.g., Bowman, *Beyond the Modern Mind*). Some theologians acknowledge this point, while also emphasizing certain aspects of divine suffering: see Gilkey, *Reaping the Whirlwind*, 29–31, 203–8; Hall, *Imaging God*, 161–205; McFague, *Models of God*, 59–87. Although not a theologian of divine suffering, James Gustafson also demonstrated such discernment, in his development of a theocentric ethic (Gustafson, *Ethics from a Theocentric Perspective*, vol. 1).

5. Such practices and ideologies of domination have traditionally drawn primary support from the language of the priestly account of creation, where God commands humans to "have dominion over" all living things. As I have previously indicated about Gen 1:28, ancient Israel also used its two key Hebrew verbs, translated respectively as "to subdue" or "to bring into bondage" and "to rule over," to describe the rape of women and the waging of war. Thus, the meaning of the narratives in Genesis, on the relationship between human and non-human creatures, lingers not too far at all from the idea of domination. Some scholars readily admit the probable validity of such an assessment: "The *nature* of the universal human stewardship is absolute dominance" (Wolff, *Anthropology of the Old Testament*, 163). Other biblical scholars resist this understanding of the priestly emphasis upon dominion. "It means the full responsibility of the ruler for the welfare of the people and country entrusted to him. Whenever the king is not capable of bringing about and guaranteeing the welfare of those entrusted to him, then he has forfeited his dominion. There is thus no textual basis when, in the contemporary discussion about *dominium terrae*, an unscrupulous exploitation of our earth's resources refers itself to the granting of dominion in the creation story. Every form of exploitation of the earth is contempt for God's commission" (Westermann, *Elements of Old Testament Theology*, 98–99).

charge, trust, responsibility, or even property. Once again, however, such traditions have construed the human as the wisest of all beings, able to make the best judgments and to enact the best decisions about and for *its* world. Construing the cosmos as a human *responsibility* has also enabled humans thoroughly to enslave every aspect of the non-human world, to enlist the entire creation in the service of human purposes, desires, and needs. Even in the more positive expressions of this human *watch-care* over the world, this human responsibility has more often remained prudential, centered upon human concern to preserve or protect the human's own *resources, environment,* or *conditions* for life.

To the contrary, the Christian symbol of divine suffering presupposes something slightly different about human interaction with and responsibility for the cosmos. This symbol's theocentric character perceives the entire cosmos as an other-than-God, which God created precisely to fulfill that alterity. As a creaturely other, composed of countless created others, the cosmos possesses an intrinsic value, irrespective in one sense of the value of humans who depend upon its resources. Hence, the Christian symbol of divine suffering presupposes a different conception of *imago Dei* as the world's steward. Because of human intelligence, as the Christian symbol of divine suffering readily acknowledges, the human has developed great powers with which to manipulate many features and dimensions of the world. As a result, the human can no longer merely assume a place as one aspect of the world, a "comrade" without its developed and heightened powers and abilities, alongside an equally or a less vulnerable population of created others.[6] Rather,

6. See Lynn White's modified version of this viewpoint. White described this view of Christian compassion as "spiritual comity," human "comradeship with the other creatures" (L. White, "Future of Compassion," 99–109). One study from the turn of the twentieth century differently emphasized "comradeship with God" in the suffering of pain or death that humans experienced "for the sake of others" (H. Wright, "Self-Sacrificing God and the Problem of Evil," 749). Also consider the similar viewpoint in Hall's "ontology of communion" (Hall, *Imaging God*, 113–205). Hall seemed to succumb, however, to the ancient tendency to place the human at the pinnacle of creation, in his understanding of the human as "*homo loquens*," the speaking human. For Hall, God makes the human function as the representative creature, or "priest" for the non-human world of creatures, speaking with gratitude to God for a mute and instinctively-moved creation. In one sense, Hall's viewpoint greatly limits both non-human creatures as well as God. For Hall, the human, as *homo loquens*, is the image of God—*Deus loquens!* Thus, unfortunately, in spite of his excellent challenges to distortions of the Christian tradition, Hall defines his concept of God almost completely, if not exclusively, on the basis of one Protestant Christian tradition, a proclamation trajectory (particularly

because of human freedom and power, though the human neither can legitimately actualize itself toward the world as a "dominating overlord" nor can realistically co-exist with the non-human creaturely world as a sort of "comrade" without intervention, humans can exercise a sort of "comrade stewardship." Though humans remain fellow creatures alongside all created others (in this sense, comrades), they nevertheless still exercise enormous power by their knowledge (though not always by their wisdom) and, therefore, have a responsibility to use it properly vis à vis the world. As a task, that comrade-stewardship grows very complex because of the complexity of the world's dimensions.

Dimensions of the Cosmos

Thus, in the answers to my previous questions, two dimensions of worldhood appear. On the one hand, because the world as a whole has a developmental or an evolutionary priority in time and place to the human as participant in the world, the human vitally depends upon the world. On the other hand, because the human possesses such powerful intellectual, emotional, and volitional capacities, the world also vitally depends upon the human. Through the two insights that comprise this dialectic of interdependence, between the world as a whole and the human as part of the world, the two fundamental dimensions of the world's worldhood appear: the world as *natural* cosmos and the world as *historical* cosmos.

Natural Cosmos

The Christian symbol of divine suffering presupposes a conception of the world or cosmos, first, as a community of nature or as the natural world. The world is first an interrelated network of communities of interdependence: one large ecosystem composed of multitudes of smaller ecosystems. Often, Christian traditions identify this aspect of the cosmos almost exclusively as the world. Thus, these traditions understand

---

Barthian and, therefore, quite reformed); in many ways, then, he ignores legitimate manifestation-trajectories within the Christian traditions. Paul Ricoeur and David Tracy carefully developed a distinction between manifestation and proclamation trajectories in Christian traditions (e.g., Ricoeur, "Manifestation et Proclamation," 57–76; Tracy, *Analogical Imagination*, 193–229). I far prefer the Augustinian, and even biblical, viewpoint that all creatures in their own ways love God, having already received the divine love!

nature as that with which the human (in its history) must struggle and, therefore, that which the human must conquer and control. In spite of the power in this perspective, it remains blind to one very obvious factor: the human remains first of all an organic and a quite *natural* creature as well. Human life, in its individual and social forms, participates in all of the processes in which all other non-human aspects of the world participate: birth, growth, development, adaptation, degeneration, death, decay. Furthermore, human life, despite the power of its capacities, never attains independence from the world as nature, no matter how much humans attempt to insulate themselves; both human biological reproduction and the human's protection or nurture of its offspring in family units of various kinds attest to this claim. Nevertheless, even though the natural (as created, essential, or unfallen) world often heavily afflicts its human components, it also remains moldable in many ways and, therefore, susceptible (or, more positively, receptive) to human manipulation and abuse. Other creatures also possess varying capacities to manipulate various aspects of the cosmos.

Historical Cosmos

Discernment of the world's natural side does not exhaust this symbol's insight about the cosmos. That which occurs through instinct or laws of physics, for example, with some form of predictability or *necessity* in the world's natural processes finds balance through the reality of *freedom or indeterminacy* (in its various degrees) both in human life and, in varying degrees, throughout the entire creation. The world also sustains a history that quite often (and often unwisely) runs against the course of nature. Nevertheless, human history, in all of its various social and communal forms (familial, religious, political), often actualizes itself along lines that run parallel to or remain consistent with the world's natural processes. Moreover, when humans violate the world's natural processes, their own manipulation and disruption of reality repeatedly threaten even human life and its conditions.

Thus, although humans both receive that which they can and must (to some extent at least) mold and, thereby, create their world as human community and history, for the Christian symbol of divine suffering, God gives humans to the world as that which the world also molds and incorporates as part of its greater natural community and history.

The cosmos possesses a kind of plasticity, in both its historical and natural dimensions.[7] The interrelatedness of God, neighbor, and self, as expressed through authentic human love, participates fully within the world as conceived by the Christian symbol of divine suffering.

7. Gilkey identified this dialectical interdependence between the world's natural and historical dimensions (e.g., Gilkey, *Reaping the Whirlwind*, 29–31). Expositions of the occasion for the third divine wound, analyses that will appear in volume three, require studies of the interaction between authentic or essential human life and the tragic aspects of the world as natural (divinely created and divinely valorized as good) community.

Epilogue:
From Divine Vulnerability to Divine Suffering

Introduction

IN THIS STUDY, I HAVE AIMED BOTH TO ESTABLISH AN APPROACH TO THE Christian symbol of divine suffering and to inaugurate the first stages of an interpretation of this symbol through an analysis of its two principal presuppositions. The dialectical network between these two presuppositions constitutes the symbol of divine vulnerability: the symbolic condition of possibility for all forms or modes of actual divine suffering, according to the Christian symbol of divine suffering.

My interpretation of this symbol's construal of divine vulnerability, consequently, requires me to step across, to trans-gress, the gaps between this first volume in my study of this symbol and the subsequent two volumes of this work. Together, the following thoughts, then, comprise the first step across the gaps, or the momentary dissolution of the abstractions that I have emplaced through the various methods that I have employed, between the major moments in this larger study.

From Divine Vulnerability to Divine Affliction

Concluding this first volume of my study of the Christian symbol of divine suffering with my analyses of the second presupposition, principally focusing upon the human creature as I have done, perhaps suggests a more anthropocentric construal of creation by this symbol than this symbol's resources and tendencies actually or implicitly promote. I have tried to dispel such suspicions with my brief analysis of the cosmic referentiality in the Christian symbol of divine suffering. Nonetheless, historically, many attestations to divine suffering most certainly have tended toward and encouraged various degrees of anthropocentric thought. Such oversights and distortions, however, have continued to occur especially when and insofar as testimonies to divine suffering have ignored the *tragic region of reality* or have fused this aspect of creation with their visions about the *realm of evil*.

In the Christian symbol of divine suffering, as I have interpreted it, essential reality or reality as originally created (reality untouched by evil) includes the region of tragic reality and experience. Nevertheless, in this book, I have withheld even the region of the tragic from extended consideration. This particular abstraction obviously contributes to the impression that this symbol remains hopelessly anthropocentric. My analysis of divine affliction or the third divine wound in the third volume of this work, however, releases the present brackets around the tragic region of the world in essential reality. At that point, then, this symbol's most fully theocentric character will emerge. Until then, perhaps my brief examination of the world in chapter 8 will temper undue yet understandable suspicions.

From Divine Vulnerability to Divine Grief

While this book has examined this symbol's understanding of the being or life of both creatures and God as abstracted from various forms of suffering, the second volume of studies will release one set of brackets, thus allowing an examination of these essential or created realities as the introduction of *evil*, or the negative non-essential dimensions of human experience and the historical dimension of the world, affects both of them. Nevertheless, in volume two, *Evil and Divine Suffering*, I will continue to maintain a second set of brackets around the region of tragic reality, withholding an examination of the region of the tragic dimension in creation until the third volume of studies and not allowing its dynamics to intrude upon the dynamics of evil in relation to God.

Among attestations to divine suffering, the divine response to evil historically constitutes the heart of the Christian symbol of divine suffering, even though the divine response to the region of tragic reality represents the essential and, in many ways, the primary moment in divine suffering. The reality of evil serves as the occasion, however, for the first two divine wounds, which my analysis will examine in volume two. Hence, while volume three examines only the third divine wound (divine affliction), volume two will contain my studies of the first and second divine wounds of this symbol: divine grief and divine self-sacrifice. Thus, I begin my studies of the moments of divine suffering (rather than studies of divine vulnerability or the conditions of possibility for divine suffering) with analyses of the moments that God has not created that occasion divine suffering, that which the beloved human creation has introduced in betrayal of the divine lover.

Occasions for and Responses of Divine Suffering

Because the three major moments of divine suffering arise from the interaction of the two presuppositions that this present book has examined, transition to volumes two and three of this study requires one additional preparatory discussion. I repeat the two fundamental presuppositions of the Christian symbol of divine suffering: *First, the God whose being is love limits the divine self when creating; second, God creates the human in the image of the God whose being is love.* These two presuppositions underlie the entire structure and dynamism of this religious symbol.

Occasions Not Causes of Divine Suffering

Divine suffering results neither from a conflict within the divine life nor from a divine struggle to subjugate, dominate, or conquer a second eternal principle or reality of opposition; God does not suffer as the result of any primal warfare between *eternal* realities of good and evil. Hence, God suffers only because this God of love has chosen to create creatures in the divine image. The divine choice itself required God's self-limitation. As a consequence, nothing other than God *causes* divine suffering, except that to which God has always already consented or opened the divine life. Strictly speaking, as the ultimate source of the conditions that permit the appearance of creaturely *occasions* for divine suffering, God does cause God's own suffering: here I refer to appearances of both evil in and the tragic realities of creation. In volume three, I will analyze in more detail the meaning of this aspect of divine responsibility for divine suffering in the Christian symbol of divine suffering.

As a consequence of these complications, the Christian symbol of divine suffering distinguishes between *causes* and *occasions* for divine suffering.[1] For this symbol, to claim that something causes divine suffering implies a reality that remains totally external to and independent

1. Other theologians of divine suffering develop this distinction similarly: see Heschel, *Prophets*, 2:5; J. Lee, *God Suffers for Us*, 41, 49–52.

from God, something equally as ultimate as, or even more ultimate than, the suffering God. Nonetheless, when this symbol construes ultimate reality as the God who limits the divine self for the purpose of bringing an other-than-God into existence, then the symbol properly describes a cause of divine suffering—even if God causes such divine suffering indirectly. Thus, this symbol qualifies its usage of causal language with the awareness that, as self-limiting, God remains the ultimate, though not always the immediate, cause of God's own suffering.

Rather than continuing to use the problematic language of cause and effect, however, I have employed the term "occasion" with which to describe the creaturely source or origin for each moment in divine suffering. The term, "occasion," more precisely indicates the way in which most Christian testimonies to divine suffering construe the relationship between divine vulnerability and creaturely freedoms. According to the Christian symbol of divine suffering, God has principally created only the conditions of possibility for these occasions, not the occasions themselves. Of course, in volume three, my studies of the third divine wound, divine affliction, will *significantly qualify* this very general assessment. At this stage, the Christian symbol of divine suffering construes *an occasion for divine suffering*, therefore, in the following way: *As a situation or state of affairs that God's creatures principally initiate, within the limitations and through the freedoms created by God, and to which God has made the divine self vulnerable.*

Passive and Active Stages of Divine Suffering

Moreover, in the divine responses to the creaturely occasions of divine suffering, all three divine wounds exhibit both passive and active stages, although the order of the active and passive stages oscillates from one divine wound to the next. One might introduce an alternative terminology for these two stages in each divine wound: *voluntary* (the active stage) and *involuntary* (the passive stage). Due to problems with these particular terms, which I will identify in the studies that the following volumes contain, however, I have decided not to employ this alternative terminology. Consequently, I have developed the distinction between active and passive forms of divine suffering, a distinction that operates in most attestations to divine suffering.[2] Few attestations to or theologians of divine suffering, however, explicitly perceive or acknowledge the passive stages in the three divine wounds. Some of these theologians even refuse to attribute to God any capacity for passive suffering whatsoever.[3] Nonetheless, careful analysis of testimonies to divine suffering discloses, at least, an implicit awareness of both active and passive divine responses of suffering to creaturely occasions. As a consequence, I will examine both active and passive stages of divine suffering in the following studies of all three divine wounds.

Each moment in the Christian symbol of divine suffering, then, contains the basic structure of all religious symbols, as displayed through its references to God, the world (in historical as well as natural dimensions), and the human. In addition, the interaction between the two presuppositions, which I have previously described in the chapters of this book, determines the specific characteristics of each divine wound. Thus, a creaturely occasion and divine responses to it constitute each moment in the Christian symbol of divine suffering. The character of each creaturely occasion influences or conditions the particular mode of suffering through which God responds to the creation. Naturally, then, an analysis of the various modes or types of divine suffering also requires an analysis even of the *creaturely occasions* for each mode of divine suffering, as essential components in those *divine modes* of suffering.

In the subsequent two volumes of this study, therefore, my interpretation of the Christian symbol of divine suffering will follow the basic pattern that I have identified in this first part of my hermeneutic of the Christian symbol of divine suffering. The order of my examination of the divine, human, and worldly referents in this symbol, however,

---

2. God's "... suffering is not to be conceived of as merely passive pain and certainly not as helpless endurance, but as active travail" (Hughes, *Christian Idea of God*, 215).

3. For example, after distinguishing *pain* ("defined in terms of a sensation bound to the body") from *suffering* (defined "in terms of a loving relationship bound to time"), Jung Young Lee divides suffering into the two categories of *voluntary* and *involuntary* sufferings. "The former is often called redemptive suffering, while the latter is penal suffering. When we attribute suffering to the divine, we mean the former, namely the pure form of vicarious and redemptive suffering" (J. Lee, *God Suffers for Us*, 5). In his analysis, not only does Lee deny God's capacity for passive forms of suffering, but he also refuses to attribute to God forms of suffering other than the redemptive or sacrificial form that relates to the second divine wound.

will shift as the rhythm of the relationship between God and creation changes in the logic of this symbol. In this present study, I began with a discussion of the symbol's representation of the divine lover as the self-limiting creator, followed by analyses of the beloved creation, precisely because, in this Christian symbol, that order and pattern represents the fundamental conviction about the origin of all things in a divine creator. In volume two, *Evil and Divine Suffering*, the title reflects the order of my interpretation of the rationality in the first two divine wounds: the *imago Dei*, actualized as *cupiditas*, introduces the reality of evil into creation, which produces the occasions for the first two divine wounds. In the third volume, *Divine Suffering and Tragic Reality*, however, the title reflects a different order in my study of the third divine wound: because God has created the features of the world that constitute tragic reality, my analysis of the divine referent in this symbol appears as the presupposition of that study, which the title reflects as well.

With the previous transitions, then, I complete my sketch of the symbol of divine vulnerability, the twofold symbolic presupposition of the major and explicit moments in the Christian symbol of divine suffering. Through this study, I have aimed to provide an approach to the Christian symbol of divine suffering that will allow the most profound dimensions of its terrible sublimity to appear. I can only hope, as the features of divine vulnerability have emerged, that this study has begun to fulfill that goal at least in part.

Bibliography

Abbott, Eric. *The Compassion of God and the Passion of Christ: A Scriptural Meditation for the Weeks of Lent.* New York: McKay, 1963.

Abe, Masao. "Kenotic God and Dynamic Sunyata." In *The Emptying God: A Buddhist-Jewish-Christian Conversation,* edited by John B. Cobb Jr. and Christopher Ives, 3–65. Faith Meets Faith Series. Edited by Paul F. Knitter. Maryknoll: Orbis Books, 1990. Reprint, Eugene, OR: Wipf & Stock, 2005.

———. "The Problem of Self-Centeredness as the Root-Source of Human Suffering." *Japanese Religions* 15 (1989) 15–25.

Abramowski, Luise. "Die Schrift Gregors des Lehrers 'ad Theopompum' und Philoxenus von Mabbug." *Zeitschrift für Kirchengeschichte* 89 (1978) 273–90.

Ahlers, Rolf. "Theory of God and Theological Method." *Dialog* 22 (1983) 235–40.

Allen, Diogenes. "Natural Evil and the Love of God." *Religious Studies* 16 (1980) 439–56.

Althaus, Paul. *The Theology of Martin Luther.* Translated by Robert C. Schultz. Philadelphia: Fortress, 1966.

Alves, Rubem A. *A Theology of Human Hope.* Washington DC: Corpus, 1969.

Amundsen, Darrel W. "The Developing Role of Suffering in Salvation History." *Crux* 20 (1984) 12–25.

Anastos, Milton V. "Justinian's Despotic Control over the Church as Illustrated by His Edicts on the Theopaschite Formula and His Letter to Pope John II in 533." *Recueil de travaux de l'institut d'études byzantines (Mélanges Georges Ostrogorsky 2)* 8.2 (1964) 1–11.

Angelus Silesius. *The Cherubinic Wanderer.* Translated by Maria Schrady. The Classics of Western Spirituality. Edited by John Farina. New York: Paulist, 1986.

Anglin, Bill, and Stewart Goetz. "Evil is Privation." *International Journal for Philosophy of Religion* 13 (1982) 3–12.

Aquinas, Thomas. *The Sermon-Conferences of St. Thomas Aquinas on the Apostles' Creed.* Translated by Nicholas Ayo. Notre Dame: University of Notre Dame Press, 1988.

Araya, Victorio. *God of the Poor: The Mystery of God in Latin American Liberation Theology.* Translated by Robert R. Barr. Maryknoll: Orbis, 1987.

Aristotle. *The Complete Works of Aristotle: The Revised Oxford Translation.* Edited by Jonathan Barnes. 2 vols. The Bollingen Series. Princeton: Princeton University Press, 1984.

Attfield, D. G. "Can God Be Crucified: A Discussion of J. Moltmann." *Scottish Journal of Theology* 30 (1977) 47–57.

Augustine. *Confessions.* Translated by Henry Chadwick. The World's Classics Series. Oxford: Oxford University Press, 1991.

————. *Sancti Augustini Confessionum Libri XIII.* In *Corpus Christianorum: Series Latina* 27. Turnholt: Brepols, 1981.

————. *A Select Library of the Nicene and Post-Nicene Fathers of the Christian Church.* Edited by Philip Schaff. Vol. 1. *The Confessions and Letters of St. Augustine with a Sketch of His Life and Work.* 1886. Reprint, Grand Rapids: Eerdmans , 1979.

————. *A Select Library of the Nicene and Post-Nicene Fathers of the Christian Church.* Edited by Philip Schaff. Vol. 2. *St. Augustine's City of God and Christian Doctrine.* 1886. Reprint, Grand Rapids: Eerdmans, 1979.

Aulén, Gustaf. *Christus Victor: An Historical Study of the Three Main Types of the Idea of Atonement.* Translated by A. G. Hebert. New York: Macmillan , 1969.

————. *The Faith of the Christian Church.* Translated by Eric H. Wahlstrom. Philadelphia: Fortress, 1960.

Avis, Paul. *Eros and the Sacred.* Wilton, CT: Morehouse , 1990.

Awes, L. H. "Theology of Crisis and the Problem of Evil." *Lutheran Church Quarterly* 5 (1932) 25–35.

Ayali, Meir. "Gottes und Israels Trauer über die Zerstörung des Tempels." *Kairos: Zeitschrift für Religionswissenschaft und Theologie* 23 (1981) 215–31.

Ayer, Alfred J. *Language, Truth, and Logic.* 1936; 2nd ed. London: Victor Gollancz; New York: Dover, 1946.

Bachmann, Michael. "Hohepriesterliches Leiden: Beobachtungen zu Hebr 5:1–10." *Zeitschrift für die Neutestamentliche Wissenschaft und die Kunde der Älteren Kirche* 78 (1987) 244–66.

Baillie, D. M. *God Was in Christ: An Essay on Incarnation and Atonement.* New York: Scribner, 1948.

Baillie, John. *The Place of Jesus Christ in Modern Christianity.* New York: Scribner, 1929.

Baker, John Robert. "The Christological Symbol of God's Suffering." In *Religious Experience and Process Theology: The Pastoral Implications of a Major Modern Movement,* edited by Harry James Cargas and Bernard Lee, 93–105. New York: Paulist, 1976.

Barbour, John D. "Tragedy and Ethical Reflection." *Journal of Religion* 63 (1983) 1–25.

————. *Tragedy as a Critique of Virtue: The Novel and Ethical Reflection.* Chico, CA: Scholars, 1984.

Barnes, E. W. "Apparent Helplessness of God." *Christian Century* 43 (6 May 1926) 580–81.

Barnhart, J. E. *Religion and the Challenge of Philosophy.* Totowa, NJ: Littlefield, Adams, 1975.

Barr, James. *The Scope and Authority of the Bible.* Philadelphia: Westminster, 1980.

Barth, Hans-Martin. "Angesichts des Leiden von Gott reden." *Pastoral-Theologie* 75 (1986) 116–31.

Barth, Karl. *Church Dogmatics.* Translated by G. T. Thompson, Harold Knight, T. H. L. Parker, W. B. Johnston, et al. 4 vols. Edinburgh: T. & T. Clark, 1936–1969.

————. *Dogmatics in Outline.* Translated by G. T. Thomson. 1949. Reprint, New York: Harper and Row, 1959.

————. *The Epistle to the Romans.* 6th ed. Translated by Edwyn C. Hoskyns. London: Oxford University Press, 1933.

———. *The Humanity of God.* Translated by Thomas Wieser and John Newton Thomas. Atlanta: John Knox, 1960.

———. *The Word of God and the Word of Man.* Translated by Douglas Horton. 1956. Reprint, Gloucester: Peter Smith, 1978.

Basinger, David. *Divine Power in Process Theism: A Philosophical Critique.* SUNY Series in Philosophy. New York: State University of New York Press, 1988.

———, and Randall Basinger, editors. *Predestination and Free Will: Four Views of Divine Sovereignty and Human Freedom.* Downers Grove: InterVarsity, 1986.

Batstone, David. *From Conquest to Struggle: Jesus of Nazareth in Latin America.* Albany: State University of New York Press, 1991.

———. "The Transformation of the Messianic Ideal in Judaism and Christianity in Light of the Holocaust: Reflections on the Writings of Elie Wiesel." *Journal of Ecumenical Studies* 23 (1986) 587–600.

Battles, Ford L. "God Was Accommodating Himself to Human Capacity." *Interpretation* 31 (1977) 19–38.

Bauckham, Richard J. "In Defence of *The Crucified God*." In *The Power and Weakness of God: Impassibility and Orthodoxy: Papers Presented at the Third Edinburgh Conference in Christian Dogmatics, 1989,* edited by Nigel M. de S. Cameron, 93–118. Edinburgh: Rutherford, 1990.

———. "Moltmann's Eschatology of the Cross." *Scottish Journal of Theology* 30 (1977) 301–11.

———. "Moltmanns Eschatologie des Kreuzes." In *Diskussion über Jürgen Moltmanns Buch "Der gekreuzigte Gott,"* edited by Michael Welker, 43–53. Munich: Kaiser, 1979.

———. "'Only the Suffering God Can Help': Divine Passibility in Modern Theology." *Themelios* 9 (1984) 6–12.

———. "Theodicy from Ivan Karamazov to Moltmann." *Modern Theology* 4 (1987) 83–97.

———. "Universalism: A Historical Survey." *Evangelical Review of Theology* 15 (1991) 22–35.

Bauer, Walter. *Orthodoxy and Heresy in Earliest Christianity.* 2nd ed. Translated by the Philadelphia Seminar on Christian Origins. Edited by Robert A. Kraft and Gerhard Krodel. Philadelphia: Fortress, 1971.

Bayer, Oswald. "Tempus Creatura Verbi." In *Gottes Zukunft-Zukunft der Welt: Festschrift für Jürgen Moltmann zum 60 Geburtstag,* edited by Hermann Deuser, Gerhard Marcel Martin, Konrad Stock, and Michael Welker, 3–13. Munich: Kaiser, 1986.

Bayes, Jonathan. "Divine ἀπάθεια in Ignatius of Antioch." In *Studia Patristica,* edited by Elizabeth A. Livingstone, 21:27–31. Leuven: Peeters, 1989.

Beattie, Paul H. "The Tragic View of Life." *Religious Humanism* 19 (1985) 54–61, 100.

Beauchamp, Paul. *L'Un et l'Autre Testament: Essai de lecture.* Paris: Seuil, 1977.

Beecher, Charles. *Redeemer and Redeemed: An Investigation of the Atonement and of Eternal Judgment.* Boston: Lee and Shepard, 1864.

Beecher, Edward. *The Concord of Ages: or The Individual and Organic Harmony of God and Man.* New York: Derby and Jackson, 1860.

———. *The Conflict of Ages: or The Great Debate on the Moral Relations of God and Man.* Boston: Phillips, Sampson, 1853.

Beek, Martinus A. "Das Mit-Leiden Gottes: eine masoretische Interpretation von Jes. 63,9." In *Symbolae Biblicae et Mesopotamicae: Francisco Mario Theodoro de Liagre Böhl dedicatae*, edited by Martinus A. Beek et al, 23–30. Leiden: Brill, 1973.

Beker, J. Christiaan. *Suffering and Hope: The Biblical Vision and the Human Predicament*. Philadelphia: Fortress, 1987.

Benjamin, Walter. *Illuminations*. Edited by Hannah Arendt. Translated by Harry Zohn. New York: Schocken, 1968.

Berdyaev, Nicolas. *The Destiny of Man*. 3rd ed. Translated by Natalie Duddington. London: Geoffrey Bles, 1937.

———. *The Divine and the Human*. Translated by R. M. French. London: Geoffrey Bles, 1949.

———. *Freedom and the Spirit*. Translated by Oliver Fielding Clark. New York: Books for Libraries, 1972.

———. *Slavery and Freedom*. Translated by R. M. French. New York: Scribner, 1944.

———. "Unground and Freedom." In *Six Theosophic Points and Other Writings*, by Jacob Boehme, v–xxxvii. Translated by John Rolleston Earle. Ann Arbor: University of Michigan Press, 1958.

Berkouwer, G. C. *Man: The Image of God*. Grand Rapids: Eerdmans, 1962.

Berkovits, Eliezer. "Dr. A. J. Heschel's Theology of Pathos." *Tradition* 6 (1964) 67–104.

Bernard of Clairvaux. *On the Song of Songs IV: Sermons 67–86*. Translated by Irene Edmonds. Cistercian Fathers Series 40. Kalamazoo, MI: Cistercian, 1980.

Bertocci, Peter. *Introduction to the Philosophy of Religion*. Englewood Cliffs, NJ: Prentice-Hall, 1951.

———. *The Person God Is*. London: Allen and Unwin, 1970.

———. "Theistic Temporalistic Personalism and the Problem of Good and Evil." *Proceedings of the American Catholic Philosophical Association* 51 (1977) 57–65.

Bhattacharyya, Kalidas. "Does God Suffer?" *Visvabharati Journal of Philosophy* 7 (1970) 34–47.

Blake, William. *The Complete Poetry and Prose of William Blake*. Edited by David V. Erdman. Revised ed. Garden City, NY: Doubleday, 1982.

———. *The Paintings of William Blake*. Edited by Raymond Lister. Cambridge: Cambridge University Press, 1986.

Blancy, Alain. " 'Der gekreuzigte Gott' von Jürgen Moltmann." In *Diskussion über Jürgen Moltmanns Buch "Der gekreuzigte Gott,"* edited by Michael Welker, 118–25. Munich: Kaiser, 1979.

Blank, Sheldon H. "'Doest Thou Well to Be Angry?' A Study in Self-Pity." *Hebrew Union College Annual* 26 (1955) 29–41.

Blanksby, A. J. "A Reappraisal of the Doctrine of God Derived from the New Testament." PhD diss., Durham University, 1961–1962.

Bleske, Elisabeth. "Failure in the Lifelong Project of Fidelity." In *Concilium: Coping with Failure*, edited by Norbert Greinacher and Norbert Mette, 105–16. Philadelphia: Trinity, 1990.

Blocher, Henri. "Divine Immutability." In *The Power and Weakness of God: Impassibility and Orthodoxy: Papers Presented at the Third Edinburgh Conference in Christian Dogmatics, 1989*, edited by Nigel M. de S. Cameron, 1–22. Edinburgh: Rutherford, 1990.

Blumenfeld, David. "On the Compossibility of the Divine Attributes." *Philosophical Studies* 34 (1978) 91–103.

Bodem, Anton. "'Leiden Gottes': Erwägungen zu einem Zug im Gottesbild der gegenwärtigen Theologie." In *Veritati Catholicae: Festschrift für Leo Scheffczyk zum 65 Geburtstag,* edited by Anton Ziegenaus, Franz Courth, and Philipp Schäfer, 586–611. Aschaffenburg: Paul Pattloch Verlag, 1985.

Boehme, Jacob. *Six Theosophic Points and Other Writings.* Translated by John Rolleston Earle. Ann Arbor: University of Michigan Press, 1958.

Boespflug, François. "The Compassion of God the Father in Western Art." *Cross Currents* 42 (1992–1993) 491–93.

Boeyink, David E. "Pain and Suffering." *Journal of Religion and Ethics* 2 (1974) 85–98.

Boff, Leonardo. *Passion of Christ, Passion of the World: The Facts, Their Interpretation, and Their Meaning Yesterday and Today.* Translated by Robert R. Barr. Maryknoll: Orbis, 1987.

Bolz, Norbert. "Leiderfahrung als Wahrheitsbedingung." In *Leiden,* edited by Willi Oelmüller, 9–19. *Kolloquium Religion und Philosophie* 3. Paderborn: Ferdinand Schöning, 1986.

Bomberger, C. G. "Jesus Christ in Human Suffering: A Theology of Suffering Interpreted through the Incarnation." PhD diss., University of Edinburgh, 1967–1968.

Bonhoeffer, Dietrich. *Act and Being.* Translated by Bernard Noble. 1961. Reprint, New York: Octagon, A Division of Hippocrene, 1983.

———. *The Communion of Saints: A Dogmatic Inquiry into the Sociology of the Church.* Translated by R. Gregor Smith. New York: Harper and Row, 1963.

———. "Concerning the Christian Idea of God." *Journal of Religion* 12 (1932) 177–85.

———. *Gesammelte Schriften.* Edited by Eberhard Bethge. 6 vols. Munich: Kaiser, 1958–1974.

———. *Letters and Papers from Prison.* Enlarged 3rd ed. Edited by Eberhard Bethge. Translated by Reginald Fuller, Frank Clarke, and John Bowden. New York: Macmillan, 1972.

———. *No Rusty Swords: Letters, Lectures and Notes 1928–1936.* Translated by Edwin H. Robertson and John Bowden. New York: Harper and Row, 1965.

Bonhoeffer, Thomas. "Gotteslehre: Eine pastoralpsychologische Zuspitzung." *Theologische Literaturzeitung* 113 (1988) 865–72.

Boreham, L. "The Semantic Development of πάσχω." *Glotta: Zeitschrift für griechische und lateinische Sprache* 49 (1971) 231–44.

Borg, Marcus J. *Jesus, A New Vision: Spirit, Culture, and the Life of Discipleship.* San Francisco: Harper and Row, 1987.

Bouchard, Larry D. *Tragic Method and Tragic Theology: Evil in Contemporary Drama and Religious Thought.* University Park: Pennsylvania State University Press, 1989.

Bourel, Dominique. "'Bien qu'il tarde' . . . Théodicée dans le Judaïsme contemporain?" *Archivio di Filosofia* 56 (1988) 139–46.

Boutry, Aubert. "La souffrance du Seigneur." *Bible et Vie Chrétienne* 25 (1959) 59–68.

Bowker, John. "Suffering as a Problem of Religions." In *The Meaning of Human Suffering*, edited by Flavian Dougherty, 15–54. New York: Human Sciences, 1982.

Bowman, Douglas C. *Beyond the Modern Mind: The Spiritual and Ethical Challenge of the Environmental Crisis*. New York: Pilgrim, 1990.

Braaten, Carl E. "A Trinitarian Theology of the Cross." *Journal of Religion* 56 (1976) 113–21.

Brabant, F. H. "God and Time." In *Essays on the Trinity and the Incarnation: By Members of the Anglican Communion*, edited by A. E. J. Rawlinson, 323–60. London: Longmans, Green, 1933.

Bracken, Joseph A. "Process Philosophy and Trinitarian Theology." *Process Studies* 11 (1981) 83–96.

Bradley, A. C. *Oxford Lectures on Poetry*. London: Macmillan, 1917.

Brandy, Hans Christian. "Vom Leiden des Menschen und vom Leiden Gottes." *Kerygma und Dogma* 51 (2005) 290–307.

Brantschen, J. B. "Die Macht und Ohnmacht der Liebe. Randglossen zum dogmatischen Satz: Gott ist unveränderlich." *Freiburger Zeitschrift für Philosophie und Theologie* 27 (1980) 224–46.

Brasnett, Bertrand R. *The Suffering of the Impassible God*. New York: Macmillan, 1928.

Braybrooke, Marcus. "The Suffering of God: New Perspectives in the Christian Understanding of God since the Holocaust." In *Jews and Christians During and After the Holocaust*, edited by Yehuda Bauer et al, 702–8. *Remembering for the Future: Working Papers and Addenda* 1. New York: Pergamon, 1989.

Breton, Stanislas. "Human Suffering and Transcendence." In *The Meaning of Human Suffering*, edited by Flavian Dougherty, 55–94. New York: Human Sciences, 1982.

Brightman, Edgar Sheffield. *A Philosophy of Religion*. New York: Prentice Hall, 1940.

———. *The Problem of God*. New York: Abingdon, 1930.

———. "A Temporalist View of God." *Journal of Religion* 12 (1932) 544–55.

Brock, Rita Nakashima. *Journeys by Heart: A Christology of Erotic Power*. New York: Crossroad, 1988.

Brown, Robert F. "God's Ability to Will Moral Evil." *Faith and Philosophy* 8 (1991) 3–20.

———. "Schelling and Dorner on Divine Immutability." *Journal of the American Academy of Religion* 53 (1985) 237–49.

Brown, Robert. *Analyzing Love*. Cambridge Studies in Philosophy, edited by Sydney Shoemaker. Cambridge: Cambridge University Press, 1987.

Brümmer, Vincent. "Atonement and Reconciliation." *Religious Studies* 28 (1992) 435–52.

———. "God and the Union of Love." *Bijdragen* 52 (1991) 254–72.

———. *The Model of Love: A Study in Philosophical Theology*. Cambridge: Cambridge University Press, 1993.

———. "Moral Sensitivity and the Free Will Defence." *Neue Zeitschrift für systematische Theologie und Religionsphilosophie* 29 (1987) 86–100.

———. *Speaking of a Personal God*. Cambridge: Cambridge University Press, 1992.

Bruce, Alexander Balmain. *The Providential Order of the World*. New York: Scribner, 1897.

Brueggemann, Walter. "The Formfulness of Grief." *Interpretation* 31 (1977) 263–75.

———. "From Hurt to Joy, From Death to Life." *Interpretation* 28 (1974) 3-19.

———. *Genesis*. Interpretation: A Bible Commentary for Teaching and Preaching. Series edited by James L. Mays. Old Testament edited by Patrick D. Miller. Atlanta: John Knox, 1982.

———. "The Rhetoric of Hurt and Hope: Ethics Odd and Crucial." In *The Annual of the Society of Christian Ethics*, edited by D. M. Yeager, 73–92. Washington DC: Georgetown University Press, 1989.

———. "A Shape for Old Testament Theology, II: Embrace of Pain." *Catholic Biblical Quarterly* 47 (1985) 395–415.

Brunner, Heinrich Emil. *Dogmatics*. Vol. 1. *The Christian Doctrine of God*. Translated by Olive Wyon. London: Lutterworth, 1949.

———. *Dogmatics*. Vol. 2. *The Christian Doctrine of Creation and Redemption*. Translated by Olive Wyon. Philadelphia: Westminster, 1952.

———. *Dogmatics*. Vol. 3. *The Christian Doctrine of the Church, Faith and the Consummation*. Translated by David Cairns in collaboration with T. H. L. Parker. London: Lutterworth, 1962.

———. *Man in Revolt: A Christian Anthropology*. Translated by Olive Wyon. Philadelphia: Westminster, 1939.

Buber, Martin. *Eclipse of God: Studies in the Relation Between Religion and Philosophy*. New York: Harper and Brothers, 1952.

———. *I and Thou*. 2nd ed. Translated by Ronald Gregor Smith. New York: Scribner, 1958.

Buckham, John Wright. *The Humanity of God: An Interpretation of the Divine Fatherhood*. New York: Harper and Brothers, 1928.

Bulgakov, Sergius. *The Wisdom of God: A Brief Summary of Sophiology*. Translated by Patrick Thompson, O. Fielding Clarke, and Xenia Braikevitch. London: Williams and Norgate, 1937.

Bultmann, Rudolf. *The History of the Synoptic Tradition*. 2nd ed. Translated by John Marsh. New York: Harper and Row, 1968.

———. *The Johannine Epistles*. Edited by Robert W. Funk. Translated by R. Philip O'Hara, Lane C. McGaughy, and Robert W. Funk. Hermeneia—A Critical and Historical Commentary on the Bible. Philadelphia: Fortress, 1973.

———. *Theology of the New Testament*. Vol. 1. Translated by Kendrick Grobel. New York: Scribner, 1951.

Burkle, Howard R. *God, Suffering, and Belief*. Nashville: Abingdon, 1977.

Burnley, W. F. E. "Impassibility of God." *Expository Times* 67 (1955) 90–91.

Burrell, David S. "René Girard: Violence and Sacrifice." *Cross Currents* 38 (1988–1989) 443–47.

Burtness, James H. "Sharing the Suffering of God in the Life of the World: From Text to Sermon on I Peter 2:21." *Interpretation* 23 (1969) 277–88.

Bushnell, Horace. *Forgiveness and Law: Grounded in Principles Interpreted by Human Analogies*. New York: Scribner, Armstrong, 1874.

———. *The Vicarious Sacrifice: Grounded in Principles Interpreted by Human Analogies*. 2 vols. New York: Scribner, 1877.

Cahill, Lisa Sowle. "Consent in Time of Affliction: The Ethics of a Circumspect Theist." *Journal of Religious Ethics* 13 (1985) 22–36.

Caillard, Emma Marie. "The Suffering God: A Study in St. Paul." *The Living Age: A Weekly Magazine of Contemporary Literature and Thought* 228 (1901) 577–84.

Cain, Clifford C. "A Passionate God?" *Saint Luke's Journal of Theology* 25 (1981) 52–57.

Caird, John. *The Fundamental Ideas of Christianity.* 2 vols. Glasgow: James MacLehose, 1899.

Cairns, David. *The Image of God in Man.* London: SCM, 1953.

Calvin, John. *Institutes of the Christian Religion.* 2 vols. Edited by John T. McNeill. Translated by Ford Lewis Battles. The Library of Christian Classics. Philadelphia: Westminster, 1960.

Cameron, Nigel M. de S., ed. *Issues in Faith and History: Papers Presented at the Second Edinburgh Conference on Dogmatics, 1987.* Edinburgh: Rutherford, 1989.

————, ed. *The Power and Weakness of God: Impassibility and Orthodoxy: Papers Presented at the Third Edinburgh Conference on Christian Dogmatics, 1989.* Edinburgh: Rutherford, 1990.

Campbell, Antony F. "Psalm 78: A Contribution to the Theology of Tenth Century Israel." *Catholic Biblical Quarterly* 41 (1979) 51–79.

Campbell, John McLeod. *The Nature of the Atonement and Its Relation to Remission of Sins and Eternal Life.* London. 1873. Reprinted 4th ed., London: James Clarke, 1959.

Campbell, Mary Margaret. "Critical Theory and Liberation Theology: A Comparison of the Works of Jürgen Habermas and Gustavo Gutiérrez." PhD diss., Graduate Theological Union, 1990.

Campbell, R. J. "God and the Suffering Servant." *Homiletic Review* 91 (1926) 149–52.

Cantalamessa, R. "Incarnazione e immuabilitá di Dio. Una soluzione moderna nella patristica?" *Rivista di filosofia neo-scolastica* 57 (1975) 631–47.

Caputo, John D. *Radical Hermeneutics: Repetition, Deconstruction, and the Hermeneutic Project.* Studies in Phenomenology and Existential Philosophy, edited by James M. Edie. Bloomington: Indiana University Press, 1987.

————. *The Weakness of God: A Theology of the Event.* Indiana Series in the Philosophy of Religion, edited by Merold Westphal. Bloomington: Indiana University Press, 2006.

Cargas, Harry James and Lee, Bernard, eds. *Religious Experience and Process Theology: The Pastoral Implications of a Major Modern Movement.* New York: Paulist, 1976.

Carr, Anne. "The God Who Is Involved." *Theology Today* 38 (1981) 314–28.

————. *Transforming Grace: Christian Tradition and Women's Experience.* San Francisco: Harper and Row, 1988.

Carr-Wiggin, Robert. "God's Omnipotence and Immutability." *The Thomist* 48 (1984) 44–51.

Case-Winters, Anna. *God's Power: Traditional Understandings and Contemporary Challenges.* Louisville: Westminster/John Knox, 1990.

Casey, Robert P. "Clement of Alexandria and the Beginnings of Christian Platonism." *Harvard Theological Review* 18 (1925) 39–101.

Caskey, Marie. *Chariot of Fire: Religion and the Beecher Family.* New Haven: Yale University Press, 1978.

Cassel, Eric J. "The Nature of Suffering and the Goals of Medicine." *The New England Journal of Medicine* 306 (1982) 639–45.

Chalmers, Thomas. *Lectures on the Epistle of Paul the Apostle to the Romans.* 7th ed. New York: Robert Carter, 1850.

Chéné, Jean. "Unus de Trinitate passus est." *Recherches de Science Religieuse* 53 (1965) 545–88.

Cherbonnier, Edmund LaB. "Biblical Faith and the Idea of Tragedy." In *The Tragic Vision and the Christian Faith*, edited by Nathan A. Scott, Jr., 23–55. New York: Association, 1957.

———. "Logic of Biblical Anthropomorphism." *Harvard Theological Review* 55 (1962) 187–206.

Chopp, Rebecca S. *The Praxis of Suffering: An Interpretation of Liberation and Political Theologies.* Maryknoll: Orbis, 1986.

Chung, Paul. "Trinity and Asian Theology of Divine Dukkar." *Asia Journal of Theology* 16 (2002) 131–47.

Clark, Ted R. "The Doctrine of a Finite God." *Review and Expositor* 52 (1955) 21–43.

Clarke, Bowman L. and Eugene T. Long, eds. *God and Temporality.* God: The Contemporary Discussion Series. New York: Paragon , 1984.

Clarke, O. Fielding. *God and Suffering.* Derby: Peter Smith, 1964.

Clarke, W. Norris. "A New Look at the Immutability of God." In *God Knowable and Unknowable*, edited by Robert J. Roth, 43–72. New York: Fordham University Press, 1973.

Clarke, William Newton. *The Christian Doctrine of God.* New York: Scribner, 1909.

———. *An Outline of Christian Theology.* New York: Scribner, 1898.

Clifford, Paul R. "Omnipotence and the Problem of Evil." *Journal of Religion* 41 (1961) 118–28.

Cobb, John B., Jr. *God and the World.* Philadelphia: Westminster, 1969.

——— and Ives, Christopher, eds. *The Emptying God: A Buddhist-Jewish-Christian Conversation.* Faith Meets Faith Series. Maryknoll: Orbis, 1990.

Cohen, Arthur A. *The Tremendum: A Theological Interpretation of the Holocaust.* New York: Crossroad, 1981.

Coldman, A. T. "The Self-Limitation of God." *Church Quarterly Review* 98 (1924) 36–50.

Cole, G. A. "Towards a New Metaphysic of the Exodus." *Reformed Theological Review* 42 (1983) 75–84.

Commissio Theologica Internationalis. "Theologia-Christologia-Anthropologia: Quaestiones Selectae. Altera Series (Sessio Plenaria 1981, relatio conclusive)." *Gregorianum* 64 (1983) 20–24.

Cone, James H. *God of the Oppressed.* New York: Seabury, 1975.

Cook, David. "Weak Church, Weak God: The Charge of Anthropomorphism." In *The Power and Weakness of God: Impassibility and Orthodoxy: Papers Presented at the Third Edinburgh Conference on Christian Dogmatics, 1989*, edited by Nigel M. de S. Cameron, 69–92. Edinburgh: Rutherford, 1990.

Cook, Katherine. "To Be Suffering Servants." *Christian Ministry* 16 (1985) 20–22.

Cooke, Bernard J. "The Mutability-Immutability Principle in St. Augustine's Metaphysics." *Modern Schoolman* 23 (1945) 175–93; 24 (1946) 37–49.

Cooper, Burton Z. "Education for Suffering and the Shifting of the Catena." *Religious Education* 84 (1989) 26–36.

———. "How Does God Act in Our Time? An Invitation to a Dialogue between Process and Liberation Theologies." *Union Seminary Quarterly Review* 32 (1976) 25–35.

———. "Why, God? A Tale of Two Sufferers." *Theology Today* 42 (1986) 423–34.

Cowburn, John. *Shadows and the Dark: The Problems of Suffering and Evil.* London: SCM, 1979.

Cox, Harvey. "Complaining to God: Theodicy and the Critique of Modernity in the Resurgence of Traditional Religion. The Example of Latin American Liberation Theology." *Archivio di Filosofia* 56 (1988) 311–25.

———. "Gedanken über Jürgen Moltmanns Buch: Der gekreuzigte Gott." In *Diskussion über Jürgen Moltmanns Buch "Der gekreuzigte Gott,"* edited by Michael Welker, 126–39. Munich: Kaiser, 1979.

———. *God's Revolution and Man's Responsibility.* Valley Forge: Judson, 1965.

Cox, R. L. "Tragedy and the Gospel Narratives." *The Yale Review* 57 (1968) 545–70.

Cox, Samuel. "Man's Inhumanity and God's Humanity." *The Sunday Magazine* 28 (1891) 227–30.

Crawford, R. G. "The Atonement in Karl Barth." *Theology* 74 (1971) 355–58.

Creel, Richard E. *Divine Impassibility: An Essay in Philosophical Theology.* Cambridge: Cambridge University Press, 1986.

———. "Process Theology Debate Continues." *Christian Century* 104 (1987) 225–27.

Crenshaw, James L. "The Human Dilemma and Literature of Dissent." In *Tradition and Theology in the Old Testament*, edited by Douglas A. Knight, 235–58. Philadelphia: Fortress, 1977.

———. "Introduction: The Shift from Theodicy to Anthhropodicy." In *Theodicy in the Old Testament*, edited by James L. Crenshaw, 1–16. Issues in Religion and Theology Series, edited by Douglas Knight and Robert Morgan. Philadelphia: Fortress, 1983.

———. "The Problem of Theodicy in Sirach: On Human Bondage." *Journal of Biblical Literature* 94 (1975) 47–64. Also in *Theodicy in the Old Testament*, edited by James L. Crenshaw, 119–40. Issues in Religion and Theology Series, edited by Douglas Knight and Robert Morgan. Philadelphia: Fortress, 1983.

———, ed. *Theodicy in the Old Testament.* Issues in Religion and Theology Series, edited by Douglas Knight and Robert Morgan. Philadelphia: Fortress, 1983.

——— and Sandmel, Samuel, eds. *The Divine Helmsman: Studies on God's Control of Human Events, Presented to Lou H. Silberman.* New York: KTAV, 1980.

Crombie, George M. "Fate and Faith: A Reflection on Australian Culture." *Colloquium: The Australian and New Zealand Theological Review* 20 (1987) 22–30.

Crouzel, Henri. "La passion de l'impassible; un essai apologétique et polémique du IIIe siècle." In *Exgèse et patristique*, 269–79. *L'Homme devant Dieu: Mélanges offerts au Père Henri de Lubac* 1. Théologie: Études publiées sous la direction de la faculté de théologie S. J. de Lyon–Fourvière 56. Paris: Aubier, 1963.

Cyril of Alexandria. *Select Letters*. Edited and translated by Lionel R. Wickham. Oxford Early Christian Texts, edited by Henry Chadwick. Oxford: Clarendon, 1983.

D'Arcy, Charles F. "Love and Omnipotence." In *God and the Struggle for Existence*, edited by B. H. Streeter, 44–60. London: SCM, 1919.

D'Arcy, Martin. "The Immutability of God." *Proceedings of the American Catholic Philosophical Association* 41 (1967) 19–26.

Dalferth, Ingolf U. "Gott und Sünde." *Neue Zeitschrift für Systematische Theologie und Religionsphilosophie* 33 (1991) 1–22.

Davis, Stephen T., ed. *Encountering Evil: Live Options in Theodicy*. Atlanta: John Knox, 1981.

———. "Universalism, Hell, and the Fate of the Ignorant." *Modern Theology* 6 (1990) 173–86.

Davison, W. T. "God and the World: A Theodicy." *London Quarterly Review* 125 (1916) 1–21.

Dawe, Donald G. *The Form of a Servant: A Historical Analysis of the Kenotic Motif.* Philadelphia: Westminster, 1963.

De Andia, Y. "Passione di Cristo passione di Dio." *Communio* 49 (1980) 45–57.

De Diétrich, Suzanne. " 'You Are My Witnesses': A Study of the Church's Witness." *Interpretation* 8 (1954) 273–79.

De Margerie, Bertrand. "De la souffrance de Dieu?" *Esprit et Vie* 93 (1983) 110–12.

De Schrijver, Georges. "From Theodicy to Anthropodicy: The Contemporary Acceptance of Nietzsche and the Problem of Suffering." In *God and Human Suffering*, Louvain Theological and Pastoral Monographs, vol. 3, edited by Jan Lambrecht and Raymond F. Collins, 95–119. Louvain: Peeters, 1990.

———. "Theodicy, Justification, and Justice: A Critique of Leibniz from the Perspective of Latin American Liberation Theology." *Archivio di Filosofia* 56 (1988) 291–310.

Dearborn, Timothy A. "God, Grace and Salvation." In *Christ in Our Place: The Humanity of God in Christ for the Reconciliation of the World: Essays Presented to Professor James Torrance*, edited by Trevor A. Hart and Daniel P. Thimell, 265–93. Exeter: Paternoster, 1989.

Dearing, Richard N. "Ministry and the Problem of Suffering." *Journal of Pastoral Care* 39 (1985) 58–68.

DeBellis, Robert, et al, eds. *Suffering: Psychological and Social Aspects in Loss, Grief and Care*. New York: Haworth, 1986.

Denzinger, Henricus and Adolfus Schönmetzer, eds. *Enchiridion Symbolorum: Definitionum et Declarationum de Rebus Fidei et Morum*. 33rd ed. Freiburg im Breisgau: Verlag Herder, 1965.

Depoortere, Kristiaan. "'You Have Striven with God' (Gen 32:28): A Pastoral-Theological Reflection on the Image of God and Suffering." In *God and Human Suffering*, Louvain Theological and Pastoral Monographs, vol. 3, edited by Jan Lambrecht and Raymond F. Collins, 211–34. Louvain: Peeters, 1990.

Derrett, J. Duncan M. "'Love Thy Neighbor as a Man Like Thyself'?" *The Expository Times* 83 (1971) 55–56.

Deuser, Hermann, et al, eds. *Gottes Zukunft-Zukunft der Welt: Festschrift für Jürgen Moltmann zum 60 Geburtstag*. Munich: Kaiser, 1986.

DeWolf, Harold. *A Theology of the Living Church.* New York: Harper and Brothers, 1953.

DeYounge, Kevin. "Divine Impassibility and the Passion of Christ in the Book of Hebrews." *Westminster Theological Journal* 68 (2006) 41–50.

Dietrich, Ernst Ludwig. "Die rabbinische Kritik an Gott." *Zeitschrift für Religions und Geistesgeschichte* 7 (1955) 193–224.

Dillard, Raymond B. "Reward and Punishment in Chronicles: The Theology of Immediate Retribution." *Westminster Theological Journal* 46 (1984) 164–72.

Dillistone, F. W. *The Christian Understanding of the Atonement.* Philadelphia: Westminster, 1968.

Dinsmore, Charles Allen. *Atonement in Literature and Life.* Boston: Houghton, Mifflin, 1906.

Doctrine in the Church of England (1938): The Report of the Commission on Christian Doctrine Appointed by the Archbishops of Canterbury and York. London: SPCK, 1938.

Doctrine in the Church of England: The Report of the Commission on Christian Doctrine Appointed by the Archbishops of Canterbury and York in 1922. London: SPCK, 1938; 1982 edition.

Dodds, Michael J. "Thomas Aquinas, Human Suffering, and the Unchanging God of Love." *Theological Studies* 52 (1991) 330–44.

———. *The Unchanging God of Love: A Study of the Teaching of Thomas Aquinas on Divine Immutability in View of Certain Contemporary Criticism of This Doctrine.* Studia Friburgensia: Travaux Publiés sous la Direction des Dominicains Professeurs l'Université de Fribourg Suisse. Novelle Série, vol. 66. Fribourg, Switzerland: Éditions Universitaires Fribourg Suisse, 1986.

Doherty, Catherine de Hueck. "The Meaning of Suffering—A Personal Witness." In *The Meaning of Human Suffering,* edited by Flavian Dougherty, 343–48. New York: Human Sciences, 1982.

Donceel, Joseph. "Second Thoughts on the Nature of God." *Thought* 46 (1971) 346–70.

Dorner, Isaac August. *Divine Immutability: How God's Immutability Should Be Understood.* Translated by Robert R. Williams and Claude Welch. Minneapolis: Fortress, 1994.

———. "Dogmatic Discussion of the Doctrine of the Immutability of God." In *God and Incarnation in Mid-Nineteenth Century German Theology: G. Thomasius, I. A. Dorner, A. E. Biedermann,* edited and translated by Claude Welch, 115–80. A Library of Protestant Thought, edited by John Dillenberger et al. New York: Oxford University Press, 1965.

———. *A System of Christian Doctrine.* Vol. 2. Translated by J. S. Banks. Edinburgh: T. & T. Clark, 1881.

Dougherty, Flavian, ed. *The Meaning of Human Suffering.* New York: Human Sciences, 1982.

Dreher, Martin N. "A theologia crucis de Lutero e o tema da teologia da libertaçâo." *Estudos Teológicos* 28 (1988) 137–52.

Duclow, Donald F. "'My Suffering Is God': Meister Eckhart's Book of Divine Consolation." *Theological Studies* 44 (1983) 570–86.

Duncan, J. Ligon III. "Divine Passibility and Impassibility in Nineteenth-Century American Confessional Presbyterian Theologians." *Scottish Bulletin of Evangelical Theology* 8 (1990) 1–15.

Dunn, Geoffrey D. "Divine Impassibility and Christology in the Christmas Homilies of Leo the Great." *Theological Studies* 62 (2001) 71–85.

Duquoc, Christian. "The Folly of the Cross and 'The Human.'" *Concilium* 155 (1982) 65–73.

Durham, John I. "שלם and the Presence of God." In *Proclamation and Presence: Old Testament Essays in Honour of Gwynne Henton Davies*, edited by John I. Durham and J. R. Porter, 272–93. Richmond: John Knox, 1970.

Dussel, Enrique. "The People of El Salvador: The Communal Sufferings of Job." *Concilium* 169 (1983) 61–68.

Dvorácek, Jan A. "Vom Leiden Gottes: Markus 15, 29–34." *Communio Viatorum* 14 (1971) 224–45.

Ebach, Jürgen. "'Lord, why have you done evil to this people?' Lamentation before God and Accusation against God in the Experience of Failure." In *Concilium: Coping with Failure*, edited by Norbert Greinacher and Norbert Mette, 117–27. Philadelphia: Trinity, 1990.

———. "Die Welt, 'in der Erlösung nicht vorweggenommen werden kann' (G. Scholem) *oder*: Wider den 'Trug für Gott' (Hi 13, 7) Thesen zum Hiobbuch." In *Leiden*, edited by Willi Oelmüller, 20–27. *Kolloquium Religion und Philosophie*, vol 3. Paderborn: Ferdinand Schöning, 1986.

Eckardt, Burnell F. "Luther and Moltmann: The Theology of the Cross." *Concordia Theological Quarterly* 49 (1985) 19–28.

Edwards, Rem B. "Pagan Dogma of the Absolute Unchangeableness of God." *Religious Studies* 14 (1978) 305–13.

Ehrlich, A. *Randglossen zur hebräischen Bibel*. 2 vols. Leipzig, 1909.

Eibach, Ulrich. "Prayer and Conceptions of God." In *Concilium: Asking and Thanking*, edited by Christian Duquoc and Casiano Florestan, 60–74. Philadelphia: Trinity, 1990.

———. "Die Sprache leidender Menschen und der Wandel des Gottesbildes." *Theologische Zeitschrift* 40 (1984) 34–65.

Eichrodt, Walther. "Faith in Providence and Theodicy in the Old Testament." In *Theodicy in the Old Testament*, edited by James L. Crenshaw, 17–41. Issues in Religion and Theology Series, edited by Douglas Knight and Robert Morgan. Philadelphia: Fortress, 1983.

———. *Theology of the Old Testament*. Vol. 2. Translated by J. A. Baker. The Old Testament Library Series. Philadelphia: Westminster, 1967.

Eidem, Erling. *Den Lidande Guden: Nagra Subjektiva Betraktelser över Det Högsta Objektiva*. Stockholm: Sveriges Kristliga Studentrörelses Förlag, 1921.

———. *The Suffering God: A Few Subjective Meditations on the Highest Objective Reality*. Translated by S. G. Hägglund. Rock Island: Augustana, 1938.

Eigo, Francis A., ed. *Suffering and Healing in Our Day*. Villanova: Villanova University Press, 1990.

———. ed. *Whither Creativity, Freedom, Suffering? Humanity, Cosmos, God*. Pittsburgh: Villanova University Press, 1981.

Eisland. Nancy L. and Amy Contopulos (illustrator). "Encountering the Disabled God." *Other Side* 38 (2002) 10–15.

Elert, Werner. *Der Ausgang der altkirchlichen Christologie: Eine Untersuchung über Theodor von Pharan und seine Zeit als* Einführung *in die alte Dogmengeschichte*. Edited by Wilhelm Maurer and Elisabeth Bergsträsser. Berlin: Lutherisches Verlagshaus, 1957.

———. "Die Theopaschitische Formel." *Theologische Literaturzeitung* 75 (1950) 195–206.

Eliade, Mircea. *Myth and Reality*. Translated by Willard R. Trask. New York: Harper and Row, 1963.

Ellis, Robert. "From Hegel to Whitehead." *Journal of Religion* 61 (1981) 403–21.

Elmore, Joe Earl. "The Theme of the Suffering of God in the Thought of Nicholas Berdyaev, Charles Hartshorne, and Reinhold Niebuhr." PhD diss., Columbia University, 1963.

Elphinstone, Andrew. *Freedom, Suffering and Love*. Edited by G. R. Dunstan. London: SCM, 1976.

Endo, Shusaku. "Concerning the Novel 'Silence'." *Japan Christian Quarterly* 36 (1970) 100–3.

England, Eugene. "The Weeping God of Mormonism." *Dialogue* 35 (2002) 63–80.

Enuma Elish. "The Creation Epic." Translated by E. A. Speiser. In *Ancient Near Eastern Texts Relating to the Old Testament*, edited by James A. Pritchard, 60–72. Princeton: Princeton University Press, 1950.

Erickson, Millard J. *The Word Became Flesh*. Grand Rapids: Baker, 1991.

Estess, Ted L. "Elie Wiesel and the Drama of Interrogation." *Journal of Religion* 56 (1976) 18–34.

Exum, J. Cheryl. *Tragedy and Biblical Narrative: Arrows of the Almighty*. Cambridge: Cambridge University Press, 1992.

Eyzaguirre, Samuel Fernandez. " '*Passio Caritatis*' according to Origen in *Ezechielem Homiliae* VI in the Light of DT 1.31." *Vigiliae christianae* 60 (2006) 135–47.

Fackenheim, Emil L. "New Hearts and the Old Covenant: On Some Possibilities of a Fraternal Jewish-Christian Reading of the Jewish Bible Today." In *The Divine Helmsman: Studies on God's Control of Human Events, Presented to Lou H. Silberman*, edited by James L. Crenshaw and Samuel Sandmel, 191–203. New York: KTAV, 1980.

Fackre, Gabriel. "Almighty God and the Problem of Evil." *Pacific Theological Review* 15 (1980) 11–16.

Fagnani, C. P. "Humanity of God." *Christian Century* 40 (1923) 429–30.

Fairbairn, Andrew Martin. *The Place of Christ in Modern Theology*. 1912 ed. New York: Scribner, 1893.

Farley, Edward. *Divine Empathy: A Theology of God*. Minneapolis: Fortress, 1996.

———. *Ecclesial Reflection: An Anatomy of Theological Method*. Philadelphia: Fortress, 1982.

———. "God as Dominator and Image Giver: Divine Sovereignty and the New Anthropology." *Journal of Ecumenical Studies* 6 (1969) 354–75.

———. *Good and Evil: Interpreting a Human Condition*. Minneapolis: Fortress, 1990.

Farley, Wendy. *Tragic Vision and Divine Compassion: A Contemporary Theodicy.* Louisville: Westminster/John Knox, 1990.

Feitsma, Muus. *Het Theopaschitisme: Een Dogma-Historische Studie over de Ontwikkeling van het Theopaschitisch Denken.* Kampen: J. H. Kok N. V., 1956.

Felt, James W. "The Temporality of Divine Freedom." *Process Studies* 4 (1974) 252–62.

Ferrar, W. J. "Modern View of God." *London Quarterly Review* 148 (1927) 236–48.

Feuerbach, Ludwig. *The Essence of Christianity.* Translated by George Eliot. 2nd ed., 1843. New York: Harper and Row, Harper Torchbooks, 1957.

Feuillet, André. *L'Agonie de Gethsémani.* Paris: Gabalda, 1977.

———. "Souffrance et confiance en Dieu: Commentaire du Psaume XXII." *Nouvelle Revue Théologique* 70 (1948) 137–49.

Fiddes, Paul S. *The Creative Suffering of God.* Oxford: Clarendon, 1988.

———. "*The Cross of Hosea* Revisited: The Meaning of Suffering in the Book of Hosea." *Review and Expositor* 90 (1993) 175–90.

———. *Past Event and Present Salvation: The Christian Idea of Atonement.* Louisville: Westminster/John Knox, 1989.

Fiorenza, Francis P. "Joy and Pain as Paradigmatic for Language about God." In *Concilium: Religion in the Seventies.* Vol. 10. *Theology of Joy,* edited by Johann Baptist Metz and Jean–Pierre Jossua, 67–80. New York: Herder and Herder, 1974.

Fishbane, Michael. "Sin and Judgment in the Prophecies of Ezekiel." *Interpretation* 38 (1984) 131–50.

Fleming, James R. "Restoration through Indemnity and the Problem of Suffering." In *Restoring the Kingdom,* edited by Deane William Ferm, 33–43. Unification Studies Series. New York: Paragon, 1984.

Ford, Lewis S. "Divine Persuasion and the Triumph of Good." In *Process Philosophy and Christian Thought,* edited by Delwin Brown, Ralph E. James, Jr., and Gene Reeves, 287–304. Indianapolis: Bobbs-Merrill, 1971.

———. *The Lure of God: A Biblical Background for Process Theism.* Philadelphia: Fortress, 1978.

———. "Our Prayers as God's Passions." In *Religious Experience and Process Theology: The Pastoral Implications of a Major Modern Movement,* edited by Harry James Cargas and Bernard Lee, 429–38. New York: Paulist, 1976.

"Formula of Concord," "Part II: Solid Declaration." In *The Book of Concord: The Confessions of the Evangelical Lutheran Church,* translated and edited by Theodore G. Tappert, 463–636. Philadelphia: Fortress, 1959.

Forster, Peter R. "Divine Passibility and the Early Christian Doctrine of God." In *The Power and Weakness of God: Impassibility and Orthodoxy: Papers Presented at the Third Edinburgh Conference in Christian Dogmatics, 1989,* edited by Nigel M. de S. Cameron, 23–51. Edinburgh: Rutherford, 1990.

Forsyth, P. T. *The Justification of God: Lectures for War-Time on a Christian Theodicy.* New York: Scribner, 1917.

———. *The Person and Place of Jesus Christ.* Boston: Pilgrim, 1909.

Foster, Durwood and Paul Mojzes, eds. *Society and Original Sin: Ecumenical Essays on the Impact of the Fall.* New York: Paragon, 1985.

Frankenberry, Nancy. "Some Problems in Process Theodicy." *Religious Studies* 17 (1981) 179–97.

Fretheim, Terence E. "The Repentance of God: A Key to Evaluating Old Testament God-Talk." *Horizons in Biblical Theology* 10 (1988) 47–70.

———. "The Repentance of God: A Study of Jeremiah 18:7–10." *Hebrew Annual Review* 11 (1987) 81–92.

———. "Suffering God and Sovereign God in Exodus: A Collision of Images." *Horizons in Biblical Theology* 11 (1989) 31–56.

———. *The Suffering of God: An Old Testament Perspective.* Overtures to Biblical Theology Series, edited by Walter Brueggemann and John Donahue. Philadelphia: Fortress, 1984.

Freud, Sigmund. *Totem and Taboo: Some Points of Agreement between the Mental Lives of Savages and Neurotics.* Translated by James Strachey. New York: W. W. Norton, 1950.

Frey, Chr. "Ewige Passion Gottes." *Lutherische Monatshefte* 21 (1982) 90–91.

Frey, Robert Seitz. "The Holocaust and the Suffering of God." In *Remembering for the Future: Working Papers and Addenda.* Vol. 1. *Jews and Christians During and After the Holocaust,* edited by Yehuda Bauer et al, 612–21. New York: Pergamon Press, 1989.

———. "The Nature of God and Images of Humankind." *Encounter* 49 (1988) 93–107.

———. "Post-Holocaust Theodicy: Images of Deity, History, and Humanity." *Bridges: An Interdisciplinary Journal of Theology, Philosophy, History, and Science* 3 (1991) 9–21.

Fries, Heinrich. "Der christliche Glaube vor der Herausforderung der Leidensproblematik." In *Communicatio Fidei: Festschrift für Eugen Biser zum 65 Geburtstag,* edited by Horst Bürkle and Gerhold Becker, 99–109. Regensburg: Verlag Friedrich Pustet, 1983.

———. "Praesentia Christi im Leiden." In *Praesentia Christi: Festschrift für Johannes Betz zum 70 Geburtstag dargebracht von Kollegen, Freunden, Schülern,* edited by Lothar Lies, 385–95. Düsseldorf: Patmos Verlag, 1984.

Fritz, Maureena. "A Midrash: The Self-Limitation of God." *Journal of Ecumenical Studies* 22 (1985) 703–14.

Frohnhofen, Herbert. *Apatheia Tou Theou: Über die Affektlosigkeit Gottes in der griechischen Antike und bei den griechischsprachigen Kirchenvätern bis zu Gregorios Thaumaturgos.* Europäische Hochschulschriften. Series 23. *Theologie* 318. Frankfurt am Main: Verlag Peter Lang, 1987.

Fromm, Erich. *You Shall Be as Gods: A Radical Interpretation of the Old Testament and Its Tradition.* Greenwich, CT: Fawcett , 1966.

Furnish, Victor Paul. *Theology and Ethics in Paul.* Nashville: Abingdon, 1968.

Gajardo-Velasquez, Joel. "Suffering Coming from the Struggle against Suffering." In *The Meaning of Human Suffering,* edited by Flavian Dougherty, 266–300. New York: Human Sciences, 1982.

Galot, Jean. *Dieu souffre-t-il?* Paris: P. Lethielleux, 1976.

———. "Le Dieu Trinitaire et la passion du Christ." *Nouvelle Revue Théologique* 104 (1982) 70–87.

———. "Le mystère de la souffrance de Dieu." *Esprit et Vie* 100 (1990) 261–68.

———. "Necessità di una teologia della sofferenza di Dio secondo uno studio di J. Maritain." In *La Sapienza della Croce Oggi: Atti del Congresso internazionale Roma, 13–18 Ottobre 1975*, vol. 1, *La Sapienza della Croce nella Rivelazione e nell' Ecumenismo*, 356–62. Torino: Leumann, 1976.

———. "La réalité de la souffrance de Dieu." *Nouvelle Revue Théologique* 101 (1979) 224–44.

———. "La révélation de la souffrance de Dieu." *Science et Esprit* 31 (1979) 159–71.

———. *Vers une nouvelle christologie.* Paris: Duculot-Lethielleux, 1971.

Gammie, John G. *Holiness in Israel.* Overtures to Biblical Theology Series, edited by Walter Brueggemann, John R. Donahue, Elizabeth Struthers Malbon, and Christopher R. Seitz. Minneapolis: Fortress, 1989.

García-Mateo, Rogelio. "Erlösung als Selbstrechtfertigung Gottes: Leiden und Tragik im Denken Miguel de Unamunos." In *Auf der Suche nach dem verborgenen Gott: Zur theologischen Relevanz neuzeitlichen Denkens*, edited by Alois Halder, Klaus Kienzler, and Joseph Möller, 274–87. Düsseldorf: Patmos Verlag, 1987.

Garrison, Jim. *The Darkness of God: Theology after Hiroshima.* Grand Rapids: Eerdmans, 1982.

Gavrilyuk, Paul. "Theopatheia: Nestorius's Main Charge against Cyril of Alexandria." *Scottish Journal of Theology* 56 (2003) 190–207.

Geertz, Clifford. *The Interpretation of Cultures: Selected Essays.* New York: Basic Books, 1973.

Geffre, Claude. *The Risk of Interpretation: On Being Faithful to the Christian Tradition in a Non-Christian Age.* Translated by David Smith. New York: Paulist, 1987.

Geisler, Norman L. *The Roots of Evil.* 2nd ed. Dallas: Word/Probe, 1989.

Gerstenberger, Erhard S. and Wolfgang Schrage. *Suffering.* Translated by John E. Steely. Nashville: Abingdon, 1980.

Gervais, M. "Incarnation et immuabilité divine." *Revue des sciences religieuses* 50 (1976) 215–34.

Gesché, Adolphe. "Odyssée de la théodicée: Dieu dans l'objection." *Archivio di Filosofia* 56 (1988) 453–68.

———. "Topiques de la question du mal." *Revue théologique de Louvain* 17 (1986) 393–418.

Geyer, Carl-Friedrich. "Das Theodizeeproblem—ein historischer und systematischer Überblick." In *Theodizee—Gott vor Gericht?* edited by Willi Oelmüller, 9–32. Munich: Wilhelm Fink Verlag, 1990.

———. "Wirkungsgeschichtliche Aspekte der biblischen Hiobdichtung." In *Leiden*, edited by Willi Oelmüller, 28–39. *Kolloquium Religion und Philosophie*, vol 3. Paderborn: Ferdinand Schöning, 1986.

Gilkey, Langdon. *Catholicism Confronts Modernity.* New York: Seabury, 1975.

———. "The Christian Understanding of Suffering." *Buddhist-Christian Studies* 5 (1985) 49–65

———. "The Concept of Providence in Contemporary Theology." *Journal of Religion* 43 (1963) 171–92.

———. "Cosmology, Ontology, and the Travail of Biblical Language." *Journal of Religion* 41 (1961) 194–205.

———. "Creation, Being and Nonbeing." In *God and Creation: An Ecumenical Symposium*, edited by David B. Burrell and Bernard McGinn, 226–41. Notre

Dame: University of Notre Dame Press, 1990. Also in, Gilkey, *Through the Tempest*, 89–100.

———. "God." In *Christian Theology: An Introduction to Its Traditions and Tasks*, edited by Peter C. Hodgson and Robert H. King, 88–113. Revised and enlarged ed. Philadelphia: Fortress, 1985. Also as "The Christian Understanding of God." In *Through the Tempest: Theological Voyages in a Pluralistic Culture* by Langdon Gilkey, edited by Jeff B. Pool, 69–88. Minneapolis: Fortress, 1991.

———. *Maker of Heaven and Earth: The Christian Doctrine of Creation in the Light of Modern Knowledge*. 1959. Reprint, New York: University Press of America, 1985.

———. "The Meaning of Jesus the Christ." In *The Christ and The Bodhisattva*, edited by Donald S. Lopez Jr. and Steven C. Rockefeller, 193–207. Albany: State University of New York Press, 1987.

———. "Meditation on Death and Its Relation to Life." *Archivio di Filosofia* 49 (1981) 19–32.

———. *Message and Existence: An Introduction to Christian Theology*. New York: Seabury, 1981.

———. *Naming the Whirlwind: The Renewal of God-Language*. Indianapolis: Bobbs-Merrill, 1969.

———. "Power, Order, Justice, and Redemption." In *The Voice from the Whirlwind: Interpreting the Book of Job*, edited by Leo G. Perdue and W. Clark Gilpin, 159–71. Nashville: Abingdon, 1992.

———. *Reaping the Whirlwind: A Christian Interpretation of History*. New York: Seabury, 1976.

———. "The Roles of the 'Descriptive' or 'Historical' and of the 'Normative' in Our Work." *Criterion* 20 (1981) 10–17.

———. *Society and the Sacred: Toward a Theology of Culture in Decline*. New York: Crossroad, 1981.

———. "Symbols, Meaning, and the Divine Presence." *Theological Studies* 35 (1974) 249–67; also in Gilkey, *Through the Tempest*, 49–65.

———. *Through the Tempest: Theological Voyages in a Pluralistic Culture*. Edited by Jeff B. Pool. Minneapolis: Fortress, 1991.

Gillet, Lev. "Le Dieu souffrant." *Contacts: Revue Français de l'Orthodoxie* 17 (1965) 239–54.

Gillon, Louis-B. "Tristesse et miséricorde du Père." *Angelicum* 55 (1978) 3–11.

Glatt, Melvin J. "God the Mourner—Israel's Companion in Tragedy." *Judaism* 28 (1979) 72–79.

Glennon, Fred. "Divine Pathos and Human Sympathy: Saying Yes and No to Gustafson's Theocentric Ethics." *Perspectives in Religious Studies* 17 (1990) 237–51.

Godet, Frederic. *Commentary on the Gospel of John with an Historical and Critical Introduction*. Vol. 1. 3d ed. Translated by Timothy Dwight. New York: Funk and Wagnall's, 1886.

Godsey, John D. "Bonhoeffer's Doctrine of Love." In *New Studies in Bonhoeffer's Ethics*, edited by William J. Peck, 189–234. Toronto Studies in Theology Series, vol. 30, Bonhoeffer Series, no. 3. Lewiston, New York: Edwin Mellen, 1987.

Goetz, Ronald. "The Divine Burden." *Christian Century* 95 (22 March 1978) 298–302.

————. "Karl Barth, Juergen Moltmann and the Theopaschite Revolution." In *Festschrift: A Tribute to Dr. William Hordern*, edited by Walter Freitag, 17–28. Saskatoon: University of Saskatchewan, 1985.

————. "Process Theology Debate Continues." *Christian Century* 104 (4 March 1987) 224–25.

————. "The Suffering God: The Rise of a New Orthodoxy." *Christian Century* 103 (16 April 1986) 385–89.

Goitein, S. D. "YHWH the Passionate: The Monotheistic Meaning and Origin of the Name YHWH." *Vetus Testamentum* 6 (1956) 1–9.

Gonnet, Dominique. *Dieu aussi* connaît *la souffrance*. Paris: Les éditions du cerf, 1990.

Gonzalez, Faus. "La teologia del dolor de Dios." *Estudios eclesiàsticos* 48 (1973) 5–40.

Gordon, George Angier. *The New Epoch for Faith*. Boston and New York: Houghton, Mifflin, 1901.

Gore, Charles. *Belief in God*. New York: Scribner, 1922.

Gotthard, Fuchs. "Does God Fail? Theological Considerations with a Practical Intent." In *Concilium: Coping with Failure*, edited by Norbert Greinacher and Norbert Mette, 128–37. Philadelphia: Trinity, 1990.

Goulder, Michael, ed. *Incarnation and Myth: The Debate Continued*. Grand Rapids: Eerdmans, 1979.

Grant, Colin. "The Abandonment of Atonement." *King's Theological Review* 9 (1986) 1–8.

————. "Possibilities for Divine Passibility." *Toronto Journal of Theology* 4 (1988) 3–18.

Grant, Frederick C. *Roman Hellenism and the New Testament*. New York: Scribner, 1962.

Grant, Robert M. *The Early Christian Doctrine of God*. Charlottesville: University of Virginia Press, 1966.

————. *Gods and the One God*. Library of Early Christianity Series, edited by Wayne A. Meeks. Philadelphia: Westminster, 1986.

———— and David Tracy. *A Short History of the Interpretation of the Bible*. 2nd ed. Philadelphia: Fortress, 1984.

Grassi, Joseph A. "'I Was Hungry and You Gave Me to Eat' (Matt 25:35ff.): The Divine Identification Ethic in Matthew." *Biblical Theology Bulletin: A Journal of Bible and Theology* 11 (1981) 81–84.

Greenberg, Simon. "God in the Biblical–Rabbinic Tradition." In *God in Contemporary Thought: A Philosophical Perspective*, edited by Sebastian A. Matczak, 301–48. Philosophical Questions Series, vol. 10, edited by Sebastian A. Matczak. Jamaica, New York: Learned Publications, 1977.

Gregg, Robert C. "The Centrality of Soteriology in Early Arianism." In *Studia Patristica* 15.1, edited by Elizabeth A. Livingstone, 305–16. Berlin: Academie-Verlag, 1984.

———— and Dennis E. Groh. "The Centrality of Soteriology in Early Arianism." *Anglican Theological Review* 59 (1977) 260–78.

Greider, Kathleen J. "'Too Militant?': Aggression, Gender, and the Construction of Justice." *The Occasional Paper* 3 (1993) 1–8.

Greshake, G. "Leiden und Gottesfrage." *Geist und Leben* 50 (1977) 102–21.

Griffin, David Ray. *Evil Revisited: Responses and Reconsiderations*. Albany: State University of New York Press, 1991.

———. *God, Power, and Evil: A Process Theodicy*. Philadelphia: Westminster, 1967.

———. "Holy Spirit: Compassion and Reverence for Being." In *Religious Experience and Process Theology: The Pastoral Implications of a Major Modern Movement*, edited by Harry James Cargas and Bernard Lee, 107–20. New York: Paulist, 1976.

———. "Religious Pluralism: Generic, Identist, and Deep." In *Deep Religious Pluralism*, edited by David Ray Griffin, 3–38. Louisville: Westminster John Knox, 2005.

———. "The Rationality of Belief in God: A Response to Hans Küng." *Faith and Philosophy* 1 (1984) 16–26.

Griffin, George. *The Sufferings of Christ*. 2nd ed. New York: Harper and Brothers, 1846.

Grislis, Egil. "Luther's Understanding of the Wrath of God." *Journal of Religion* 41 (1961) 277–92.

Gruber, L. F., and F. H. Foster. "Theory of a Finite and Developing Deity Examined; Discussion." *Bibliotheca Sacra* (Oberlin) 75 (1918) 475–526; 76 (1919) 125–32.

Gruber, Mayer I. *The Motherhood of God and Other Studies*. No. 57, South Florida Studies in the History of Judaism. Atlanta: Scholars, 1992.

Gruchy, John De. "Salvation as Healing and Humanization." In *Christ in Our Place: The Humanity of God in Christ for the Reconciliation of the World: Essays Presented to Professor James Torrance*, edited by Trevor A. Hart and Daniel P. Thimell, 32–47. Exeter: Paternoster, 1989.

Guroian, Vigen. "The Suffering God of Armenian Christology: Toward an Ecumenical Theology of the Cross." *Dialog* 32 (1993) 97–101.

Gustafson, James M. *Ethics from a Theocentric Perspective*. Vol. 1. *Theology and Ethics*. Chicago: University of Chicago Press, 1981.

———. *Ethics from a Theocentric Perspective*. Vol. 2. *Ethics and Theology*. Chicago: University of Chicago Press, 1984.

———. "A Response to the Book of Job." In *The Voice from the Whirlwind: Interpreting the Book of Job*, edited by Leo G. Perdue and W. Clark Gilpin, 172–84, 251. Nashville: Abingdon, 1992.

Gutiérrez, Gustavo. *On Job: God-Talk and the Suffering of the Innocent*. Translated by Matthew J. O'Connell. Maryknoll: Orbis, 1987.

Habermas, Jürgen. *Knowledge and Human Interests*. Translated by Jeremy J. Shapiro. Boston: Beacon, 1971.

Hall, Charles Cuthbert. *The Gospel of Divine Sacrifice: A Study in Evangelical Belief with Some Conclusions Touching Life*. New York: Dodd, Mead, 1898.

Hall, Douglas John. *God and Human Suffering: An Exercise in the Theology of the Cross*. Minneapolis: Augsburg, 1986.

———. *Imaging God: Dominion as Stewardship*. Grand Rapids: Eerdmans; New York: Friendship, 1986.

Hallman, Joseph M. *The Descent of God: Divine Suffering in History and Theology*. Minneapolis: Fortress, 1991.

———. "Divine Suffering and Change in Origen and *Ad Theopompum*." *The Second Century* 7 (1990) 85–98.

———. "The Emotions of God in the Theology of St. Augustine." *Recherches de théologie ancienne et médiévale* 51 (1984) 5–19.

———. "The Mutability of God: Tertullian to Lactantius." *Theological Studies* 42 (1981) 373–93.

———. "The Necessity of the World in Thomas Aquinas and Alfred North Whitehead." *Modern Schoolman* 60 (1983) 264–72.

Halperin, Sarah. "Tragedy in the Bible." *Semitics* 7 (1980) 28–39.

Hammer, Robert Alan. "The God of Suffering." *Conservative Judaism* 31 (1976–1977) 34–41.

Hankey, Wayne. "Aquinas and the Passion of God." In *Being and Truth: Essays in Honour of John Macquarrie*, edited by Alistair Kee and Eugene T. Long, 318–33. London: SCM, 1986.

Hanson, Geddes. "The Hope: God's Suffering in Man's Struggle." *Reformed World* 36 (1980) 72–79.

Hanson, R. P. C. "The Arian Doctrine of the Incarnation." In *Arianism, Historical and Theological Reassessments: Papers from the Ninth International Conference on Patristic Studies*, edited by Robert C. Gregg, 181–211. Philadelphia: Philadelphia Patristic Foundation, 1985.

———. *The Search for the Christian Doctrine of God: The Arian Controversy 318–381*. Edinburgh: T. & T. Clark, 1988.

Hardin, Garrett. "The Tragedy of the Commons." *Science* 162 (1968) 1243–8.

Hardmeier, Christof. *Texttheorie und biblische Exegese: zur rhetorischen Funktion der Trauermetaphorik in der Prophetie*. Munich: Kaiser, 1978.

Harnack, Adolf von. *History of Dogma*. Vol. 1. 3rd ed. Translated by Neil Buchanan. Boston: Roberts Brothers, 1897.

———. *History of Dogma*. Vol. 4. 3rd ed. Translated by Neil Buchanan. Boston: Little, Brown, 1898.

———. *What is Christianity?* Translated by Thomas Bailey Saunders. Fortress Texts in Modern Theology. 1957. Reprint, Philadelphia: Fortress, 1986.

Harrington, Wilfrid. *The Tears of God: Our Benevolent Creator and Human Suffering*. Collegeville, MN: Liturgical, 1992.

Harris, John. *The Great Teacher: Characteristics of Our Lord's Ministry*. 16th ed. Boston: Gould and Lincoln, 1859.

Harrison, William Pope. "Can the Divine Nature Suffer?" *Methodist Quarterly Review* 25 (1887) 119–21.

Hart, David B. "No Shadow of Turning: On Divine Impassibility." *Pro Ecclesia* 11 (2002) 184–206.

Hart, Trevor A. and Daniel P. Thimell, eds. *Christ in Our Place: The Humanity of God in Christ for the Reconciliation of the World: Essays Presented to Professor James Torrance*. Exeter: Paternoster, 1989.

Hartshorne, Charles. "The Formally Possible Doctrines of God." In *Process Philosophy and Christian Thought*, edited by Delwin Brown, Ralph E. James, Jr., and Gene Reeves, 188–214. Indianapolis: Bobbs-Merrill Company, 1971.

———. "Is Whitehead's God the God of Religion?" *Ethics* 53 (1943) 219–27.

———. "A New Look at the Problem of Evil." In *Current Philosophical Issues: Essays in Honor of Curt John Ducasse*, edited by Frederick C. Dommeyer, 201–12. Springfield, IL: Charles C. Thomas, 1966.

———. "Tillich and the Other Great Tradition." *Anglican Theological Review* 43 (1961) 245–59.

———. "Whitehead and Berdyaev: Is There Tragedy in God?" *Journal of Religion* 37 (1957) 71–84.

——— and William L. Reese, eds. *Philosophers Speak of God*. 1953. Reprint, Chicago: University of Chicago Press, 1976.

Hatcher, Brian A. "Eternal Punishment and Christian Missions: The Response of the Church Missionary Society to Broad Church Theology." *Anglican Theological Review* 72 (1990) 39–61.

Haughton, Rosemary. *The Passionate God*. New York: Paulist, 1981.

Hauken, A. I. "Incarnation and Hierarchy: The Christ according to Ps-Dionysius." In *Studia Patristica* 15:1, edited by Elizabeth A. Livingstone, 317–20. Berlin: Academie-Verlag, 1984.

Hayman, Eric. *Disciplines of the Spiritual Life*. London: SPCK, 1957.

Hays, Richard B. *The Moral Vision of the New Testament: Community, Cross, New Creation*. San Francisco: HarperSanFrancisco, Harper Collins, 1996.

Hebblethwaite, Brian. *Evil, Suffering and Religion*. London: Sheldon, 1976.

———. "The Moral and Religious Value of the Incarnation." In *Incarnation and Myth: The Debate Continued*, edited by Michael Goulder, 87–100. Grand Rapids: Eerdmans, 1979.

Hedinger, Ulrich. *Wider die Versöhnung Gottes mit dem Elend: eine Kritik des christlichen Theismus und A-theismus*. Basler Studien zur historischen und systematischen Theologie 60, edited by Max Geiger. Zurich: Theologischer Verlag, 1972.

Hegel, G. W. F. *The Christian Religion: Lectures on the Philosophy of Religion. Part 3: The Revelatory, Consummate, Absolute Religion*. Edited and translated by Peter C. Hodgson. American Academy of Religion Texts and Translations Series 2, edited by James A. Massey. Missoula: Scholars, 1979.

———. *Hegel on Tragedy*. Edited by Anne and Henry Paolucci. Garden City: Doubleday, 1962

———. *Phenomenology of Spirit*. Translated by A. V. Miller. Oxford: Clarendon, 1977.

Heidegger, Martin. *Being and Time*. 7th ed. Translated by John Macquarrie and Edward Robinson. New York: Harper and Row, 1962.

———. *Sein und Zeit*. 7th ed. Tübingen: Max Niemeyer Verlag, 1953.

Heine, Heinrich. *Religion and Philosophy in Germany: A Fragment*. Translated by John Snodgrass. Boston: Houghton, Mifflin, 1882.

Helle, Horst Jürgen. "Stufen der Theodizee und der Familie." In *Communicatio Fidei: Festschrift für Eugen Biser zum 65 Geburtstag*, edited by Horst Bürkle and Gerhold Becker, 253–66. Regensburg: Verlag Friedrich Pustet, 1983.

Helm, Paul. "The Impossibility of Divine Passibility." In *The Power and Weakness of God: Impassibility and Orthodoxy: Papers Presented at the Third Edinburgh Conference in Christian Dogmatics, 1989*, edited by Nigel M. de S. Cameron, 119–40. Edinburgh: Rutherford, 1990.

Helm, Thomas E. "Enchantment and the Banality of Evil." *Religion in Life* 49 (1980) 81–95.

Hendry, George S. "Nothing." *Theology Today* 39 (1982) 274–89.

Hengel, Martin. *Jews, Greeks and Barbarians: Aspects of the Hellenization of Judaism in the Pre-Christian Period*. Translated by John Bowden. Philadelphia: Fortress, 1980.

Henrichs, Albert. "Loss of Self, Suffering, Violence: The Modern View of Dionysus from Nietzsche to Girard." In *Harvard Studies in Classical Philology*, edited by D. R. Shackleton Bailey, 205–40. Cambridge, MA: Harvard University Press, 1984.

Herdt, Jennifer A. "The Rise of Sympathy and the Question of Divine Suffering." *Journal of Religious Ethics* 29 (2001) 367–99.

Hermann, Wilhelm. *Systematic Theology*. Translated by Nathaniel Micklem and Kenneth Saunders. London: George Allen and Unwin, 1927.

Heron, Alasdair I. C. "The Time of God." In *Gottes Zukunft—Zukunft der Welt: Festschrift für Jürgen Moltmann zum 60 Geburtstag*, edited by Hermann Deuser, Gerhard Marcel Martin, Konrad Stock, and Michael Welker, 231–39. Munich: Kaiser, 1986.

Herzog, Frederick. "Praxis Passionis Divini." *Evangelische Theologie* 44 (1984) 563–75.

Heschel, Abraham J. "The Divine Pathos: The Basic Category of Prophetic Theology." *Judaism* 2 (1955) 61–67.

———. *God in Search of Man: A Philosophy of Judaism*. New York: Farrar, Straus, and Giroux, 1955.

———. *Man Is Not Alone: A Philosophy of Religion*. New York: Farrar, Straus, and Young, 1951.

———. *The Prophets*. 2 vols. New York: Harper and Row, 1962; Harper Colophon, 1975.

Hick, John. *Evil and the God of Love*. San Francisco: Harper and Row, 1966.

———, ed. *The Myth of God Incarnate*. Philadelphia: Westminster, 1977.

Hicks, David C. "Moral Evil as Apparent Disvalue." *Religious Studies* 13 (1977) 1–16.

Hiebert, D. Edmond. "Following Christ's Example: An Exposition of 1 Peter 2:21–25." *Bibliotheca Sacra* 139 (1982) 32–45.

Higgins, Jean. "The Feminine Image of God in Shusaku Endo." In *God and Temporality*, edited by Bowman L. Clarke and Eugene T. Long, 99–117. New York: Paragon, 1984.

———. "The Inner Agony of Endo Shusaku." *Cross Currents* 34 (1984–1985) 414–26.

Highfield, Ron. "Divine Self-Limitation in the Theology of Jürgen Moltmann: A Critical Appraisal." *Christian Scholar's Review* 32 (2002) 49–71.

Hill, William J. "Does Divine Love Entail Suffering in God?" In *God and Temporality*, edited by Bowman L. Clarke and Eugene T. Long, 55–71. New York: Paragon, 1984.

———. "The Historicity of God." *Theological Studies* 45 (1984) 320–33.

Hiller, G. E. "Jacob Boehme on the Divine Nature." *Methodist Review* 109 (1926) 724–31.

Hinson-Hasty, Elizabeth. "Violence, Vulnerabilty and the Suffering of God." *Church and Society* 92 (2002) 129–32.

Hinton, James. *The Mystery of Pain: A Book for the Sorrowful*. New York: Mitchell, Kennerley, 1914; originally published, 1866.

Hitchcock, Roswell Dwight. *Eternal Atonement*. New York: Scribner, 1888.

Hodgson, Leonard. "The Incarnation." In *Essays on the Trinity and the Incarnation: By Members of the Anglican Communion*, edited by A. E. J. Rawlinson, 361–402. London: Longmans, Green, 1933.

Hodgson, Peter C. *New Birth of Freedom: A Theology of Bondage and Liberation*. Philadelphia: Fortress, 1976.

———. *Winds of the Spirit: A Constructive Christian Theology*. Louisville, KY: Westminster John Knox, 1994.

Holditch, Elisabeth. "Theodicy and the God of Hiroshima." In *Theology against the Nuclear Horizon*, edited by Alan Race, 117–26. London: S. C. M. Press Ltd., 1988.

Hopko, Thomas. "You Shall Be Holy, For I Am Holy." *Living Pulpit* 10 (July–September 2001) 8.

Hori, Ichiro. "Three Types of Redemption in Japanese Folk Religion." In *Types of Redemption: Contributions to the Theme of the Study-Conference Held at Jerusalem 14th to 19th July 1968*, edited by R. J. Zwi Werblowsky and C. Jouco Bleeker, 105–19. *Studies in the History of Religions (Supplements to Numen)* 18. Leiden: Brill, 1970.

House, Francis. "The Barrier of Impassibility." *Theology* 83 (1980) 409–15.

Howe, Leroy T. "God's Power and God's Personhood." *The Iliff Review* 37 (1980) 35–50.

Hryniewicz, Waclaw. "Le Dieu souffrant? Réflexions sur la notion chrétienne de Dieu." *Église et Théologie* 12 (1981) 333–56.

Hübmaier, Balthasar. "Eighteen Dissertations Concerning the Entire Christian Life and of What it Consists: Propositions Upheld at Waldshut by Dr. Balthasar Friedberger, and Others, 1524." In *Baptist Confessions of Faith*, revised edition, edited by William L. Lumpkin, 18–21. Valley Forge: Judson, 1969.

Hughes, Henry Maldwyn. *The Christian Idea of God*. London: Duckworth, 1936.

———. *What Is the Atonement? A Study in the Passion of God in Christ*. New York: George H. Doran, 1924.

Humphreys, W. Lee. *The Tragic Vision and the Hebrew Tradition*. Overtures to Biblical Theology Series. Philadelphia: Fortress, 1985.

Hunsinger, George. "The Crucified God and the Political Theology of Violence." *Heythrop Journal* 14 (1973) 379–95.

Hutcheson, Robert Joseph, Jr. "Twentieth-Century Settings of the Passion: An *Opusculum* on the Powerless God." PhD diss., Washington University, 1976.

Hux, Samuel. "The Holocaust and the Survival of Tragedy." *Worldview* 20 (1977) 4–10.

Hyman, Frieda Clark. "Job, or The Suffering of God." *Judaism* 42 (1993) 218–28.

Idel, Moshe. *Kabbalah: New Perspectives*. New Haven: Yale University Press, 1988.

Ignatius of Antioch. "Epistle to the Romans." In *The Apostolic Fathers—Justin Martyr—Irenaeus*, edited by Alexander Roberts and James Donaldson. Vol. 1. *The Ante-Nicene Fathers: The Writings of the Fathers Down to A. D. 325*. Reprint, Grand Rapids: Eerdmans, 1987.

Ilsar, Yehiel. "Theological Aspects of the Holocaust." *Encounter* 42 (1981) 115–31.

Irwin, Alexander C. *Eros toward the World: Paul Tillich and the Theology of the Erotic*. Minneapolis: Fortress, 1991.

Irwin, William A., H. and H. A. Frankfort, John A. Wilson, and Thorkild Jacobson. *The Intellectual Adventure of Ancient Man: An Essay on Speculative Thought in the Ancient Near East*. Chicago: University of Chicago Press, 1946.

Jackson, Timothy P. *The Priority of Love: Christian Charity and Social Justice*. New Forum Books Series. Princeton: Princeton University Press, 2003.

Jacob, Edmond. "Le Dieu souffrant: un thème théologique vétérotestamentaire." *Zeitschrift für die alttestamentliche Wissenschaft* 95 (1983) 1–8.

———. *Theology of the Old Testament*. Translated by Arthur W. Heathcote and Philip J. Allcock. New York: Harper and Row, 1958.

Jaggar, William L. "The Passibility of God as Atonement Motif in the Theology of Martin Luther." PhD diss., Southwestern Baptist Theological Seminary, 1989.

Jakovljevic, Radivoj. "The Sense of Ebed Yahweh's Suffering." *Communio Viatorum* 30 (1987) 59–62.

James, William. *Essays in Radical Empiricism and a Pluralistic Universe*. Edited by Ralph Barton Perry. New York: Longmans, Green, 1947.

Janßen, Hans-Gerd. "Theodizee als neuzeitliches Problem versöhnender Praxis." In *Leiden*, edited by Willi Oelmüller, 40–50. Vol. 3. *Kolloquium Religion und Philosophie*. Paderborn: Ferdinand Schöning, 1986.

———. *Das Theodizee-Problem der Neuzeit: Ein Beitrag zur historisch-systematischen Grundlegung politischer Theologie*. Vol 198. European University Studies. Series 23, Theology. Frankfurt am Main: Peter Lang, 1982.

Jantzen, Grace M. *God's World, God's Body*. London: Darton, Longman and Todd, 1984.

———. "Healing Our Brokenness: The Spirit and Creation." *Ecumenical Review* 42 (1990) 131–42.

———. "On Worshipping an Embodied God." *Canadian Journal of Philosophy* 8 (1978) 511–19.

———. "Reply to Taliaferro." *Modern Theology* 3 (1987) 189–92.

Jaspers, Karl. *Philosophy*. Vol. 3. Translated by E. B. Ashton. Chicago: University of Chicago Press, 1971.

———. *Tragedy Is Not Enough*. Translated by Harald A. T. Reiche, Harry T. Moore, and Karl W. Deutsch. Boston: Beacon, 1952.

Jenkins, David E. *The Contradiction of Christianity*. London: SCM, 1976.

———. *Living with Questions: Investigations into the Theory and Practice of Belief in God*. London: SCM, 1969.

———. *Still Living with Questions*. London: SCM, 1990.

John Paul II, Pope. "Salvifici Doloris: The Christian Meaning of Human Suffering." *Origins* 13 (1984) 609, 611–24.

Johnson, Elizabeth A. *Consider Jesus: Waves of Renewal in Christology*. New York: Crossroad, 1993.

———. *She Who Is: The Mystery of God in Feminist Theological Discourse*. New York: Crossroad, 1992.

Johnson, William Hallock. "Is God Almighty?" *Princeton Theological Review* 21 (1923) 202–22; (1923) 521–40.

Johnstone, Brian V. "Learning through Suffering: The Moral Meaning of Negative Experience." In *History and Conscience: Studies in Honour of Father Sean*

O'Riordan, CSsR, edited by Raphael Gallagher and Brendan McConvery, 144–60. Dublin: Gill and Macmillan, 1989.

Jonas, Hans. "The Concept of God after Auschwitz: A Jewish Voice." *Journal of Religion* 67 (1987) 1–13.

———. "Is Faith Still Possible? Memories of Rudolf Bultmann and Reflections on the Philosophical Aspects of His Work." *Harvard Theological Review* 75 (1982) 1–23.

———. *The Gnostic Religion: The Message of the Alien God and the Beginnings of Christianity*. 2nd ed. Boston: Beacon, 1963.

———. *Der Gottesbegriff nach Auschwitz: Eine jüdische Stimme*. Frankfurt am Main: Suhrkamp Verlag, 1987.

Jones, H. "The Immutability of God Considered with Reference to Prayer." *Christian Spectator: New Series* 1 (1827) 565–70.

Julian of Norwich. *Revelations of Divine Love*. Translated by Clifton Wolters. Middlesex: Penguin, 1966.

Jüngel, Eberhard. *Death: The Riddle and the Mystery*. Translated by Iain and Ute Nicol. Philadelphia: Westminster, 1974.

———. *The Doctrine of the Trinity: God's Being Is in Becoming*. Grand Rapids: Eerdmans, 1976.

———. "Das dunkle Wort vom Tode Gottes." *Evangelische Kommentare* 2 (1969) 133–38, 198–202.

———. *God as the Mystery of the World: On the Foundation of the Theology of the Crucified One in the Dispute Between Theism and Atheism*. Translated by Darrell L. Guder. Grand Rapids: Eerdmans, 1983.

———. "Gott ist Liebe: Unterscheidung von Glaube und Liebe." In *Festschrift für Ernst Fuchs*, edited by Gerhard Ebeling, Eberhard Jüngel, and Gerd Schunack, 193–202. Tübingen: Mohr/Siebeck, 1973.

———. *Unterwegs zur Sache: Theologische Bemerkungen*. Munich: Kaiser, 1972.

———. "What Does It Mean to Say, 'God Is Love'?" In *Christ in Our Place: The Humanity of God in Christ for the Reconciliation of the World: Essays Presented to Professor James Torrance*, edited by Trevor A. Hart and Daniel P. Thimell, 294–312. Exeter: Paternoster, 1989.

Justinian I. *On the Person of Christ: The Christology of Emperor Justinian*. Translated by Kenneth Paul Wesche. Crestwood, New York: St. Vladimir's Seminary Press, 1991.

Kagawa, Tyohiko. *The Religion of Jesus and Love, the Law of Life*. Translated by J. Fullerton Gressitt. Philadelphia, Pennsylvania: John C. Winston, 1931.

Kammer, Charles. "Liberation and Love: Concepts in Conversation." *Word and World* 10 (1990) 260–69.

Kamp, Jean. "Présence du Dieu souffrant." *Lumière et Vie* 25 (1976) 54–66.

———. *Souffrance de Dieu, vie du monde*. Tournai: Casterman, 1971.

Kane, G. Stanley. "Evil and Privation." *International Journal for Philosophy of Religion* 11 (1980) 43–58.

Kaplan, L. J. "Maimonides, Dale Patrick, and Job XLII 6." *Vetus Testamentum* 28 (1978) 356–57.

Kasper, Walter. *The God of Jesus Christ*. Translated by Matthew J. O'Connell. New York: Crossroad, 1984.

————. "Revolution im Gottesverständnis? Zur Situation des ökumenischen Dialogs nach Jürgen Moltmanns 'Der gekreuzigte Gott.'" In *Diskussion über Jürgen Moltmanns Buch "Der gekreuzigte Gott,"* edited by Michael Welker, 140–48. Munich: Kaiser, 1979.

Katz, Steven T. *Post-Holocaust Dialogues: Critical Studies in Modern Jewish Thought.* New York: New York University Press, 1983.

Kazantzakis, Nikos. *The Suffering God: Selected Letters to Galatea and to Papastephanou.* Translated by Philip Ramp and Katerina Anghelaki Rooke. New Rochelle: Caratzas Brothers, 1979.

Keller, James A. "Some Basic Differences between Classical and Process Metaphysics and Their Implications for the Concept of God." *International Philosophical Quarterly* 22 (1982) 3–20.

Kelly, Geffrey B. "Sharing in the Pain of God: Dietrich Bonhoeffer's Reflections on Christian Vulnerability." *Weavings* 8 (1993) 6–15.

Kelly, J. N. D. *Early Christian Creeds.* 3rd ed. Singapore: Longman, 1972.

————. *Early Christian Doctrines.* Revised ed. San Francisco: Harper and Row, 1978.

Kempis, Thomas à. *Of the Imitation of Christ.* New Canaan, CT: Keats, 1973.

Khan, Abraham H. "God Suffers: Sense or Nonsense." *The Indian Journal of Theology* 28 (1979) 91–99.

Kierkegaard, Søren. *Concluding Unscientific Postscript.* Translated by David F. Swenson and Walter Lowrie. Princeton: Princeton University Press, 1941.

————. *Fear and Trembling and the Sickness unto Death.* Translated by Walter Lowrie. Princeton: Princeton University Press, 1968.

————. *Philosophical Fragments or a Fragment of Philosophy.* Translated by David Swenson. Translation revised by Howard V. Hong. Princeton: Princeton University Press, 1962.

————. *Training in Christianity and the Edifying Discourse which "Accompanied" It.* Translated by Walter Lowrie. Princeton: Princeton University Press, 1967.

Kim, Chung Choon. "The Hope: God's Suffering in Man's Struggle (2)." *Reformed World* 36 (1980) 13–19.

Kim, Young Oon. *Unification Theology and Christian Thought.* Revised ed. New York: Golden Gate, 1976.

King, Henry Churchill. *Reconstruction in Theology.* New York: Hodder and Stoughton, 1909; London and New York: Macmillan, 1901.

King-Farlow, John and Niall Shanks. "Theodicy: Two Moral Extremes." *Scottish Journal of Theology* 41 (1988) 153–76.

Kitagawa, Shin. "Unchangeableness and Changeableness of God." In *Gottes Zukunft— Zukunft der Welt: Festschrift für Jürgen Moltmann zum 60 Geburtstag,* edited by Hermann Deuser, Gerhard Marcel Martin, Konrad Stock, and Michael Welker, 224–30. Munich: Kaiser, 1986.

Kitamori, Kazoh. "Buchbesprechung." In *Diskussion über Jürgen Moltmanns Buch "Der gekreuzigte Gott,"* edited by Michael Welker, 108–10. Munich: Kaiser, 1979.

————. "The Theology of the Pain of God." *Japan Christian Quarterly* 19 (1953) 318–20.

————. *Theology of the Pain of God.* 5th ed. Translated by M. E. Bratcher. Richmond: John Knox, 1965.

Kittel, Gerhard. "The Metaphorical Use of Image in the NT." In *D–H*, edited by Gerhard Kittel, translated and edited by Geoffrey W. Bromiley. Vol. 2. *Theological Dictionary of the New Testament*. Grand Rapids: Eerdmans, 1964.

Klappert, Bertold. "Die Gottverlassenheit Jesu und der gekreuzigte Gott. Beobachtungen zum Problem einer theologia crucis in der Christologie der Gegenwart." In *Diskussion über Jürgen Moltmanns Buch "Der gekreuzigte Gott,"* edited by Michael Welker, 57–73. Munich: Kaiser, 1979.

———. "Weg und Wende Dietrich Bonhoeffers in der Israelfrage—Bonhoeffer und die theologischen Grundentscheidungen des Rheinischen Synodalbeschlusses 1980." In *Ethik im Ernstfall: Dietrich Bonhoeffers Stellung zu den Juden und ihre Aktualität*, edited by Wolfgang Huber and Ilse Tödt, 77–135. Vol. 4. Internationales Bonhoeffer Forum Forschung und Praxi. Munich: Kaiser, 1982.

Knierim, Rolf. "Cosmos and History in Israel's Theology." *Horizons in Biblical Theology* 3 (1981) 59–123.

Knight, Harold. *The Hebrew Prophetic Consciousness*. London: Lutterworth, 1947.

Kobusch, Theo. "Kann Gott Leiden? Zu den philosophischen Grundlagen der Lehre von der Passibilität Gottes bei Origenes." *Vigiliae Christianae* 46 (1992) 328–33.

Koch, Klaus. "Is There a Doctrine of Retribution in the Old Testament?" In *Theodicy in the Old Testament*, edited by James L. Crenshaw, 57–87. Issues in Religion and Theology Series, edited by Douglas Knight and Robert Morgan. Philadelphia: Fortress, 1983.

Kondoleon, Theodore J. "The Immutability of God: Some Recent Challenges." *The New Scholasticism* 58 (1984) 293–315.

König, Adrio. "The Idea of 'The Crucified God': Some Systematic Questions." *Journal of Theology for Southern Africa* 39 (1982) 55–61.

Koslowski, Peter. "Der leidende Gott." In *Leiden*, edited by Willi Oelmüller, 51–57. Vol. 3. *Kolloquium Religion und Philosophie*. Paderborn: Ferdinand Schöning, 1986.

———. "Der leidende Gott." *Theologie und Philosophie* 61 (1986) 562–65.

———. "Der leidende Gott: Theodizee in der christlichen Philosophie und im Gnostizismus." *Internationale katholische Zeitschrift "Communio"* 19 (1990) 352–76.

———. "Der leidende Gott: Theodizee in der christlichen Philosophie und im Gnostizismus." In *Theodizee-Gott vor Gericht?* edited by Willi Oelmüller, 33–66. Munich: Wilhelm Fink Verlag, 1990.

Koyama, Kosuke. "The Hand Painfully Open." *Lexington Theological Quarterly* 22 (1987) 33–43.

———. "Reflections on War and Peace for an Ecumenical Theology 40 Years after Hiroshima." *Mid-Stream* 25 (1986) 141–54.

Kraus, Wolfgang. "Leiden als Flucht und Selbstbestrafung." In *Leiden*, edited by Willi Oelmüller, 58–65. Vol. 3. *Kolloquium Religion und Philosophie*. Paderborn: Ferdinand Schöning, 1986.

Krause, Burghard. *Leiden Gottes—Leiden des Menschen: Eine Untersuchung zur Kirchlichen Dogmatik Karl Barths*. Stuttgart: Calwer Verlag, 1980.

Kremers, Heinz. "Leidensgemeinschaft mit Gott im Alten Testament: Eine Untersuchung der 'biographischen' Berichte im Jeremiabuch." *Evangelische Theologie* 13 (1953) 122–40.

Krötke, Wolf. "Teilnehmen am Leiden Gottes: Zu Dietrich Bonhoeffers Verständnis eines 'religionslosen Christentums.'" In *450 Jahre Evangelische Theologie in Berlin*, edited by Gerhard Besier and Christof Gestrich, 439–57. Göttingen: Verlag Vandenhoeck and Ruprecht, 1989.

Kümmel, Werner Georg. *The Theology of the New Testament: According to Its Major Witnesses Jesus–Paul–John*. Translated by John E. Steely. Nashville: Abingdon, 1973.

Küng, Hans. *Gott und das Leid*. Theologische Meditationen Series, edited by Hans Küng. Zürich: Benziger Verlag, 1967.

———. *On Being a Christian*. Translated by Edward Quinn. New York: Doubleday, 1976.

———. *The Incarnation of God: An Introduction to Hegel's Theological Thought as a Prolegomena to a Future Christology*. Translated by J. R. Stephenson. New York: Crossroad, 1987.

Kucharek, Casimir. *The Byzantine-Slav Liturgy of St. John Chrysostom: Its Origin and Evolution*. Allendale: Alleluia, 1971.

Kuhn, Peter. *Gottes Selbsterniedrigung in der Theologie der Rabbinen*. Munich: Kössel-Verlag, 1968.

———. *Gottes Trauer und Klage in der rabbinischen Uberlieferung (Talmud und Midrash)*. Leiden: Brill, 1978.

Kuitert, H. M. *De Mensvormigheid Gods: Een dogmatisch-hermeneutische studie over de anthropomorfismen van de Heilige Schrift*. Kampen: J. H. Kok, 1962.

Kuramatsu, Von Isao. "Die gegenwärtige Kreuzestheologie und Luther, besonders in Rücksicht auf die Theologie des Schmerzes Gottes von Kazo Kitamori." *Kerygma und Dogma: Zeitschrift für theologische Forschung und kirchliche Lehre*" 36 (1990) 273–83.

Kuyper, Lester, J. "The Repentance of God." *Reformed Review: A Quarterly Journal of the Western Theological Seminary* 18 (1965) 3–16.

———. "The Suffering and the Repentance of God." *Scottish Journal of Theology* 22 (1969) 257–77.

La Rochefoucauld, François. *Maxims*. Translated by Leonard Tancock. Middlesex, England: Penguin, 1959.

LaCugna, Catherine Mowry. *God For Us: The Trinity and Christian Life*. San Francisco: HarperSanFrancisco, 1991.

Ladd, George T. "The Biblical and the Philosophical Conception of God." *The Old and New Testament Student* 12 (1891) 20–27.

Laeuchli, S. "Prolegomena to a Structural Analysis of Ancient Christian Salvation." In *Studia Patristica* 15.1, edited by Elizabeth A. Livingstone, 337–60. Berlin: Academie-Verlag, 1984.

Lake, Kirsopp, trans. *Epistle to Diognetus*. In *The Shepherd of Hermas, The Martyrdom of Polycarp, The Epistle of Polycarp. The Apostolic Fathers*. Vol. 2. The Loeb Classical Library. 1913. Reprint, Cambridge, MA: Harvard University Press, 1976.

Lamb, Matthew L. *Solidarity with Victims: Toward a Theology of Social Transformation*. New York: Crossroad, 1982.

Lambert, George E. "The Prior Suffering of God as a Tool in Pastoral Care of Trauma and of Traumatic Loss." DMin thesis, Trinity Lutheran Seminary, 1986.

Lambrecht, Jan. "Paul and Suffering." In *God and Human Suffering*, no. 3. Louvain Theological and Pastoral Monographs, edited by Jan Lambrecht and Raymond F. Collins, 47–67. Louvain: Peeters, 1990.

————, ed. *Hoelang Nog en Waarom Toch? God, Mens en Lijden*. Leuven/Amersfoort: Acco, 1988.

Lambrecht, Jan and Collins, Raymond F., eds. *God and Human Suffering*, no.3. Louvain Theological and Pastoral Monographs. Louvain: Peeters, 1990.

Lan, Kwok Pui. "God Weeps with Our Pain." In *New Eyes for Reading: Biblical and Theological Reflections by Women from the Third World*, edited by John S. Pobee and Bärbel von Wartenberg-Potter, 90–95. Geneva: World Council of Churches, 1986.

Lang, P. Justin. "Der Schmerz Gottes: Zur Theologie des Leids." *Franziskanische Studien* 62 (1980) 180–92.

Larson, Lawrence A. "Christian Symbolism and the 'Tragic' Point of View." *Encounter* 24 (1963) 77–88.

Lawrie, R. "Passion." *Philosophy and Phenomenological Research* 41 (1980) 106–26.

Leclercq, Jean. *The Love of Learning and the Desire for God: A Study of Monastic Culture*. Translated by Catharine Misrahi. New York: Fordham University Press, 1961.

Lee, Bernard. "The Appetite of God." In *Religious Experience and Process Theology: The Pastoral Implications of a Major Modern Movement*, edited by Harry James Cargas and Bernard Lee, 369–84. New York: Paulist, 1976.

————. "The Helplessness of God: A Radical Re-appraisal of Divine Omnipotence." *Encounter* 38 (1977) 325–36.

Lee, Jung Young. *God Suffers for Us: A Systematic Inquiry into a Concept of Divine Passibility*. The Hague: Martinus Nijhoff, 1974.

————. "The Suffering of God: A Systematic Inquiry into a Concept of Divine Passibility." ThD diss., Boston University School of Theology, 1968.

————. *The Theology of Change: A Christian Concept of God in an Eastern Perspective*. Maryknoll: Orbis, 1979.

Leith, John H., ed. *Creeds of the Churches: A Reader in Christian Doctrine from the Bible to the Present*. 3rd ed. Atlanta: John Knox, 1982.

Lepargneur, François-H. "Sickness in a Christian Anthropology." In *The Mystery of Suffering and Death*, edited by Michael J. Taylor, 71–80. Staten Island: Alba, 1973.

Leplay, Michel. "La faiblesse de Dieu comme élément de la théologie de Peguy." *Foi et Vie* 87 (1988) 93–114.

Lester, Andrew D., ed. *When Children Suffer: A Sourcebook for Ministry with Children in Crisis*. Philadelphia: Westminster, 1987.

Levenson, Jon D. *Creation and the Persistence of Evil: The Jewish Drama of Divine Omnipotence*. San Francisco: Harper and Row, 1988.

Levinas, Emmanuel. "God and Philosophy." *Philosophy Today* 22 (1978) 127–45.

————. "La souffrance inutile." *Giornale di Metafisica: Nuova Serie* 4 (1982) 13–26.

Lewis, Alan E. "The Burial of God: Rupture and Redemption as the Story of Salvation." *Scottish Journal of Theology* 40 (1987) 335–62.

Lewis, F. Warburton. "The Suffering of God." *The Expositor: Sixth Series* 12 (1905) 40–46.

Liderbach, Daniel Patrick. "Martin Luther's Theology of Suffering in Modern Translation: A Comparative Study of Dietrich Bonhoeffer's Theology of Suffering." PhD diss., St. Michael's University, 1979.

Lifton, Robert Jay. "Apathy and Numbing—A Modern Temptation." In *The Meaning of Human Suffering*, edited by Flavian Dougherty, 196–231. New York: Human Sciences, 1982.

Lind, Millard C. "Hosea 5:8–6:6." *Interpretation* 38 (1984) 398–403.

Lochman, Jan M. "The Hope: God's Suffering in Man's Struggle (1)." *Reformed World* 36 (1980) 5–12.

———. "Ökumenische Begegnungen in Korea." *Reformatio: Evangelische Zeitschrift für Kultur und Politik* 28 (1979) 580–84.

——— and Dembowski, Hermann. "Gottes Sein ist im Leiden. Zur trinitarischen Kreuzestheologie Jürgen Moltmanns." In *Diskussion über Jürgen Moltmanns Buch "Der gekreuzigte Gott*," edited by Michael Welker, 26–38. Munich: Kaiser, 1979.

Loeschen, John. "The God Who Becomes: Eckhart on Divine Relativity." *The Thomist* 35 (1971) 405–22.

Longinus. "On the Sublime." In *Critical Theory since Plato*, edited by Hazard Adams, 76–102. New York: Harcourt Brace Jovanovich, 1971.

Loomer, Bernard M. "Dimensions of Freedom." In *Religious Experience and Process Theology: The Pastoral Implications of a Major Modern Movement*, edited by Harry James Cargas and Bernard Lee, 323–39. New York: Paulist, 1976.

Lorenzen, Thorwald. "The Meaning of the Death of Jesus Christ." *American Baptist Quarterly* 4 (1985) 3–34.

Lowe, Walter James. "Cosmos and Covenant." *Semeia* 19 (1981) 107–11.

Lübbe, Hermann. "Theodizee als Häresie." In *Leiden*, edited by Willi Oelmüller, 167–76. Vol. 3. *Kolloquium Religion und Philosophie*. Paderborn: Ferdinand Schöning, 1986.

Lucas, J. R. "Foreknowledge and the Vulnerability of God." In *The Philosophy in Christianity*, edited by Godfrey Vesey, 119–28. Cambridge: Cambridge University Press, 1989.

———. *Freedom and Grace: Essays by J. R. Lucas*. London: SPCK, 1976.

Ludwig, Theodore Mark. "The Suffering Love of God: The Tension between Judgment and Grace in the Pre-Exilic Prophets." PhD diss., Concordia Seminary, 1968.

Luther, Martin. "Confession Concerning Christ's Supper, 1528." Translated by Robert H. Fischer. In *Word and Sacrament* 3, edited by Robert H. Fischer and Helmut T. Lehmann, 161–372. *Luther's Works* 37. Philadelphia: Muhlenberg, 1961.

———. "The Freedom of a Christian." Translated by W. A. Lambert. In *Career of the Reformer: 1*, edited by Harold J. Grimm and Helmut T. Lehmann, 333–77. *Luther's Works* 31. Philadelphia: Fortress, 1957

———. "Heidelberg Disputation, 1518." Translated by Harold J. Grimm. In *Career of the Reformer 1*, edited by Harold J. Grimm and Helmut T. Lehmann, 39–70. *Luther's Works* 31. Philadelphia: Fortress, 1957.

———. *Luther's Works*. Vol. 2. *Lectures on Genesis: Chapters 6-14*. Edited by Jaroslav Pelikan. Translated by George V. Schick. Saint Louis: Concordia, 1960.

———. *Luther's Works*. Vol. 17. *Lectures on Isaiah: Chapters 40-66*. Edited by Hilton C. Oswald. Translated by Herbert J. A. Bouman. Saint Louis: Concordia, 1972.

―――. *Luther's Works.* Edited by Jaroslav Pelikan and Helmut T. Lehmann. Vol. 25. *Lectures on Romans: Glosses and Scholia*, edited by Hilton C. Oswald. Saint Louis: Concordia, 1972.

―――. "A Meditation on Christ's Passion, 1519." Translated by Martin H. Bertram. In *Devotional Writings*, edited by Martin O. Dietrich and Helmut T. Lehmann, 7–14. *Luther's Works* 42. Philadelphia: Fortress, 1969.

―――. "On the Councils and the Church, 1539." Translated by Charles M. Jacobs and Eric W. Gritsch. In *Church and Ministry* 3, edited by Eric W. Gritsch and Helmut T. Lehmann, 9–178. *Luther's Works* 41. Philadelphia: Fortress, 1966.

―――. "A Treatise on the New Testament, that is, the Holy Mass, 1520." Translated by Jeremiah J. Schindel and E. Theodore Bachmann. In *Word and Sacrament* 1, edited by E. Theodore Bachmann. *Luther's Works* 35, edited by Helmut T. Lehmann. Philadelphia: Muhlenberg, 1960.

Luyten, Jos. "Het Lijden van God volgens het Oude Testament." *Collationes* 21 (1991) 21–36.

―――. "Perspectives on Human Suffering in the Old Testament." In *God and Human Suffering*, edited by Jan Lambrecht and Raymond F. Collins, 1–30. Louvain Theological and Pastoral Monographs, vol. 3. Louvain: Peeters, 1990.

Maas, Wilhelm. *Unveränderlichkeit Gottes: zum Verhältnis von griechisch-philosophischer und christlicher Gotteslehre.* Munich: Verlag Ferdinand Schöning, 1974.

MacGregor, Geddes. "Does Scripture Limit the Power of God?" *Hibbert Journal* 53 (1955) 382–86.

―――. *He Who Lets Us Be: A Theology of Love.* New York: Seabury, 1975.

Macintosh, Douglas Clyde. *Theology as an Empirical Science.* New York: Macmillan, 1919.

MacKay, Donald G. M. "The Relation of God and Man in the Writings of Nicolas Berdyaev." *Scottish Journal of Theology* 3 (1950) 380–96.

Mackie, J. L. "Evil and Omnipotence." *Mind* 64 (1955) 200–12.

Mackintosh, Hugh Ross. *The Christian Experience of Forgiveness.* New York: Harper and Brothers, 1927.

―――. "The Conception of a Finite God." *The Expositor: Eighth Series* 16 (1918) 346–61.

―――. *Sermons.* New York: Scribner, 1938.

―――. *Some Aspects of Christian Belief.* New York: George H. Doran, 1924.

―――. "The Vicarious Penitence of Christ." *The Expositor: Eighth Series* 11 (1916) 81–96.

Macquarrie, John. *The Humility of God.* Philadelphia: Westminster, 1978.

―――. *In Search of Deity: An Essay in Dialectical Theism.* New York: Crossroad, 1987.

―――. *Jesus Christ in Modern Thought.* London: SCM, 1990.

―――. *Principles of Christian Theology.* New York: Scribner, 1966.

Madden, Edward H. "The Riddle of God and Evil." In *Current Philosophical Issues: Essays in Honor of Curt John Ducasse*, edited by Frederick C. Dommeyer, 185–200. Springfield, IL: Charles C. Thomas, 1966.

Maimonides, Moses. *The Guide of the Perplexed.* Translated by Shlomo Pines. Chicago: University of Chicago Press, 1963.

Margull, Hans J. "Tod Jesu und Schmerz Gottes." In *Leben angesichts des Todes; beiträge zum theologischen Problem des Todes; Helmut Thielicke zum 60 Geburtstag*, edited by M. L. Henry, 269–76. Tübingen: Mohr, 1968.

Maritain, Jacques. *God and the Permission of Evil*. Translated by Joseph W. Evans. Christian Culture and Philosophy Series, edited by Donald A. Gallagher and Idella Gallagher. Milwaukee: Bruce, 1966.

Marmorstein, A. *The Doctrine of Merits in Old Rabbinical Literature and The Old Rabbinic Doctrine of God*. New York: KTAV, 1968.

Marquard, Odo. "Bemerkungen zur Theodizee." In *Leiden*, edited by Willi Oelmüller, 213–18. Vol. 3. *Kolloquium Religion und Philosophie*. Paderborn: Ferdinand Schöning, 1986.

———. "Schwierigkeiten beim Ja-Sagen." In *Theodizee-Gott vor Gericht?* edited by Willi Oelmüller, 87–102. Munich: Wilhelm Fink Verlag, 1990.

Marquardt, Friedrich-Wilhelm. "Christsein nach Auschwitz." In *Glaube und Hoffnung nach Auschwitz: Jüdisch-christliche Dialoge, Vorträge, Diskussionen*, edited by Peter von der Osten–Sacken and Martin Stöhr, 62–76. Berlin: Selbstverlag Institut Kirche und Judentum, 1980.

Marsh, James L. *Critique, Action, and Liberation*. SUNY Series in the Philosophy of the Social Sciences, edited by Lenore Langsdorf. Albany, New York: State University of New York Press, 1995.

———. *Process, Praxis, and Transcendence*. SUNY Series in the Philosophy of the Social Sciences, edited by Lenore Langsdorf. Albany, New York: State University of New York Press, 1999.

Marshall, G. D. "On Being Affected." *Mind* 77 (1968) 243–59.

Martensen, Hans Lassen. *Christian Dogmatics: A Compendium of the Doctrines of Christianity*. Translated by William Urwick. Edinburgh: T. & T. Clark, 1878.

Marti, Kurt. "Leiden, nicht dulden." *Reformatio: Evangelische Zeitschrift für Kultur und Politik* 31 (1982) 147–50.

Martinez de Pison, Ramon. "Le Dieu qui est 'victime': Le problème du mal dans la pensée de Maurice Zundel." *Science et Esprit* 43 (1991) 55–68.

Mascall, E. L. "Does God Change? Mutability and Incarnation: A Review Discussion." *The Thomist* 50 (1986) 447–57.

Mason, David R. "Some Abstract, Yet Crucial Thoughts about Suffering." *Dialogue* 16 (1977) 91–100.

Matthews, Walter Robert. *God in Christian Thought and Experience*. London: Nisbet, 1930.

May, Gerhard. *Creatio Ex Nihilo: The Doctrine of 'Creation out of Nothing' in Early Christian Thought*. Translated by A. S. Worrall. Edinburgh: T. & T. Clark, 1994.

McCabe, Herbert. "The Involvement of God." *New Blackfriars* 66 (1985) 464–76.

McCarthy, Dennis J. *Treaty and Covenant*. Rome: Pontifical Biblical Institute, 1963.

McConnell, Francis John. *Is God Limited?* New York: Abingdon, 1924.

McCreary, George B. "The Finite God." *Bibliotheca Sacra* (Oberlin) 80 (1923) 421–39.

McDaniel, Jay. "The God of the Oppressed and the God Who Is Empty." *Journal of Ecumenical Studies* 22 (1985) 687–702.

McDowall, Stewart Andrew. *Evolution and the Need of Atonement*. Cambridge: Cambridge University Press, 1912.

McFague, Sallie. *The Body of God: An Ecological Theology.* Minneapolis: Fortress, 1993.

———. *Models of God: Theology for an Ecological, Nuclear Age.* Philadelphia: Fortress, 1987.

———. *Super, Natural Christians: How We Should Love Nature.* Minneapolis: Fortress, 1997.

McGiffert, Arthur Cushman. *The God of the Early Christians.* New York: Scribner, 1924.

McGill, Arthur C. "Human Suffering and The Passion of Christ." In *The Meaning of Human Suffering,* edited by Flavian Dougherty, 159–93. New York: Human Sciences, 1982.

———. *Suffering: A Test of Theological Method.* Philadelphia: Westminster, 1982.

McGuckin, J. A. "Sacrifice and Atonement: An Investigation into the Attitude of Jesus of Nazareth towards Cultic Sacrifice." In *Jews and Christians During and After the Holocaust,* edited by Yehuda Bauer et al, 648–61. Vol. 1. *Remembering for the Future: Working Papers and Addenda.* New York: Pergamon, 1989.

———. "The 'Theopaschite Confession' (Text and Historical Context): A Study in the Cyrilline Re-interpretation of Chalcedon." *Journal of Ecclesiastical History* 35 (1984) 239–55.

McKenzie, John L. "Divine Passion in Osee." *Catholic Biblical Quarterly* 17 (1955) 167–79.

McWilliams, Warren. "Daniel Day Williams' Vulnerable and Invulnerable God." *Encounter* 44 (1983) 73–89.

———. "Divine Suffering in Contemporary Theology." *Scottish Journal of Theology* 33 (1980) 35–53.

———. "God the Friend: A Test Case in Metaphorical Theology." *Perspectives in Religious Studies* 16 (1989) 109–20.

———. "A Kenotic God and the Problem of Evil." *Encounter* 42 (1981) 15–27.

———. "The Pain of God in the Theology of Kazoh Kitamori." *Perspectives in Religious Studies* 8 (1981) 184–200.

———. "The Passion of God and Moltmann's Christology." *Encounter* 40 (1979) 313–26.

———. *The Passion of God: Divine Suffering in Contemporary Protestant Theology.* Macon: Mercer University Press, 1985.

Meeks, M. Douglas. "The 'Crucified God' and the Power of Liberation." In *Philosophy of Religion and Theology: 1974 Proceedings,* edited by James Wm. McClendon Jr., 31–43. Tallahassee: American Academy of Religion (Florida State University), 1974.

———. "God's Suffering Power and Liberation." *Journal of Religious Thought* 33 (1976) 44–54.

Meesen, Frank. *Unveränderlichkeit und Menschwerdung Gottes: Eine theologie-geschichtlich-systematische Untersuchung.* Freiburg: Herder, 1989.

Meland, Bernard E. "Toward a Valid View of God." *Harvard Theological Review* 24 (1931) 197–208.

Melito of Sardis. *On Pascha and Fragments: Texts and Translations.* Edited by Stuart George Hall. Oxford Early Christian Texts, edited by Henry Chadwick. Oxford: Clarendon, 1979.

Mendenhall, George E. "Covenant Forms in Israelite Tradition." *Biblical Archaeologist* 17 (1954) 50–76.

Merkle, John C. "Heschel's Theology of Divine Pathos." *Louvain Studies* 10 (1984) 151–65.

Mesnard, Pierre. "La conception de l'humilité dans l'imitation de Jésus–Christ." In *Du moyen age au siècle des lumières*, 199–222. Vol. 2. *L'Homme devant Dieu: Mélanges offerts au Père Henri de Lubac*. Théologie: Études publiées sous la direction de la faculté de théologie S. J. de Lyon-Fourvière 57. Paris: Aubier, 1964.

Mettinger, Tryggve N. D. "Fighting the Powers of Chaos and Hell—Towards the Biblical Portrait of God." *Studia Theologica* 39 (1985) 21–38.

———. *In Search of God: The Meaning and Message of the Everlasting Names.* Translated by Frederick H. Cryer. Philadelphia: Fortress, 1988.

Metz, Johann Baptist. *Faith in History and Society: Towards a Practical Fundamental Theology*. Translated by David Smith. New York: Seabury, 1980.

———. "The Future in the Memory of Suffering." In *New Questions on God*, edited by Johann Baptist Metz, 9–25. *Concilium: Religion in the Seventies* 76. New York: Herder and Herder, 1972.

———. "Theologie als Theodizee?" In *Theodizee—Gott vor Gericht?* edited by Willi Oelmüller, 103–18. Munich: Wilhelm Fink Verlag, 1990.

Meyendorff, John. *Christ in Eastern Christian Thought*. 2nd ed. Translated by Yves Dubois. Crestwood, NY: St. Vladimir's Seminary Press, 1975.

Michaelis, Wilhelm. "μιμέομαι, μιμητής, συμμιμητής." In *Theological Dictionary of the New Testament*. Vol. 4. *L—N*. Edited by Gerhard Kittel. Translated and edited by Geoffrey W. Bromiley. Grand Rapids, Michigan: William B. Eerdmans Publishing Company, 1967.

Michiels, Robrecht. "Jesus and Suffering—The Suffering of Jesus." In *God and Human Suffering*, edited by Jan Lambrecht and Raymond F. Collins, 31–45. Vol. 3. Louvain Theological and Pastoral Monographs. Louvain: Peeters, 1990.

Migliore, Daniel L. *Faith Seeking Understanding: An Introduction to Christian Theology*. Grand Rapids: Eerdmans, 1991.

———. "Der gekreuzigte Gott." In *Diskussion über Jürgen Moltmanns Buch "Der gekreuzigte Gott,"* edited by Michael Welker, 39–42. Munich: Kaiser, 1979.

———. "God's Freedom and Human Freedom." In *Gottes Zukunft—Zukunft der Welt: Festschrift für Jürgen Moltmann zum 60 Geburtstag*, edited by Hermann Deuser, Gerhard Marcel Martin, Konrad Stock, and Michael Welker, 240–49. Munich: Kaiser, 1986.

———. "The Passion of God and the Prophetic Task of Pastoral Ministry." In *The Pastor as Prophet*, edited by Earl E. Shelp and Ronald H. Sunderland, 114–34. New York: Pilgrim, 1985.

———. *The Power of God*. Library of Living Faith Series. Edited by John H. Mulder. Philadelphia: Westminster, 1983.

Milazzo, G. Tom. *The Protest and the Silence: Suffering, Death, and Biblical Theology*. Minneapolis: Fortress, 1992.

Miller, Jerome A. *The Way of Suffering: A Geography of Crisis*. Washington DC: Georgetown University Press, 1988.

Miller, Randolph Crump. "The Problem of Evil and Religious Education." *Religious Education* 84 (1989) 5–15.

Miller-McLemore, Bonnie J. *Death, Sin and the Moral Life: Contemporary Cultural Interpretations of Death.* American Academy of Religion Academy Series 59, edited by Susan Thistlethwaite. Atlanta: Scholars, 1988.

Miskotte, Hermannus Heiko. "Das Leiden ist in Gott: Über Jürgen Moltmanns trinitarische Kreuzestheologie." In *Diskussion über Jürgen Moltmanns Buch "Der gekreuzigte Gott,"* edited by Michael Welker, 74–93. Munich: Kaiser, 1979.

Mollenkott, Virginia Ramey. *The Divine Feminine: The Biblical Imagery of God as Female.* New York: Crossroad, 1986.

Molnar, Paul D. "The Function of the Trinity in Moltmann's Ecological Doctrine of Creation." *Theological Studies* 51 (1990) 673–97.

Moltmann, Jürgen. "Antwort auf die kritik an 'Der gekreuzigte Gott.'" In *Diskussion über Jürgen Moltmanns Buch "Der gekreuzigte Gott,"* edited by Michael Welker, 165–90. Munich: Kaiser, 1979.

———. "'Begnadete Angst': Religiös integrierte Angst und ihre Bewältigung." In *Angst und Gewalt: Ihre Präsenz und ihre Bewältigung in den Religionen*, edited by Heinrich von Stietencron, 137–53. Düsseldorf: Patmos Verlag, 1979.

———. "The Crucified God." *Theology Today* 31 (1974) 6–18.

———. *The Crucified God: The Cross as the Foundation and Criticism of Christian Theology.* Translated by R. A. Wilson and John Bowden. New York: Harper and Row, 1974.

———. "The 'Crucified God': A Trinitarian Theology of the Cross." *Interpretation* 26 (1972) 278–99.

———. *The Future of Creation: Collected Essays.* Translated by Margaret Kohl. Philadelphia: Fortress, 1979.

———. "Gesichtspunkte der Kreuzestheologie heute." *Evangelische Theologie* 33 (1973) 346–65.

———. "God and the Nuclear Catastrophe." *Pacifica* 1 (1988) 157–70.

———. "The Motherly Father: Is Trinitarian Patripassianism Replacing Theological Patriarchalism?" In *God as Father?* edited by Johann Baptist Metz, Edward Schillebeeckx, and Marcus Lefébure, 51–56. *Concilium: Religion in the Eighties* 143. New York: Seabury, 1981.

———. *The Passion for Life: A Messianic Lifestyle.* Translated by M. Douglas Meeks. Philadelphia: Fortress, 1978.

———. "Passion of Life." *Currents in Theology and Mission* 4 (1977) 3–9.

———. "Theology of Mystical Experience." *Scottish Journal of Theology* 32 (1979) 501–20.

———. "The Trinitarian History of God." *Theology* 78 (1975) 632–46.

———. *The Trinity and the Kingdom: The Doctrine of God.* Translated by Margaret Kohl. San Francisco: Harper and Row, 1981.

Mondin, Battista. "Der gekreuzigte Gott." In *Diskussion über Jürgen Moltmanns Buch "Der gekreuzigte Gott,"* edited by Michael Welker, 94–107. Munich: Kaiser, 1979.

———. "The Pneumatic Structure of the Church: Charisms and Evangelical Counsels." In *Gottes Zukunft—Zukunft der Welt: Festschrift für Jürgen Moltmann zum 60 Geburtstag*, edited by Hermann Deuser, Gerhard Marcel Martin, Konrad Stock, and Michael Welker, 190–98. Munich: Kaiser, 1986.

Moon, Sun Myung. *Divine Principle.* Washington DC: The Holy Spirit Association for the Unification of World Christianity, 1973.

Moore, Michael S. "Human Suffering in Lamentations." *Revue Biblique* 90 (1983) 534–55.

Moore, Sebastian. "God Suffered." *Downside Review* 77 (1958–1959) 122–40.

Morgan, G. Campbell. *The Bible and the Cross.* New York: Fleming H. Revell, 1909.

Morgan, John H. "Karl Barth in Pursuit of God's Humanity." *Religion in Life* 45 (1976) 324–38.

Morris, S. J. "Anthropopathy." *The Methodist Review* 22 (1885) 545–56.

Mozley, J. K. "The Impassibility of God." DD diss., Cambridge University, 1926.

———. *Some Tendencies in British Theology: From the Publication of Lux Mundi to the Present Day.* London: SPCK, 1952.

———. *The Impassibility of God.* Cambridge: Cambridge University Press, 1926.

Mühlen, Heribert. *Die Veränderlichkeit Gottes als Horizont einer zukünftigen Christologie: auf dem Wege zu einer Kreuzetheologie in Auseinandersetzung mit der altkirchlichen Christologie.* Münster: Verlag Aschendorff, 1976.

Muilenberg, James. "The Form and Structure of the Covenantal Formulations." *Vetus Testamentum* 9 (1959) 357–60.

Müller, G. L. "Tod und Auferstehung Gottes heute. Zur Überwindung des neuzeitlichen Atheismus in Bonhoeffers theologia crucis." *Zeitschrift für katholische Theologie* 104 (1982) 172–90.

Muller, Richard A. "Incarnation, Immutability, and the Case for Classical Theism." *Westminster Theological Journal* 45 (1983) 22–40.

Mullins, Edgar Young. *The Christian Religion in Its Doctrinal Expression.* Philadelphia: Judson, 1917.

Mura, G. *Da Kierkegaard a Moltmann, Giobbe e la "sofferenza di Dio."* Rome: Città Nuova, 1982.

Muraoka, T. "A Syntactic Problem in Lev. XIX.18b." *Journal of Semitic Studies* 23 (1978) 291–97.

Murphey, Roland E. "Biblical Insights into Suffering: Pathos and Compassion." In *Whither Creativity, Freedom, Suffering? Humanity, Cosmos, God,* edited by Francis A. Eigo, 53–75. Pittsburgh: Villanova University Press, 1981.

Myers, C. Mason. "Free Will and the Problem of Evil." *Religious Studies* 23 (1987) 289–94.

Nabert, Jean. *Le Désir de Dieu.* Paris: Aubier-Montaigne, 1966.

Nelson, Derek. "The Vulnerable and Transcendent God: the Postliberal Theology of William Placher." *Dialog* 44 (2005) 273–84.

Newell, Roger. "Participation and Atonement." In *Christ in Our Place: The Humanity of God in Christ for the Reconciliation of the World: Essays Presented to Professor James Torrance,* edited by Trevor A. Hart and Daniel P. Thimell, 92–101. Exeter: Paternoster, 1989.

Ngien, Dennis. "God Who Suffers: If God Does Not Grieve, Then Can He Love at All? An Argument for God's Emotions." *Christianity Today* 41 (1997) 38–42.

———. " 'The Most Moved Mover': Abraham Heschel's Theology of Divine Pathos in Response to the 'Unmoved Mover' of Traditional Theism." *Evangelical Review of Theology* 25 (2001) 137–53.

———. *The Suffering of God According to Martin Luther's Theologia Crucis.* New York: Peter Lang, 1995.

———. "Trinity and Divine Passibility in Martin Luther's 'Theologia Crucis.'" *Scottish Bulletin of Evangelical Theology* 19 (2001) 31–64.

Nicolas, Jean-Hervé. "Aimante et bienheureuse Trinité." *Revue Thomiste* 78 (1978) 271–92.

———. "Les discours sur Dieu." *Revue Thomiste* 85 (1985) 635–57.

———. "La souffrance de Dieu?" *Nova et Vetera* 53 (1978) 56–64.

Nicolin, Friedhelm. "Unbekannte Aphorismen Hegels aus der Jenaer Periode." *Hegel-Studien* 4 (1967) 9–16.

Niebuhr, H. Richard. *Radical Monotheism and Western Culture, With Supplementary Essays.* New York: Harper and Row, 1960; Harper Torchbooks, 1970.

———. *The Responsible Self: An Essay in Christian Moral Philosophy.* New York: Harper and Row, 1963.

———, Daniel Day Williams, and James M. Gustafson. *The Purpose of the Church and its Ministry: Reflections on the Aims of Theological Education.* New York: Harper and Row, 1956.

Niebuhr, Reinhold. *Beyond Tragedy: Essays on the Christian Interpretation of History.* New York: Scribner, 1937.

———. *An Interpretation of Christian Ethics.* 1935. Reprint, New York: Seabury, 1963.

———. *The Nature and Destiny of Man.* Vol. 1. *Human Nature.* New York: Scribner, 1941.

———. *The Nature and Destiny of Man.* Vol. 2. *Human Destiny.* New York: Scribner, 1943

Nietzsche, Friedrich. *The Complete Works of Friedrich Nietzsche: The First Complete and Authorised English Translation.* Edited by Oscar Levy. Vol. 12. *Beyond Good and Evil: Prelude to a Philosophy of the Future,* translated by Helen Zimmern. New York: Russell and Russell, 1964.

———. *The Portable Nietzsche.* Edited and translated by Walter Kaufmann. New York: Viking, 1954.

Noddings, Nel. *Women and Evil.* Berkeley: University of California Press, 1989.

Norment, Owen Lennon, Jr. "George Angier Gordon: Theologian of the Humanity of God." PhD diss., Duke University, 1968.

Noro, Yoshio. "*Impassibilitas Dei.*" ThD diss., Union Theological Seminary, 1955.

Norris, R. A., Jr. *God and World in Early Christian Theology: A Study in Justin Martyr, Irenaeus, Tertullian, and Origen.* New York: Seabury, 1965.

Northam, Joan. "The Kingdom, the Power, and the Glory." *Expository Times* 99 (1988) 300–3.

Nouwen, Henri J. M. "The Vulnerable God." *Weavings* 8 (1993) 28–35.

Nussbaum, Martha C. *The Fragility of Goodness: Luck and Ethics in Greek Tragedy and Philosophy.* Cambridge: Cambridge University Press, 1986.

Nygren, Anders. *Agape and Eros.* Translated by Philip S. Watson. Chicago: University of Chicago Press, 1982.

O'Brien, George Dennis. "Prolegomena to a Dissolution to the Problem of Suffering." *Harvard Theological Review* 57 (1987) 301–23.

O'Donnell, John. "In Search of Christian Spirituality Today." In *History and Conscience: Studies in Honour of Father Sean O'Riordan, CSsR,* edited by Raphael Gallagher and Brendan McConvery, 253–73. Dublin: Gill and Macmillan, 1989.

O'Donovan, Leo J. "The Mystery of God as a History of Love: Eberhard Jüngel's Doctrine of God." *Theological Studies* 42 (1981) 251–71.

O'Hanlon, Gerard F. *The Immutability of God in the Theology of Hans Urs von Balthasar.* Cambridge: Cambridge University Press, 1990.

O'Sullivan, Michael A. "Blood, Sweat, and Tears: Suffering for the Kingdom." In *Restoring the Kingdom,* edited by Deane William Ferm, 101–11. Unification Studies Series. New York: Paragon, 1984.

Oakes, Robert A. "The Wrath of God." *International Journal for the Philosophy of Religion* 27 (1990) 129–40.

Oates, Wayne E. "Forms of Grief: Diagnosis, Meaning, and Treatment." In *The Meaning of Human Suffering,* edited by Flavian Dougherty, 232–65. New York: Human Sciences, 1982.

Odell, Willis P. "The Christian Conception of God." *The Methodist Review* 78 (1896) 728–34.

Oden, Thomas C. *The Living God: Systematic Theology.* San Francisco: Harper and Row, 1987.

O'Donnell, J. J. "Trinity and Temporality: The Christian Doctrine of God in the Light of Process Theology and the Theology of Hope." PhD diss., Oxford University, 1980.

Oeing-Hanhoff, Ludger. "Thesen zum Theodizeeproblem." In *Leiden,* edited by Willi Oelmüller, 218–28. Vol. 3. *Kolloquium Religion und Philosophie.* Paderborn: Ferdinand Schöning, 1986.

Oelmüller, Willi. "Philosophische Antwortversuche angesichts des Leidens." In *Theodizee-Gott vor Gericht?* edited by Willi Oelmüller, 67–86. Munich: Wilhelm Fink Verlag, 1990.

———. "Zum Selbstverständnis leidender Menschen in den Erfahrungshorizonten Gott, Natur, Kultur." In *Leiden,* edited by Willi Oelmüller, 176–91. Vol. 3. *Kolloquium Religion und Philosophie.* Paderborn: Ferdinand Schöning, 1986.

———, ed. *Kolloquium Religion und Philosophie.* Vol. 3, *Leiden.* Paderborn: Ferdinand Schöning, 1986.

———, ed. *Theodizee—Gott vor Gericht?* Munich: Wilhelm Fink Verlag, 1990.

Ogden, Schubert. "The Meaning of Christian Hope." In *Religious Experience and Process Theology: The Pastoral Implications of a Major Modern Movement,* edited by Harry James Cargas and Bernard Lee, 195–212. New York: Paulist, 1976.

———. "The Metaphysics of Faith and Justice." In *Gottes Zukunft—Zukunft der Welt: Festschrift für Jürgen Moltmann zum 60 Geburtstag,* edited by Hermann Deuser, Gerhard Marcel Martin, Konrad Stock, and Michael Welker, 511–19. Munich: Kaiser, 1986.

———. "On the Trinity." *Theology* 83 (1980) 97–102.

———. *The Reality of God and Other Essays.* New York: Harper and Row, 1963.

———. "Toward a New Theism." In *Process Philosophy and Christian Thought,* edited by Delwin Brown, Ralph E. James Jr., and Gene Reeves, 173–87. Indianapolis: Bobbs-Merrill, 1971.

Ogletree, Thomas W. "A Christological Assessment of Dipolar Theism." In *Process Philosophy and Christian Thought,* edited by Delwin Brown, Ralph E. James, Jr., and Gene Reeves, 331–46. Indianapolis: Bobbs-Merrill, 1971.

Oguro-Opitz, Bettina. *Analyse und Auseinandersetzung mit der Theologie des Schmerzes Gottes von Kazoh Kitamori.* Series 23. Europäische Hochschulschriften, vol. 133. *Theologie.* Frankfurt am Main: Verlag Peter Lang, 1980.

Ohlrich, Charles. *The Suffering God: Hope and Comfort for Those Who Hurt.* Downers Grove: Intervarsity, 1982.

Olson, Roger E. "Trinity and Eschatology: The Historical Reign of God in the Theology of Wolfhart Pannenberg." PhD diss., Rice University, 1984.

Origen. *Selections from the Commentaries and Homilies of Origen.* Translated by R. B. Tollington. London: SPCK, 1929.

Orr, James. *God's Image in Man and Its Defacement in the Light of Modern Denials.* Grand Rapids: Eerdmans, 1948.

Osborne, Thomas P. "Guidelines for Christian Suffering: A Source-Critical and Theological Study of I Peter 2:21–25." *Biblica* 64 (1983) 381–408.

Osthathios, Geevarghese Mar. "Justice to the Poor on the Trinitarian Model." In *Gottes Zukunft—Zukunft der Welt: Festschrift für Jürgen Moltmann zum 60 Geburtstag,* edited by Hermann Deuser, Gerhard Marcel Martin, Konrad Stock, and Michael Welker, 213–23. Munich: Kaiser, 1986.

Otto, Randall E. "Japanese Religion in Kazoh Kitamori's Theology of the Pain of God." *Encounter* 52 (1991) 33–48.

Otto, Rudolf. *The Idea of the Holy: An Inquiry into the Non-Rational Factor in the Idea of the Divine and Its Relation to the Rational.* 2nd edition. Translated by John W. Harvey. Oxford: Oxford University Press, 1950.

Ottolander, P. Den. *Deus Immutabilis: Wijgerige Beschouwing Over Onveranderlijkheid en Veranderlijkheid Volgens de Theo-ontologie Van Sint-Thomas en Karl Barth.* Assen: Van Gorcum and Comp. N. V., 1965.

Outka, Gene. *Agape: An Ethical Analysis.* New Haven: Yale University Press, 1972.

Outler, Albert C. "God's Providence and the World's Anguish." In *The Mystery of Suffering and Death,* edited by Michael J. Taylor, 3–23. Staten Island: Alba, 1973.

Owen, O. T. "Does God Suffer?" *Church Quarterly Review* 158 (1957) 176–84.

Page, Ruth. "Human Liberation and Divine Transcendence." *Theology* 85 (1982) 184–90.

Pailin, David A. "The Utterly Absolute and the Totally Related: Change in God." *New Blackfriars* 68 (1987) 243–55.

Pannenberg, Wolfhart. *The Apostles' Creed in the Light of Today's Questions.* Translated by Margaret Kohl. Philadelphia: Westminster, 1975.

Parente, Pascal P. "The Book of Job: Reflections on the Mystic Value of Human Suffering." *Catholic Biblical Quarterly* 8 (1946) 213–19.

Park, Andrew Sung. *The Wounded Heart of God: The Asian Concept of Han and the Christian Doctrine of Sin.* Nashville: Abingdon, 1993.

Pasewark, Kyle A. *A Theology of Power: Being beyond Domination.* Minneapolis: Fortress, 1993.

Patrick, Dale. "Job's Address of God." *Zeitschrift für die Alttestamentliche Wissenschaft* 91 (1979) 268–82.

———. "The Translation of Job XLII 6." *Vetus Testamentum* 26 (1976) 369–71.

Paul, Robert S. *The Atonement and the Sacraments.* London: Hodder and Stoughton, 1961.

Pawlikowski, John. "The Holocaust and Contemporary Christology." In *Concilium: The Holocaust as Interruption*, edited by Elisabeth Schüssler Fiorenza and David Tracy, 43–49. Edinburgh: T. & T. Clark, 1984.

Peacocke, Arthur. *Intimations of Reality: Critical Realism in Science and Religion.* Notre Dame: University of Notre Dame Press, 1984.

———. *Theology for a Scientific Age: Being and Becoming—Natural, Divine, and Human.* Theology and the Sciences Series, edited by Kevin J. Sharpe. Enlarged edition. Oxford: Basil Blackwell, 1990; Minneapolis: Fortress, 1993.

Pelagius. "Letter to Demetrias." In *Theological Anthropology*, translated and edited by J. Patout Burns, 39–55. Sources of Early Christian Thought Series, edited by William G. Rusch. Philadelphia: Fortress, 1981.

Pelikan, Jaroslav. *The Christian Tradition: A History of the Development of Doctrine.* Vol. 1. *The Emergence of the Catholic Tradition (100–600).* Chicago: University of Chicago Press, 1971.

———. *The Christian Tradition: A History of the Development of Doctrine.* Vol. 2. *The Spirit of Eastern Christendom* (600–1700). Chicago: University of Chicago Press, 1974.

———. *The Christian Tradition: A History of the Development of Doctrine.* Vol. 3. *The Growth of Medieval Theology (600–1300).* Chicago: University of Chicago Press, 1978.

———. *The Christian Tradition: A History of the Development of Doctrine.* Vol. 4. *Reformation of Church and Dogma (1300–1700).* Chicago: University of Chicago Press, 1984.

———. *The Christian Tradition: A History of the Development of Doctrine.* Vol. 5. *Christian Doctrine and Modern Culture (since 1700).* Chicago: University of Chicago Press, 1989.

Perdue, Leo G. "Job's Assault on Creation." *Hebrew Union Annual Review* 10 (1986) 295–315.

——— and W. Clark Gilpin, eds. *The Voice from the Whirlwind: Interpreting the Book of Job.* Nashville: Abingdon, 1992.

Perkins, Moreland. "Emotion and Feeling." *The Philosophical Review* 75 (1966) 139–60.

Perry, R. M. "Jahweh, the God of Love: A Study in Old Testament Theology." PhD diss., University of Edinburgh, 1937.

Peters, Ted. *God—the World's Future: Systematic Theology for a Postmodern Era.* Minneapolis: Fortress, 1992.

Pétré, H. " 'Misericordia': Histoire du mot et de l'idee du paganisme au christianisme." *Revue des Études Latines* 12 (1934) 376–89.

Petrie, J. C. "Canon Streeter's View of God." *Christian Century* 45 (1928) 1585–88.

Petuchowski, Jakob Josef. "Mehschlich reden von Gott: Erzählende Theologie aus Israels Lehrhäusern." In *Mut zur Tugend: Über die Fähigkeit, menschlicher zu leben*, edited by Karl Rahner and Bernhard Welte, 145–52. Freiburg: Verlag Herder, 1979.

———. *Theology and Poetry: Studies in the Medieval Piyyut.* The Littman Library of Jewish Civilization. Edited by David Goldstein, Louis Jacobs, and Lionel Kochan. London: Routledge and Kegan Paul, 1978.

Pfeil, H. "Die Frage nach der Veränderlichkeit und Geschichtlichkeit Gottes." *Münchener theologische Zeitschrift* 31 (1980)1–23.

Phillips, Anthony. "The Servant: Symbol of Divine Powerlessness." *Expository Times* 90 (1979) 370–74.

Phillips, Mickey Arnold. "A Theological Analysis of Suffering as a Christian Lifestyle in the New Testament." PhD diss., Southern Baptist Theological Seminary, 1978.

Piepmeier, Rainer. "Philosophische Reflexionen zum Phänomen des Leidens." In *Leiden,* edited by Willi Oelmüller, 66–82. Vol. 3. *Kolloquium Religion und Philosophie.* Paderborn: Ferdinand Schöning, 1986.

Pike, Nelson. "Omnipotence and God's Ability to Sin." *American Philosophical Quarterly* 6 (1969) 208–16.

Pinnock, Clark. "God Limits His Knowledge." In *Predestination and Free Will: Four Views of Divine Sovereignty and Human Freedom,* edited by David Basinger and Randall Basinger, 143–62. Downers Grove: InterVarsity, 1986.

———. "The Need for a Scriptural, and therefore a Neo-Classical Theism." In *Perspectives on Evangelical Theology,* edited by Kenneth Kantzer and Stanley Gundry, 37–42. Grand Rapids: Baker, 1979.

Pire, Henri-Dominique. "Sur l'emploi des termes *apatheia* et *eleos* dans les oeuvres de Clément d'Alexandrie." *Revue des Sciences Philosophiques et Théologiques* 27 (1938) 427–31.

Placher, William C. "Narratives of a Vulnerable God." *Princeton Seminary Bulletin, New Series* 14 (1993) 134–51.

———. *Narratives of a Vulnerable God: Christ, Theology, and Scripture.* Louisville: Westminster John Knox, 1994.

Plank, Karl A. "The Scarred Countenance: Inconstancy in the Book of Hosea." *Judaism* 32 (1983) 343–54.

Plathow, Michael. "Menschenleid als Leiden an Gottes Verborgenheit: Theologische Überlegungen zur psychoanalytischen Sicht von menschlicher Sünde und göttlichem Zorn." *Theologische Zeitschrift* 40 (1984) 275–95.

Pohlenz, Max. *Vom Zorne Gottes. Eine Studie über den Einfluss der griechischen Philosophie auf das alte Christentum.* Göttingen: Vandenhoeck and Ruprecht, 1909.

Polen, Nehemia. "Divine Weeping: Rabbi Kalonymos Shapiro's Theology of Catastrophe in the Warsaw Ghetto." *Modern Judaism* 7 (1987) 253–69.

Poling, James N. "Child Sexual Abuse: A Rich Context for Thinking about God, Community, and Ministry." *Journal of Pastoral Care* 42 (1988) 58–61.

Pollard, T. E. "The Impassibility of God." *Scottish Journal of Theology* 8 (1955) 353–64.

Pool, Jeff B. *Against Returning to Egypt: Exposing and Resisting Credalism in the Southern Baptist Convention.* Macon, GA: Mercer University Press, 1998.

———. "Baptist Infidelity to the Principle of Religious Liberty." *Perspectives in Religious Studies* 17 (1990) 13–30.

———. "Beyond Postliberal Foundationalism: The Theological Method of Langdon Gilkey." In *The Theology of Langdon B. Gilkey: Systematic and Critical Studies,* edited by Jeff B. Pool and Kyle A. Pasewark, 57–166. Macon, GA: Mercer University Press, 1999.

———. "Chief Article of Faith: The Preamble of the *Baptist Faith and Message (1963).*" In *Sacred Mandates of Conscience: Interpretations of the Baptist Faith and Message*, 37–101. Edited by Jeff B. Pool. Macon, GA: Smyth & Helwys, 1997.

———. "Christ, Conscience, Canon, Community: Web of Authority in the Baptist Vision." *Perspectives in Religious Studies* 24 (1997) 417–45.

———. "Conscience and Interpreting Baptist Tradition." In *Sacred Mandates of Conscience: Interpretations of the Baptist Faith and Message (1963)*, edited by Jeff B. Pool, 1–36. Macon, GA: Smyth & Helwys, 1997.

———. "God's Wounds: Structure and Dynamism in the Christian Symbol of Divine Suffering." PhD diss., University of Chicago, 1994.

———. "The Heart of Christian Confession." *American Baptist Quarterly* 24 (2005) 376–90.

———. "No Entrance into Truth Except through Love: Contributions of Augustine of Hippo to a Contemporary Christian Hermeneutic of Love." *Review and Expositor* 101 (2004) 629–66.

———. " '*Non Intratur in Veritatem, Nisi per Charitatem*': Toward a Christian Hermeneutic of Love." *Communio Viatorum* 43 (2001) 159–88.

———. "Toward a Christian Hermeneutic of Love: Problem and Possibility." *Perspectives in Religious Studies* 28 (2001) 257–83.

———, ed. *Sacred Mandates of Conscience: Interpretations of the Baptist Faith and Message (1963)*. Macon, GA: Smyth & Helwys, 1997.

———, ed. *Through the Tempest: Theological Voyages in a Pluralistic Culture* by Langdon Gilkey. Minneapolis: Fortress, 1991.

——— and Kyle Pasewark, eds. *The Theology of Langdon B. Gilkey: Systematic and Critical Studies*. Macon, GA: Mercer University Press, 1999.

Pope, Stephen J. *The Evolution of Altruism and the Ordering of Love*. Moral Traditions and Moral Arguments Series, edited by James F. Keenan. Washington DC: Georgetown University Press, 1994.

Porter, Jean M. "The Feminization of God: Second Thoughts on the Ethical Implications of Process Theology." *St. Luke's Journal of Theology* 29 (1986) 251–60.

Post, Stephen G. "The Inadequacy of Selflessness: God's Suffering and the Theory of Love." *Journal of the American Academy of Religion* 56 (1988) 213–28.

———. "The Purpose of Neighbor-Love." *Journal of Religious Ethics* 18 (1990) 181–93.

———. *A Theory of Agape: On the Meaning of Christian Love*. Lewisburg: Bucknell University Press; London and Toronto: Associated University Presses, 1990.

Power, William L. "The Doctrine of the Trinity and Whitehead's Metaphysics." *Encounter* 45 (1984) 287–302.

Prestige, G. L. *God in Patristic Thought*. 2nd ed. London: SPCK, 1952; SPCK Paperback, 1964.

Prichard, J. "The Immutability of God." *The Thinker* 6 (1894) 338–44.

Pringle-Pattison, A. Seth. *The Idea of God in the Light of Recent Philosophy*. New York: Oxford University Press, 1917.

Proudfoot, Charles Merrill. "The Apostle Paul's Understanding of Christian Suffering." PhD diss., Yale University, 1956.

Pseudo-Dionysius. "The Divine Names." In *Pseudo Dionysius: The Complete Works*. Translated by Colm Luibheid. The Classics of Western Spirituality: A Library of the Great Spiritual Masters. Edited by John Farina. New York: Paulist, 1987.

———. *The Divine Names and the Mystical Theology*. Translated by C. E. Rolt. London: SPCK, 1940.

Quick, Oliver Chase. *Christian Beliefs and Modern Questions*. London: SCM, 1923.

———. *Doctrines of the Creed: Their Basis in Scripture and Their Meaning Today*. London: Nisbet, 1938.

———. *Essays in Orthodoxy*. London: Macmillan, 1916.

———. *The Gospel of Divine Action*. New York: E. P. Dutton, 1933.

Quinn, John M. "Triune Self-Giving: One Key to the Problem of Suffering." *The Thomist* 44 (1980) 173–218.

Raabe, Paul R. "The Suffering of God." *Concordia Journal* 12 (1986) 147–52.

Rae, Elanor and Bernice Marie-Day. *Created in Her Image: Models of the Feminine Divine*. New York: Crossroad, 1990.

Rahner, Karl. "Reflections on the Unity of the Love of Neighbour and the Love of God." In *Theological Investigations*. Vol. 6. *Concerning Vatican Council II* by Karl Rahner, 231–49. Translated by Karl H. Kruger and Boniface Kruger. New York: Crossroad Publishing Company, 1982.

Ramsey, Paul. *Basic Christian Ethics*. New York: Scribner, 1952.

Randles, Marshall. *The Blessed God: Impassibility*. London: Charles H. Kelly, 1900.

Rashdall, Hastings. *The Idea of Atonement in Christian Theology*. London: Macmillan, 1919.

Rattigan, Mary T. "The Concept of God in Process Thought." *Irish Theological Quarterly* 49 (1982) 206–15.

Rauschenbusch, Walter. *A Theology for the Social Gospel*. New York: Macmillan, 1917.

Rawlinson, A. E. J., ed. *Essays on the Trinity and the Incarnation: By Members of the Anglican Communion*. London: Longmans, Green, 1933.

Rehm, M. "Eli, Eli, lamma sabacthani." *Biblische Zeitschrift* 2 (1958) 275–78.

Reichenbach, Bruce. "God Limits His Power." In *Predestination and Free Will: Four Views of Divine Sovereignty and Human Freedom*, edited by David Basinger and Randall Basinger, 101–24. Downers Grove: InterVarsity, 1986.

Reid, Duncan. "Without Parts or Passions? The Suffering God in Anglican Thought." *Pacifica* 4 (1991) 257–72.

Relton, H. Maurice. "The Christian Conception of God: I." *Church Quarterly Review* 111 (1931) 227–53.

———. "The Christian Conception of God: II." *Church Quarterly Review* 112 (1931) 37–64.

———. *Cross and Altar: A Study of the Way Christ Saves Us*. London: Skeffinton and Son, 1947.

———. "Patripassianism." In *Studies in Christian Doctrine* by H. Maurice Relton, 61–91. London: Macmillan, 1960.

———. *Studies in Christian Doctrine*. London: Macmillan, 1960.

Rentsch, Thomas. "Theodizee als Hermeneutik der Lebenswelt: Existential-anthropologische und ethische Bemerkungen." In *Leiden*, edited by Willi

Oelmüller, 83–91. Vol. 3. *Kolloquium Religion und Philosophie.* Paderborn: Ferdinand Schöning, 1986.

Richard, Jean. "Dieu tout-puissant et souffrant." *Laval théologique et philosophique* 47 (1991) 39–52.

Richard, Lucien. "Kenotic Christology in a New Perspective." *Église et théologie* 7 (1976) 5–39.

———. *What Are They Saying about the Theology of Suffering.* New York: Paulist, 1992.

Richard, Marcel. "Proclus de Constantinople et le Théopaschisme." *Revue D'Histoire Ecclésiastique* 38 (1942) 303–31.

Richardson, James T. and Rex Davis. "Experiential Fundamentalism: Revisions of Orthodoxy in the Jesus Movement." *Journal of the American Academy of Religion* 51 (1983) 397–425.

Ricoeur, Paul. "Biblical Hermeneutics." *Semeia* 4 (1975) 29–148.

———. *The Conflict of Interpretations: Essays in Hermeneutics.* Edited by Don Ihde. Evanston: Northwestern University Press, 1974.

———. "Le Dieu crucifié de Jürgen Moltmann." *Les quatres fleuves: cahiers de recherche et de réflexion religieuses (Le Christ visage de Dieu)* 4 (1975) 109–14.

———. "Entre philosophie et théologie: la régle d'or en question." *Revue D'Histoire et de Philosophie Religieuses* 69 (1989) 3–9.

———. "Evil, A Challenge to Philosophy and Theology." *Journal of the American Academy of Religion* 53 (1985) 635–48.

———. *Fallible Man.* Translated by Charles A. Kelbley. Chicago: Henry Regnery, 1965.

———. *Freedom and Nature: The Voluntary and the Involuntary.* Translated by Erazim V. Kohák. Evanston: Northwestern University Press, 1966.

———. *Freud and Philosophy: An Essay on Interpretation.* Translated by Denis Savage. New Haven: Yale University Press, 1970.

———. "Der gekreuzigte Gott von Jürgen Moltmann." In *Diskussion über Jürgen Moltmanns Buch "Der gekreuzigte Gott,"* edited by Michael Welker, 17–25. Munich: Kaiser, 1979.

———. "The Golden Rule: Exegetical and Theological Perplexities." *New Testament Studies* 36 (1990) 392–97.

———. "The Hermeneutical Function of Distanciation." *Philosophy Today* 17 (1973) 129–41.

———. "The Hermeneutics of Testimony." *Anglican Theological Review* 61 (1979) 435–61.

———. "Hope and the Structure of Philosophical Systems." *Proceedings of the American Catholic Philosophical Association* 44 (1970) 55–69.

———. *Interpretation Theory: Discourse and the Surplus of Meaning.* Fort Worth: Texas Christian University Press, 1976.

———. "The Language of Faith." In *The Philosophy of Paul Ricoeur: An Anthology of His Work*, edited by Charles E. Reagan and David Stewart, 223–38. Boston: Beacon, 1978.

———. *Liebe und Gerechtigkeit = Amour et Justice.* Translated into German by Matthias Raden. Edited by Oswald Bayer. Tübingen: Mohr/Siebeck, 1990.

———. "Manifestation et Proclamation." *Archivio di Filosofia, Il Sacro* (1974) 57–76.

————. "Naming God." *Union Seminary Quarterly Review* 34 (1979) 215–27.

————. *Oneself as Another.* Translated by Kathleen Blamey. Chicago: University of Chicago Press, 1992.

————. "Philosophy and Religious Language." *Journal of Religion* 54 (1974) 71–85.

————. *Political and Social Essays.* Edited by David Stewart and Joseph Bien. Athens: Ohio University Press, 1974.

————. "The Problem of the Foundation of Moral Philosophy." *Philosophy Today* 22 (1978) 175–92.

————. *The Rule of Metaphor: Multi-Disciplinary Studies of the Creation of Meaning in Language.* Translated by Robert Czerny. Toronto: University of Toronto Press, 1977.

————. *The Symbolism of Evil.* Translated by Emerson Buchanan. Boston: Beacon, 1967.

————. *Time and Narrative.* Vol. 1. Translated by Kathleen McLaughlin and David Pellauer. Chicago: University of Chicago Press, 1984.

Ridderbos, Herman. *Paul: An Outline of His Theology.* Translated by John Richard De Witt. Grand Rapids: Eerdmans, 1975.

Riedlinger, Helmut. "Den Schmerz Gottes erleiden: Besinnung auf Geduld, die aus dem Glauben kommt." In *Mut zur Tugend: Über die Fähigkeit, menschlicher zu leben,* edited by Karl Rahner and Bernard Welte, 200–7. Freiburg: Verlag Herder, 1979.

Ritschl, Albrecht. *The Christian Doctrine of Justification and Reconciliation: The Positive Development of the Doctrine.* Translated and edited by H. R. Mackintosh and A. B. Macaulay. Edinburgh: T. & T. Clark, 1900.

Ritschl, Dietrich. "Gott wohnt in der Zeit: Auf der Suche nach dem verlorenen Gott." In *Gottes Zukunft—Zukunft der Welt: Festschrift für Jürgen Moltmann zum 60 Geburtstag,* edited by Hermann Deuser, Gerhard Marcel Martin, Konrad Stock, and Michael Welker, 250–61. Munich: Kaiser, 1986.

Roberts, Preston T., Jr. "A Christian Theory of Dramatic Tragedy." In *The New Orpheus: Essays toward a Christian Poetic,* edited by Nathan A. Scott, Jr., 255–85. New York: Sheed and Ward, 1964.

Robertson, John C., Jr. "Does God Change?" *The Ecumenist* 9 (1971) 61–64.

Robinson, Forbes. *The Self-Limitation of the Word of God as Manifested in the Incarnation and An Essay on the Evidential Value of O.T. Prophecy.* London: Longmans, Green, 1914.

Robinson, H. Wheeler. *The Christian Experience of the Holy Spirit.* New York: Harper and Brothers, 1928.

————. *The Cross in the Old Testament.* London: SCM, 1955.

————. *Redemption and Revelation in the Actuality of History.* New York: Harper and Brothers, 1942.

————. *Suffering, Human and Divine.* New York: Macmillan, 1938.

————. *Two Hebrew Prophets: Studies in Hosea and Ezekiel.* London: Lutterworth, 1948.

Rolt, Clarence E. *The World's Redemption.* London: Longmans, Green, 1913.

Rosenthal, Gilbert S. "Omnipotence, Omniscience and a Finite God." *Judaism* 39 (1990) 55–72.

Rosenzweig, Franz. *The Star of Redemption.* Translated by William W. Hallo. 1971. Reprint, Notre Dame: University of Notre Dame Press, 1985.

Ross, James F. "Job 33:14–30: The Phenomenology of Lament." *Journal of Biblical Literature* 94 (1975) 38–46.

Ross, Susan A. "The Human Face of Suffering and Healing." In *Suffering and Healing in Our Day*, edited by Francis A. Eigo, 1–28. Villanova: Villanova University Press, 1990.

Rossé, Gérard. *The Cry of Jesus on the Cross: A Biblical and Theological Study.* Translated by Stephen Wentworth Arndt. New York: Paulist, 1987.

Rothuizen, Gerard Th. "Who Am I? Bonhoeffer and Suicide." In *New Studies in Bonhoeffer's Ethics*, edited by William J. Peck, 167–85. Vol. 30. Toronto Studies in Theology Series, no. 3, Bonhoeffer Series. Lewiston, New York: Edwin Mellen, 1987.

Rüther, Theodor. *Die sittliche Forderung der Apatheia in den beiden ersten christlichen Jahrhunderten und bei Klemens von Alexandrien: Ein Beitrag zur Geschichte des christlichen Vollkommenheitsbegriffes.* No. 63. Freiburger theologische Studien, edited by Arthur Allgeier and Johannes Vincke. Freiburg: Verlag Herder, 1949.

Ruether, Rosemary Radford. *Sexism and God-Talk: Toward a Feminist Theology.* Boston: Beacon, 1983.

Russell, Brian. "A Nuclear End: Would God Ever Let It Happen?" In *Theology against the Nuclear Horizon*, edited by Alan Race, 103–16. London: SCM, 1988.

Russell, John M. "Impassibility and Pathos in Barth's Idea of God." *Anglican Theological Review* 70 (1988) 221–32.

Ryssel, Victor. *Gregorius Thaumaturgus: Sein Leben und Seine Schriften.* Leipzig: Verlag von L. Fernau, 1880.

Sabant, Philippe. "Christ, Freedom and Salvation in the Thought of Nicholas Berdyaev." *Ecumenical Review* 26 (1974) 483–94.

Sachs, John R. "Current Eschatology: Universal Salvation and the Problem of Hell." *Theological Studies* 52 (1991) 227–54.

Sands, Kathleen M. *Escape from Paradise: Evil and Tragedy in Feminist Theology.* Minneapolis: Fortress, 1994.

Sarot, Marcel. "Auschwitz, Morality and the Suffering of God." *Modern Theology* 7 (1991) 135–52.

———. *God, Passibility and Corporeality.* Studies in Philosophical Theology Series, edited by H. J. Adriaanse and Vincent Brümmer. Kampen, Netherlands: Kok Pharos, 1992.

———. "Het lijden van God? Enkele terminologische notities bij een hedendaagse theologische discussie." *Nederlands Theologisch Tijdschrift* 44 (1990) 35–50.

———. "Omnipotence and Self-Limitation." In *Christian Faith and Philosophical Theology: Essays in Honour of Vincent Brümmer*, edited by Gijsbert van den Brink, Luco J. van den Brom, and Marcel Sarot, 172–85. Kampen, Netherlands: Kok Pharos, 1992.

———. "Omniscience and Experience." *Philosophy of Religion* 30 (1991) 89–102.

———. "De Passibilitas Dei in de Hedendaagse Westerse Theologie: Een Literatuuroverzicht." *Kerk en Theologie* 40 (1989) 196–206.

———. "Patripassianism, Theopaschitism and the Suffering of God: Some Historical and Systematic Considerations." *Religious Studies* 26 (1990) 363–75.

————. "Suffering of Christ, Suffering of God?" *Theology* 95 (1992) 113–19.

Sartre, Jean-Paul. *Being and Nothingness: An Essay in Phenomenological Ontology.* Translated by Hazel E. Barnes. Secaucus, NJ: Citadel, 1956.

Saussy, Carroll. *God Images and Self Esteem: Empowering Women in a Patriarchal Society.* Louisville: Westminster John Knox, 1991.

Sauter, Gerhard. "'Leiden' und 'Handeln.'" *Evangelische Theologie* 45 (1985) 435–58.

Schaeder, Erich. *Theozentrische Theologie: Eine Untersuchung zur dogmatischen Prinzipienlehre, Erster, geschichtlicher Teil.* Leipzig: Werner Scholl, 1916.

————. *Theozentrische Theologie: Eine Untersuchung zur dogmatischen Prinzipienlehre, Zweiter, systematischer Teil.* Leipzig: Werner Scholl, 1914.

Schaff, Philip and Henry Wace, eds. *A Select Library of Nicene and Post-Nicene Fathers of the Christian Church: Second Series.* Vol. 14. *The Seven Ecumenical Councils.* Reprint, Grand Rapids: Eerdmans, 1983.

Scharbert, Josef. *Der Schmerz im alten Testament.* Bonn: Hanstein, 1955.

Scheffczyk, Leo. "Die Frage nach der Hellenizierung des Christentums unter modernem Problemaspekt." *Münchener theologische Zeitschrift* 33 (1982) 195–205.

————. "Die 'Gott-ist-tot'-Theologie." In *Gott die Frage unserer Zeit*, edited by Heinrich Fries, 120–31. Munich: Don Bosco Verlag, 1973.

————. *Tendenzen und Brennpunkte der neueren Problematik um die Hellenisierung des Christentums.* Munich: Bayerische Akademie der Wissenschaften, 1982.

Scheler, Max. "The Meaning of Suffering." In *Max Scheler (1874–1928): Centennial Essays*, edited by M. S. Fringes, 121–63. The Hague: Martinus Nijhoff, 1974.

————. "On the Tragic." *Cross Currents* 4 (1954) 178–91.

————. "*Ordo Amoris.*" In *Selected Philosophical Essays* by Max Scheler, translated by David R. Lachterman, 98–135. Evanston: Northwestern University Press, 1973.

Schelling, Friedrich. *The Ages of the World.* Translated by Frederick de Wolfe Bolman, Jr. New York: Columbia University Press, 1942.

————. *Philosophical Inquiries into the Nature of Human Freedom.* Translated by James Gutmann. La Salle, IL: Open Court, 1936.

Schiffers, Norbert. "Suffering in History." In *Concilium: Religion in the Seventies.* Vol. 76, *New Questions on God*, edited by Johann Baptist Metz, 38–47. New York: Herder and Herder, 1972.

Schiller, F. C. S. "Man's Limitations or God's?" *Hibbert Journal* 32 (1933) 41–55.

Schilling, Sylvester Paul. *God and Human Anguish.* Nashville: Abingdon, 1977.

————. "God and Suffering in Christian Hymnody." *Religion in Life* 48 (Autumn 1979) 323–36.

Schiwy, Günter. "Vom Leiden am Gotteswort." *Geist und Leben* 39 (1966) 1–3.

Schleiermacher, Friedrich. *The Christian Faith.* 2nd ed. Edited by H. R. Mackintosh and J. S. Stewart. Philadelphia: Fortress, 1976.

Schlesinger, George N. "Grappling with the Problem of Suffering." In *Encounter: Essays on Torah and Modern Life*, edited by H. Chaim Schimmel and Aryeh Carmell, 22–41. Jerusalem: Feldheim, 1989.

Schmied, A. "Gotteslehre als trinitarische Kreuzestheologie." *Theologie der Gegenwart* 16 (1973) 246–51.

Schöndorf, Harald. "Warum musste Jesus leiden? Eine neue Konzeption der Soteriologie." *Zeitschrift für katholische Theologie* 124 (2002) 440–67.

Scholem, Gershom G. *Major Trends in Jewish Mysticism*. New York: Schocken, 1941.

Schoonenberg, Piet. "Chalcedon and Divine Immutability." *Theology Digest* 29 (1981) 103–7.

———. "De lijdende God in de Britse Theologie." *Gereformeerd Theologisch Tijdschrift* 89 (1989) 154–70.

———. "Lijden van God?" *Ons Geestelijk Leven Tijdschrift voor Informatie, Bezinning en Gesprek* 56 (1979) 33–42.

———. "Process or History in God?" *Louvain Studies* 4 (1973) 303–9.

Schottroff, Luise, et al. *Essays on the Love Commandment*. Translated by Reginald H. Fuller and Ilse Fuller. Philadelphia: Fortress, 1978.

Schrage, Wolfgang. *The Ethics of the New Testament*. Translated by David E. Green. Philadelphia: Fortress, 1988.

Schüngel, Paul H. "Der leidende Vater." *Orientierung* 41 (1977) 49–50.

Schulweis, H. M. "Karl Barth's Job: Morality and Theodicy." *Jewish Quarterly Review* 65 (1975) 156–67.

Schwan, Alexander. "Leiden an und in der Politik: Eine Skizze in 7 Thesen." In *Leiden*, edited by Willi Oelmüller, 92–96. Vol. 3. *Kolloquium Religion und Philosophie*. Paderborn: Ferdinand Schöning, 1986.

Schwanz, Peter. *Imago Dei als christologisch-anthropologisches Problem in der Geschichte der Alten Kirche von Paulus bis Clemens von Alexandrien*. Leipzig: Max Niemeyer Verlag, 1970.

Schwartz, Matthew B. "The Meaning of Suffering: A Talmudic Response to Theodicy." *Judaism* 32 (1983) 444–51.

Schweiker, William. *Mimetic Reflections: A Study in Hermeneutics, Theology, and Ethics*. New York: Fordham University Press, 1990.

———. *Theological Ethics and Global Dynamics: In the Time of Many Worlds*. Oxford, United Kingdom: Blackwell, 2004.

Schweitzer, Wolfgang. "Theologia crucis als Basis der Christusverkündigung heute." In *Christus Allein—Allein das Christentum? Vorträge der vierten theologischen Konferenz zwischen Vertretern der Evangelischen Kirche in Deutschland und der Kirche von England*, edited by Klaus Kremkau, 68–80. Beiheft zur Ökumenischen Rundschau Series 36. Frankfurt am Main: Verlag Otto Lembeck, 1979.

Schwöbel, Christoph. "Exploring the Logic of Perfection: Divine Attributes and Divine Agency." In *Christian Faith and Philosophical Theology: Essays in Honour of Vincent Brümmer*, edited by Gijsbert van den Brink, Luco J. van den Brom, and Marcel Sarot, 197–217. Kampen, Netherlands: Kok Pharos, 1992.

Scott, Nathan A., ed. *The Tragic Vision and the Christian Faith*. New York: Association, 1957.

Seeberg, Reinhold. *Text-Book of the History of Doctrines*. Vol. 1. *History of Doctrines in the Ancient Church*. Translated by Charles E. Hay. Grand Rapids: Baker, 1952.

Seeskin, Kenneth. "The Reality of Radical Evil." *Judaism* 29 (1980) 440–53.

Selling, Joseph A. "Moral Questioning and Human Suffering: In Search of a Credible Response to the Meaning of Suffering." In *God and Human Suffering*, edited by Jan Lambrecht and Raymond F. Collins, 155–82. Louvain Theological and Pastoral Monographs 3. Louvain: Peeters, 1990.

Sewall, Richard B. *The Vision of Tragedy*. New Haven: Yale University Press, 1959.

Shaull, Richard. "The Redemptive Suffering of the Poor." In *Suffering and Healing in Our Day*, edited by Francis A. Eigo, 167–200. Villanova: Villanova University Press, 1990.

Shedd, William G. T. *Dogmatic Theology*. Vol. 2. 2nd ed. New York: Scribner, 1889.

———. *Theological Essays*. New York: Scribner, Armstrong, 1877.

Shields, George W. "Hartshorne and Creel on Impassibility." *Process Studies* 21 (1992) 44–59.

Shusaku, Endo. *A Life of Jesus*. Translated by Richard Schuchert. New York: Paulist, 1973.

———. *The Samurai*. Translated by Van C. Gessel. New York: Harper and Row, 1982.

———. *Silence*. Translated by William Johnston. New York: Taplinger, 1969.

Sia, Santiago. "A Changing God?" *Word and Spirit* 8 (1986) 13–30.

Simon, David Worthington. *Reconciliation by Incarnation: The Reconciliation of God and Man by the Incarnation of the Divine Word*. Edinburgh: T. & T. Clark, 1898.

———. *The Redemption of Man: Discussions Bearing on the Atonement*. Edinburgh: T. & T. Clark, 1889.

Simonis, W. "Über das 'Werden' Gottes. Gedanken zum Begriff der ökonomischen Trinität." *Münchener theologische Zeitschrift* 33 (1982) 133–39.

Sinclair, J. C. "Is God Finite?" *Methodist Review* 112 (1929) 604–6.

Slonimsky, Henry. "The Philosophy Implicit in the Midrash." *Hebrew Union College Annual* 27 (1956) 235–90.

Slusser, Michael. "The Scope of Patripassianism." In *Studia Patristica*, edited by Elizabeth A. Livingstone, 17.2: 169–75. New York: Pergamon, 1982.

Smiley, Jane. *A Thousand Acres*. New York: Knopf, 1992.

Smith, David. *The Atonement in the Light of History and the Modern Spirit*. London: Hodder and Stoughton, 1920.

Smith, E. A. "Historicity of God." *Journal of Religion* 43 (1963) 20–34.

Smith, J. Warren. "Suffering Impassibly: Christ's Passion in Cyril of Alexandria's Soteriology." *Pro Ecclesia* 11 (2002) 463–83.

Smith, Richmond, ed. "Seoul Theological Consultation 1979: Reporting the Event." *Reformed World* 36 (1980) 3–4.

Snaith, Norman H. *The Distinctive Ideas of the Old Testament*. New York: Schocken, 1964.

Snodgrass, Klyne R. "Justification by Grace—to the Doers: An Analysis of the Place of Romans 2 in the Theology of Paul." *New Testament Studies* 32 (1986) 72–93.

Sölle, Dorothee. "Blood of the Dragon, Blood of the Lamb." *The Other Side* 23 (1987) 26–27.

———. *Christ the Representative: An Essay in Theology after the 'Death of God.'* Translated by David Lewis. Philadelphia: Fortress, 1967.

———. "God's Pain and Our Pain." In *The Future of Liberation Theology: Essays in Honor of Gustavo Gutiérrez*, edited by Marc H. Ellis and Otto Maduro, 326–33. Maryknoll: Orbis, 1989.

———. "God's Pain and Our Pain: How Theology Has to Change after Auschwitz." In *Judaism, Christianity, and Liberation: An Agenda for Dialogue*, edited by Otto Maduro, 110–21. Maryknoll: Orbis, 1991.

————. "Gott und das Leiden." In *Diskussion über Jürgen Moltmanns Buch "Der gekreuzigte Gott,"* edited by Michael Welker, 111–17. Munich: Kaiser, 1979.

————. "Remembrance, Pain and Hope." *The Witness* 74 (1991) 24–27.

————. *Suffering*. Translated by Everett R. Kalin. Philadelphia: Fortress, 1975.

Sobrino, Jon. *Christology at the Crossroads: A Latin American Approach*. Translated by John Drury. Maryknoll: Orbis, 1978.

————. "A Crucified People's Faith in the Son of God." *Concilium* 153 (1982) 23–28.

Sockman, Ralph W. *The Meaning of Suffering*. Nashville: Abingdon, 1961.

Sommer, Manfred. "Bewußtlosigkeit: Eine phänomenologische Skizze." In *Leiden*, edited by Willi Oelmüller, 97–103. Vol 3. *Kolloquium Religion und Philosophie*. Paderborn: Ferdinand Schöning, 1986.

Song, Choan-Seng. *The Compassionate God*. Maryknoll: Orbis, 1982.

————. *Jesus and the Reign of God*. Minneapolis: Fortress, 1993.

————. "The Role of Christology in the Christian Encounter with Eastern Religions." *South East Asia Journal of Theology* 5 (1964) 13–31.

Sonneborn, John Andrew. "God, Suffering and Hope: A Unification View." In *Unity in Diversity: Essays in Religion by Members of the Faculty of the Unification Theological Seminary*, edited by Henry O. Thompson, 163–239. New York: Rose of Sharon, 1984.

Sontag, Frederick. "God and Evil." *Religion in Life* 34 (1965) 215–23.

————. "The Holocaust God." *Encounter* 42 (1981) 163–67.

Sorrentino, Sergio. " 'Sofferenza di Dio' e 'theologia crucis' in D. Bonhoeffer." In *La Sapienza della Croce nella Rivelazione e nell' Ecumenismo*, 600–11. Vol. 1. *La Sapienza della Croce Oggi: Atti del Congresso internazionale Roma, 13–18 Ottobre 1975*. Torino: Leumann, 1976.

Spaemann, Robert. "Die christliche Sicht des Leidens." In *Leiden*, edited by Willi Oelmüller, 104–10. Vol. 3. *Kolloquium Religion und Philosophie*. Paderborn: Ferdinand Schöning, 1986.

Sparn, Walter. *Leiden-Erfahrung und Denken: Materialien zum Theodizeeproblem*. Vol. 67. Theologische Bücherei: Neudrucke und Berichte aus dem 20 Jahrhundert, edited by Gerhard Sauter. Munich: Kaiser, 1980.

Spence, Brian J. "The Hegelian Element in Von Balthasar's and Moltmann's Understanding of the Suffering of God." *Toronto Journal of Theology* 14 (1998) 45–60.

Spera, Salvatore. "Tristezza di Dio e annichilamento del Figlio: Prospettive della filosofia della religione di Schelling." In *La Sapienza della Croce nella Cultura e nella Pastorale*, 116–23. Vol. 3. *La Sapienza della Croce Oggi: Atti del Congresso internazionale Roma, 13–18 Ottobre 1975*. Torino: Leumann, 1976.

Spohn, William C. "Notes in Moral Theology: 1990: Passions and Principles." *Theological Studies* 52 (1991) 69–87.

Sponheim, Paul R. *Faith and the Other: A Relational Theology*. Minneapolis: Fortress, 1993.

————. *God—The Question and the Quest: Toward a Conversation Concerning Christian Faith*. Philadelphia: Fortress, 1985.

Springsted, Eric O. "Is There a Problem with the Problem of Evil?" *International Philosophical Quarterly* 24 (1984) 303–12.

Spufford, Margaret. "The Reality of Suffering and the Love of God." *Theology* 88 (1985) 441–46.

Staudinger, Hansjürgen. "Das Leiden in der Natur." In *Leiden*, edited by Willi Oelmüller, 111–18. Vol. 3. *Kolloquium Religion und Philosophie*. Paderborn: Ferdinand Schöning, 1986.

Stead, G. Christopher. "The Platonism of Arius." *Journal of Theological Studies* 15 (1964) 16–31.

———. "The Scriptures and the Soul of Christ in Athanasius." *Vigiliae Christianae* 36 (1982) 233–50.

Steen, Marc. "Een God Die met Ons Lijdt?" *Collationes* 21 (1991) 37–56.

———. "Het Actuele Thema van de Lijdende God: Vooronderstellingen, Illustratie en Evaluatie van Recent Theopaschitisme." PhD diss., Leuven, 1990.

———. "Jürgen Moltmann's Critical Reception of K. Barth's Theopaschitism." *Ephemerides Theologicae Lovanienses* 67 (1991) 278–311.

———. "The Theme of the Suffering God: An Exploration." In *God and Human Suffering*, edited by Jan Lambrecht and Raymond F. Collins, 69–93. Louvain Theological and Pastoral Monographs 3. Louvain: Peeters, 1990.

Steffen, Bernhard. *Das Dogma vom Kreuz: Beitrag zu einer staurozentrischen Theologie*. Gütersloh, Germany: Verlag von C. Bertelsmann, 1920.

Stern, Leonard W. "A Contemporary Jewish View of Suffering and God." In *God in Contemporary Thought: A Philosophical Perspective*, edited by Sebastian A. Matczak, 1053–65. Philosophical Questions Series, vol. 10, edited by Sebastian A. Matczak. Jamaica, New York: Learned, 1977.

Stevens, George Barker. *The Christian Doctrine of Salvation*. New York: Scribner, 1923.

Stockdale, Fairbank Barnes. "Does God Suffer?" *Methodist Quarterly Review* 81 (1899) 87–92.

Storr, Vernon F. *The Development of English Theology in the Nineteenth Century: 1800–1860*. London: Longmans, Green, 1913.

———. *The Living God*. London: Hodder and Stoughton, 1925.

———. *The Problem of the Cross*. London: John Murry, 1919.

Stott, John R. W. *The Cross of Christ*. Downers Grove: Inter-Varsity, 1986.

———. "God on the Gallows: How Could I Worship a God Immune to Pain?" *Christianity Today* 31 (1987) 28–30.

Streeter, Burnett Hillman. "The Suffering of God." *Hibbert Journal* 12 (1913–1914) 603–11.

———. *Reality: A New Correlation of Science and Religion*. New York: Macmillan, 1926.

———, ed. *God and the Struggle for Existence*. London: SCM, 1919.

Strong, Augustus Hopkins. *Christ in Creation and Ethical Monism*. Philadelphia: Roger Williams, 1899.

———. "God's Self-Limitations." *Baptist Quarterly Review* 13 (1891) 521–32.

———. "Modern Exaggerations of the Divine Immanence." *Christian Literature* 3 (1891) 276–83.

Strong, Edmund Linwood. *Lectures on the Incarnation of God*. London: Longmans, Green, 1917.

Stroumsa, Gedaliahu. "The Incorporeality of God: Context and Implications of Origen's Position." *Religion* 13 (1983) 345–58.

Studdert-Kennedy, Geoffrey A. *The Hardest Part*. London: Hodder and Stoughton Ltd., 1918.

———. *The Sorrows of God and Other Poems*. New York: Richard R. Smith, 1930; George H. Doran, 1924.

Stuhlmueller, Caroll. "Voices of Suffering in Biblical Prophecy and Prayer." In *The Meaning of Human Suffering*, edited by Flavian Dougherty, 97–158. New York: Human Sciences, 1982.

Suchocki, Marjorie Hewitt. *The End of Evil: Process Eschatology in Historical Context*. Albany: State University Press of New York, 1988.

Sullivan, Thomas D. "Omniscience, Immutability, and the Divine Mode of Knowing." *Faith and Philosophy* 8 (1991) 21–35.

Sundermeier, Theo. "Das Kreuz in japanischer Interpretation." *Evangelische Theologie* 44 (1984) 417–40.

Surin, Kenneth. "Atonement and Christology." *Neue Zeitschrift für systematische Theologie und Religionsphilosophie* 24 (1982) 131–49.

———. "The Impassibility of God and the Problem of Evil." *Scottish Journal of Theology* 35 (1982) 97–115.

———. "Theodicy?" *Harvard Theological Review* 76 (1983) 225–47.

———. *Theology and the Problem of Evil*. Signposts in Theology. Oxford: Basil Blackwell, 1986.

Sutherland, Denis. "Impassibility, Asceticism and the Vision of God." *Scottish Bulletin of Evangelical Theology* 5 (1987) 197–210.

Sykes, S. W. "The Strange Persistence of Kenotic Christology." In *Being and Truth: Essays in Honour of John Macquarrie*, edited by Alistair Kee and Eugene T. Long, 349–75. London: SCM, 1986.

Talbott, Thomas. "The Doctrine of Everlasting Punishment." *Faith and Philosophy* 7 (1990) 19–42.

Taliaferro, Charles. "The Incorporeality of God." *Modern Theology* 3 (1987) 179–88.

———. "The Passibility of God." *Religious Studies* 25 (1989) 217–24.

Tan, C. B. "The Idea of 'Suffering with Christ' in the Pauline Epistles: An Exegetical and Historical Study." PhD diss., University of Manchester, 1978.

Tappert, Theodore G., trans. and ed. *The Book of Concord: The Confessions of the Evangelical Lutheran Church*. Philadelphia: Fortress, 1959.

Tatian. *Oratio ad Graecos and Fragments*. Edited and translated by Molly Whittaker. Oxford Early Christian Texts. Edited by Henry Chadwick. Oxford: Clarendon, 1982.

Taubes, Jacob. "Theodicy and Theology: A Philosophical Analysis of Karl Barth's Dialectical Theology." *Journal of Religion* 34 (1954) 231–43.

Taylor, Mark C. *Erring: A Postmodern A/theology*. Chicago: University of Chicago Press, 1984.

Taylor, Michael J., ed. *The Mystery of Suffering and Death*. Staten Island, New York: Alba, 1973.

Taylor, Patty. "Participating in the Sufferings of God." *TSF Bulletin* 5 (1982) 2–5.

Telepneff, Gregory. "Theopaschite Language in the Soteriology of Saint Gregory the Theologian." *Greek Orthodox Theological Review* 32 (1987) 403–16.

Temple, William. *Christus Veritas: An Essay*. London: Macmillan, 1924.

———. *The Faith and Modern Thought*. London: Macmillan, 1913.

———. *Mens Creatrix: An Essay*. London: Macmillan, 1917.

Tennant, F. R. "The Conception of a Finite God." *Expository Times* 31 (1919–1920) 89–91.

Terrien, Samuel. *The Elusive Presence: Toward a New Biblical Theology*. Vol. 26. Religious Perspectives Series, edited by Ruth Nanda Anshen. New York: Harper and Row, 1978.

———. *Job: Poet of Existence*. Indianapolis: Bobbs-Merrill, 1957.

Thaumaturgus, Gregory. "Ad Theopompum, De Passibili et Impassibili in Deo." In *Analecta Sacra* 4, edited by Johannes B. Pitra, 363–76. 1883. Reprint, Farnborough, England: Gregg, 1966.

Thompson, John. "The Humanity of God in the Theology of Karl Barth." *Scottish Journal of Theology* 29 (1976) 249–69.

Thompson, William M. "A Suffering World, A Loving God? A Moderate Panentheistic View." In *Suffering and Healing in Our Day*, edited by Francis A. Eigo, 63–94. Villanova: Villanova University Press, 1990.

Thomsen, Mark W. "Jesus Crucified and the Mission of the Church." *International Review of Mission* 77 (1988) 247–64.

Tilley, Terrence W. "The Use and Abuse of Theodicy." *Horizons* 11 (1984) 304–19.

Tillich, Paul. *Biblical Religion and the Search For Ultimate Reality*. Chicago: University of Chicago Press, 1955.

———. *The Construction of the History of Religion in Schelling's Positive Philosophy: Its Presuppositions and Principles*. Translated by Victor Nuovo. Lewisburg: Bucknell University Press, 1974.

———. *The Interpretation of History*. Translated by N. A. Rasetzki and Elsa L. Talmey. New York: Scribner, 1936.

———. *Systematic Theology*. 3 vols. Chicago: University of Chicago Press, 1951–1963.

Tilliette, Xavier. "L'exinanition du Christ: Théologies de la kénose." *Les quatre fleuves: cahiers de recherche et de réflexion religieuses (Le Christ visage de Dieu)* 4 (1975) 48–60.

———. "Der Kreuzesschrei." *Evangelische Theologie* 43 (1983) 3–15.

Tinker, Melvin. "Purpose in Pain—Teleology and the Problem of Evil." *Themelios* 16 (April–May 1991) 15–18.

Tinsley, John. "Tragedy and Christian Beliefs." *Theology* 85 (1982) 98–106.

Torrance, Alan. "Does God Suffer? Incarnation and Impassibility." In *Christ in Our Place: The Humanity of God in Christ for the Reconciliation of the World: Essays Presented to Professor James Torrance*, edited by Trevor A. Hart and Daniel P. Thimell, 345–68. Exeter: Paternoster, 1989.

Tracy, David. *The Analogical Imagination: Christian Theology and the Culture of Pluralism*. New York: Crossroad, 1981.

———. *Blessed Rage for Order: The New Pluralism in Theology*. New York: Seabury, 1975.

Traets, Cor. "The Sick and Suffering Person: A Liturgical/Sacramental Approach." In *God and Human Suffering*, edited by Jan Lambrecht and Raymond F. Collins,

183–210. Louvain Theological and Pastoral Monographs 3. Louvain: Peeters, 1990.

Traina, Mariano. "Teologia del dolore di Dio e filosofia di Scoto." In *Sectio Generalis*, edited by Camille Bérubé, 401–16. *Regnum Hominis et Regnum Dei: Acta Quarti Congressus Scotistici Internationalis* 1. Rome: Societas Internationalis Scotistica, 1978.

Trethowan, Illtyd. "A Changing God." *Downside Review* 84 (1966) 247–61.

———. "Christology Again." *Downside Review* 98 (1977) 1–10.

———. "God's Changelessness." *Word and Spirit* 8 (1986) 31–43.

Trible, Phyllis. *God and the Rhetoric of Sexuality*. Overtures to Biblical Theology Series, edited by Walter Brueggemann and John Donahue. Philadelphia: Fortress, 1978.

Troeltsch, Ernst. *The Christian Faith*. Edited by Gertrud von le Fort. Translated by Garrett E. Paul. Fortress Texts in Modern Theology. Minneapolis: Fortress, 1991.

———. *Glaubenslehre. Nach Heidelberger Vorlesungen aus den Jahren 1911 und 1912*. Munich: Verlag von Duncker und Humbolt, 1925.

Tsambassis, Alexander Nicholas. "Evil and the 'Abysmal Nature' of God in the Thought of Brightman, Berdyaev, and Tillich." PhD diss., Northwestern University, 1957.

Tymms, T. Vincent. *The Christian Idea of Atonement*. London: Macmillan, 1904.

Ullendorff, E. "Thought Categories in the Hebrew Bible." In *Studies in Rationalism, Judaism and Universalism in Memory of Leon Roth*, edited by R. Loewe, 273–88. London: Routledge 1966.

Unamuno, Miguel de. *The Tragic Sense of Life in Men and Nations*. Translated by Anthony Kerrigan. Princeton: Princeton University Press, 1972.

Vacek, Edward Collins. *Love, Human and Divine: The Heart of Christian Ethics*. Moral Traditions and Moral Arguments Series. Series edited by James F. Keenan. Washington D C: Georgetown University Press, 1994.

Van Bavel, Tarsicius Johannes. "Le Dieu souffrant." *Stauros Bulletin* (1975).

———. "De lijdende God." *Tijdschrift voor Theologie* 14 (1974) 131–50.

———. "The Meaninglessness of Suffering and Attempts at Interpretation." In *God and Human Suffering*, edited by Jan Lambrecht and Raymond F. Collins, 121–36. No. 3. Louvain Theological and Pastoral Monographs. Louvain: Peeters, 1990.

———. "Where Is God when Human Beings Suffer?" In *God and Human Suffering*, edited by Jan Lambrecht and Raymond F. Collins, 137–53. No. 3. Louvain Theological and Pastoral Monographs. Louvain: Peeters, 1990.

Van den Brink, Gijsbert. "Natural Evil and Eschatology." In *Christian Faith and Philosophical Theology: Essays in Honour of Vincent Brümmer*, edited by Gijsbert van den Brink, Luco J. van den Brom, and Marcel Sarot, 39–55. Kampen, Netherlands: Kok Pharos, 1992.

———, Gijsbert, Van den Brom, Luco J., and Sarot, Marcel, eds. *Christian Faith and Philosophical Theology: Essays in Honour of Vincent Brümmer*. Kampen, Netherlands: Kok Pharos, 1992.

Van den Brom, Luco J. "God's Omnipresent Agency." *Religious Studies* 20 (1984) 637–55.

Van der Ven, Johannes A. "Theodicee: Traditioneel of Modern." *Wijsgerig Perspectief* 30 (1989–1990) 71–78.

———. "Towards an Empirical Theodicy." *Archivio di Filosofia* 56 (1988) 359–80.

Van Egmond, A. *De lijdende God in de Britse Theologie van de negentiende Eeuw: De bijdrage van Newman, Maurice, McLeod Campbell en Gore aan de christelijke theopaschitische traditie*. Amsterdam: VU Uitgeverij, 1986.

———. "Theopaschitische Tendenzen in de Na-Oorlogse Protestantse Theologie." *Gereformeerd Theologisch Tijdschrift* 79 (1979) 161–77.

Vanhoutte, Johan. "God as Companion and Fellow–Sufferer: An Image Emerging from Process Thought." *Archivio di Filosofia* 56 (1988) 191–225.

Vann, Gerald. *The Divine Pity: A Study in the Social Implications of the Beatitudes*. New York: Sheed and Ward, 1946.

———. *The Pain of Christ and the Sorrow of God*. 3rd ed. London: Blackfriars, 1952.

Vanstone, W. H. *The Risk of Love*. New York: Oxford University Press, 1978.

Varillon, François. "Bóg pokorny i cierpiacy." *Znak* 30 (1978) 549–60.

———. *L'humilité de Dieu*. Paris: Editions du Centurion, 1974.

———. *The Humility and Suffering of God*. Translated by Nelly Marans. New York: Alba, 1983.

———. *La souffrance de Dieu*. Paris: Editions du Centurion, 1975.

Vermilye, Robert G. "The Suffering of God." *Boston Review* 5 (1865) 1–31.

Vidal, Marciano. "Structural Sin: A New Category in Moral Theology?" In *History and Conscience: Studies in Honour of Father Sean O'Riordan, CSsR*, edited by Raphael Gallagher and Brendan McConvery, 181–98. Dublin: Gill and Macmillan, 1989.

Vitali, Theodor. "Organicism, Evil and Divine Redemption." *Archivio di Filosofia* 56 (1988) 227–44.

Von Balthasar, Hans Urs. *The von Balthasar Reader*. Edited by Medard Kehl and Werner Löser. Translated by Robert J. Daly and Fred Lawrence. New York: Crossroad, 1982.

Von Hügel, Baron Friedrich. "Suffering and God." In *Essays and Addresses on the Philosophy of Religion: Second Series*, by Baron Friedrich von Hügel, 165–213. London: J. M. Dent and Sons, 1926.

Von Loewenich, Walther. *Luther's Theology of the Cross*. Translated by Herbert J. A. Bouman. Minneapolis: Augsburg, 1976.

Von Rad, Gerhard. *Genesis: A Commentary*. Translated by John H. Marks. The Old Testament Library. Series edited by G. Ernest Wright, John Bright, James Barr, and Peter Ackroyd. Philadelphia: Westminster, 1972.

———. *Old Testament Theology*. Vol. 1. *The Theology of Israel's Historical Traditions*. Translated by D. M. G. Stalker. New York: Harper and Row, 1962.

———. *Old Testament Theology*. Vol. 2. *The Theology of Israel's Prophetic Traditions*. Translated by D. M. G. Stalker. New York: Harper and Row, 1965.

Vorgrimler, H. "Das Leiden Gottes." *Theologie der Gegenwart* 30 (1987) 20–26.

Vos, Antonie. "Immutabilitas Dei." *Nederlands Theologisch Tijdschrift* 35 (1981) 111–33.

———. "The Possibility of Impeccability." In *Christian Faith and Philosophical Theology: Essays in Honour of Vincent Brümmer*, edited by Gijsbert van den Brink, Luco J. van den Brom, and Marcel Sarot, 227–39. Kampen, Netherlands: Kok Pharos, 1992.

Vroom, H. M. "God and Goodness." In *Christian Faith and Philosophical Theology: Essays in Honour of Vincent Brümmer*, edited by Gijsbert van den Brink, Luco

J. van den Brom, and Marcel Sarot, 240–57. Kampen, Netherlands: Kok Pharos, 1992.

Waldenfels, Bernhard. "Das überbewältigte Leiden: Eine pathologische Betrachtung." In *Leiden*, edited by Willi Oelmüller, 129–40. Vol. 3. *Kolloquium Religion und Philosophie*. Paderborn: Ferdinand Schöning, 1986.

Waliggo, John M. "African Christology in a Situation of Suffering." In *Faces of Jesus in Africa*, edited by Robert J. Schreiter, 164–80. Faith and Cultures Series. Edited by Robert J. Schreiter. Maryknoll: Orbis, 1991.

Walker, D. P. *The Decline of Hell: Seventeenth-Century Discussions of Eternal Torment.* Chicago: University of Chicago Press, 1964.

Walker, Theodore, Jr. "Hartshorne's Neoclassical Theism and Black Theology." *Process Studies* 18 (1989) 240–58.

Wallace, Mark I. *Finding God in the Singing River: Christianity, Spirit, Nature.* Minneapolis: Fortress, 2005.

———. *Fragments of the Spirit: Nature, Violence, and the Renewal of Creation.* New York: Continuum, 1996.

———. "The World of the Text: Theological Hermeneutics in the Thought of Karl Barth and Paul Ricoeur." *Union Seminary Quarterly Review* 41 (1986–1987) 1–15.

Walls, Jerry L. "Can God Save Anyone He Will?" *Scottish Journal of Theology* 38 (1985) 155–72.

———. *Hell: The Logic of Damnation.* Library of Religious Philosophy, edited by Thomas V. Morris. South Bend: University of Notre Dame Press, 1992.

———. "Is Molinism as Bad as Calvinism?" *Faith and Philosophy* 7 (1990) 85–98.

Walsh, P. G. "The Pain of This World." *The Way* 21 (1981) 261–69.

Walsh, Thomas. "The Response to Suffering." In *Society and Original Sin: Ecumenical Essays on the Impact of the Fall*, edited by Durwood Foster and Paul Mojzes, 119–32. New York: Paragon, 1985.

Walters, Kerry. "Hell, This Isn't Necessary after All." *International Journal for Philosophy of Religion* 29 (1991) 175–86.

Ward, Keith. *Holding Fast to God: A Reply to Don Cupitt.* London: SPCK, 1982.

———. *Rational Theology and the Creativity of God.* New York: Pilgrim, 1982.

———. *A Vision to Pursue: Beyond the Crisis in Christianity.* London: SCM, 1991.

Warren, W. "The Atonement in Modern Theology." *The Thinker* 6 (1894) 53–62.

Watson, G. "The Problem of the Unchanging in Greek Philosophy." *Neue Zeitschrift für systematische Theologie und Religionsphilosophie* 27 (1985) 57–69.

We Believe in God: A Report by the Doctrine Commission of the General Synod of the Church of England. Wilton, CT: Church, 1987.

Weatherhead, Leslie Dixon. *Why Do Men Suffer?* New York and Nashville: Abingdon-Cokesbury, 1936.

Weber, Otto. *Foundations of Dogmatics.* Vol. 1. Translated by Darrell L. Guder. Grand Rapids: Eerdmans, 1981.

Weddle, D. L. "God the Redeemer: Sovereignty and Suffering." *Christianity Today* 13 (1969) 12–15.

Weil, Simone. *Gravity and Grace.* Translated by Arthur Wills. New York: G. P. Putnam's Sons, 1952.

———. *Waiting for God*. Translated by Emma Craufurd. New York: G. P. Putnam's Sons, 1951.

Weinandy, Thomas G. *Does God Change? The Word's Becoming in the Incarnation*. Still River, MA: St. Bede's, 1985.

———. *Does God Suffer?* Notre Dame: University of Notre Dame, 2000.

———. "Does God Suffer?" *First Things* 117 (2001) 35–41.

———. "Easter Saturday and the Suffering of God: The Theology of Alan E. Lewis." *International Journal of Systematic Theology* 5 (2003) 62–76.

Welch, Claude, ed. *God and Incarnation in Mid-Nineteenth Century German Theology: G. Thomasius, I. A. Dorner, A. E Biedermann*. Translated by Claude Welch. A Library of Protestant Thought. New York: Oxford University Press, 1965.

Welker, Michael, ed. *Diskussion über Jürgen Moltmanns Buch "Der gekreuzigte Gott."* Munich: Kaiser, 1979.

Wells, Paul. "God and Change: Moltmann in the Light of the Reformed Tradition." In *The Power and Weakness of God: Impassibility and Orthodoxy: Papers Presented at the Third Edinburgh Conference in Christian Dogmatics, 1989*, edited by Nigel M. de S. Cameron, 53–68. Edinburgh: Rutherford, 1990.

Wesley, John. *John Wesley's Theology: A Collection from His Works*. Edited by Robert W. Burtner and Robert E. Chiles. Nashville: Abingdon, 1982.

———. *A Plain Account of Christian Perfection*. London, England: Epworth, 1952.

Westermann, Claus. *Elements of Old Testament Theology*. Translated by Douglas W. Stott. Atlanta: John Knox, 1982.

———. *Genesis 1–11: A Commentary*. Translated by John J. Scullion. Minneapolis: Augsburg, 1984.

———. "The Role of Lament in the Theology of the Old Testament." *Interpretation* 28 (1974) 20–38.

Westley, Dick. *Redemptive Intimacy: A New Perspective for the Journey to Adult Faith*. Mystic, CT: Twenty-Third, 1981.

Weth, Rudolf. "Heil im gekreuzigten Gott." *Evangelische Theologie* 31 (1971) 227–43.

———. "Über den Schmerz Gottes. Zur Theologie des Schmerzes Gottes von Kazoh Kitamori." *Evangelische Theologie* 33 (1973) 431–36.

Wetz, Franz Josef. "Gibt es ein Leiden am Denken?" In *Leiden*, edited by Willi Oelmüller, 119–28. Vol. 3. *Kolloquium Religion und Philosophie*. Paderborn: Ferdinand Schöning, 1986.

White, Douglas. *Forgiveness and Suffering: A Study of Christian Belief*. Cambridge: Cambridge University Press, 1913.

White, Lynn, Jr. "The Future of Compassion." *Ecumenical Review* 30 (1978) 99–109.

———. "The Historical Roots of the Ecological Crisis." *Science* 155 (1967) 120–37.

Whitehead, Alfred North. *Adventures of Ideas*. New York: Free, 1961.

———. *Process and Reality: An Essay in Cosmology*. Corrected ed. Edited by David Ray Griffin and Donald W. Sherburne. New York: Free, 1978.

Whitelaw, David P. "A Theology of Anguish." *Theologia Evangelica* 15 (1982) 38–48.

Whitney, Barry L. "Divine Immutability in Process Philosophy and Contemporary Thomism." *Horizons* 7 (1980) 49–68.

———. "God, Man and Evil: The Question of Theodicy in the Neoclassical Metaphysics of Charles Hartshorne." PhD diss., McMaster University, 1977.

———. *Theodicy: An Annotated Bibliography on the Problem of Evil 1960–1991.* Bowling Green, OH: Philosophy Documentation Center, Bowling Green University, 1998.

Wiesel, Elie. *Night.* 25th anniversary ed. Translated by Stella Rodway. New York: Bantam, 1986.

Wifall, Walter. "Models of God in the Old Testament." *Biblical Theology Bulletin: A Journal of Bible and Theology* 9 (1979) 179–86.

Wigram, W. A. *The Separation of the Monophysites.* 1923. Reprint, New York: AMS, 1978.

Wild, Robert. *Who I Will Be: Is There Joy and Suffering in God?* Denville: Dimension Books, 1976.

Wiles, Maurice. "In Defence of Arius." *Journal of Theological Studies* 13 (1962) 339–47.

Williams, Daniel Day. "Deity, Monarchy, and Metaphysics: Whitehead's Critique of the Theological Tradition." In *Essays in Process Theology* by Daniel Day Williams, edited by Perry LeFevre, 51–70. Chicago: Exploration, 1985.

———. *The Demonic and the Divine.* Edited by Stacy A. Evans. Minneapolis: Fortress, 1990.

———. *The Spirit and the Forms of Love.* New York: Harper and Row, 1968.

———. "Suffering and Being in Empirical Theology." In *The Future of Empirical Theology*, edited by Bernard E. Meland, 175–94. *Essays in Divinity* 7. Chicago: University of Chicago Press, 1969.

———. "Tillich's Doctrine of God." In *Essays in Process Theology* by Daniel Day Williams, edited by Perry LeFevre, 233–43. Chicago: Exploration, 1985.

———. "Tragedy and the Christian Eschatology." *Encounter* 24 (1963) 61–76.

———. "The Vulnerable and the Invulnerable God." *Christianity and Crisis* 22 (1962) 27–30; also in, *Union Seminary Quarterly Review* 17 (1962) 223–29.

———. *What Present Day Theologians Are Thinking.* New York: Harper and Row, 1967.

Williams, John Milton. "Divine Limitation." *Bibliotheca Sacra* (Oberlin) 47 (1890) 253–66.

Williams, Robert R. "Theodicy, Tragedy, and Soteriology: The Legacy of Schleiermacher." *Harvard Theological Review* 77 (1984) 395–412.

Williams, Stephen. "On Giving Hope in a Suffering World: Response to Moltmann." In *Issues in Faith and History: Papers presented at the Second Edinburgh Conference on Dogmatics, 1987*, edited by Nigel M. de S. Cameron, 3–19. Edinburgh: Rutherford, 1989.

Wilson, Bruce. "The God Who Suffers: A Re-Examination of the Theology of Unjust Suffering." *St. Mark's Review* 140 (1990) 21–31.

Wilson, James Maurice. *The Gospel of the Atonement.* London: Macmillan, 1899.

Wilson, Paul Eddy. "The Bearing of Process Thought on the Problem of Theodicy." PhD diss., University of Tennessee, 1989.

Wimberly, Edward P. "The Suffering God." In *Preaching on Suffering and a God of Love*, edited by Henry J. Young, 56–62. Philadelphia: Fortress, 1978.

Winslow, D. F. "Soteriological 'Orthodoxy' in the Fathers." In *Studia Patristica*, edited by Elizabeth A. Livingstone, 15.1: 393–95. Berlin: Academie-Verlag, 1984.

Witt, Douglas A. "'And God Repented': Heschel's Theology of Pathos and Our Contemporary Portrait of God." *Journal of Theology* 91 (1987) 67–73.

Woelfel, James W. "Death of God: A Belated Personal Postscript." *Christian Century* 93 (29 December 1976) 1175–78.

Wolf, William J. *No Cross, No Crown: A Study of the Atonement.* Garden City, NY: Doubleday, 1957.

Wolff, Hans Walter. *Anthropology of the Old Testament.* Translated by Margaret Kohl. Philadelphia: Fortress, 1974.

Wolterstorff, Nicholas. "Suffering Love." In *Philosophy and the Christian Faith,* edited by Thomas V. Morris, 196–237. University of Notre Dame Studies in the Philosophy of Religion 5. Notre Dame: University of Notre Dame Press, 1988.

Wondra, Gerald. "The Pathos of God." *Reformed Review: A Quarterly Journal of the Western Theological Seminary* 18 (1964) 28–35.

Woodbridge, John. "God Without Passions." *Literary and Theological Review* 1 (1834) 42–61.

Woollcombe, Kenneth J. "The Pain of God." *Scottish Journal of Theology* 20 (1967) 129–48.

Wright, G. Ernest and Reginald H. Fuller. *The Book of the Acts of God: Contemporary Scholarship Interprets the Bible.* Garden City, NY: Doubleday, 1957; Anchor, 1960.

Wright, Henry W. "A Self-Sacrificing God and the Problem of Evil." *Open Court: A Monthly Magazine* 19 (1905) 745–51.

Wright, John H. "Problem of Evil, Mystery of Sin and Suffering." *Communio* 6 (1979) 140–56.

Wynkoop, Mildred Bangs. *A Theology of Love: The Dynamic of Wesleyanism.* Kansas City, MI: Beacon Hill, 1972.

Wyschogrod, Edith. "Empathy and Sympathy as Tactile Encounter." *Journal of Medicine and Philosophy* 6 (1981) 25–43.

Yancey, Philip. "Distress Signals." *Christianity Today* 34 (1990) 33–35.

Yates, Roy. "Christ and the Powers of Evil in Colossians." *Studia Biblica* 3 (1978) 461–68.

———. "The Powers of Evil in the New Testament." *Evangelical Quarterly* 52 (1980) 97–111.

Young, Frances M. "A Cloud of Witnesses." In *The Myth of God Incarnate,* edited by John Hick, 13–47. Philadelphia: Westminster, 1977.

———. *Face to Face: A Narrative Essay in the Theology of Suffering.* Edinburgh: T. & T. Clark, 1990.

———. "Incarnation and Atonement: God Suffered and Died." In *Incarnation and Myth: The Debate Continued,* edited by Michael Goulder, 101–3. Grand Rapids: Eerdmans, 1979.

———. "A Reconsideration of Alexandrian Christology." *Journal of Ecclesiastical History* 22 (1971) 103–14.

Young, Henry James. "Does Christianity Proclaim Redemption in and through or despite Suffering—Special Emphasis on the Black Experience." In *The Meaning of Human Suffering,* edited by Flavian Dougherty, 301–42. New York: Human Sciences, 1982.

———. "Process Theology and Black Liberation: Testing the Whiteheadian Metaphysical Foundations." *Process Studies* 18 (1989) 259–67.

———, ed. *Preaching on Suffering and a God of Love*. Philadelphia: Fortress, 1977.

Zahl, Paul F. M. "The Historical Jesus and Substitutionary Atonement." *Saint Luke's Journal of Theology* 26 (1983) 313–32.

Zahrnt, Heinz. *Wie kann Gott das zulassen? Hiob—Der Mensch im Leid*. Munich: Piper, 1985.

Zimany, Roland D. "Moltmann's Crucified God." *Dialog* 16 (1977) 49–57.

Zoffoli, Enrico. *"Mistero della sofferenza di Dio"? Il pensiero di S. Tommaso*. Vol. 34. Studi Tomistici. Città del Vaticano: Libreria Editrice Vaticana, 1988.

Index of Scriptures

Index of Persons

Index of Topics

Aaron, 162n.54
Abraham, 162n.54
abstractions, methodological,
   20–22, 65, 92–93, 94–95,
   101, 105, 107, 111, 112, 113,
   117, 130, 134, 166, 176, 180,
   196, 198, 211, 222, 235–36,
   263, 264
abstrahentium non est mendacium,
   65
abuse, 192, 257, 260
academic freedom, xiii, xiv
actu exercito, 175
actu signato, 175
Adam, 154n.32, 183n.6
affliction, divine, 14, 95, 98, 101,
   102, 264, 266
affliction, human, 91, 96, 98, 260
agapé, 118, 119n.13, 120n.13,
   123n.17, 125n.23, 129, 199,
   200n.26, 208, 208n.41, 209,
   210n.43
agapic dimension of divine life,
   117–19, 121, 132, 140, 147,
   241
agapic dimension of human life,
   198, 199–201, 203, 208, 209,
   210, 240, 241, 247, 248, 251
agapic love for God, human, 200–1
agony, divine, 145
aheb, 118, 199
alienation, human, 98, 99, 211,
   217, 224, 227n.23, 228n.26,
   230n.29
allegorical interpretation, 40

all-in-all, divine, 139, 141, 142, 148,
   160, 161, 167
alterity, 139, 140, 140n.12, 141, 142,
   144, 146, 147, 148, 149, 150,
   152, 160, 161, 163, 167, 168,
   170n.70, 171, 195, 207, 208,
   209, 231n.30, 234, 239, 243,
   244, 245, 246, 247, 249, 250,
   251, 253, 255n.2, 258
altruism, human, 193n.18
amor Dei, 197
amor sui, 197
Anabaptist testimony, 35n.16
analogia entis, 41
analogical discourse, 106, 107
analysis, ontological, 119n.13
anathemas, 4n.9, 5n.9
anthropocentricity, 73n.15,
   192n.18, 193, 193n.18, 264
anthropological principle, 78–91,
   92, 96n.2, 101, 154n.32
anthropology, ancient, 186n.9
anthropology, biblical, 185n.8,
   197n.22, 212n.1
anthropology, Christian, 190n.13,
   193n.18, 195n.19, 210n.43,
   224n.21
anthropology, contemporary and
   modern, 186n.9
anthropomorphism, 1n.1, 25
apatheia, divine, 155n.34
appetite, divine, 121n.14
appropriateness to Christian tradition, criterion, 75
arché, 147, 188n.12

hope, divine, 151
humans as cosmocentric, 256
humility, divine, 132–33, 132n.32,
 132n.33, 136, 140, 160

identity, divine, 115, 116
identity, human, 207–8, 234, 244,
 246, 250, 251
id ipsum et id ipsum, 132
Iliad, 10n.20
image of God, Christ as, 180n.1
imagination, human, 223, 223n.20,
 224, 224n.20
imago, 177n.3
imago Dei, 14, 56, 97, 105, 106, 151,
 152, 154, 168, 171, 175–78,
 177n.3, 177n.4, 179–210,
 212n.1, 213–17, 229n.27,
 243, 248, 250, 255, 256, 257,
 258, 265, 268
imago Dei as love, formal dimensions, 183–95
imago Dei as love, material dimensions, 195–210
imitatio Christi, 212n.1, 217–24
imitatio Dei, 14, 72n.13, 106,
 175–78, 194n.19, 211–53,
 212n.1, 213n.1, 218n.9,
 223n.20, 229n.27
immanence, divine, 188n.12
immutability, divine, 2n.2, 4, 4n.9,
 5n.9, 25, 27, 30n.8, 31, 61,
 130n.29, 131n.30, 138n.9,
 168n.66, 189n.13, 190n.13
impassibility, divine, 2n.2, 4, 4n.9,
 5n.9, 7, 12, 25, 27, 30, 30n.8,
 31, 34, 61, 64n.1, 166n.63,
 168n.66
imperative, the, 213, 214, 214n.4,
 222
imperialism, 245n.41
impotence (divine), 166, 166n.63
incarnation (divine), 2n.1, 4n.9,
 147n.20, 186n.9

incomprehensibility (divine), 2n.2
incorporeality (divine), 2n.2
indeterminacy, 260
indicative, the, 213, 214, 214n.4,
 222
indivisibility, divine, 2n.2
in facto esse, 215
infantilism, spiritual, 146n.19
in fieri, 215
infinitum capax finiti, 158n.43
infinity, 158n.43, 203
injustice, 199
in medias res, xi
Institute for the Advanced Study of
 Religion, xi, xiv
interdependence, divine, 203
interdependence, human, 207, 259
International Baptist Theological
 Seminary (Prague, Czech
 Republic), xvi
interreligious dialogue, 245n.41
in transitu, xi
invisibility, divine, 160
ipseity, 209, 234, 249
Isaiah, Second, 115, 115n.6, 145
Isaiah, Third, 95, 115
Israel, history of, 115

James, the apostle, 3
Jerusalem, 161, 202n.30
Jesus as mother, 146n.19
Jesus of Nazareth, 3, 7, 30, 71,
 72n.13, 73, 73n.15, 74, 75,
 78, 88, 88n.35, 89, 114, 116,
 117, 118, 130, 132, 134,
 146n.19, 152n.30, 161n.51,
 175, 176, 178, 179, 180, 181,
 182, 183, 184, 185, 186n.9,
 191, 192, 194, 195, 196,
 198, 198n.23, 199, 199n.24,
 201, 201n.27, 201n.28, 202,
 202n.29, 202n.30, 202n.31,
 202n.32, 204, 206, 211, 212,
 212n.1, 213, 216n.7, 217,

Solid Declaration, 4n.8
solidarity, 204, 206, 210, 237, 243,
    244, 245, 249, 253
Solomon, King, 86
soteriology, 51, 55–56, 114–16, 180,
    188n.12
soul, human, 186n.9
Southern Baptist Convention, xii,
    xii n.7
Southwestern Baptist Theological
    Seminary, xii, xvi
space, 160, 257
spatiality, 160
spirit, 197n.22
spirit, human, 186n.9
staurocentric theology, 4n.8
stewardship of creation, human,
    192, 257n.5, 258, 259
story, x
storyteller, x
sublime, experience of, 14
sublimity, terrible, 1, 10, 10n.20, 14,
    16, 183, 268
suffering, 267n.3
suffering, divine (active), 266–67
suffering, divine (passive), 266–67
suffering, human, 12, 50, 80–84, 85,
    85–86n.28, 88n.35, 89
suffering, involuntary, 267n.3
suffering, ontology of, 80
suffering, penal, 267n.3
suffering, redemptive, 267n.3
suffering, reflexive divine, 171n.70,
    231n.30
suffering, transitive divine, 171n.70
suffering, vicarious, 267n.3
suffering, voluntary, 267n.3
surprise, divine, 168n.67
susceptibility, divine, 169n.69,
    170n.69
swounds, ix n.1
symbol, 1–2n.1
symbol, religious, 34–50, 178, 254,
    267

symbol, theocentric character of,
    258
symbols, function of religious,
    49–50
symbols, creatures as, 194n.19
symbolization, process of, 41
symbols, theological, 2n.1
sympathy, divine, 170, 227n.23
sympathy, human, 227n.23
Synoptic Gospels, 71n.12, 222n.18,
    226n.22

télos, 147, 188n.12, 208, 248
temporality, 162
temporality, divine, 129, 129n.28,
    130, 130n.29
temptation, 250
theandric, human as, 188n.12,
    195–96
theater of divine-human drama,
    world as, 257
theatrum gloriae Dei, 255n.2
theism, classical Christian, xii, 2,
    2–3n.2, 4, 4n.8, 6, 7, 9, 12, 15,
    28, 29, 106, 112, 112n.2, 122,
    132, 137n.7, 148, 154n.32,
    158n.42, 168n.66, 170n.69,
    186n.9, 189n.13, 190n.13,
    235, 239
theocentric postures, typology of,
    51–54
theocentric theology, 50–57
theocentricity, 193, 198, 264
theodicy, 137n.7
theogony, 145n.18
theology, Calvinist, 100n.5, 255n.2
theology, constructive (systematic),
    58–62, 64n.1, 67n.6, 68, 69,
    101, 114n.3, 180n.2
theology, continental, 27n.4
theology, eschatological, 137n.7
theology, feminist, 149n.23
theology of divine suffering,
    British, 26–27n.4

32602307R00213

Made in the USA
Lexington, KY
26 May 2014